Saluki

Saluki

The Desert Hound and the English Travelers Who Brought It to the West

BRIAN PATRICK DUGGAN

Foreword by SIR TERENCE CLARK

McFarland & Company, Inc., Publishers

Jefferson, North Carolina, and London

LIBRARY OF CONGRESS CATALOGUING-IN-PUBLICATION DATA

Brian Patrick Duggan, 1953–
Saluki : the desert hound and the English travelers who brought it to
the west / Brian Patrick Duggan ; foreword by Sir Terence Clark.
p.   cm.
Includes bibliographical references and index.

ISBN-13: 978-0-7864-3407-7
softcover : 50# alkaline paper ∞

1. Saluki — History.   I. Title.
SF429.S33D84   2009   636.753'2 — dc22   2008047030

British Library cataloguing data are available

On the cover: (*detail*) Florence Amherst walking her Salukis, 1931;
Saluki and desert ©2008 Shutterstock

Manufactured in the United States of America

McFarland & Company, Inc., Publishers
Box 611, Jefferson, North Carolina 28640
www.mcfarlandpub.com

To my late father, James,
who taught me to love history and eloquence;
my mother, Betty,
who gave me the love of dogs;
and to my wife, Wendy,
who brought Salukis into my life and patiently
supported this seemingly endless endeavor.

And for Spike, Djordii, Naziir, L.B., Sinan,
and Ildico — faithful hounds all.

Acknowledgements

It occurs to me that the research for this book was much like sorting through jigsaw puzzle pieces scattered over a tennis court. The pieces were variously face down, face up, damaged, intact, duplicate, extraneous, and missing. Writing this book has been a process of discovering and collecting the pieces, deciding which were relevant, and then figuring out how to assemble them into the most complete picture possible. I could never have told this story alone and am grateful to my relatives, friends and colleagues, as well as to complete strangers, who kindly helped by providing one, two or several pieces of the puzzle. I would like to acknowledge these contributors here (some of whom have retired or moved on to other jobs since I worked with them). If I have neglected anyone, I offer my sincere apologies.

At the Bodleian Library, assistance with T.E. Lawrence's unpublished letters came from my good friend Dr. Judith Priestman and Colin Harris, Anna Dunn, Richard Bell, Melissa Dalziel, and John Slater of its Nuneham Courtney Repository (and the Bodleian porter — whose name I've forgotten — who let me out after I was locked in one night); and permission to quote the letters was given by Mr. M.V. Carey of Vizards Tweedie, London, and the Seven Pillars of Wisdom Trust. Alan Williams at the Imperial War Museum plowed through a great number of photographs and found the Goslett gems for me; Claire Horton and Emily Burdis at Marist College originally located a copy of the Lowell Thomas photograph of the Aqabah Staff back in 1993, and John Ansley most recently assisted with their archive of Lowell Thomas photos; Ann N. Patera and Linda Briscoe Myers at the Harry Ransom Humanities Research Center at the University of Texas at Austin found the un-cropped version of the Aqabah Staff photo; and Kaveri Subbarao, Esq., of ReedSmith LLP, facilitated permission to publish the Lowell Thomas photographs.

Paul Smith, archivist for Thomas Cook UK, Ltd., allowed me access to the company accounts for 1895 and gave permission for two images to be used in this book; at the Natural History Museum, London, Daphne Hills allowed me to examine Luman's skeleton and Katie Anderson assisted with permissions for photographs of the dog exhibit at Tring; Peter Foynes of the Hackney Archives at the Rose Lipman Library in London helped me with their Amherst ephemera; Lucinda O'Donovan of the Mary Evans Picture Library tracked down the Thomas Fall photograph of Florence Amherst, Zobeid, and Farhan; Allison Maloney of the Eastern Counties Newspapers, Norfolk, let me scour their chilly basement full of *Thetford and Watton Times* back issues; and at the Norfolk Record Office, Frank Meeres, Jean Kennedy, Tom Townsend, and William Monaghan directed me to Amherst material in their holdings, and Norfolk photographer Gary Hacon made a digital copy of their Lord Amherst photo.

Three canine archives provided important materials and gracious assistance: Barbara Walker, Elaine Camroux, Monica Smith, all formerly of the Kennel Club Library, London;

Barbara Kolk and her staff at the American Kennel Club Library, New York; and Terry O'Neill, Dolores Nugent, and Karen Murphy of the Irish Kennel Club, Dublin. Lorraine Budge of the Central Library in Bromley unearthed considerable information about Francis Joan Mitchell and Brigadier Lance (and has been a continuing source of encouragement); Melissa Paul, curator of the W.K. Kellogg Arabian Horse Library at California State Polytechnic University, Pomona, brought to my notice many sources on Arabian horses which contained pertinent side notes about Salukis; Cathleen Baldwin, research coordinator of the archives at Biltmore Estate, Asheville, North Carolina, brought to my attention other sources of Amherst information; Barbara McNab of the Museum of the Dog, St. Louis, Missouri, arranged a viewing of and provided details about two of the most important Saluki paintings extant. Thanks also to Mike Meakin and Kate Ferguson of the Zoological Society of London library — particularly the latter who pointed me towards the Giza Zoo information and returned my misplaced address book by airmail.

Miscellaneous historical and biographical puzzle pieces were provided by Robert Hale of the Berkshire Record Office; Elizabeth Finn and M.A. Sims of the Oxfordshire Archives; Debbie Saunders of the Centre for Kentish Studies; Susan McGann, archivist, Royal College of Nursing; Christina Grindon of *The Field*, IPC Magazines, Ltd.; Wendy Sage, deputy librarian, Wye College, University of London; Howard Grey for a discussion of Florence Amherst's last London residence with me; and Dr. Andrew Kitchener, National Museums, Scotland, for information on their mounted Saluki.

Dr. Roxanne Robbin shared her knowledge about Cellini and his Saluki bronze; Dr. Amin Elmallah and his family settled some points on Egyptian geography; Dr. Farid S. Haddad, MD, FACS, of Phoenix, Arizona, put me in touch with Dr. Walid Kamhawi of Amman, Jordan, who in turn provided information about Francis Joan Mitchell's hospital in Nablus; Susan Waltman brought to my attention the Saluki mention in Rudyard Kipling's *Kim*; D. Lawrence, director of the Oriental and India Office Collections, the British Library, sent me some obscure details about Brigadier Lance's military records; Paul Evans of the Royal Artillery Museum, Woolwich, London, sent details on Major Bayne-Jardine's army career; Marion Harding of the National Army Museum looked into the army records of Capt. Goslett and Jennings-Bramly; and Mrs. Jean McKenzie of Canada gave me permission to quote her father, James Trimbee, about his experiences as a gardener at Didlington Hall.

Mr. Paul Cooper of the British Museum Library gave me the first real lead on the elusive Wilfred Jennings-Bramly by dexterously locating two of his scientific articles. Locating documentation about Jennings-Bramly's survey work began with Dr. Peter Mellini of Stanford whose few paragraphs about Jennings-Bramly and the Aqabah Incident in his book led me to Dr. Bob Harrison of Southern Oregon State University, who made me aware of archives at the Royal Geographical Society, London. There, I had the excellent assistance of Dr. Andrew Tatham and Sarah Strong with Jennings-Bramly's papers, which then took me to the Palestine Exploration Fund, where, on my last day in London on one trip, Dr. Rupert Chapman gave me access to their collection of his letters and later Felicity Cobbing assisted with permissions and verifying their holdings. Clare Brown, keeper of the Middle Eastern Collection, St. Antony's College, Oxford, produced further material by Jennings-Bramly, and put me in touch with James Offer, the nephew of Wing Commander A.R.M. Rickards. Professional genealogist Edward R. Lowe, M.A., C.G.R.S., found Francis Joan Mitchell's and Jennings-Bramly's descendents in England, and that started a friendship with his grandson, Jasper Scovil, who generously shared family information with me.

John Goslett and Dr. Colin Bayne-Jardine were kind enough to talk about their fathers with a complete stranger over excellent luncheons in Oxford; Venetia Chattey kindly let me read her grandmother's Egyptian journals; at her home in Hartfordshire, Avril Berrisford shared information about her great aunt, Francis Joan Mitchell; and the Earl of Portland gave me a warm welcome one Halloween and talked at great length about his great uncle Arthur Bentinck over dinner. Adrien Sturgeon, of the Wrotham and Fairseat Societies, energetically provided facts about the history of the Lances and their home in Kent (and set me straight on a few points). Mrs. Zahra Freeth graciously gave me information about her parents the Dicksons, and their life in Kuwait. My friend Carole Tipler of New Zealand was the contact for Judy Lance, who sent along biographical information, and just before my submission deadline, Carolyn Potts of Australia put me in touch with the Brigadier's grandson, Trevor Lance, with whom I've had several delightful and informative conversations about his family's history.

Colonel Pierce Joyce's personal and military history came out of Galway, Ireland, in various ways. My father's good friend, the late Sonny Molloy, put me in touch with Peadar O'Dowd, president of the Galway Archæological and Historical Society. From Peadar, the leads spread out to include Marie Mannion of the Galway Family History Society West Ltd., Michael Kilroy of Royal Tara China (the Joyce's former manor house), Sgt. McDonagh and Sgt. Major MacGowan of the Irish Army at Renmore Barracks, and, most recently, Dr. David Murphy of Dublin. From Joyce's second cousin and family historian, Gordon St. George Mark of Winnetka, Illinois, came the history of the Merry Joyces in Galway and his own biographical notes on the colonel. Frank Keegan of Dublin was kind enough to share with me the story of his mother's willful Saluki.

Insights on T.E. Lawrence and officers of the Arab Revolt came from the late St. John Armitage, C.B.E., Jeremy Wilson and his admirable Web site and e-mail listserv, and Christopher Matheson (who learned of my work through the Liddell Harte Center for Military Archives in London, and got in touch with me with their help — only to learn that we lived only 70 miles apart at that time).

T.G.H. James's book, *Howard Carter: The Path to Tutankahmun*, provided leads on a number of sources for Amherst documents, and Professor James kindly advised me on aspects of ancient Egyptian Salukis and the phenomenon of "Tutmania." Dr. James P. Allen, former curator of the Department of Egyptian Art at the Metropolitan Museum of Art, New York, and now at Brown University, helped me with matters concerning the Amherst Sekhmet statues and Saluki hieroglyphics. Patricia Spencer at the Egypt Exploration Society searched without luck for Carter-Amherst letters in their archives and Mr. Terry J. Eva did the same with his collection; Diana Magee of the Griffith Institute, Ashmolean Museum, Oxford, looked into Howard Carter's reproduction of the Rekhmire tomb painting; and David Butters of the Swaffam Museum contributed information on Howard Carter and the Amhersts.

Nuggets of Amherst family history came generously from Florence's relatives — Venetia Chattey, George Cecil of the Biltmore Estate, Asheville, North Carolina, and the present Lord Amherst of Hackney. Angela Knapp put me in touch with the owners of the new Didlington Manor, Elizabeth Sutcliffe and Fiona Dixon — who once threw me off the premises as a trespasser and then welcomed me back the following year to help me sort out questions about the old Didlington Hall.

For matters aerial, Peter Elliott, senior keeper of the Royal Air Force Museum, Hendon, and Allan Janus of the National Air and Space Museum, the Smithsonian Institution, gave me useful answers that helped shape the passages concerning Salukis flying in airplanes. On the customs, language, and hunting practices of the Middle East, I am grateful to Sir Terence Clark, K.B.E., C.M.G., C.V.O., and Dr. John Burchard.

Thanks must go to the librarians who assisted me in getting my hands on a lot of very old books and periodicals in between my trips overseas: Edith Amrine, Eric Striker, Julia Graham, Laura McClanahan and the rest of the Inter-Library Loan staff of McHenry Library at the University of California, Santa Cruz. At California State University, Stanislaus, librarians Amy Andres, Arthur Buell, and the Inter-Library Loan staff of Julie Ruben, Deb Travers, and Texas Keo were particularly tolerant and obliging about my odd requests. Encouragement came from Allan Dyson, university librarian, Rita Bottoms (who let me sit in Robert Heinlein's chair) and Christine Bunting of Special Collections, McHenry Library, University of California, Santa Cruz, and Ed Jajko, formerly of the Middle Eastern Collection of the Hoover Institute, Stanford University.

Every effort has been made to secure the required permissions for photographs and illustrations appearing in *Saluki: The Desert Hound and the English Travelers who Brought It to the West.* For permission to reproduce images and journal entries I wish to acknowledge the following people and institutions: Lowell Thomas Jr.; John Goslett; Dr. Colin Bayne-Jardine; the Earl of Portland, Timothy Bentinck; Trevor Lance; Venetia Chattey; James Offer; Nigel Nicolson; John and Margaret Moss; Jasper Scovil; Zahra Freeth; the Metropolitan Museum of Art; Royal Geographical Society; Palestine Exploration Fund; Bodleian Library; the Harry Ransome Humanities Research Center, University of Texas at Austin; Marist College; National Monuments Record; Mary Evans Picture Library; National History Museum; Norfolk Record Office; Imperial War Museum; Thomas Cook UK Ltd.; the Kennel Club; and the Saluki or Gazelle Hound Club Committee.

A grateful nod goes to go to my mapmakers, Tammy White and Dennis Leinfelder, as well as to Melanie Birdsall and Gail Garret who assisted with early stages of proofreading. Friends and colleagues who bounced my theories back at me, read parts or all of my manuscript and offered helpful suggestions include Dr. Ken and Mary Ellen Gorske, Ken and Diana Allan, Warren Cook, Dr. Steven Caton, Danny Carnahan, Peg DeMouthe, and David Keymer. Special thanks to Dr. Nancy Taniguchi for her continuing advice and support.

Saluki historians who provided me with information and pedigrees and a sounding board for my ideas are, in England, Hope and David Waters, Ann Birrell (who generously spent time with me and opened up her private collection), Viv Davies and Betty Chanter, Nick and Marie Bryce-Smith, Chris Ormsby, Diana Allan, Michael and Helen Williams (who loaned their back issues of *The Saluki*), Clair Chryssolor, and the sagacious Dr. John Hudson; and, in the United States, Mary Ellen Gorske, Carol Ann Lantz, Sue Anne Pietros, Marilyn LaBrache Brown, Catherine and Carlene Kuhl, Patsy Hoy, Frank Cassano, and Ann Mayea. And elsewhere in the world, Peter Van Arkel of the Netherlands, Dagmar Hintzenberg-Freisleben of Germany, and Ingrid Romanowski, Roberta Pattison, and Lin Jenkins of Canada.

Sadly, several people have died since contributing to this book: my courageous friend and occasional patron, Carl Oakley, who told me the amazing story of his visit with Florence Amherst; Nigel Nicolson of Sissinghurst Castle, who answered my questions about the fate of poor Zurcha; Wilfred Jennings-Bramly's daughter, Vivien Betti, who had me to tea and talked freely about her amazing father; Baroness Strange and Lady Lanyon, who wrote to me about Florence Amherst and her family; the Brigadier's son, John Waterlow Fitzhugh Lance, who wrote to me about the Saronas; Ngaire Coe, an early supporter of the book; my uncle Patrick "Mogan" Duggan, a great hurler and rower in his day and a breeder of racing greyhounds who gave me the insight about tourists posing with animals they did not own; and my father, James Duggan, who always reminded me that I had "the autonomy of the author."

This book would not have been possible had it not been for my family and friends in England and Ireland who gave me warm hospitality during my vagabonding research, put up with my odd comings and goings, and listened patiently to my ramblings about the day's discoveries. I am sure that they still think of me as the Yank who was always lost on the "B" roads and late for dinner. My thanks go to Gerry, Lia, Hannah, Tom and Daisy Duggan; Catherine Pickup; Brendan, Helen, Anna, Danny, Seán, Fiona Noctor; Michael Noctor; my aunt Mary Duggan; Pearse, Kathleen, and Jade Duggan; Ken and Diana Allan (who did a considerable amount of legwork for me and provided some of the photos from the early days of the SGHC); Nick and Marie Bryce-Smith; Martin and Kathy Webb; Michael and Helen Williams; Joanne and Paul Mahon; Denis and Jane Pyatt; and Doreen and Eric Stansfield (who have since emigrated to Australia). In the States, Terry Smith and Dan Bunn, Cori Solomon and Ken Bornstein, and Barbara Nackerud and Verial Whitten hosted me on a couple of research trips. On both sides of the Atlantic, all gave me transport, a spare bed, and good cheer.

Several dear friends and relatives have made it their mission to keep me motivated (with dangling carrots and swift kicks) so that this book actually would get published during our lifetimes. These include Dr. Craig and Karen Robertson, Dr. Ken and Mary Ellen Gorske, Abbe Altman, Diane Divin, Seán Duggan, Anna Fuchs, and Fiona Duggan-Fuchs, Kevin Duggan, my uncle Jim Trayler, Verial Whitten, Barbara Nackerud, John Smith, Robert Jones, John and Tracy Skupny, Amy Andres, Margaret Coe, Susan Schroder, and Diana Allan (who prodded persistently and had me take tea at the Orchard in Grantchester for inspiration).

Finally, I owe the greatest of debts to my wife, my friend, and my love, Wendy, for this book could never have been completed without her forbearance and help over the last fourteen years while my head was buried in the manuscript and household projects went uncompleted.

Table of Contents

Foreword by Sir Terence Clark

Brian Patrick Duggan has achieved the distinction of writing a most readable book, with some wonderfully evocative illustrations, that will delight not only the specialists who are interested in knowing more about the origins of their Salukis but also the general reader who enjoys learning about the history of the Middle East in the heyday of the British Empire. He is eminently well-qualified to undertake this task, which has clearly taken many years of research, as he is at the same time a professional educator at the California State University, Stanislaus, and, with his wife Wendy, a most successful breeder of coursing and show Salukis at their Kyzyl Kum kennels.

The central character of the Honorable Florence Amherst, who threads her way through the latter period of Queen Victoria's reign and the turbulent years between the two World Wars, started with all the advantages of wealth and position in society, yet through a chance encounter in Egypt, while on the Grand Tour with her family, she chose to devote much of her life to fostering in the West the captivating breed of hunting hound that she met there. Brian Duggan brings her story alive by revealing previously unpublished material from the Amherst family archives as well as from other sources that are not easy for the general reader to access. Thus we find detailed descriptions of the high life of the expatriate community in Cairo at the end of the 19th century, where the imagination of Florence was fired by the rather eccentric keeper of the Zoological Gardens at Giza, Wilfred Jennings-Bramly, through whom she probably saw her first Salukis and from whom she certainly obtained her foundation breeding pair in 1895 (not 1897, as is commonly and mistakenly reported). She was smitten not only by their graceful beauty and athletic form but also by their impressive history carved into the walls of the tombs of the pharaohs, which she and her family visited as they made their slow progression down the Nile to Luxor. On their return to England she determined to find out everything that she could about the history and development of the breed. She could draw on the considerable library assembled by her father and she also exploited the family connections with a range of personalities in the Middle East, including notably T. E. Lawrence ("Lawrence of Arabia"), by bombarding them with requests for information. Over the next four decades she bred a staggering 50 litters and registered 199 puppies. Although beset by increasing financial problems, which finally limited her ambitions, she also employed her knowledge and experience to write authoritatively about the breed with the object of popularising it in the West.

Brian Duggan brings into the story a range of other great travellers, whose names are still familiar in Middle Eastern circles, such as Lady Jane Digby, Lady Anne Blunt, Austen Layard and Gertrude Bell, who all fell under the spell of their Salukis. He also cites a greater number of less-well-known people, mainly military officers who served in the region and became addicted to hunting with their hounds in the deserts of Iraq, Syria, Palestine and Egypt: an addiction that they sought to replicate on their return home. Among them was Captain (later Brigadier-General) Frederick Lance, who with his wife Gladys shared the object of popularising the breed but who came to dominate it through their well-developed organisational skills. However, they joined forces with Florence in establishing the Saluki or Gazelle Hound Club (SGHC) in 1923 and in putting together an admirably flexible breed standard to take account of the diversity of the hounds' origins that in large measure has withstood the test of time. They clearly struggled to find a name for the breed from the many conflicting usages — from Slughi to Tazi — and the resulting compromise is not the happiest. They should have listened rather to the expert advice of the Reverend H.W. Bush, Florence's only rival in regards to knowledge of Saluki history, who correctly suggested that the proper transliteration of the Arabic name was *Saluqi*.

Nevertheless the relationship between Florence and the Lances was not all smooth sailing and they retained to the end a difference of opinion about breed type, echoes of which continue to be heard to the present day. Florence and her supporters preferred the so-called "lighter Mesopotamian type" as exemplified by the Amherstias of her own breeding over the "heavier Syrian type" as exemplified by the Saronas of the Lances' breeding. The irony is that her foundation hounds did not come from Mesopotamia at all but from a tribe in Lower Egypt with close connections to Syria and she tended to refer to them as *Slughi Shami*, meaning from Syria. Sadly her smaller and lighter hounds, which she once described as being 22 to 24 inches at the shoulder, found less and less favour in the show ring before the more numerous and flashier hounds from the Lance kennels and it has long been a cause for regret among some of the older judges that her type has virtually disappeared. However, until the introduction of the ban on hunting with dogs in Britain in 2003, it was more often to be seen among the coursing community where its light, short-coupled, manoeuvrable frame was well suited to pursuing the wily hare.

Although this book is largely historical, it is also important for the future of the breed in the West. Above all it serves as a salutary reminder of Florence Amherst's belief in the significance of new blood for the gene pool, which motivated her donation to the SGHC of the Amherstia Perpetual Trophy for the best imported dog or bitch. Brian Duggan records that in 1924–28, despite all the difficulties of the six-month quarantine regime then in force, there were at least 35 imports from Transjordan, Egypt, Iraq and the Gulf, with Iraq as the main source, and the leading breeders were keen to outcross their lines with the latest imports. Many breeders were, however, forced to put down their hounds because of food shortages during the Second World War and some of the beneficial effects were therefore lost. Although the former sources are not so prolific as they once were, there are still large populations of hounds in the countries of origin. My hope is that this book will inspire some of the more adventurous to seek them out and bring them back to provide new blood for maintaining the legacy of the pioneers in the breed.

Sir Terence Clark
London

Preface

Serendipity has always played an important part in my life and the idea for this book resulted from two serendipitous coincidences — both of which were a confluence of my long-time interests in the British soldier's experience, early photography, and Salukis. The first was an article in *Saluki Heritage* (1990) about the previous year's sale by Christies in London of the effects of Lt. Col. Walter F. Stirling, D.S.O., M.C., who was Lawrence's chief of staff during the Arab Revolt. Illustrating the article was a photograph of Stirling in his uniform and Arab headdress with a white Saluki by his side, taken on the day that Damascus surrendered in 1917. It was an amazing image and I was glad the auction was long over as I never could have afforded even an opening bid on Stirling's medals and photographs. I mentally filed the image away as an interesting curiosity and forgot about it.

The second coincidence (and ultimately the catalyst) occurred three years later on an impromptu trip to a used bookstore with Jo Ann Van Arsdale, where I stumbled across a 1967 edition of *With Lawrence in Arabia* by Lowell Thomas. I already had a 1924 first edition and did not need a second copy, but I noticed that this one had additional photographs as well as a newly added commentary on the film *Lawrence of Arabia* by Thomas and the surviving participants of the Arab Revolt. Well, those two factors alone made the expenditure of $7.50 worthwhile, but it was not until I actually had the book at home that I noticed the poor reproduction of the photo of Lawrence and his staff at Aqaba — which included Captain Goslett and his Saluki. At that moment the image of Stirling and his Saluki came flooding back to me.

After my wife Wendy calmed me down, I began to think about the two different Salukis in photographs from the same campaign. Figuring that they must be more than a coincidence, I set out to discover what documentation existed about Salukis and the Arab Revolt. The trail led me to the T.E. Lawrence–Florence Amherst letters and then Captain Goslett's photographs at the Imperial War Museum. To my great surprise, these were unknown to breed historians. In the course of further digging, I began to unearth more material about English men and women with Salukis in the desert than could fit in one article, so I started filing away these references — wondering what I was going to do with them. When my article on the Lawrence/Arab Revolt–Saluki connection, "Dear Miss Amherst ... Yours Sincerely, T.E. Lawrence" (*Saluki International*, 1994), won a top award in 1995 from the Dog Writers Association of America, I realized that there might be a story here beyond the interest of just Saluki fanciers — that and a work much larger than a few articles was needed to properly tell the story.

There was an astonishing amount of information turning up and I had a hard time coming to grips with how to tell the story in a logical fashion. It was not until I went to England in 1995 on my first research trip that my friend and Saluki historian Ann Birrell gave me the nucleus for the book's structure with an insightful comment: "None of these people went to the Middle East looking for Salukis, but they found these dogs and liked them enough as companions to bring them back home." What was the attraction to the elite hunting hound of the Bedouin and why were those particular human-canine bonds so strong? Combining that theme with the historical events of the early 20th century seemed to be the key to the story.

I was learning a lot about the first English Saluki owners who were independent and often eccentric. They came from different classes, moved in disparate social circles, changed careers, and even disagreed with each other as to the correct Saluki breed type. The settings ranged from the Valley of the Kings to Jazz-Age London and from the Afghanistan frontier to the lands of the Bible. Syria, Jordan, and Iraq became countries during this time period and oil was discovered in the Persian Gulf. Fascinating stuff, yet I still could not see how to bring these Saluki stories together into a cohesive narrative.

Serendipity stepped in again when an idle thought prompted me to draw an affinity diagram of the characters' relationships and create a timeline of their lives and involvement with the breed. From the diagrams, it became clear that the key champions of the breed, Florence Amherst, Brigadier Lance and his wife Gladys, had Salukis for longer than anyone else in the period. Their biographies became the "red thread" of the book, with the rest of the stories interwoven in around their lives. And that became the concept for the book — the true adventures of people and their dogs set against the tapestry of history.

Two books greatly influenced my thinking in writing the book — *After the Fact: The Art of Historical Detection* (1982) by James West Davidson and Mark Hamilton Lytle (which was given to me by my father), and *The Historian as Detective* (1968), a book of essays edited by Robin W. Winks. These added a dimension to solving historical problems by suggesting that understanding *why* a particular event happened often helps to answer the questions of *what*, *when*, and *how*. The general circumstances of how the Saluki breed came to England were known — but no one had ever asked the *whys*. As the fortunes of three people were tied inextricably to the rise and fall of the Saluki in England, in many respects, the red thread becomes a limited biography of Florence Amherst and the Lances. *The Cruelest Miles: The Heroic Story of Dogs and Men in a Race Against an Epidemic* by Gay & Laney Salisbury (2003) proved that there was interest in the sort of book I wanted to write. It is a great narrative about the race with sled dogs to get life-saving serum to Nome, Alaska, in the terrible winter and diphtheria epidemic of 1925 — a brilliant human/canine adventure story and a real page-turner.

While *Saluki: The Desert Hound and the English Travelers Who Brought It to the West* does cover aspects of the breed's history, it is not comprehensive nor is it a litany of pedigrees — sire and dam information have been included where it bears on human relationships and the story. It would serve no purpose for me to detail pedigrees when other breed scholars have already done so.

It may occur to the reader that in the cast of players, I have omitted a number of famous Middle Eastern travelers. The names of Lady Hester Stanhope, Sir Richard Burton, Alois Musil, Carl Raswan, Wilfred Thesiger, and Freya Stark are instantly recognizable to anyone who studies the desert and its peoples, and all have written at least a little about Salukis. Some of these, such as Doughty, Burton, or Stark, never owned a Saluki and only mentioned them briefly in their writing. The book needed limits, and I confined myself to writing about the men and women who owned or had some important connection to Salukis in the formative years of their importation into England — essentially from 1895 to 1939.

Similarly, there is no shortage of excellent biographical material about T.E. Lawrence, Gertrude Bell, and Vita Sackville-West. As these three individuals had lesser, but nonetheless interesting, experiences with Salukis, it was my intention to reveal this less well-known facet of their lives. As Mr. M.V. Carey of the Seven Pillars of Wisdom Trust so kindly wrote about my article on Lawrence-Amherst letters, "I think that you are right (or your editor is) in the comment that this story has never been told before. It does not appear in any biography of T.E. Lawrence known to me."

Long-distance research can be particularly frustrating and my overseas correspondents have been both obliging and patient — I can certainly now better appreciate Florence Amherst's situation of having to write to strangers and hoping they would reply with the Saluki information she was seeking. When I first began researching this book, the Internet was primitive at best and of no real use, but that has changed exponentially in the last few years. Astonishing amounts of information related to this story can now be found on the Web, although original source materials (which will probably never be broadcast on the Web) are only available to the intrepid researcher who visits the library, archive, or newspaper morgue to take notes by hand.

The period of the book is the fascinating borderland between the Victorian and modern eras. It was a time of great and rapid change — motorcars, motion pictures, jazz, radio, telephones, airplanes, and war technology on a scale that had been previously inconceivable. Social circles could be both wide and small at the same time, and I was continually struck by connections between the classes when there was a common interest such as archaeology or Salukis. Women were gaining independence and leaving corsets behind, yet there were still serious debates about whether it was medically safe or hygienic for women to ride astride. To give the reader some insight into this different age and way of life, wherever possible I have tried to keep their own charming English, rather than using modern idiom or paraphrases. Reading reference material from both sides of the Great Herring Pond has made me slightly dyslexic about the differences between American and English spelling (e.g., "honorable" vs. "honourable"), but for the book I have tried to be consistent in using American spelling conventions.

It is appropriate to address here the use of Arab words and names in the interest of accuracy and clarity. These can be quite confusing when looking at primary sources over one hundred years old whose authors used varying English phonetic pronunciations of both the classical and colloquial languages of Egypt, Arabia, Palestine, Syria, Persia and Mesopotamia. Methods of transliterating Arabic into English with or without diacritical marks have changed in the years I have been working on this book and even current maps and scholars disagree with each other. With the guidance of linguist and former diplomat Sir Terence Clark, K.B.E., C.M.G., C.V.O., I have tried to use modern transliterations of Arabic words and names wherever possible so that the reader may be more easily able to find these places on conventional maps. In some cases, I could find no modern transliteration and have left certain obscure place names as the author wrote them. The erratic and phonetic spelling of Arabic words by both Wilfred Jennings-Bramly and T.E. Lawrence will give the reader some flavor of their letters. I have included a glossary of foreign words at the end of the book, and with Sir Terence's advice, have given not only the Arabic meaning, but a common English spelling of the word along with a more correct modern spelling.

On that same topic, there is the spelling issue of "Saluki" versus "Saluqi." While the latter version is linguistically correct, I have chosen to use "Saluki" in this book as it is the breed name adopted by the kennel clubs in English-speaking countries and consequently more familiar to the reader. More important, I have used "Saluki" because it is what Florence Amherst and her contemporaries used.

To quote Lord Lonsdale, "I have had lots of fun and some of my greatest fun has been among my dogs." Like him, I've had a great deal of fun writing this book (with Ildico napping under my desk), and I hope you find it worthwhile and enjoyable.

Brian Patrick Duggan
Turlock, California
Spring 2009

Prologue: Unanswered Letters

"I'll write to the greyhound fancier ... but she will get nothing out of me. I've finished with the East; & forgotten it."

T.E. Lawrence[1]

Once again, something was missing from the handful of letters that came in the Honorable Florence Amherst's morning post — the reply from Colonel Lawrence. For some reason, he was ignoring her inquiries about Saluki dogs, the greyhound of the Bedouin. Florence was sixty-four and England's reigning expert on the rare breed. After nearly thirty years of research, she was still indefatigable in sleuthing out their recondite history. She knew that Lawrence had considerable experience in the desert and that his current fame might be a way to help establish her Salukis in the public eye and achieve the sort of lasting popularity that Borzoi fanciers enjoyed. After all, Salukis had become somewhat trendy the year before in 1923, during the Egyptian craze that followed the opening of Tutankhamun's tomb.

Prior to the Great War, when T.E. Lawrence had been a young archaeologist in Northern Syria, he had once supplied Florence with some local folklore about Salukis. She still had three of his letters preserved in her files. True, their acquaintance had been slight and Lawrence had been an erratic correspondent, but she could not fathom his current silence. Being a baron's daughter, she was accustomed to a modicum of deference, to say nothing of common courtesy. Surely one letter was not too much to ask of a former correspondent who was now a war hero?

Florence poured tea into her cup — it mixed with the milk until it was light brown. She added her usual dose of sugar and then sat back in her armchair to ponder the next step. The walls around her were crowded with paintings and photographs of Salukis, Egyptian scenes, and family portraits. The bookshelves were overflowing with photo albums, research notes, boxes of correspondence from around the world, and volumes on history, art, archaeology, dogs, and the Middle East. The Amherst family all had a great passion for scholarly learning, art, and travel, and in happier times their wealth had given them the leisure to indulge both their pleasures and researches.

When Florence first imported Salukis in 1895, she set about to learn everything she could about them and their unique place in Bedouin culture. Because of the dearth of reliable information about Salukis in books about dog breeds, she depended primarily on receiving information via a stream of letters to and from archaeologists and diplomats working in the Middle East. In the fall of 1911, David Hogarth of the Ashmolean Museum suggested that she write to one of his employees, Lawrence, who was currently excavating the Hittite palace mound at Carchemish in northern Syria. Now, twelve years later, Florence knew that Hogarth was still in touch with Lawrence and she wondered if perhaps he could intercede again for her.

Lawrence had met Florence only once — for tea and sandwiches at her London town house in January of 1913.[2] She was a gracious host and, having worked with her father's private collection of Egyptian and Babylonian artifacts, was quite knowledgeable about archaeology herself. They discussed his work at the Hittite mound but the aristocratic Salukis were the primary focus of the meeting. She had her kennel man trot out several for display — including the magnificent Sultan who had been doing a fair amount of winning at dog shows. Even though Lawrence did not like dogs, he could appreciate their beauty and graceful athleticism.

They parted that day with Lawrence helpfully agreeing to send her more information from Syria and to see if a breeding pair could be charmed away from a sheikh to increase her stock. His intentions were good but work would cause them to fade and they finally disappeared when war against Germany was declared in 1914. Lawrence enlisted in the army and would eventually find his niche in the guerrilla warfare campaign in Arabia. Florence's attention turned to the pressing problems of helping the war effort, dealing with food shortages, and the difficulties caused by the steadily diminishing Amherst fortune.

In the years after the armistice, the American journalist and showman Lowell Thomas produced a hugely popular lecture about the Middle Eastern campaign. In it, Thomas used sets, images, music and his own narration to romanticize the events of the Arab Revolt, and Thomas named Colonel Lawrence "the Uncrowned King of Arabia" — much to the latter's embarrassment and discomfort.

While Lawrence's hit-and-run tactics against the Turks had been highly successful, from his perspective, the war had ended badly. At the Peace Conference in 1919, the British and French governments carved up the former Ottoman Empire according to a long-standing agreement — despite the efforts of Lawrence and Prince Faisal to secure an independent Arab state. Thomas's show generated a barrage of unwanted attention for Lawrence, including letters requesting lectures, favors, and even marriage.[3] His own book about the Arab Revolt was *Seven Pillars of Wisdom*, which would have its first printing in 1922. To avoid the uncomfortable public attention, he changed his name and rejoined the RAF later that year, not with the rank of an officer, but as an enlisted man — a lowly ranker.

Now that Lawrence was an unwilling celebrity, "the greyhound fancier" was after him again and he justifiably suspected that she wanted to capitalize on his fame to promote her dogs. As it happened, he had indeed seen several Salukis during the campaign but wanted to put his desert experience far behind him. He had determined to ignore Florence, but in early 1924 a letter arrived from David Hogarth, diplomatically suggesting that Lawrence might at least write a short note to her.

If Florence was annoyed at his lack of response, then Lawrence was equally annoyed at her persistence — and that she would presume upon a slight acquaintance from long ago to pester him about such trivial matters as dogs. She refused to take the hint of unanswered letters and had now involved Hogarth. Baron's daughter or no, this was the last straw — but to mollify his friend, Lawrence agreed to write to Florence Amherst one last time.

PART I: DISCOVERY

1

The Bibliophile and His Daughters

*"His collection of travels in Palestine and of herbals both start with the earliest printed
books devoted to these subjects."*

Alfred W. Pollard[1]

The first Baron Amherst of Hackney, his wife and four daughters celebrated New
Year's Eve 1894 in the lounge of an Egyptian boat anchored on the moonlit banks of the Nile.
They had dressed formally for the occasion—Lord Amherst in his white collar and dinner
jacket, and the ladies in their evening gowns and jewelry. Taking the time from the patriarch's pocket watch, at midnight the loving family toasted each other with champagne
and sang "God Save the Queen" and "Auld Lang Syne" as the *dehabiyeh* swayed gently on the
Nile.

The New Year would see the births of the future King George VI, the American libret-
tist Oscar Hammerstein, baseball hero Babe Ruth, and the nation of Rhodesia. The ill-
fated Czar Nicholas II had just assumed the throne of Russia and Louis Pasteur would
die that year. Art Nouveau was all the rage and Oscar Wilde would serve time in prison.
While *The Time Machine* and *Quo Vadis* took the public's reading fancy, Mr. Sherlock
Holmes was back in Baker Street after years in hiding. St. Petersburg saw the first complete
performance of *Swan Lake* and motion pictures made their debut at a Parisian hotel. King
C. Gillette invented the safety razor and Lily Langtry, actress and former lover of the Prince
of Wales, had £40,000 worth of jewels stolen from a Union Bank safe. Marconi's radio-
telegraphy became practical and William Röentgen's newly discovered "invisible radiations of
light" caused a sensation by producing a remarkable image of hand bones after an exposure
of only fifteen to twenty minutes. "Clarke's World Famed Blood Mixture," "Carter's Little
Liver Pills," "Dr. William's Pink Pills for Pale People," and "Dr. Knight's Spheroids—A
Special Pill for Ladies" all guaranteed cures for a bewildering variety of ailments in the year
1895.

The *dehabiyeh* was gaily decorated for the holiday with the colored drapes and palm
fronds which had been purchased for their bon voyage party in Cairo. On New Year's Day,
the Amherst daughters, Florence, Sybil, Margaret, and Alicia, hired donkeys and rode through
cultivated fields to marvel at the giant statues of Ramesses II in the ruins of Memphis. Riding west from the colossi and dodging the crowds from a Cook's steamer tour, they explored
the necropolis of Saqqara and neighboring tombs. The Amhersts were thoroughly enjoying
the beginning of their holiday in Egypt and knowing that Norfolk was buried in the cold
snows of winter made the warm weather all the sweeter. For Florence Amherst, the trip to
Egypt would change her life in a manner that she could never have imagined. In the shad-

ows of the Giza pyramids, she would first see Salukis — a rare breed of hound that would fire
her imagination and inspire devotion for the rest of her years.

Florence Margaret was born on January 25, 1860, to William and Margaret Tyssen-
Amhurst* of Didlington Hall, Norfolk.† She was their third daughter and named after both
her father's younger sister and her mother. The Tyssen-Amhursts were wealthy gentry with a
respectable family name. William's ancestor, Francis Tyssen of Flushing, Holland, had become
a naturalized English citizen in the late 17th century. His sons were to make wise property
investments in Hackney near London town, for by the 1880s there were no less than seven
railway stations on the Amhurst Hackney properties. In 1852, after generations of marriages
and alliances, the family name had become Tyssen-Amhurst.§ The Amhurst side of the family could trace their Kentish ancestry back to the time of Henry III. Florence's father would
make one final modification to the family name in August 1877 when the spelling was changed
to mark the distant connection to the descendants of William Pitt, the Earls of Amherst.

As a child, William Amhurst Tyssen-Amhurst was privately tutored at Hethel Hall just
a few miles from Norwich and later attended boarding school at Eton. In May of 1853 he was
enrolled in Christ Church College, Oxford. A daguerreotype of William at that time shows
his mild expression in a thoughtful pose. His oval face was framed by lank, brown hair —
carefully parted on one side and worn long enough to curl up over his ears. Of average height
and sturdy build, he sported a wispy mustache as soon as there was enough growth to look
intentional. William's school chums knew him as a genial fellow with unassuming manners
and an appreciation for the pleasures of outdoor life. He was an avid cricket player and a
scholar who spent countless hours in the Bodleian Library and Ashmolean Museum. His fascination with rare books and antiquities would become deep and abiding passions.

From all accounts, he was a kind and generous man with an excellent education and a
deep aesthetic sensibility. After finishing school, he would later become, in succession, high
sheriff for Norfolk, then member of Parliament (Conservative) for West Norfolk and Southwest Norfolk. He would also be provincial grand master for the Masons, a member of several charitable organizations, and a noted breeder of Norfolk Red Poll cattle.** His mother,
Mary, had died at the recently purchased Didlington Hall in February 1854 while he was in
school. Almost exactly two years later, January 1856, his father also died in their new home.
His brother and two sisters benefited from the will, but as the eldest, William inherited the
bulk of the property and estates (consisting of some 10,000 acres in Norfolk and 2,500 acres
in the Hackney borough of London) and became master of the villages of Didlington and
Buckenham. He also now owned the smaller estate of Foulden, a London house at 88 Brook
Street, off Grosvenor Square, a house or two in Hackney, and a villa in the south of France.

With a respectable surname and prospect of a substantial inheritance, William could reasonably expect the finest that life could offer. He was a most eligible bachelor but it was not
long before he removed himself from the competition. At one of the endless rounds of social

---

*The spelling was later changed to "Amherst."
†Southwest of Swaffham and near the village of Foulden.
§The surname Amhurst entered the family around 1800, through a Captain Amhurst of the Royal Navy. He
married the illegitimate but wealthy Mary Tyssen (Florence's great-great-grandmother). Mary was fortunate to
have not only her own inheritance but also those of her two unmarried brothers (also illegitimate) on their deaths.
**An ancient breed in that part of England, Red Poll cattle were used both for beef and milk production.

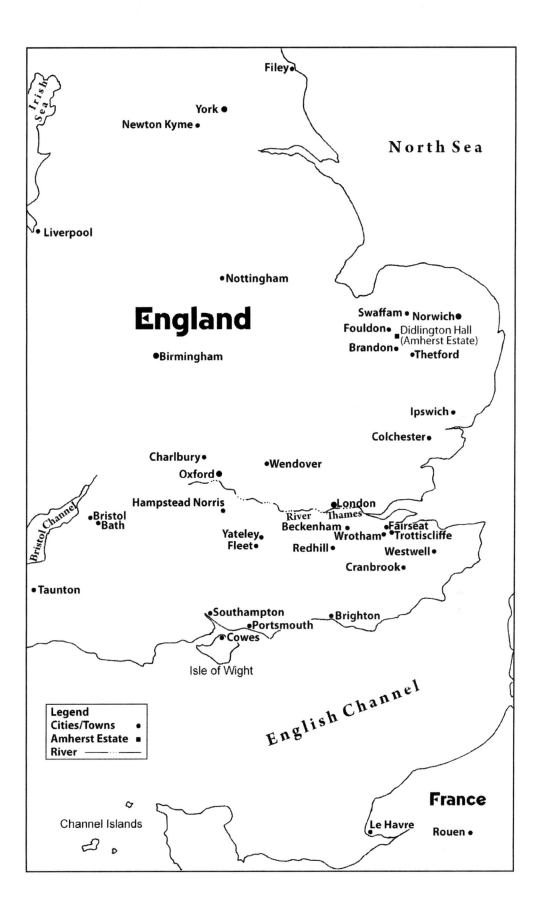

Irish Sea

Filey●

York ●

Newton Kyme ●

North Sea

●Liverpool

●Nottingham

England

Swaffam ● Norwich●
Fouldon● ■ Didlington Hall
Brandon● (Amherst Estate)
●Thetford

●Birmingham

Ipswich●

Colchester●

Charlbury●

●Wendover

Oxford●

Bristol Channel

Hampstead Norris●
River Thames
●London
Beckenham●
●Bristol
●Bath

●Fairseat
Wrotham●●Trottiscliffe
Yateley●
Fleet●
Redhill●
Westwell●

Cranbrook●

●Taunton

●Southampton
●Portsmouth ●Brighton
●Cowes

Isle of Wight

Legend
Cities/Towns ●
Amherst Estate ■
River ———

English Channel

France

Channel Islands

●Le Havre
Rouen ●

functions, William met and fell in love with Margaret Susan, the only daughter of Admiral Robert Mitford. Margaret had a marvelous mezzo-soprano voice and used to captivate her audiences when she sang at gatherings and dinners. She was an excellent wood carver and would decorate portions of Didlington Hall with work she produced in the lathe room. Her special accomplishments included the ability to carve an interlocking ivory puzzle-ball, and her woodworking skills won her the freedom* of the Worshipful Company of Turners. Her family would remember her as a "good amateur surgeon"—presumably the result of ample practice on the pets and her active daughters.[2] William and Margaret became engaged, and on June 4, 1856, they were married at the admiral's estate—Hunmanby Hall, Yorkshire. On their honeymoon, they hired a special railway carriage and the front of the locomotive engine was covered with flowers. They were both 21 years old.

Mr. and Mrs. Tyssen-Amhurst settled into Didlington Hall and their new life together. Three hours from London by train and coach, Didlington was located in the wild and beautiful Norfolk countryside. The grand neo–Georgian manor was constructed of red and white brick in an Italian style and if one looked closely, architectural elements of a much older building could be seen here and there within the Hall.[†] There were no less than forty-six bedrooms (including one reserved for royal visits), twelve reception rooms, grand ballroom, library, seven bathrooms, offices, and a museum. The outbuildings consisted of two guesthouses, coach house, large stables, kennels, greenhouses and hothouses, boathouse, and falconer's lodge. Situated on 7,105 acres, Didlington boasted a large reflecting pool, private cricket ground, trout stream, artificial lake, folly, deer park, and sixty acres of parks and tended grounds. With neighboring estates belonging to the Prince of Wales, the Earl of Albermarle, the Earl of Leicester, and Lord Walsingham, the Tyssen-Amhursts were in distinguished company in their corner of Norfolk.

Margaret took charge of the household and saw that there was an adequate domestic staff to keep the manor alive and running smoothly. The small army of servants including major-domo, housekeeper, butlers, footmen, cooks, and maids for the upstairs, downstairs, and scullery, made Didlington Hall a community of its own. In all, twenty-five house servants lived in seventeen rooms, segregated by gender. The grounds staff included gardeners, builders, coachmen, and gamekeeper—all of whom had their own cottages on the estate.

Tyssen-Amhurst asked his childhood tutor, the Reverend F.A. Bickmore of Hethel Hall, to be both the rector of St. Michael's Church on the estate grounds and the nearby church at Cranwich. St. Michael's medieval baptismal font would do yeoman service for the family. Their first child was born a year after their marriage and six other daughters were to follow between 1858 and 1869: Mary Rothes Margaret ("May") in 1857, Sybil Margaret ("Sib") in 1858, Florence Margaret ("Flo" or "Fluff") in 1860, Margaret Mitford ("Maggie") in 1864, Alicia Margaret ("Ally") in 1865, Geraldine Margaret ("Cherry") in 1867, and Beatrice Margaret ("Bee") in 1869. All of the girls were named after their mother, Margaret.[§]

Florence, who was also named after William's youngest sister, had blue eyes, a fair complexion, and an abundance of fine, curly hair. Growing up, she was taught watercolor paint-

---

Dating back to medieval times, a man who was granted the freedom of guild or a city had certain privileges or rights not available to vassals. Its American equivalent, although more ceremonial, is the custom of an honored guest being given the key to a city.

†In "The Return from Hawking," a romantic hunting scene commissioned by Lord Francis Egerton (later the Earl of Ellesmere), Sir Edwin Landseer, R.A., included a Didlington stable archway as the backdrop.

§I am indebted to the late Baroness Strange for her notes on the Amherst family.

South view of Didlington Hall, 1910. The Sekhmet statues can just be seen between the windows of the Museum Room. © English Heritage, National Monuments Record. #BB87/06342.

ing, music, and the domestic arts that a Victorian lady was expected to be proficient in — including needlework, flower arranging, and planning elaborate dinner parties. The estate at Didlington had many fine riding trails and a stable of horses. She learned to ride sidesaddle (decent women could ride no other way) and would become a superior horsewoman. In winter, the girls would dress in fur hats and woolen skirts, lace skates to their shoes and go ice skating on the lake. Florence in particular excelled in tracing precise, delicate figures.

She had a lovely, low soprano voice and adored dancing. Florence mastered the piano, and a family friend and celebrated virtuoso of the day, Guido Papini, taught her to play the violin.* In 1897 a song written by Florence, Sybil, and Mary was included in the children's pamphlet, *A Child's Book of Song and Praise*. Needing a male voice to work out their compositions, Florence and Maggie would frequently summon under-gardener James Trimbee to assist.

The Honorable Florence Margaret Tyssen Amherst, circa 1880. With the kind permission of Mrs. Venetia Chattey.

*Lord Amherst owned several rare stringed instruments, including a cello and violin made by Antonio Stradivari (Cozio Publishing Ltd., http://www.cozio.com/, accessed on September 27, 2007).

The young man was delighted to oblige the two ladies as his own recreational preference was St. Michael's choir — which he thought a more fitting pastime than joining the estate's beer-soaks down the road at the White Hart pub.*

Devoted to her father, Florence would often assist "Fardie" with his correspondence and studies. Once during a sailing holiday, Tyssen-Amhurst lay ill on his yacht and Florence took dictation for his chapter notes on an incident in Spanish history. According to family tradition, she spoke French, German, and Spanish, and once surprised her family by conversing in Russian on their 1888 holiday trip to St. Petersburg.

The maze of rooms at Didlington was perfect for hide and seek, and the halls would echo with the laughter of the girls and, in later years, with that of nieces, nephews, and grandchildren. Didlington Hall was filled with rare tapestries, antiques, armor, hunting trophies, military loot, statues, and paintings — including portraits of the family by the well-known pre–Raphaelite artist the Honorable John Collier. Two of the most remarkable architectural features were works of art in their own right. There was the 300-square-foot Vernet Room (with walls covered in Spanish leather painted by the room's namesake) and the Octagon Room, whose walls were filled with paintings of grotesque animals and birds, all capped by a sun dome. Here in this visually rich environment, Florence and her sisters played, studied, and flourished.

For the adventuresome children, Didlington held innumerable outdoor pastimes. There was riding, rowing, croquet, and lawn tennis. The well-kept pet cemetery and carved wooden dogs on the family pews in St. Michael's were tangible signs of the family's affection for their dogs. The gardens, lawns, woods, lake, dovecote, and the River Wissey provided plenty of opportunity for games and walks. Picnics on Birdcage Island or playing at knights and damsels at the Castle Cave tower (a pseudo-medieval folly) were always a great treat. With the lakes and woods at Didlington teeming with trout, pike, otter, heron, pheasant, woodcock, snipe, quail, geese, rabbit, hare, fox, and deer, nature study and sketching were engaging pastimes. When the weather was too foul to be outdoors, Florence and her sisters would sharpen their artistic talents by drawing the Egyptian artifacts in their father's private museum.

Tyssen-Amhurst hospitality was a byword of society and they hosted regular dinners, balls, and shooting parties when they were not traveling abroad. Mrs. Tyssen-Amhurst's delicate carvings were much admired by Didlington's guests, and audiences were said to weep when she hit the last note of "Ave Maria." They were equal to any hospitality need — even when royalty came to visit. In December of 1888, they were honored with a visit from Albert, Prince of Wales, his son Albert Victor, the Duke of Clarence, Prince Louis Estherhazy, Lord and Lady Cecil and other nobles of the court. Tyssen-Amhurst was a crack shot, but no doubt took pains to see that he did not outdo his royal guest. The Prince of Wales was particularly satisfied with his large bag of quail and pronounced Didlington as one of the best preserves for cover shooting in the country.[3] The affair was a great success and suitably noted in the society columns of the day.

The family was active and energetic, and the seven daughters as indefatigable as their father. They spent their leisure in scholarly pursuits, charity, and travel. Tyssen-Amhurst was a knight justice and secretary of the Order of St. John of Jerusalem in England — an order dedicated to ambulance work and hospital assistance. Florence, Mary, and Sybil would become

---

*I am grateful to Mrs. J. MacKenzie for permission to quote her father's autobiography, A Trail of Trials, Pentland Press.

lady justices of that same order. Their mother instilled in the girls the importance of charity and they took great interest in the welfare of their tenants — attending to children's education, food for the poor, care of the sick, and re-building churches and schools. The North Eastern Hospital for Children in Hackney* was a favorite cause for Mrs. Tyssen-Amhurst. In 1885, to benefit the hospital, she published *In a Good Cause*, an anthology of poems and stories which included "Le Jardin des Tuileries" by the promising poet Oscar Wilde, and a prequel to *King Solomon's Mines* entitled "Hunter Quatermain's Story" by H. Rider Haggard.

The Tyssen-Amhurst women appeared regularly as dignitaries at charitable bazaars and Christmas fetes, and were often prize-givers at county fair competitions. A considerate and generous employer, Tyssen-Amhurst cared deeply about his workers and had no hesitation in hiring extra men as needed. So that his gardeners and groundskeepers would have a salary during the winter, he set them to work on special projects on the lake and wetlands.[4] He employed 300 men on his estates and paid out a total of £200 per month in old-age pensions — an extremely liberal amount for the time.[5] Tyssen-Amhurst had given instructions that a large copper pot in the butler's pantry should be always filled with beer for the staff. Anyone was welcome to a mug and this was a great relief on hot days, particularly as the White Hart pub was two miles down the road and beer sold for twopence a pint. James Trimbee noted in his memoirs that some of the senior gardeners took advantage of Amherst's generosity and found several excuses a day to visit the kitchen and sample the contents of the pot.[†] Trimbee had been at Didlington for only a few years, but on announcing his intention to emigrate to Canada to improve himself, the kindly Amherst called him into his library and gave him his best wishes along with four golden sovereigns as a parting gift.[6]

The splendid library was the spiritual heart of Didlington. Amherst's collection of incunabula was his pride and joy. Nearly a thousand rare volumes were housed in the large library and filled floor-to-ceiling bookshelves. Proudly displayed were several books written by himself and his family. Through a solitary door concealed behind a bookcase, Florence and her sisters would enter the library and work at several tables dedicated to their projects. Here in warm sisterhood, they would work on their sketches and translations, read *Punch*, *Country Life Magazine*, the newspapers from London and Norfolk, Tyssen-Amhurst's scholarly journals and the library's wondrous books.

Each of the daughters had her particular hobbies: Florence researched Egyptology; Sybil specialized in the husbandry of Emden geese. Bee loved painting, rowing, and caring for the family pets, and Mary was an expert ornithologist and skilled at needlepoint. Maggie sculpted and freely translated Spanish, Alicia was an accomplished photographer and an authority on the history of English gardening, and Cherry was a knowledgeable geologist and graphologist, and could decipher hieroglyphics as well as sculpt. All the daughters were talented watercolorists and their project tables were loaded with paraphernalia — Limoges enamels, Russian grammars, geological handbooks, photographs, sketches, sextants, prismatic compasses, and microscopes. From his desk in front of the stone fireplace, Fardie would adoringly watch his daughters at work — their hair ringed with halos from the light of the solitary window. On the painted ceiling above, the nine muses watched over the scholarly pursuits of the family.

Not only concerned for the intellectual sustenance of his family, the Master of Didlington was also very keen on comfort and convenience. He gave every thought to domestic

---

Still located on Hackney Road, Bethnal Green, and now known as the Queen Elizabeth Hospital for Children.
[†]*Quoted with the kind permission of Ms. Jean Trimbee McKenzie.*

Lord Amherst's library at Didlington Hall, with the painting of the nine muses on the ceiling. © English Heritage, National Monuments Record #BB87/06344.

improvements and took pride in equipping his home with the latest of these. There was an underground ice house, a model laundry, a darkroom (complete with plumbing) for Alicia's photography, a steam-powered fire engine, cloth escape chutes for the upper stories, a motor-car garage, a petrol generator and glass-jar accumulators (batteries) to provide electric lights, electricians to maintain them, and a hydraulic ram which pumped lake water up to a cistern in the observatory tower. From there, gravity delivered ample water pressure throughout the manor, as well as providing power to the lathe in Mrs. Tyssen-Amhurst's woodworking room in the tower.

They adored travel and sailing. The squire of Didlington commissioned the construction of a yawl to accommodate the family of nine, a couple of guests, and crew. He took an active interest in all the aspects of the two-masted boat's design and construction, and had a careful eye for detail — the ship builder was even instructed to see that the yacht's bookshelves were large enough to hold his copy of *Gulliver's Travels*, most appropriate reading for a scholar-sailor. Tyssen-Amhurst joined the Royal Yachting Society and passed the test for his own master's license so that he could take the helm himself. Christened *The Dream*, the yacht was ready for its maiden voyage in 1874 and Mr. C.R. Chapman was engaged as the ship's master. That year the family took an extended cruise around England, Scotland, and Ireland, and *The Dream* was permanently berthed at the fashionable harbor of Cowes on the Isle of Wight.

In 1871, on a trip to Paris and Switzerland, the family came down with dysentery and recuperated at a chateau on Lake Thun. In 1877, the year that they changed the spelling of their name, the Tyssen-Amhersts contracted scarlet fever and were confined to their house in Grosvenor Square. When they were well enough to travel, they moved to Devonshire and rented a villa in Sidmouth to speed their complete recuperation. From 1878 to 1880, they toured Spain and the Pyrenees, cruised the Mediterranean and traveled extensively in France, Italy, and Norway. Tyssen-Amhurst built a villa called Lou Casteou in the small town of Valescure, near Saint Raphael on the French Riviera. They would spend months on holiday there and use it as a rest stop on the way home from longer journeys abroad. They had grand adventures, but the togetherness of family holidays was not to be enjoyed much longer.

In January of 1880, Tyssen-Amherst's younger brother, Francis, died at sea while returning to England from his sugar plantation in the Solomon Islands. Tragedy struck again in November of the following year when Beatrice, the youngest daughter, contracted typhoid fever while on holiday in Cannes and died. She was just twelve. The family was inconsolable at the loss of Bee, their bright little pixie. Consumed with grief, the family accompanied her body back to Didlington and saw her interred in the family vault at St. Michael's.

Happier events would further diminish the family. In 1885, the eldest daughter, Mary, married Lord William Cecil, C.V.O., the son of the Marquess of Exeter and a well-connected personage in court circles. In 1890, Geraldine, the sixth daughter, married Captain Malcolm Drummond and became the mistress of Megginch Castle in Errol, Perthshire. Mrs. Tyssen-Amherst arranged for the estate gardeners to send cut flowers to her married daughters every week. The family now numbered six.

In 1892, at the age of 57, the graying William Tyssen-Amherst was still a vigorous and sturdy man — but his eyelids were beginning to droop, and, as if to balance his balding pate, he sported a magnificent full beard. In August of that year, he was elevated to the peerage with great ceremony and invested with the crimson velvet mantle trimmed with ermine and silver gilt coronet emblematic of his rank. He was now the Right Honorable Baron William Amhurst Tyssen-Amherst of Hackney, his daughters were entitled to have the prefix "The Honorable" attached to their own names and their mother was now Lady Tyssen-Amherst. Gradually the Tyssen portion of their surname fell into disuse. The Baron now signed his letters "Amherst of Hackney."

If rare books and travel were two of Lord Amherst's great passions, the third was his museum of archaeology, which at the time held the largest private collection of Egyptian and Assyrian artifacts in England. He had purchased three private collections and from these formed the bulk of the Didlington museum. He was a committee member of the Egypt Exploration Fund, and a fellow of the Society of Antiquities, and privately financed archaeologists on their expeditions — with the understanding that he would be able to purchase some of the choicest finds for his collection. Despite the fact that Amherst was methodical in his approach to most projects, some of his large purchases of tablets and papyri were not cataloged until years after he bought them, and by that time he often could not remember where or when they had been obtained or how much he had paid for them.

Early on, Florence caught her father's interest in archaeology — which was fitting as the Didlington Collection was begun in the year she was born. She often handled his correspondence with dealers of antiquities and museum experts. The Amherst Egyptian collection had outstanding examples of sculpture, canopic jars, papyri, mummies, jewelry, and Babylonian tablets. A group of scrolls that would come to be known as the "Amherst Papyri," contained a wealth of information about tomb robbing, a harem conspiracy to depose Ramesses III, a geographical survey of Lower Egypt, literature, and several Books of the Dead. Perhaps the most remarkable feature of the collection was seven diorite statues of the lion-headed goddess, Sekhmet — the sun-scorching, destroyer of the wicked in the afterlife.*

The massive, dark-gray figures ranged in size from five to seven feet tall and weighed nearly two tons each. Placed outdoors between the windows of the museum, the Sekhmets kept watch over the lawn and Italian garden. The author H. Rider Haggard lived in Ditchingham, in eastern Norfolk, and was a frequent visitor to Didlington and its museum. He was said to have been inspired to write the novel *She* from the expression on the painted face of a wooden *shawabty* figure in the collection.† Amongst the many treasures, Amherst had the mummy and case of Amenhotep I — the first mummy case brought to England in 1730, four other human mummies, and assorted cats, hawks, ibis, and crocodiles collected by Grenfell, the famous Egyptologist. The macabre exhibits were too much for the superstitious country girls employed as maids. Frightened of dusting glass cases containing desiccated corpses and painted sarcophagi, the downstairs maids resigned on a regular basis — provoking periodic staff shortages for Lady Amherst.§ But the exhibits were to have more significance than enlightening the Amhersts or alarming country maids. It was at Didlington Hall that the discoverer of Tutankhamun's tomb first became fascinated by the antiquities of Egypt.

In the neighboring county of Suffolk, local artists Samuel Carter and his son, Howard, were making names for themselves doing landscapes and portraiture. Despite class differences, friendly ties developed between the Amhersts and the Carters, and Lord Amherst eventually purchased Sporle Road House in the nearby town of Swaffham for the use of the Carter family.[7] The elder Carter had painted for the Amhersts since the 1850s and at the request of Lady Amherst had provided three illustrations for the Hunter Quatermain story in her charity publication, *In a Good Cause*. In the course of painting Lord Amherst's commissions, Samuel introduced his son to the family benefactor. Impressed with the boy's artistic abilities and his interest in the Egyptian collection, Amherst gave young Howard Carter the freedom of the private museum. The ancient statues, jewelry, and pottery fragments mesmerized the lad, and he came to prefer antiquities to the portraits of lapdogs and squire's wives that were the primary source of the Carter family income. Lord and Lady Amherst would become his patrons and Howard Carter would not only prove a loyal friend to them in difficult times, but also play an unsuspecting role in helping Florence to gain breed recognition for her beloved Salukis.

Her counterpart, Bastet, was depicted as a domestic cat which represented, in addition to domestic virtues, gentle and beneficial sunshine.

†*From the Amherst collection (most likely a gift), Haggard acquired an 18th Dynasty copper and gold ring adorned with Akhenaton's name. Two months before he died in May 1925, Haggard gave it to his good friend, Rudyard Kipling, as a belated birthday present (Morton Cohen, ed., Rudyard Kipling to Rider Haggard: The Record of a Friendship [Florham, NJ: Fairleigh Dickinson University Press, 1965], 146–148).*

§*The less affluent satisfied their interest in Egyptology by visiting the popular exhibits at the British Museum or indulging in the strange Victorian pastime of purchasing a mummy and then unwrapping it at a party.*

2

Didlington Up the Nile

"Those who have drunk from the Nile will always return to drink from it again."
Egyptian proverb

Toward the latter part of 1860, Amherst asked his sister Amelie and his uncle and aunt, Charles and Rose Fountaine, to accompany Margaret and him on a trip up the Nile. The Fountaines were well aware of the difficulties of traveling in Egypt, for in the days before Thomas Cook and Sons' tours, travelers had to fend for themselves as best as their wits and purses could manage. Charles Fountaine was a photographer, and in addition to the extensive quantity of luggage that was necessary for a gentleman or lady on tour, there was a wooden tripod and camera, crates of glass photographic plates, and bottles of chemicals that would need to be transported by porter, donkey, camel, and native boat. Knowing the possible hardships but fond of the legendary Amherst hospitality, Charles agreed to go "if it is Didlington up the Nile."[1]

At the time of the Amhersts' trip to Egypt in the winter of 1860, Florence was under a year old, and stayed at home with toddlers Mary and Sybil, and their nanny. The trip was a great success and the Amhersts vowed to return one day. The Amhersts traveled to the Middle East a second time in June 1864, and Amelie came along again. In Syria, they met the remarkable expatriate Jane Digby (formerly Lady Ellenborough) who escorted their camel expedition to the ruins of Palmyra (Tadmur), the capital of the legendary warrior Queen Zenobia. Amelie had painted several excellent watercolors of Didlington and applied her talents to capturing Middle Eastern scenes.* Jane much admired her faithful rendering of the desert colors — but did not care much for "her prodigality of 'Indian yellow' on her buildings."

In the early years of their marriage, Lord and Lady Amherst made frequent trips to Egypt and Palestine — always with relatives or friends along for company. During the gala opening of the Suez Canal in 1869, Thomas Cook realized that there was money to be made in organized tours of Egypt and Palestine. With the birth of his world-famous agency, travel in exotic places became much easier. By the early 1890s, Florence and her three sisters were very keen to see Egypt. The Amhersts had recommended Howard Carter for an apprenticeship in the British Museum and by 1892 he was excavating at Tell el–Amarna under tutelage of the eminent Flinders Petrie, with Lord Amherst's patronage. Carter had sent statuary fragments of

Amelie's paintings are still treasured by William Tyssen-Amherst's descendants.

19

Akenaten and Nefertiti to add to the Didlington collection and the Amhersts daughters were eager to see the places where their treasures had been excavated.

Advertising helped fuel the fire of interest. The 1894–95 season in Egypt promised to be "unusually brilliant" according to Cook's publication *Excursionist and Tourist Advisor*— and they had recently built new luxury boats to cater to their upper-class clients. The four daughters persuaded their Fardie that the time had come for them to see Egypt. Noting an advertisement for the new flotilla of luxury Nile steamers, Lord Amherst booked one of the best boats and planned the long-awaited holiday in Egypt with his wife and spinster daughters.*

On Tuesday, December 4, 1894, Lord and Lady Amherst, Sybil, Florence, Margaret, and Alicia (then aged 37, 34, 31, and 30, respectively) along with family friend, Ernest, departed Victoria Station for Dover and the continent. They had twenty pieces of luggage between them ("four huge bags and sixteen packages"), including Alicia's photographic gear† and the family pet, a small dog named Ducker. At Calais, they attended the new opera *Thais* and then traveled by rail south to Marseilles, and then east along the French coast through Toulon, Cannes, and Nice. Crossing into Italy, they stopped at Genoa and then headed south to Rome, coming at last to Brindisi on the heel of the Italian boot. There, on the Adriatic Sea, they boarded the 6,000-ton P. & O. steamer, S.S. *Arcadia*.§

Carrying three hundred passengers and burning 100 tons of coal a day, with an engine that generated 700 horsepower, the *Arcadia* was fully equipped with modern conveniences, including electric lights and "ice chambers" cooled to 10° Fahrenheit. Alicia described the *Arcadia* as being "all lit up at night — like a moving town."[2] Florence, Sybil, Margaret, Alicia, and Ducker shared a four-bunk cabin and their parents had the same for themselves. Stewards, crisply uniformed in white, glided about the ship attending to the needs of the First Class passengers. As the *Arcadia* steamed across the Mediterranean, every night there were concerts and entertainments. Excellent dancers all, the Amherst women in their best dresses skipped through the polkas, lancers, and schottisches played by the ship's band — who avoided waltzes due to the potential hazardous combination of gliding dance steps and a rolling deck. On a raised stage there were even *tableaux vivants* to help the evenings pass merrily. Florence and her sisters were no vaporish, hothouse flowers, and they seized every experience that the voyage had to offer. One day they appeared above decks, blackened with coal dust and grinning from ear to ear. Excitedly, they told their bemused parents that they had persuaded the ship's engineer to let them stoke one of the enormous iron boilers.[3]

The *Arcadia* passed the tall lighthouse of Port Said, and docked amidst the jumble of buildings on either side of the north end of the Suez Canal at 2:00 P.M., Tuesday, December 18. While the ship was coaling, the Amhersts went off to sample the local scenery. It was customary for newcomers to buy their first topees or pith helmets here. As long as one was in Africa or India, they were worn from the first light of day until sundown, and not packed

---

Commonly used in Victorian times, "spinster," "bachelor," and "widow" merely denoted marital status and were not considered to be insults unless used as such.

†*This would have consisted of a large plate camera, wooden tripod, boxes of glass plates and chemicals, enamel trays, and a dark tent for developing the exposed plates on location—an elaborate and cumbersome process. The Amhersts may have also had one of the small and easy-to-use Eastman box cameras that took pictures on rolled celluloid film. George Eastman had been steadily improving this model since first patenting the Kodak camera in 1888. The November 1894* Cook's Excursionist and Tourist Advertiser *contained an ad for the Eastman box camera—which could take up to 100 pictures without "recharge," perfect for the amateur photographer.*

§*I am indebted to Mrs. Venetia Chattey for kindly allowing me to study and quote her grandmother's marvelous journal.*

away until the homeward bound ship left Port Said. The Amhersts visited a mosque and the women were delighted at having to leave their shoes in a basket at the door (presumably Ducker waited outside on leash with one of the daughters). The streets rang with a cacophony of vendors, hawkers, beggars, braying donkeys, and grunting camels — all haranguing one another to get out of the way or pay more. Alicia would write in her journal, "The whole thing was most killingly Eastern — the Arabs laughing noisy, dirty, loudly talking." She voiced the general opinion of the time, which characterized Port Said as an awful place: "The scum of all the nations of the world they say they are here."*

Once the dirty coaling operation was completed and the pervasive black dust was sluiced off the decks and cabins, the *Arcadia* was fit to have her passengers on board once again. Cruising up the Suez Canal, the ship stopped at Ismailiya (Isma'iliya) to allow the passengers to transfer to the Cairo train. It was 3:00 A.M. and the Amhersts were looking forward to a night in proper beds, but this meant re-packing their shipboard luggage and hiring a dragoman to handle their arrangements and see that the rest of their trunks in the hold were transported to the correct hotel. The nocturnal disembarkation at Isma'iliya was standard procedure for passenger ships arriving from Port Said and the inconvenience of having to wait until the following day to catch a train was noted in the travel guides of the day. The Amhersts managed to get a few hours' sleep in the Hotel Victoria, a curious building designed for warm-weather living, with wide verandas and airy rooms that had only one opening serving as both door and window.

The next morning, the still sleepy Amhersts boarded the train to Cairo. They had booked rooms in the Hotel Continental, which was not quite as smart and modern as Shepheard's Hotel (the center of social activities in Cairo and the headquarters of Thomas Cook & Sons) but which had the cachet of exclusivity and aristocratic patronage. Overlooking Opera Square in a quiet area of the fashionable Ezbekia quarter and near an English church, it was on a par with the best hotels on the Riviera. The Continental was a first-rate establishment with sumptuous decorations, shady verandas, large rooms, "modern sanitary arrangements," and a reputation for fancy dress balls. After the carriage ride from the train station, Florence was mightily glad to be settled for a while and unpacked her tropical kit — topee, gauze scarves, blouses and skirts of cotton and linen — and rested from the two-week journey. Ducker, who was also tired of traveling, settled himself on the hotel bed.

On Friday the 21st, Lord Amherst and Alicia made the obligatory rounds in a hired carriage and left calling cards for the local nabobs and society, including General Sir Herbert Kitchener, Sirdar of the Egyptian Army†; Lord Cromer, the British Agent and Consul; and General Sir Frederick Forestier-Walker, an influential staff officer about to assume command of the administrative district west of the Nile. The whole family was eager to be in the thick of things, and their Cairo friends gave them updates on the social and political doings over tea. Because of the heat, Egypt's official business was conducted between 8:00 A.M. and 1:00 P.M. and after work there was ample time for siestas, diversion, and socializing. The English residents would drive across the Kasr-el-Nil Bridge to Ghezirah and the British-style sport-

*Forty years later, T. E. Lawrence would echo her opinion of the denizens of the Port Said docks (Seven Pillars of Wisdom, The Complete 1922 Oxford Text, 2004, 680).

†As sirdar (commander in chief of the Egyptian Army), Kitchener would soon become Britain's military lion. He would reconquer the Sudan — eventually avenging General Gordon's death at Khartoum and defeating the Mahdi's army at Omdurman, become commander in chief in South Africa during the Boer War, and served as field marshal and secretary of state for war from 1914 until his death at sea in 1916.

ing center near the old island palace. Golf, tennis, and the Ghezirah Club racecourse were popular attractions. Socializing at the track was very much the thing and there the Amhersts made acquaintances and accepted invitations amidst the excitement of races and derbies.

The Amherst holiday was a little over two weeks old when one of the daughters unwisely gave Ducker to a native porter with instructions to take the dog for a run. Understandably upset by the unfamiliar surroundings and noise, poor Ducker took fright, pulled out of his collar, and darted into the crowded street. The porter made matters worse by attempting to catch Ducker himself and not telling the Amhersts for an hour. By the time a search was organized, all witnesses to the dog's escape had disappeared. Poor Ducker was never seen again. The following day, Sybil and Alicia stayed in bed with colds while the others went to church and made social calls. That afternoon, Florence would have tea with a man who would change her life in a most unexpected way.

In the year that the Amhersts visited Egypt, twenty-three-year-old Wilfred Jennings-Bramly, late of the Customs Department in Alexandria (Al Iskandariyah), was Keeper of the Zoological Gardens at Giza. He was a handsome young man with reddish-brown hair and a pointed mustache after the style of the current military hero, Sirdar Kitchener. When not trekking in Arab robes, he was always nattily dressed and frequently wore leggings and a straw boater with his suit. He had a marvelous sense of humor, was a talented mimic and story-teller, and loved play-acting in costume — talents which served him well in his dealings with the Bedouin.*

An easy carriage drive from Cairo, his zoo sprawled over fifty lush acres and boasted a respectable collection of native and Middle Eastern species. His chief problem was how to maintain the animals and grounds with a meager budget. Animals were frequently donated to the zoo by troops returning from the Sudan or from the crews of ships passing through the Suez Canal. British "Tommies" on foreign service invariably acquired mascots to tag along with the regiment (despite orders to the contrary). When not on active campaign, officers had copious leisure time and frequently occupied themselves with amateur zoology or big-game hunting. Collecting specimens (both alive and dead) was very much the thing.

By the time that troop ships reached the Suez Canal, it no longer seemed like such a good idea to bring the likes of warthogs, crocodiles, vultures, lions, jackals, and ostriches back to England. The Giza Zoo was a convenient and obliging dumping ground for former pets and mascots. Jennings-Bramly welcomed "Oriental species" from Africa, Arabia, Persia, India, Malaya, Sumatra, China, and Australia, and anywhere that khaki-clad soldiers defended Queen Victoria's rule. The army and navy provided ample specimens to add to those captured by locals in the surrounding desert. The possibility of obtaining scientific immortality by discovering and naming an unknown species surely occurred to Jennings-Bramly (as indeed it would to any amateur naturalist in a similar position) and where better for this to happen than the zoo at the crossroads of the British Empire?

When he took over the Zoological Gardens in 1892, Jennings-Bramly's first three specimens were a gazelle, a lion, and a docile Russian wolf. His close friend and occasional civil engineer, George Fraser, would periodically live there and the two would practice their marks-

*My thanks to Jennings-Bramly's late daughter, Mrs. Vivien Betti, and his grandson, Jasper Scovil, for sharing their family information with me.

Wilfred Jennings-Bramly and his falcons at the Giza Zoological Gardens, 1896. With the kind permission of Jasper Scovil.

manship on the rats that infested the palace. An orangutan was kept in the residence because his constitution was too delicate for the outdoors. The temperamental ape would bang his bowl for meals and object to Fraser's piano playing by covering his head with a blanket. The bohemian lifestyle suited the two bachelors immensely. Jennings-Bramly was his own master and could essentially do what he liked as long as the zoo did not lose money — and that was his chief problem.

He had a modest budget for animal fodder, his own salary as keeper, and wages for his fellahin gardeners and the animal keepers. Entrusted with the care of the animals, the zoo employees were mostly Egyptian and Sudanese ex-soldiers dressed in belted khaki sweaters or white tunics, with red tarbooshes,* puttees or leggings, and white haversacks. Little money was left over for repairs, improvements, or specimen-collecting expeditions — so any augmentations to the zoo's finances had to come from admission fees and donations. What he needed was a constant stream of visitors to ensure revenue. But how was he to attract Cairo society to the zoo?

Jennings-Bramly hit on three methods to encourage repeat visits the zoological gardens. Two were sound business practices but the third could have been lifted from the marketing hoaxes of P. T. Barnum, the American showman. First, Jennings-Bramly made the grounds and lakes a pleasant setting for picnics and strolls to attract people away from the dusty city and the crowds at the Ghezirah Club. Second, he worked hard to secure donations of animals

A tarboosh is a brimless cap, similar to a fez.

so that visitors would periodically have something new and interesting to see. Finally, he and Fraser would often post a sign saying that the ostrich or some other animal was loose — which was often the case, as most of the animals were tame and allowed to wander. This would explain an empty cage and tended to generate interest (if not alarm) amongst the visitors. The Giza Zoological Gardens could be a potentially thrilling place to visit and sometimes Jennings-Bramly even *had* the animal alleged to have escaped.

By 1894, the nearly complete representation of Egyptian fauna as well as some of the more common Asiatic species was fairly impressive. Fifty acres of the old palace gardens had been revived and were now quite lush and beautiful. Not only were there manicured lawns and bedded flowers, but local flora such as the lotus, bulrush, papyrus, palm tree, and even a large banyan tree at the center of the gardens.* By December 1895, Jennings-Bramly had made the zoological gardens a popular and potentially exciting outing for Cairo society — and that was how he became friends with the Amhersts.

They had met the handsome Jennings-Bramly in their first social forays in Cairo and by the time the Amhersts were invited to tea at the zoo, they were getting along famously and calling him "Wiffy"— his boyhood nickname. His other nickname was "The Walking Englishman"— given to him by the Bedouin because of his preference for walking rather than riding a camel. At tea on December 22, Jennings-Bramly entertained the Amhersts at his residence in the middle of the zoo's paddocks and regaled them with stories of the desert. He was sorry to hear about the loss of Ducker and offered condolences along with the hope that the dog might yet turn up. Jennings-Bramly gave the family a tour of the gardens and showed off the animal exhibits and his prized hunting falcons.

While Jennings-Bramly did not own Salukis himself, his tracker Dau did and it was most likely here that Florence first glimpsed Salukis.† She was quite taken by their graceful beauty and athletic form. The golden hounds had longish hair on their ears and tail, and dark, almond-shaped eyes. Their gaze was expressive and penetrating — a feature that she would emphasize in her articles on the breed. Florence would later say that it seemed they had witnessed the history of the East but would not reveal these secrets to mere humans. Dau's hounds were aloof and demonstrated a proper reserve with the strangers. Jennings-Bramly described how Muslims did not consider Salukis to be dogs — they were *El Hor*§ — the Noble One and a gift from Allah. Contact with scavenging mongrels and guard dogs — the unclean *kalb*, was proscribed by the Qur'an. Because Salukis enjoyed the same privileged status as the falcon and horse, they lived cheek by jowl with the Bedouin, slept in their black tents, and caught game. Because of the solitary lifestyle of the nomads, Saluki breeding was said to be pure and unadulterated for centuries past. Because most Bedouin could not read or write, their history, folklore, and pedigrees of their horses and hounds were committed to memory. Intrigued by the Saluki's unique status in Bedouin culture — and perhaps missing Ducker curled up on her bed at night, Florence's interest was growing.

Jennings-Bramly and the Amhersts were mutually charmed by each other. On Christ-

---

Jennings-Bramly's scheme to make the zoo an attractive destination was a sound one despite his casual management. His successor would later expand the concept by banning liquor and dogs, offering elephant rides for children, building a refreshment stand that served afternoon tea and snacks, and instituting military band concerts on Sundays.

†*The exact circumstance of Florence's first experience with Salukis have yet to come to light, but it was either at the Giza Zoo or near Luxor.*

§*A corruption of al–Hurr.*

mas day, Alicia and her mother invited Wiffy and the Newberrys* to dinner at their suite at the Hotel Continental, while Lord Amherst, Sybil, Florence, Margaret, and Ernest dined with General Sir Frederick Forestier-Walker and his wife.

The Amhersts and their old friend Percy Newberry had mutual interests in gardens and Egyptology, so there was much to talk about. Alicia and Lady Amherst were enchanted with Newberry's descriptions of tombs and half-buried colossi. Not to be outdone, Jennings-Bramly regaled the party with tales of hashish smugglers and gave the Amhersts a board game called "The Race," as a Christmas present. As it transpired, Jennings-Bramly's friend George Fraser had worked for Percy Newberry and the Egypt Exploration Fund in surveying tombs and monuments. Newberry and Fraser had lived in an empty tomb at Beni Hasan during the excavations of 1890–91, and had to dodge bats and scorpions in the strange apartment.[4] During the second season at Beni Hasan, Fraser and another member of their team, Marcus Blackden, had committed the ungentlemanly act of archaeological "claim jumping."

Newberry and newcomer Howard Carter had discovered the quarry of Hatnub near Tell el-Amarna on Christmas Eve of 1891. When Fraser and Blackden learned of it, they raced to publish inscriptions from the quarry despite Newberry's entitlement to publication. Naturally, Fraser was persona non grata in Newberry's eyes and the fact that he was Jennings-Bramly's friend must have put a certain strain on their evening with Lady Amherst and Alicia.

After dinner, Alicia and Lady Amherst went down to the hotel ballroom, which was decorated to celebrate the season. The manager distributed presents from under the Christmas tree for everyone, and the band struck up dance music. Florence and the rest of the family returned and joined in the festivities. The daughters danced with army officers and the local gentry until the early hours of the morning. Despite the decorated tree, gifts, mince pies, and plum pudding, Alicia remarked that it did not feel very much like Christmas. Small wonder, considering the lack of snow, winter clothes, evergreen trees, and crackling fires — not to mention the fact that earlier that day the Amhersts had engaged in the most un-Christmas-like activity of touring the local pharaonic tombs.

On Boxing Day, December 26, Florence, Sybil, Margaret, and Lady Amherst paid a call on Princess Inje Hasan, the widowed sister-in-law of the late khedive. The princess was pleased to receive the Amhersts, as her sons had attended school at Harrow, and the khedive and his family had once been guests at Didlington Hall. Florence and Sybil again spent the evening with General and Lady Forestier-Walker. In their hotel sitting room, the rest of the Amhersts entertained Lady Buxton and her husband, Mr. Francis William Buxton, with parlor games and Wiffy's board game. The next morning, Florence, Sybil, and Alicia headed off to promenade on donkeys down the tree-shaded but somewhat-less-than-fashionable Shubra Road.

The whirl of social functions and touring continued unabated. The parents and their daughters visited bazaars and mosques, and were most impressed by the whirling dervishes, which they chanced upon here and there in the crowded city. On the morning of Saturday the 29th, Lord and Lady Amherst and Margaret hired a carriage and set off along the shady boulevard that led to the pyramids at Giza. Always ready for a new experience, Florence, Sybil, and Alicia rode along perched high up on their rented camels. Protected from the sun with topees, parasols, scarves, veils, and smoked-glass spectacles, the family toured the nearby

*Alicia's notes say that they had dinner with "the Newberrys" yet the famed archaeologist Percy Newberry would not marry Helene until 1907. The second Newberry may have been his elder brother, John, who also worked on the tombs and monuments.

tombs and the Great Sphinx, *Abu-el-Hol*— the "Father of Terror." Florence and her sisters were determined to climb the pyramids and generous baksheesh hired two Egyptians each to haul them up the great stone blocks. The climb took thirty minutes. Four hundred and eighty-one feet above the sand below, the Amherst women had a spectacular view of Cairo, the nearby pyramids, and the surrounding desert. The only thing to spoil the experience were the noisy boys waiting at the top to peddle highly dubious artifacts by tugging at their sleeves and shouting *"Antiquas! Antiquas!"*

On Monday they were scheduled to sail up the Nile, so Sunday afternoon saw one last social function for the Amhersts — this time on board their *dehabiyeh*, *Hathor*. Lord Amherst had spared no expense in hiring one of the best-appointed boats that Thomas Cook & Sons had to offer. Only a few years old, it was painted white and featured a 118-foot-long steel hull, a large saloon, eight cabins accommodating ten passengers, Arabesque furniture, and, in the stern cabin, "twin bedsteads with spring mattresses on improved principles."[5] At £160 per month,* the boat came with an experienced dragoman (to sort out all the logistics and details with the locals), crew, servants, qualified cook, and the best produce and meat that money could buy. Thanks to Cook's efficient organization, the level of comfort and luxury on a Nile cruise had greatly improved since the Amhersts' first trip in 1860.[†]

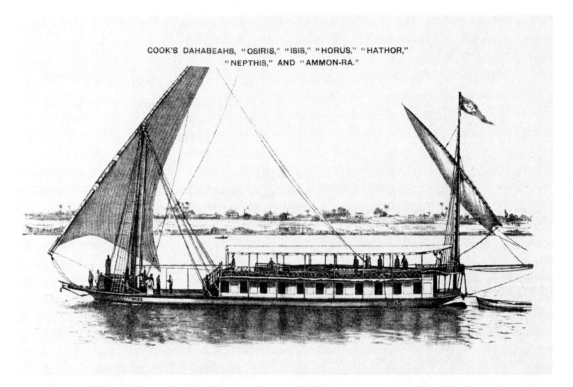

COOK'S DAHABEAHS, "OSIRIS," "ISIS," "HORUS," "HATHOR," "NEPHTHIS," AND "AMMON-RA."

Cook's luxury dehabiyeh which Lord Amherst hired for his family's Nile holiday, 1894–95. With the kind permission of Thomas Cook, UK Ltd.

*In 2006 this would amount to UK£12,698.53 ("Purchasing Power of British Pounds from 1264 to 2006," MeasuringWorth.com, accessed September 27, 2007).

†For many years, Cook's amazing organization had the only reliable source of boats and pilots for the Nile. For the relief of General Gordon at Khartoum in 1884 and the second expedition against the Mahdi in 1889, it was Thomas Cook & Sons who transported the British Army.

No strangers to life on a boat, the Amherst women had gone shopping in the specialty bazaars of Cairo to stock up on necessities and amenities for the voyage. Copperware, fabric, leather, and other merchandise each had its own bazaar and getting the best bargain took skill and bravado. A potential buyer would take a seat in a recessed area off the street and make the customary pleasantries with the shop's owner — away from the shouting of donkey boys, messengers, and the wandering vendors of vegetables, sugar cane, and drinking water in the street. After the conversational overture, the buyer would ask the price of the desired item and the shop owner would praise its virtues and name an impossibly high price. The buyer could then feign indifference and counter with an insultingly low offer or else state that the merchandise could be had elsewhere at a much cheaper price. After protracted negotiations and threats to call the whole deal off, a price would be struck somewhere in the middle — with each party claiming that the deal would send him or her to the poorhouse.

With the aid of their dragoman, the Amherst women purchased carpets, yards of striped cotton, saddle cushions for lounging, copper and brass cookware, and ornaments to decorate their cabins and the observation deck. Palm fronds added a festive touch for the *bon voyage* tea party. Porters had to be hired to carry the whole lot back to the boat and the decoration of the *Hathor* began furiously. At the appointed hour, Lord Cromer, Sirdar Kitchener, General Sir Forstier-Walker, and their wives, off-duty officers and the elite of Cairo society, all crowded on board to wish them well. Under the deck canopy, figures in white and khaki — here and there accented with tarbooshes and uniforms of red and blue, sipped tea and nibbled on sandwiches, biscuits, and cakes, and generally hobnobbed the afternoon away. The following morning, the Amherst women made one last foray into the bazaars to buy eleventh-hour treasures and necessities. The Amhersts finally got under way at 3:00 P.M. on Monday, New Year's Eve, 1894.

The *Hathor*'s main mast had a 200-foot yard with a lateen sail but a coal-fueled tug, the *Ptah*, would tow the shallow-draft *Hathor* up river whenever the winds were not fair.* There were six large oars below decks that could be manned by two fellahin apiece if wind or the *Ptah* failed. Immediately above the cabins and saloon was the observation deck, which was shaded by a full-length awning. Lord and Lady Amherst's stern cabin featured a private balcony and directly above flew Thomas Cook & Son's blue ensign. With the decorations from the bazaars, the *dehabiyeh* was the very picture indeed of Sinbad's ship from the Arabian Nights and to use Alicia's words, it must have looked "killingly Eastern."

On New Year's Day, they made the donkey ride to Saqqara and saw the colossi of Ramesses, the Step Pyramid of Djoser and temple of Mit Rahina — all the while dodging crowds from one of Cook's economy tours. The hordes of tourists disgorged from tightly scheduled steamers would be a periodic annoyance throughout the tour. In contrast, the Amherst trip up the Nile was a leisurely one — they would stop where they wished and if the local ruins were interesting enough, stay for a day or two. Alicia would take photographs and develop the exposed plates on the spot (the equipment being carried by porters and donkeys). She kept a detailed journal during the adventure and, using brown ink, filled the tiny volumes with both her notes and illustrations. The heat scheduled their daily activities — Florence and her sisters typically rose at six o'clock, breakfasted an hour later, and explored or sketched until noon when they returned for lunch. They rested until three o'clock and then

---

Hathor was the goddess of love, dance, and alcohol. She was also the mother/protector of Horus the sky god and represented by a cow-headed woman. Ptah was the creator god of the city of Memphis.

A five-person excursion at Karnak (circa 1900) similar to what the Amhersts would have enjoyed. Note the dragoman (far left) overseeing the bearers. With the kind permission of Thomas Cook, UK Ltd.

took tea. In the cool of the waning day, they might go off for a walk in the desert with a couple of the sailors for escorts.

As they progressed up the Nile, trips ashore to shoot snipe and quail provided diversion (and fresh meat for the table) but the primary attractions were the temples and tombs. Riding donkeys or walking they would travel from the riverbank to the tomb on the day's itinerary. Deep inside and far from the light of day, Florence and her intrepid sisters fended off swooping bats to poke about in crumbling sarcophagi looking for hieroglyphic tablets or relics. At the monument to Usertsen III at Dahshur, they made a rope descent thirty-nine feet below the base of the pyramid. In other tombs, they had to alternately bend double and crawl on hands and knees to reach the inner chambers. The sisters made their way, long skirts and all, through claustrophobic passages to view royal chambers by the harsh light of ignited magnesium wire. The combustible metal produced a white-blue light that was far brighter than any candle or torch but threw off sparks and noxious fumes — the latter leaving a smoky residue on the tomb walls and ceiling.* Once, deep inside a tomb in the Valley of the Kings, the metallic smoke blew into Sybil's eyes and she inhaled a lungful of fumes. On the verge of blacking out, she had to be hurriedly carried to fresh air.

In their dinner dress at night, the family would discuss their activities, compare drawings and paintings, and plan the next day's itinerary. After the meal they would sing songs, recite poetry, write letters, or read in the saloon. Dinners and parties with friends on other *dehabiyehs* would be arranged frequently. Rocking gently on the Nile in the evening, they could hear the cries of the curlew and later the hoots of owls. Now and then, a shadowy jackal could be seen prowling the banks — its eyes shining eerily green in the torchlight. The constellations were spectacular in the desert sky and the Amhersts were delighted to recognize the Southern Cross, Orion, and the Great Bear.

*Tour books of the day recommended that plenty of magnesium wire be brought for viewing tomb interiors.

Archaeology and hieroglyphic translation were constant topics of discourse, and Lord and Lady Amherst remarked on the extent of the recent excavations and how much more of the monuments were visible than when they had first seen them in 1860. They attended church on Sundays if there was a town nearby and if not, offered prayers in the saloon. Their Nile social doings included their scholarly friends from museum and archaeology circles — Newberry, the Buxtons, Howard Carter, Flinders Petrie, D. G. Hogarth and his bride, Laura, and the noted Assyriologist, Reverend Archibald Henry Sayce of the American College in Beirut and the Egypt Exploration Fund. They socialized with the passengers from other hired boats as well — Lord and Lady Egerton, Lord Compton, Lady Crossley, and the Duchess of Buckingham, who were all wintering in Egypt. The sailors on the *Hathor* grew quite fond of Lady Amherst and in her honor performed Syrian dancing and staged a play, complete with "white face" make-up and false beards. Another night, the Amhersts were invited to a fantasia on a French group's *dehabiyeh*. The festivities included dancing girls, Syrian sword dancers, and rockets. Alicia was moved greatly by the "magical effect" of the red lanterns and brilliant moonlight and stars.[6]

All along the Nile they stopped at local villages and bought souvenirs, including baskets, knives, a fine silver Qur'an case for Lady Amherst, and rhino-horn boxes. They bargained with the locals and knew enough about artifacts to ignore the late-date mummy cases offered to them by bazaar merchants. Some distance south of the village of El Sheikh 'Ibada, at a temple of *Bastet*— the cat-figured protectress of home, mothers, and children, they saw large mounds of sacred cat mummies. Florence, Alicia, Sybil, and Margaret decided that they must each have their own mummy and implored Percy Newberry to help. Generous *baksheesh* ensured the guardian's averted eyes while Newberry smuggled out a souvenir mummy for each of them.

When they reached Tell el–Amarna, Lord Amherst acquired his own special souvenir of the trip in the ruins of the old city. Howard Carter had assisted with the 1892 excavation of a site where villagers had dug up a large number of cuneiform-inscribed bricks in previous years. This was the site where, as Lord Amherst's agent, Carter had been able to earmark several choice statue fragments of Akhenaton and Nefertiti from a rubbish heap and ship them to Didlington. The excavated bricks of 'Amarna, despite the fact that they had been much damaged in their subsequent shipment to Cairo, still contained an astonishing amount of information about the relations between Egypt and Syria and other countries during the reign of Dushratta. Stopping for a day or two, Lord Amherst did a bit of digging himself and discovered a tablet that positively identified the site as "The Place of the Records of the Pharaoh" (according to Newberry's translation).[7] Amherst the bibliophile seemed to have confirmed the site of an ancient library and nothing could have delighted him more.

They stopped at the Karnak complex where moonrise over the temple was accounted to be "one of the most weird and wonderful sights imaginable."[8] There they saw the ruined temple of the great Theban goddess Mut where their seven statues of Sekhmet had been excavated in 1816 and eventually made their way to England in 1830.[9] Five hundred miles from Cairo, they saw the first cataracts of the Nile at Aswan and tomb excavations where Sir Francis Grenfell had found one of the sarcophagi in the Amherst collection. The Khalifa's Mahdist fanatics were still raiding and killing in the vicinity and there was too much danger for the garrison's officers to permit the Amhersts' planned nine-hour camel trip to a local oasis.*

*Al-Mahdi, *"the expected one," led a* jihad *or holy war against the Anglo Egpytians in the Sudan from 1881 to his death in 1885, six months after capturing Khartoum. Khalifa Abdullahi was his successor and continued the* jihad, *attacking nonbelievers wherever possible.*

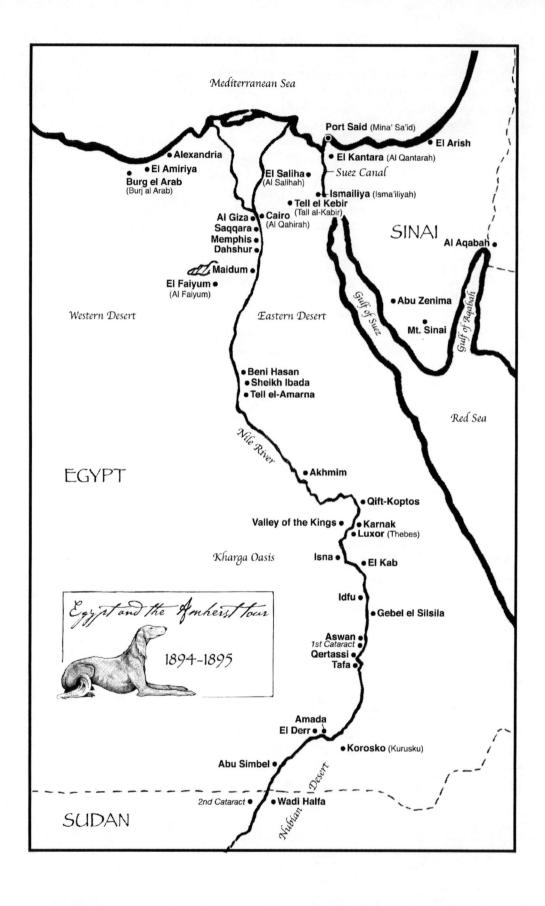

Mediterranean Sea

Port Said (Mina' Sa'id)

● El Arish

● Alexandria

● El Amiriya

Burg el Arab
(Burj al Arab)

● El Saliha
(Al Salihah)

● El Kantara (Al Qantarah)

Suez Canal

● Ismailiya (Isma'iliyah)

● Tell el Kebir
(Tall al-Kabir)

Al Giza ● ● Cairo
Saqqara ●   (Al Qahirah)
Memphis ●
Dahshur ●

SINAI

Al Aqabah ●

● Maidum

El Faiyum ●
(Al Faiyum)

Western Desert

Eastern Desert

● Abu Zenima

● Mt. Sinai

Gulf of Suez

Gulf of Aqabah

Red Sea

● Beni Hasan
● Sheikh Ibada
● Tell el-Amarna

Nile River

EGYPT

● Akhmim

● Qift-Koptos

Valley of the Kings ● ● Karnak
● Luxor (Thebes)

Kharga Oasis

Isna ●

● El Kab

Idfu ●

● Gebel el Silsila

Egypt and the Amherst tour

1894~1895

Aswan ●
1st Cataract
Qertassi ●
Tafa ●

Amada
El Derr ●

● Korosko (Kurusku)

Abu Simbel ●

Nubian Desert

2nd Cataract ● ● Wadi Halfa

SUDAN

Egypt and the Amherst Tour

from the journals
of Alicia Amherst
1894–1895

Up River (South)

Port Said, Tuesday, Dec. 18, 1894

Ismailiya, Wednesday, Dec. 19,1894

Cairo, Wednesday, Dec. 19, 1894

Al Giza, Thurday a.m., Dec. 27, 1894

Cairo, set sail at 3 p.m., Monday, Dec. 31, 1894

Saqqara & Memphis, Tuesday, Jan. 1, 1895

Dahshur

Maidum

Beni Hasan

Sheikh Ibada, Wednesday, Jan. 9, 1895

Tell el-Amarna, Thursday, Jan. 10, 1895

Akhmim, Jan. 16, 1895

Qift-Koptos

Karnak & Luxor, Sunday, Jan. 22, 1895

Idfu & Gebel el Silsila, Wednesday, Jan. 23, 1895

Aswan, Friday, Jan. 25–Saturday, Jan. 26, 1895

1st Cataract

Tafa

El Derr & Amada

Sudan Border

Abu Simbel & Wadi Halfa, Tuesday, Jan. 29–Wednesday, Jan. 30, 1895

2nd Cataract

Luxor, Tuesday, Feb. 28–Sunday, March 3, 1895 (Alica's third & fourth journal volumes have disappeared so the narrative ends here)

Thebes, Saturday, Feb. 23–Wednesday, Feb. 27, 1895

Isna

El Kab, Monday, Feb. 18, 1895

Aswan, Monday, Feb. 4–Wednesday, Feb. 13, 1895

Qertassi

Korosko, Saturday, Feb. 2, 1895

Abu Simbel, Friday, Feb. 1, 1895

Down River (North)

January 26, 1895, was Florence's thirty-fifth birthday and she celebrated by attending a review of Nubian troops with her father, Ernest, and Sybil. Later they went shopping at the local bazaar and bought skirts of leather strips, bone and mother of pearl ornaments, and silver nose rings from "naked Nubian girls." Alicia stayed on the boat and marked illustration proofs for her history of English gardening, which was to be published later that year.* Surprisingly, they met a group of friendly Bisharin tribesmen at Aswan who had been to America as part of the African exhibit at the 1893 World's Columbian Exhibition in Chicago.

As the first cataract confined the *Hathor* to the lower Nile, the Amhersts took a train around the falls and boarded a steamer to continue southward. Four days later and 200 miles from Aswan, they found themselves just inside the Sudanese border at the Nile's second cataract at the little town of Wadi Halfa. The Amhersts visited the Egyptian Army outpost on the outskirts of town and Alicia noted the peculiar officer's mess — a unique structure built by Black Watch Highlanders, which consisted of mud walls with a roof made of beer barrels and railroad ties. In the mess, talk mostly concerned the general lack of trouble from the khalifa's raiders in the previous three weeks and whether or not Kitchener would mount a campaign to reconquer the Sudan.† Captain O'Connell gave Florence a Mahdi dollar as a souvenir. Doubtless worried by the talk of the murderous attacks against Christians, Lord Amherst declared that target practice was in order. Florence was accomplished at many things but marksmanship was not one of them. Alicia and her father were the only ones of the family who were able to shatter the bottle targets.

They witnessed maneuvers and a large military review to honor the visiting Austrian Consul General, Baron von Heidler. In a "kharkee" forest of glittering sabers and lances, there were Nubian cavalry with white tarbooshes, and Egyptian lancers and the Camel Corps with their red tarbooshes. There was band music and even a detachment of mountain artillery with mules and pack howitzers. Afterward, the Amhersts went for a delightful gallop on their ponies and then reboarded the steamer to head north for Aswan and the *Hathor*.

Florence and her sisters had been drawing and painting ever since they crossed the English Channel, but the color palette of the desert sand and sunsets seduced them completely and they worked hard to reproduce the delicate tints on paper. In addition to her sketches, Alicia made good use of her camera at the tombs they visited. Nine years later, Lady Amherst would use Alicia's photographs and paintings by Florence, Sybil, and Margaret to illustrate her own book on Egyptian history. On February 12, the Cook's agent delivered letters to the Amhersts and they were surprised to learn that back in England the River Thames had frozen over. Despite daytime temperatures of 95°F on the *dehabiyeh* (Cook's economy tourists were suffering 101°F on the shaded steamer decks), Florence, Sybil, Margaret, and Alicia repeated their escapade from the S.S. *Arcadia* by going below decks and taking a turn at the *Hathor's* oars with the sailors for one stretch of the river.

At El Kab on February 18, they met Mr. Somers Clarke who was working at the tomb of Peheri. Clarke had instructed Howard Carter in the methods and techniques of tomb sur-

---

*Her book A History of Gardening in England *is still considered to be a definitive work on the topic and has been reprinted several times. Later styled Lady Rockley, C.B.E., Alicia wrote many books on gardening during her life.*

†*Kitchener did move against the khalifa's army in 1896. A series of small actions and battles reconquered the Sudan and exacted belated revenge for the murder of General Gordon at Khartoum in 1885. The Mahdist revolt effectively ended at Omdurman in 1898 and was completely finished when the khalifa was killed in 1899 at the battle of Umm Diwaykarat.*

veying and reconstruction during the work at Deir-el-Bahri in the Valley of the Kings in 1893 and he would later be appointed the Surveyor to the Fabric, St. Paul's Cathedral in 1897.[10] The architect had "gone native" and wore a turban, blue cotton nightgown, and red shoes. Despite the Amherst tolerance for unconventionality, it was a little too bohemian for them. Alicia was shocked to see that he wore no stockings and made a note of it in her journal. Down river at Esna, they met their first polygamist—a sheikh with four wives. Making a portrait of the group was practically compulsory and while it was in progress, the Amherst daughters told him that "women could do as they liked in England." Flinging his hands up in despair, the sheikh prayed that the wives had not heard this heresy. However, the old man was nothing if not philosophical and said that as he was tired of two wives in particular, that if the Amhersts liked, they could just take them along to England with them.[11]

Once again at Thebes (but without the sheikh's surplus wives), the Amhersts met up with Percy Newberry and Howard Carter on the 23rd and ate a traditional Arab meal that night. The sight of the two archaeologists tearing off hunks of lamb with their hands amused Alicia enough to add the incident to her journal. Even when not eating in Arab style, Carter's table manners left much to be desired but the Amhersts were still fond of him and always called him by his given name. He was invited to dine and sleep on board for several nights in the spare cabin. On February 25, Florence, Sybil, Ernest, and Alicia rode off to see the tombs in the Valley of the Kings. After tea with Edouard Naville, another prominent archaeologist, they visited the tomb of Rekhmire — the vizier of Tuthmosis III and Amen-hotep II, which the guidebooks considered to be the most interesting of all the non-royal tombs in Thebes.

Percy Newberry was directing the clearing and documentation of the cruciform-shaped tomb. It was filled with unusual paintings that depicted daily life as well as the official business of the vizier. Alicia, always interested in gardens, noted that while it was difficult to see in the dark, the flickering lights revealed an intriguing representation of an Egyptian garden and men buying ivory. Hunting was always depicted on north walls and here in "the Hall" (set at right angles to "the Passage") were a number of Saluki hounds coursing gazelle, oryx, hare, hyena, and wild oxen. Among Rekhmire's myriad official and priestly titles, one praise name marks his passion for hunting — "Ally of the Mistress of the Catch."

Newberry was well familiar with Egyptian representations of the hounds and had also seen these *slughis** on the walls of a tomb in the Beni Hasan complex. He also knew that the desert nomads still used the descendants of these hounds for catching game. While Rekhmire's tomb had hunting scenes aplenty, it was in connection with the vizier's official capacity that perhaps the most interesting depiction of Salukis occurs in ancient Egypt. On the south portion of the Hall's west wall, several Salukis were depicted being sent to Egypt as tribute from Nubia or Punt. A decade later, that painting would come to have special importance for Florence.

Disappointed by the canceled oasis trip at Aswan, Lord Amherst determined to have one in a safer area. He arranged with Cook's for a desert expedition from Luxor, scheduled to depart on March 3, the first Sunday of Lent. This meant more servants, large tents for both sleeping and dining, carpets, furniture, silver and crystal for dinner settings, camels to pack all this and the Amherst luggage, and of course, guides and guards. Thomas Cook & Sons could arrange just about anything desired and it is interesting to note that Amherst's request

---

*"Slughi" *being a colloquial form of the more formal* "Saluqi."

was unusual enough to be entered as a special item in their accounts for the 1894–95 season.*
Alicia wrote that they were preparing for an extended camel trek, but the guides were worried about the availability of water. Letters and telegrams were dispatched to determine the
condition of the wells while the family waited to hear if they were going or not. In a most
tantalizing Victorian cliffhanger, the second volume of Alicia's journal ends with the intriguing hint that the next volume will tell the tale.

Sadly, the third and fourth volumes of the journal have disappeared and the details of
the rest of their holiday in Egypt are unknown. Evidently, there was sufficient water at the
wells, as Lord Amherst was charged the sum of £35, ten shillings, and sixpence for his special desert tour. It was a small Egyptian fortune in those days — enough to pay one fellah's
wages for nine years.

Having taken three months to make the trip to Wadi Halfa and return as far as Luxor,
the weather was beginning to approach summer temperatures and it was time to think about
leaving Egypt. The Amhersts continued their easy pace downriver and likely stayed on for a
few weeks in Cairo before heading home by way of a leisurely stay at Lou Casteou.† But before
they packed their jumble of souvenirs and left Cairo, Florence had one more thing to do. She
visited Wiffy at the Giza Zoo and asked him to obtain a pair of Salukis for her.

---

*My thanks to Paul Smith, archivist for Thomas Cook & Sons, for access to their accounts from 1894–95 and
permission to reproduce photographs from their collection.
†The Amhersts must have journeyed elsewhere after Egypt, for the missing third and fourth volumes of Alicia's
journal covered their holiday through June 1895 and they did not return to home to Didlington until August.

3

A Sphinxitic Pastime

"The dogs are small but show great breeding, most of them being of the so-called Persian variety, with long silky ears and tails."

Lady Anne Blunt, *Bedouin Tribes of the Euphrates 1879*

The Amhersts returned home to Didlington in mid–August 1895 — eight and a half months after leaving England the previous December. On Wednesday the 14th, the family attended a fete in their honor hosted by the residents of the area. "Lord and Lady Amherst of Hackney wish to thank most sincerely all their friends and neighbors who so kindly gave them and their Daughters, such a hearty reception and welcome on their return home last Wednesday after their long absence abroad," the *Thetford and Watton Times* reported

There was much to be done now that they were home. Lord Amherst made appointments with his solicitor and estate manager, Charles Cheston, to review his affairs, business transactions, and a large pile of correspondence. Things were a bit unsettled at the estate. Elijah Palmer, the chief clerk in the estate office, had fallen seriously ill during the Amhersts' absence and much was left undone. The new housekeeper, Mrs. Parker, was still learning the myriad necessities of running the Didlington household and now that the family was back, the workload increased dramatically.* After such a long time away, Florence and her sisters were glad to be home and no longer living out of trunks and portmanteaus. Their Egyptian souvenirs and trinkets were unpacked and given special places, with the cat mummies going to join the other mummies in the Amherst museum. The family settled back into the pleasant routine and comforts of Didlington.

In November 1895, two golden Saluki puppies with feathered ears and tails arrived at Didlington. The Importation of Dogs Order, which required "isolated detention," would not be enacted for another two years, so the puppies were spared a six-month quarantine. They had gone by foot (by camel or their own locomotion) to Isma'iliyah and then by steamship through Port Said and across the Mediterranean, by train to Paris and Calais, by ship again to England, then by rail to London and on to Brandon Station. Finally a horse-drawn carriage took them to Didlington Hall. Despite the many legs of the journey, shipment from Egypt would have been a fairly swift one — perhaps as short as a week. They were just under ten months old and Florence found them to be robust in health and not suffering from the trip at all.†

---

*Elijah Palmer and Mrs. Parker would die within a month of each other in early 1896.

† The date of Florence's first importation is often incorrectly given as 1897. This stems from a mistake in Hutchinson's Dog Encyclopaedia (1935), which confused the date of import with the date of her first litter.

Jennings-Bramly had obtained the breeding pair from the brothers Saud and Magelli of the Tahawis in Lower Egypt. The tribe roamed the district around Al Salihah and Ismailia area, along the old caravan trail to Syria. The Tahawis were an Egyptian branch of the great Hamadi-Anazeh tribe who were originally from the Najd in Arabia and reputedly famous for their Syrian style Salukis and horses.* Whether or not the Al Salihah tribes had this Syrian connection, they were certainly heavily influenced by interchange with the Hejaz (Hijaz) tribes just across the Suez Canal. Saud and Magelli had named the puppies La'aman, meaning "flash of light" or "swift glance of a lady's eye," and Ayesha, after the Prophet Mohammed's second wife. Florence liked the names and decided to keep them, although "La'aman" became interchangeable with "Laaman" and "Luman" in her various writings over the years. Florence would later say that they proved themselves "hardy and as capable of standing our often erratic climate as any other breed."[1]

But what precisely were these dogs? As she had only some anecdotal notes from Jennings-Bramly, with typical Amherstian zeal, Florence applied herself to the puzzle. The quest to learn more about the enigmatic breed became her personal "Sphinxitic Pastime."[†] Naturally, she turned first to her father's extensive collection of books on travel in Palestine and the Middle East. The Norwich Free Library was next and when their holdings were thoroughly examined, it was on to London to peruse the vast holdings of the British Museum's Library in the great domed reading room. Florence first began to find scattered references in contemporary dog books that confusingly identified the breed as Persian, Oriental, and Turkish Greyhounds. The popular dog expert Dr. J. H. Walsh, writing under his more famous pen name, "Stonehenge," published the second edition of *The Dog in Health and Disease* in 1885. In it, he noted that the description of the Græcian greyhound fit the Persian greyhound admirably — the body of the smooth English Greyhound but with slightly longer hair, "wholly pendant" ears, and the tail brush of an English Setter. Oddly enough, he said that the Persian Greyhound was characterized by its hairy ears and nose. This statement was very confusing to Florence as Salukis certainly had the former but definitely not the latter.[§] The standard dog books were proving to be so full of myth and inaccuracies that they were of very little use to her.

Florence found that dog books did describe Salukis as graceful and strong, but deceptively delicate in appearance. Several even stated that they were too delicate to be of any use in coursing the English hare. Along with the obligatory (and frequently variable) description of physical characteristics, anecdotal tales of coursing were included in these publications. Here at last was information that Florence could use. Salukis were said to hunt in one of two ways, depending on the terrain and the quarry. One method involved the hounds being run in relays to wear down the gazelle or wild ass native to Syria and Persia. In the other, a hunter loosed a falcon trained to attack the head and eyes of a fleeing gazelle, thereby slowing it enough for the hounds to bring it down. The hunting stories seem to be largely derived from one or two accounts originally published in the *Field* and the *Sporting Magazine* much earlier in the century, and indeed most of the Saluki information available in 1895 had been copied many times over from a very few books.

The noted Arab horse expert, Carl Raswan, described the Al Salhiha tribe's entrance at a large Bedouin gathering in Drinkers of the Wind. *Accompanied by musicians, they entered with falcons and Salukis, and performed circus-style tricks with their horses.*

†*"Sphinxitic Pastimes" was the puzzle page in the* Thetford and Watton Times — *the local newspaper that the Amhersts read.*

§*Hairy noses are seen in Afghan puppies but not Salukis.*

Florence Amherst's foundation sire from the Egyptian desert, Luman, at the age of nine years (1904).

Finding the dog authorities to be contradictory and mostly useless, she discovered there were more reliable accounts of Salukis by people who had actually owned them in the desert. It was from this type of book that she began to piece together an accurate picture of the breed. In her mother's own book, *In a Good Cause,* Florence read accounts of summer encampments outside Jerusalem (Al Quds) by Mrs. James Finn, the wife of the British Consul for Palestine. The Finns habitually escaped the stifling buildings and spent seventeen halcyon summers living in tents near the city. Mrs. Finn was a keen naturalist and she and her husband kept "Syrian greyhounds" which hunted hyena and gazelle.[2]

From the archaeology section of her father's library and their archaeologist friend Reverend Sayce, Florence found another piece of the great puzzle. It was in the writings of Sir Austen Henry Layard — the famed diplomat and art historian who excavated the Assyrian palaces of Nineveh and Nimrud from 1845 to 1851. Layard had acquired a brace of Salukis on his earlier journeys in Mesopotamia.

In 1849, the attaché left Her Majesty's Embassy in Constantinople (Istanbul) and set out once again to dig at Nineveh.* It was on this expedition that the spectacular, winged lion statues were unearthed at Nimrud for the second time and shipped back to the British Museum. In *Discoveries at Nineveh and Babylon*, the records of his travel and excavations from 1849 to 1850, Layard talks about a Saluki given to him by a Kurdish sheikh at Redwan.†

The mound of Nineveh is now covered by the village of Kuyunjik, just across the Tigris River from present-day Al Mawsil.
†*The town of Redwan in Kurdistan (where Layard stayed with the Yezidis) is now part of eastern Turkey and near the confluence of the Tigris and Siirt rivers, southwest of Lake Van.*

> My party was increased by a very handsome black and tan greyhound with long silky hair, a present from old Akko, the Yezidi chief, who declared that he loved him as his child. The affection was amply returned. No delicacies or caresses would induce Touar, for such was the dog's name, to leave his master. He laid himself down and allowed one of the servants to drag him by a rope over the rough ground, philosophically giving tongue to his complaints in a low howl. This greyhound, a fine specimen of a noble breed, much prized by the Kurds and Persians, became, from his highly original character and complete independence, a great favourite with us. He soon forgot his old masters, and formed an equal attachment for his new.[3]

Apart from the pitiful description of the hound being dragged from his master and the seemingly contradictory statements about Touar's loyalty, the description of the hound's affectionate nature, his independence, and personality, were precisely the characteristics that Florence loved so much about her Salukis. Layard not only described the usual hunting methods, but in a letter to his mother wrote, "I have two beautiful Greyhounds of first-rate breed. I wish I could send them to you for with their silky ears and feathered tails they are quite drawing-room dogs. They catch hares capitally, but are too young yet for gazelle."[4] The phrase "drawing room dogs" would be a favorite tidbit for Florence to quote in her later efforts to advance the breed.

Florence also read the accounts of Lady Anne Blunt and her husband Wilfrid, who were enthusiastic travelers and enjoyed life in the desert. Wilfrid Scawen Blunt was a poet, diplomat, and staunch anti–imperialist who married Lady Anne Isabella Noel — an artist, musician, and the only granddaughter of Lord Byron.* Blunt also had distinguished lineage as his family came over with the Norman Conquest in 1066, but his income was far less than that of Lady Anne. They married in 1869 and by the mid–1870s were traveling to exotic locations. They journeyed farther and farther east and progressed through Spain, Barbary, Egypt, Syria, the Euphrates Valley, and finally to Arabia and Persia. In 1879, Lady Anne wrote *Bedouin Tribes of the Euphrates*, telling the story of their expedition in 1877–78. Wilfrid had his own views on narrative and edited her manuscript, changing some descriptions and rearranging a few events.

Lady Anne's first mention of Salukis appears in describing the camp of the southern Shammar tribe (who at the time were near Ash Sharqat in northern Iraq). Here she notes that they had "a great many dogs about the camp, and a few greyhounds, called by the Arabs *tazeh*."[5] "*Tazi*" or "*tazeh*" was a northern term for "Saluki," but she noted that they were called also "slouguy." They were mentioned frequently in her book but always referred to as "the dogs" or "the greyhounds." Perhaps her best description comes from a trek with the Anezah in the area southwest of Palmyra:

> A little attempt at sport was made — a bustard hawked and a fox coursed; but the Bedouins here seem to care little about such things, being in this strangely different from their relations in the Sahara. The hawk was a very large one, larger than the peregrine, and well under command; for having missed his quarry, he came back at once to his master's call. It is very pretty to see these hawks, perched two together on the croup of their master's mare, or on his wife's hówdah, and keeping their balance with wings stretched out. The greyhounds, while on the march, seemed perpetually at work coursing something or other — fox, hare, or gazelle; for the long line of camels acting as beaters puts up everything before it for miles. The dogs are small but show great breeding, most of them being of the so-called Persian variety, with long silky ears and tails.[6]

Lady Anne was the fifteenth Baroness Wentworth. Her mother was Ada Byron, a mathematical genius who developed a programming language for Charles Babbage's Analytical Engine — the Victorian prototype of the modern computer.

Although an avid fox hunter in England, Wilfrid was generally indifferent to his wife's dogs throughout their marriage. He also seems to have had an odd notion of sportsmanship, as on a later occasion he galloped after a course in progress and shot two hare from horseback before the Salukis could bring them down. He did this again when the hounds were closing a hyena, despite the danger of accidentally shooting the wrong animal. After living and trekking with a number of tribes for five months, they had developed a deep passion for the qualities of Arab horses and wanted to obtain breeding stock to take home. The Blunts returned to England in 1878 with a handful of antiquities and half a dozen pure Arabians to begin the famous Crabbet Park Stud.*

Lady Anne wrote fast and furiously about their adventures in Iraq and on the eve of publication they were off again, this time for Arabia. They started from Damascus (Dimashq or Al Sham in Arabic) on December 6, 1878, and on this trip were very keen to acquire Salukis as well as Arabians.† They tried unsuccessfully to buy the first one they came across. Just south of Damascus at Ghabaghat village they saw two hounds course and kill a fox in front of them while they were watering their camels. Wilfrid was very taken with a "blue or silver grey"§ but the old soldier who owned them would not sell at any price.[7] It was not much longer before the Blunts acquired their own brace of Salukis.

A little fawn bitch was given to them at a village fifty-five miles south of Damascus, on the fringe of Hauran territory. Lady Anne named her Shiekhah (after a type of plant) and found her to be docile, well mannered and very fond of dates. It is most probable that Shiekhah was a smooth for Lady Anne always mentions feathering on the Persian type of Saluki and she makes no such note about Shiekhah.** With the only spare fabric she had, Lady Anne made a coat from a small piece of red baize and soft canvas for a liner to keep the bitch warm at night[8]— a common enough Bedouin practice. Their second hound was a gift from a sheikh's headman traveling with them. Near the ruins of Qasr al Azraq, an 8th century hunting lodge in the eastern Transjordan, Assad gave them Sayad ("hunter"), a feathered black and tan who was aptly named. The dog "whined piteously when his master went away" and this sentiment endeared him to his new mistress.[9] The two hounds became great favorites of Lady Anne — she recorded that during a night rainstorm they were allowed to crawl under her sleeping rugs.

Sayad would prove loyal to his new owners and the two hounds traveled with them in a great loop through the Great Nafud — a desert encompassing over 55,000 square kilometers, the Jabal Shammar region and its capital, Ha'il, and then north to Baghdad.†† From there they went east and south through Luristan and Arabistan, finishing up at last in Bushire (Bushehr) on the Persian Gulf. Near Al Kut they loaded their animals onto a British steamer to cross the Tigris but 180 miles further on, near Dezful in southwestern Persia, they crossed the Dez River in fashion considerably more dangerous. The load of people, hawks, hounds, and baggage on an eight-foot-square raft of inflated goatskins and tamarisk poles was precarious at best. Lady Anne noted that "our feet were in the water all the way, and our hearts in our mouths."[10] Sheikhah and Sayad were experienced at swimming across swift rivers but who

---

The Crabbet Stud in Sussex would eventually be taken over by their daughter, Lady Wentworth. It was one of the first and most important western efforts to preserve Arabian horse lines.

†*Lady Anne owned many dogs in her life despite Wilfrid's indifference to them as pets.*

§*What would today be called a "grey grizzle."*

**Which she also spelled "Shikheh" and "Shiehah" in her writings.*

††*The Jabal Shammar or Emirate of Ha'il, was its own sovereign state until combined with the regions of Al-Hasa, Qatif, Nejd, Hijaz, and Asir to become the kingdom of Saudi Arabia in 1932.*

knows what they must have thought of this unnatural experience. The last leg of the journey through Arabistan was almost beyond endurance for human and beast alike. Throughout a two-hundred-mile stretch over rough terrain, the weather changed violently between storm and calm. The rough ground was exceedingly difficult to traverse and by the time they reached Bushehr, the horses' backs were galled, the hawk had suffered a broken leg, and the Salukis' feet were torn and bleeding. Ragged, filthy, and burned nearly black from the sun, the Blunts and their animals looked like nothing so much as the poorest of Arab beggars. As the final straw, the British Legation guards refused to believe that they could possibly be English.

From there, the Blunts went to Karachi and stayed for months in India to study Arab horses before returning to Crabbet Park. Once home, Lady Anne wrote the two volume account of their travels and titled it *A Pilgrimage to Najd, the Cradle of the Arab Race*. Wilfrid argued in the book's preface that he and Lady Anne were the first Christians to travel the Najd openly as "persons of distinction" and at leisure — or at least with as much leisure as the harsh desert permits. He contended that while three other westerners, Wallin, Guarmani, and Palgrave, had passed through the Najd before the Blunts, they had all been in disguise and were secretive about their intentions. The Blunts had developed close connections with the tribesmen — they were good friends with Jane Digby and her Bedouin husband Medjuel,* and Wilfrid had sworn an oath of brotherhood with Sheikh Faris of the Northern Shammar on their 1878 trek. When they returned in 1879, the Bedouin treated the Blunts as important relatives wherever they traveled.

Written by a sister noblewoman, *A Pilgrimage to Najd* became one of Florence Amherst's best sources of information on the breed, for the Blunts' Salukis were mentioned numerous times. There were line engravings of Lady Anne and Wilfrid in native costume posing with horse, hawk and hound.† One passage about the hardiness of Salukis made a great impression on Florence and she would refer to it several times over the years. Sayad and Sheikhah were described as coursing a hare for hundreds of yards "over ground that would have broken every bone of an English greyhound, apparently without hurting themselves."[11] If this stony ground was rough terrain for coursing, one can only imagine the hostile landscape of Arabistan that tore up their feet on their way to Bushehr. Given the adventures and privations the hounds shared with the Blunts over four and a half months, the affection which Lady Anne felt for them, and the Blunts' propensity for prestigious souvenirs, it is tempting to think that Sheikhah and Sayad were brought home to Crabbet Park — but after their arrival at Bushehr, neither Lady Anne nor Wilfrid write about their Salukis again.

While Wilfrid asserted that they were the first Christians to travel in those areas, he would not have known that another Englishman, Charles Montagu Doughty, had been in Palestine in 1875 and then spent nearly two years wandering with Bedouin in the Great Nafud from November 1876 to August 1878. Doughty partially overlapped the time period of the Blunts' Euphrates adventure and he was definitely in the Nafud before them — but did not publish *Travels in Arabia Deserta* until 1888. It was a handsome book in two volumes, with

---

*Jane Digby had fled several scandals in England and the continent, and fell in love with a sheikh named Medjuel who kept a gregarious pack of Salukis and tame gazelles. They married, had children, and alternated living between his houses in Damascus and Homs, and his desert tents. Jane could best Medjuel in a camel race as well as keep up with the men during a falcon and Saluki hunt (Mary S. Lovell, Rebel Heart: The Scandalous Life of Jane Digby, New York: W. W. Norton, 1995).

†Several of the book's illustrations had hounds, but as the London engravers had no Saluki model to work from, greyhounds were substituted.

fold-out map and several illustrations. He traveled openly as a Christian or Nasrani and, as such, relegated himself to the back of the caravan with the outcasts and low-born.

Doughty tells of a Saluki turning up its nose at a piece of cooked hedgehog, but unlike the Blunts has little to say about the hounds in his massive book. He does seem to be the first person to record how during long treks "there are the Beduin masters who in the march carry their greyhounds upon camel-back lest the burning sand should scald their tender feet."[12] This would also spare the hounds from being too fatigued to hunt should game appear. Once Doughty and a small group of Bedouin heard a strange noise at night and thought it to be a supernatural utterance by a *djinn* or an *efrit*. Doughty, in a mixture of black humor and pathos, called it "only a rumble in the empty body of Wady's starveling greyhound, for which we had no water and almost not a crumb to cast, and that lay fainting above us."[13] There was not much in Doughty's work that Florence found useful, except the line about the camel ride, which would become part of her standard breed lore.

The other explorer whose exploits Wilfrid ignored is Captain Richard F. Burton (later Sir) who had gone to elaborate lengths to prepare a disguise, which included being circumcised in London and working as a servant for Jennings-Bramly's grandfather in Alexandria in order to pass as one of the faithful and be able to enter Mecca (Makkah).[14] Burton makes one unremarkable mention of hunting Salukis in his two-volume *Personal Narrative of a Pilgrimage to Al–Medinah & Meccah*,[15] and these "greyhounds" appear in at least two stories from his famous translation of the Arabian Nights. As Florence was a great name-dropper whenever it came to publicity about her breed and Burton was certainly one of the more famous Victorian explorers, it seems likely that these tidbits escaped her notice.

Prior to Luman and Ayesha at Didlington, there had been only a handful of Salukis in England. These few were brought by travelers and soldiers and viewed as curiosities or zoological specimens, and only occasionally exhibited at dog shows, but the picturesque breed did catch the attention of English artists. John Wootton painted some of the famous Arabian horses imported to England in the early 1700s (the Darley Arabian, Byerley Turk, Bloody-Shouldered Arabian, and Godolphin Arabian) and frequently included a hound meant to be a Saluki alongside the horses and turbaned attendants. Henry Bernard Chalon (1770–1840) did the same in *Persian Horses Presented to His Majesty the King*. James Ward, R.A., the famous animal painter, had executed a life-size portrait of a magnificent red Saluki owned by Lady St. George.[16] It was entitled *The Persian Greyhound* and her hound was depicted in full chase with four other Salukis. The following description of Lady St. George's Saluki indicates that he actually coursed hare in England, most likely with greyhounds.

> This dog, so different in appearance from our English Greyhounds, is a very handsome animal, with a fine soft skin, the hair of its ears and tail appearing like silk, and resembling it in softness; his throat, toes, and inside of his ears are white; his back and upper parts of his tail a dark brown; and the rest of him a sandy hue; which, together with his handsome form and appearance, attracts the admiration of everyone who sees him. He is of gentle disposition, and possesses the same qualities as our Greyhounds, with considerable swiftness of foot, having beat several dogs which have run with him.[17]

Ward's stunning portrait was exhibited at the British Institution in 1807 and reproduced as a black and white engraving for the *Sporting Magazine* in December of that year, and later, hand colored in books. The painting disappeared into private homes for several decades and escaped Florence's notice. It returned to Saluki fanciers when Lt. Commander David and Mrs. Hope Waters (Burydown Salukis) purchased it from a gallery in the late 1950s.*

Around 1835, Zillah, an elegant black bitch with tan markings and born in the Zoological Gardens in Regent's Park, was the subject of a small but brilliant painting by the artist Charles Hamilton. She was depicted gazing at a distant hunting party, about to be slipped by her Persian master. Zillah's portrait (which Florence knew of) was converted to an engraving by F. E. Nicholson and reproduced in the *New Sporting Magazine* in 1837[18] and later in Edward Jessie's *Anecdotes of Dogs* in 1858 and 1870, and as recently as 1906.[19] Zillah's owner, Mr. George Lock of Kentish Town, London, asserted that she was the only "thoroughbred bitch at present in this country," although how she came to England was never revealed.[20] Interestingly enough, Hugh Dalziel asserted in the 1879 and 1887 editions of his book *British Dogs* that no Persian Greyhounds had been bred in England. But he was writing forty-five years after Zillah's time and either he did not know of her, or Zillah was not actually born in the Zoological Gardens and produced no offspring.

Despite their scarcity, Salukis had attracted some notice in society for they are mentioned in Thackeray's *Vanity Fair*, published in 1847, which Florence does not note anywhere. In Chapter 37, "How to Live Well on Nothing a Year," Lord Southdown misinterprets Becky Sharp's desire for an allegorical "sheep dog" (inferring both a companion and moral guardian) and suggests rather more fashionable dogs such as the giant Danish dog, a Pug, or a Persian Greyhound.

There were other Victorian descriptions of Salukis that Florence would discover much later. By the 1920s she had read Charles Doughty and Lieutenant Colonel Charles Hamilton Smith. In 1840, Smith had published two books devoted to canines and their ancestors and wrote from firsthand experience about hunting methods used by the Arabs and their Salukis. Florence noted vaguely in her writings that Smith had brought one back to England about the time that his book *Dogs* was published.

Other tantalizing Victorian Salukis appear on canvas with gilt frames. At the Royal Academy in 1880, Briton Riviere exhibited *Endymion,* which depicted the pining Greek shepherd surrounded by his three faithful hounds — two white Borzoi and a deep red Saluki. Fourteen years earlier, Sir Edwin Henry Landseer R.A., an acclaimed genius when it came to portraying horses, hounds, and stags, toyed with Orientalist fantasy when he included Salukis in one of his most famous paintings. At the Royal Academy in 1866, he exhibited his larger-than-life canvas *The Arab Tent*, depicting an Arab mare and her colt reposing within their master's tent.[†] Surrounded by Persian carpets, cut palm fronds, and wisps of incense, two Salukis cuddle on a raised, leopard-skin bed. The pair was probably modeled from life, as they are very different in color and coat from either the Ward Saluki or Zillah. Fancifully, Landseer included pet monkeys, a burning incense brazier, garishly striped fabric, and tent rigging that would be more appropriate to a three-masted brig than a Bedouin's *bait sha'r*.[§]

Florence did not know about the Landseer painting, but the fact that despite her industrious research she remained unaware of many examples of Saluki portraits is easy enough to

---

*The "Persian Greyhound" was exhibited in the Tate Gallery, London, in January 1960 and David and Hope Waters used it to illustrate cover of their book, The Saluki in History, Art, and Sport. It later passed through the hands of art collector and Saluki fancier Cynthia Woods. Retitled "Salukis," it is now in the permanent collection of the American Kennel Club's Museum of the Dog in St. Louis, Missouri.

†Currently on display in The Wallace Collection, London.

§T. E. Lawrence thought this painting to be an example of excessive Orientalism (Letter to E. T. Leeds, Dec. 16, 1910, Bodleian Library, MS. Eng. d. 3337, fol. 3 to 4).

understand. If a painting was exhibited publicly in a gallery, it might well disappear afterwards into a private collection, unless a museum thought it worthwhile to purchase. Once hung on a manor's walls, friends of the owner would certainly know the work, but it might not see the light of public exhibition until a sale or estate auction decades later. To reproduce a painting for a book or monochrome print (assuming that the owner had consented), a copyist would have to painstakingly reproduce the work as an etching or line drawing. Needless to say, this did not happen for most paintings.

Being a well-traveled scholar, Florence had seen many other examples of Salukis in pre–19th-century paintings but very few that were contemporary. She still didn't know what to properly call the breed, as conventional sources disagreed with each other. It was Arabic literature and traveler's narratives that answered many riddles about Salukis for her, but these were often contradictory as to which name properly belonged to the breed. She still did not quite know what to call them. That puzzle would take Florence over a decade to solve, and would return as a point of controversy in 1922.

4

Amherst Doings, Research, and the Walking Englishman

"His master is to him as a slave; at night he is the nearest to his cradle, and if the dog is naked he covers him with his cloak."
                    Florence Amherst, quoting the "Diwan of Abu Nuwas"

February 1897 saw the Amhersts again in the Riviera and a few months later in the Holy Land, this time with May and Willy (Mary and William Cecil). As on the Nile excursion, the Amhersts brought along another family dog. While Bluebell was spared the fate of poor Ducker, it was a close call for one of the sisters. In Jerusalem, Sybil became deathly ill and her fever rose to a dangerous 105°. Lord Amherst arranged for Sybil's treatment to be undertaken by Dr. Raphaël Rück, the chief of the French government's local medical clinic. Medicines were of little use and recovery very much depended on her own fortitude and nursing care by her sisters. Florence had always been very close to Sybil and the constant bedside vigil took its toll on both her and Alicia. It took two weeks for Sybil to pass the crisis and during that time, Alicia would become too exhausted to make her customary journal entries and sketches. Sybil recovered, but her health would always remain delicate. For the rest of her life, she would depend on Florence's tender care.

In June of that year, the Amhersts attended the London festivities for Queen Victoria's Diamond Jubilee — an exhausting array of parades, receptions, speeches, and illuminations, all occurring between June 20 and July 8. The celebrations were enough to tire a vigorous person, let alone the Queen, whose health was declining at nearly eighty years of age. June 22, was declared a bank holiday for the Queen's parade through the streets of London. Temporary stands were erected and buildings festooned with flags and bunting of red, blue, and white. The streets were lined with sailors, marines, and soldiers — shoulder to shoulder with rifles presented and sword bayonets fixed. Policemen worked the crowd behind the military cordon and kept a close eye on the crowded sidewalks, viewing stands, windows, and rooftops. The Queen was dressed in black as usual and rode in an open carriage shaded by a white parasol.* She was attended by two ladies in waiting and a pair of somber Scottish footmen. The population of London cheered madly and waved hats, kerchiefs, and flags as she passed by.

That was the day that most people celebrated the Jubilee. The Amhersts were there and had attended the numerous private celebrations for people of rank and station. Wishing to share the joyous occasion with their Norfolk neighbors, the Amhersts hosted an enormous

---

After the premature death of her husband, Albert, the Prince Consort, in 1861, she wore mourning clothes for the rest of her life.

jubilee extravaganza at Didlington a month later on Saturday, July 28. Some four to five thousand people were entertained and three thousand took advantage of the "meat tea" provided by Lord Amherst.* In addition to a ventriloquist and famous singers brought up from London, Lord Amherst hired a hand-cranked cinematograph and operator to show "animated photographs" which included footage of the Queen Victoria's grand Jubilee procession through London. One of the most remarkable features of the event was the small marquee containing two life-size figures of Queen Victoria representing her appearance in 1837 and 1897.† The Downham Volunteer and Swaffham Volunteer Bands played in concert and a one-inning match was held on the Didlington cricket pitch. The crowd watched the gentlemen players intently, and Lord Amherst's eleven ultimately lost to Mr. Johnson's eleven by 145 runs to 128. As always, Amherst hospitality was ample and gracious, and the local newspaper devoted a large amount of space to the entire event.[1]

In the large dining marquee, the popular Lord Amherst welcomed the crowd to Didlington and apologized for Lady Amherst's absence as she was away in Scotland. He made a patriotic speech to commemorate "the greatest event that had ever occurred in any of their lifetimes" and pointed out that the queen had ruled with blameless character for longer than any previous monarch. Loud cries of "Hear! Hear!" and "Huzzah!" punctuated his speech and he ended to thunderous applause when he expressed the genuine hope that he would meet them all on future occasions.[2]

The year 1897 was also a signal one for Florence, for a few weeks after the Jubilee Celebration another happy event occurred at Didlington — the birth of Florence's first litter of Saluki puppies. Luman and Ayesha were nearly three years old and had been bred sometime between May and the middle of June — possibly when the family was in London for the extended Jubilee festivities. The exact whelping date in August is unrecorded and she only registered one puppy with the Kennel Club, a bitch named Sama.§ Florence would not always register all her puppies with the Kennel Club, and how many were in that first litter is uncertain, but by 1904 she had at least ten adult Salukis at Didlington.

On Wednesday, February 16, 1898, Londoners were just beginning to learn about the destruction of the U.S.S. *Maine* in the Havana harbor the day before. For the Amhersts, the incident that sparked the Spanish-American War was overshadowed by Alicia's marriage to Evelyn Cecil, Esq. (later Baron Rockley). The bridegroom was the son of Colonel Lord Eustace and Lady Cecil, and the eldest nephew of the Prime Minister, Lord Salisbury. Evelyn was Salisbury's assistant private secretary and had written *Primogeniture*, a history of male inheritance and succession. The Amhersts were ecstatic — it was a wonderful love match and royalty, diplomats, and nobility attended the happy event.

The wedding was held at St. George's Church, Hanover Square, just three blocks from the Amherst townhouse. It was artfully decorated with palm ferns and white arum lilies. Alicia wore a rich, white, satin and lace gown with a court train of white moiré imperiale and a veil over a wreath of orange blossoms, fastened by a large diamond and pearl star — a present from Evelyn. Along with Cecil in-laws and niece Victoria Drummond, Florence, Sybil, and

---

*A more substantial meal than the usual light sandwiches, cake, or scones.
†Madame Tussaud's has no record of these figures but they were not the only company making wax likenesses at that time. The newspaper reporter was particularly impressed with the costumes on the figures.
§Florence translated this correctly as "Sky."

Margaret were bridesmaids. The sisters gave Alicia a large six-rayed-star brooch in fine diamonds, a set of silver entree dishes, and revolving-cover, silver breakfast dishes. The couple received presents from royalty, and Didlington housemaids and tenants alike. According to custom, these were put on public display at Grosvenor Square townhouse for several days prior to the wedding. The reception featured the renowned Amherst hospitality and the papers listed in minute detail the guests, their apparel, and their gifts. Alicia and her bridegroom were both thirty-three, and she was the last of the Amherst daughters to marry.

As if to balance the joy of Alicia's wedding, there were difficulties for the Amhersts during the rest of 1898. In July a young guest died at Didlington. A month later, Lady Amherst managed to break her collarbone while staying at Otterburn in Northumberland and Lord Amherst became seriously ill. Too weak to maintain his correspondence, Florence took over much of it as she had many times before. An antiquities scholar and dealer with the marvelous name of Theophilus Goldridge Pinches, LL.D,* had worked with Lord Amherst for twenty years on the Didlington collection. Pinches was translating Amherst's 120 or more cuneiform Assyrian tablets and seals for a book about their significance. Publication was scheduled for the following year and during the last months of 1898 the scholar wrote regularly to Amherst about the progress of the work and always inquired after the family's health and well-being. Over the years, Florence frequently handled her father's business correspondence with Pinches and he would send his particular regards to her. In November the Amhersts spent some recuperative time at Filey, a seaside resort in North Yorkshire, and at the beginning of December they were well enough for the journey to the sunny south of France and their haven, Lou Casteou, for a much-needed holiday which was to last several months.

So far, Florence's research on Salukis had revealed surprising evidence that the ancient breed had been a witness to western history. In addition to scouring libraries and the British Museum for the accounts and representations of the breed, family holidays on the continent provided opportunities to examine foreign museums whose treasures might not have been published as photographic facsimiles or engraved copies in the art books of the day. Salukis could be seen in the paintings of Paolo Véronèse, and two prominent examples Florence would later cite were his *Les Noces de Cana* (The Wedding Feast of Cana) in the Louvre and *The Finding of Moses* in Dresden's Gemäldegalerie.† In the latter, a brace of golden and cream Salukis stand prominently on the left, watching Moses being presented to his foster mother.

The hounds played a rather more important role in the other painting. Véronèse used a brace of Salukis as a key compositional element in *The Wedding Feast of Cana* (painted between 1562–63). One Saluki gnaws on a scrap and the other pulls at its brace lead, straining toward a cat off to the side. They are carefully centered in the lower foreground to draw the viewer's eye upward to the figure of Christ. It was not uncommon for traders and merchants to bring Salukis home from the Middle East and they show up in many paintings of the Italian Renaissance. Véronèse was fond of including them in his works and doubtless he either had his own Salukis or at least had easy access to those of his friends and patrons.

One could find painted representations of the hounds boarding the ark, looking for

---

*Doctor of Laws.

†*They are also seen in his paintings* Venus and Adonis *(The Prado, Madrid),* The Conversion of Saul *(The Hermitage, St. Petersburg),* Mary Magdalen in the House of Simon the Pharisee *(Regia Pinacoteca, Turin), and numerous others.*

scraps under banquet tables, observing the subjects of the painting, and even nuzzling Diana the Huntress. Looking further into the past, Florence discovered representations of Salukis in the stained-glass windows and knightly funeral effigies of medieval churches. Crusader knights were frequently represented with hounds having deep chests, narrow waists and lop-eared (different from the greyhound's rose-fold ear). Florence concluded that these were certainly Salukis — either feathered or smooth-coated. She advanced the theory that many of these had been brought back to England by crusaders as proof of their pilgrimage.[3] Although Florence never gives the source of this romantic story, she would later tell of a Syrian story which held that Richard the Lion-Hearted was given a Saluki during the crusades. Supposedly, Rishan — a common Saluki name meaning "feathered or hairy" — was the Arabic term for the bearded crusaders, and derived from Richard's own name.[4]

A Dresden 15th–16th century portrait of Duke Heinrich the Pious, by Lucas Cranach the Elder, gave further evidence of Salukis in European history, but Florence would not become aware of it until the 1920s. Heinrich wears magnificent puff-and-slash clothing and his Saluki stands beside him.* The playful, white-and-black parti-color hound wears an elaborate collar decorated with seashell emblems, which match those on his master's sword grip and pommel.† Florence was eager to prove her case about Salukis as evidence of a pilgrimage to the Holy Land, and cited the shell emblems in Heinrich's portrait as the badge of a pilgrim.[5] This was true enough, but rather than a trip to the Middle East, the seashell badge betokened a pilgrimage to Santiago de Compostela, Spain — believed to be the burial site of the Apostle James. Heinrich's Saluki could have easily been acquired while traveling or could have been a present from a foreign guest at his court. Obviously a dog lover as well, his wife, Catherine of Mecklenburg, was painted holding her toy "lion dog" — another exotic import from the East.[6]

Florence's appetite for information about the breed grew to be insatiable. Having scoured libraries and museums, she realized that what was now needed to augment her research were more firsthand accounts of how the hounds were used by the Bedouin, describing their place in Arab society. Her family's Egyptology and diplomatic connections provided her with access to men working in the Middle East who might be in a position to provide her with information.

Wilfred Jennings-Bramly had left his post as keeper of the Giza Zoological Gardens early in 1898. Much to the annoyance of his successor, Jennings-Bramly kept only scant records during his six years there. He had made an ill-advised expedition to Siwa (on the Libyan border) in 1896 in order to be the first Christian to penetrate the inner city. He and his guides narrowly avoided death on the return journey, and heat and thirst did kill one of his Salukis.[7] In need of new employment, he hoped that the Royal Geographical Society or the Palestine Exploration Fund (PEF) would employ him in survey work, or perhaps the philanthropic Lord Amherst might sponsor him in some fashion. The Amhersts remembered the charming man with all the stories from their visit to Cairo and particularly his assistance to Florence in obtaining a brace of Salukis.

Jennings-Bramly proposed to undertake a survey of the wells, springs, tribes, and sheikhs in the Egyptian territory in 1898 and Lord Amherst agreed to fund the project. Later in the

---

Currently in the Dresden State Art Collection, Gallery of Old Masters.
†*The fascinating collection of dog collars at Leeds Castle (some of which date back to the 15th century) has several examples of 18th century German collars that are decorated with seashells.*

year, and doubtless with Lord Amherst's endorsement, he was hired by the Palestine Exploration Fund to map large areas of Sinai and Southern Palestine. Mindful of Amherst's instructions to keep an eye out for antiquities of interest deep in the desert, Jennings-Bramly spotted a curiously engraved stone. He sent a copy of the inscription to Amherst, which was subsequently identified by the PEF as Nabatean in origin.* Lord Amherst was very interested in the artifact and seriously considered having Jennings-Bramly return to the location and haul the stone back so that it could be shipped to England.[8] In November 1898, with the theatrical panache that was his trademark, Jennings-Bramly accepted a wager that he could go from Alexandria to Sienna, Italy, dressed as a Bedouin and speaking only Arabic and traveling in steerage.[9] The amount is not recorded, but he won the bet.

As it transpired, the Palestine Exploration Fund was ultimately disappointed with the accuracy of Jennings-Bramly's maps and the lack of detail in his reports. There was considerable doubt at the time that they would ever employ him again. During Lord Amherst's illness in the fall of 1898 he had had several letters from Jennings-Bramly with news from the desert. Lord Amherst wrote back, encouraging him to finish his reports and maps so that the PEF would be disposed towards employing him again. In December, Amherst made a conciliatory gesture on Jennings-Bramly's behalf and presented the "Sinai Survey" to the Fund at his own expense. In return, Lord Amherst asked to keep Jennings-Bramly's original documents at the Didlington library.

While observing tribal practices on his expeditions, Jennings-Bramly's own interest in falconry (he had kept hawks and falcons at the Giza Zoo) coincided with that of his patron. Lord Amherst had been a founding member of the Old Falconer's Club in 1860 and the abundance of herons on the Didlington estate and falconer's lodge made it one of the club's usual hunting grounds. Well aware of Amherst's interest in falconry, during a stay with Amhersts at their Grosvenor Square townhouse in March 1899, Jennings-Bramly displayed his photographs of desert falcons and regaled them with tales of Arab hunting and his mapping adventures. The Swaffham Coursing Club had met on the Didlington grounds just a month prior to Jennings-Bramly's visit and this may have added to the Amherst enthusiasm for desert hounds. The handsome explorer was persuasive, for by June of 1900 Lord Amherst was considering funding a private publication of Jennings-Bramly's notes on falconry and coursing.

After several months of negotiations and urging by Lord Amherst in 1899, the Palestine Exploration Fund and the Royal Geographical Society agreed jointly to fund the £400 cost of Jennings-Bramly's next proposal — mapping the area around Mount Edom and east of the pilgrim's path to Mecca (Makkah) — the Haj Road.[†]

The arrangement was advantageous all around, as updated maps would not only benefit the Royal Geographical Society (RGS) and Palestine Exploration Fund, but ultimately support the British Army's safeguarding of the Suez Canal — Britain's lifeline to India. With the Suez at the frontier of the Ottoman Empire, the army was glad to have intelligence of areas under Turkish control. Scientifically noble in purpose, these surveys (which typically reported on geography, geology, ecology, zoology, anthropology and archaeology) were also a thinly disguised version of espionage. After getting authorization and funds for his Edom expedition, Jennings-Bramly made arrangements for his friend George Fraser to deposit his checks

---

Nabatea was an ancient Arabian kingdom whose capital city was Petra.

†Mt. Edom, or Gebel Seir, is located approximately 30 miles northeast of Petra and the Haj Road generally parallels the Red Sea coastline some 120 miles inland.

in a Cairo bank account before departing. With the financial support for the expedition squared away, he now needed a guide — and a disguise.

Sheikh Suleyman Ebn Amer of the Teaha was a venerable warhorse with an enormous gray beard. He was an old friend of Jennings-Bramly and for a fee he would act again as guide for the Englishman. The area to be surveyed was controlled by the Ottoman Empire but he knew that Turkish patrols were easy enough to avoid as they relied upon the sheikhs in their pay to look out for foreigners or spies.[10] The Englishman devised a clever scheme to hide the nature of his mission from watchful tribesmen. He and Sheikh Suleyman bargained for a small herd of goats and camels and pretended to be traders. The surveying took place under the pretense of driving the herd to market and every three months or so the livestock was to be sold or traded, and any profit eventually returned to his employers. To better pass as an Arab, Jennings-Bramly shaved his head and grew a bushy beard. He wrapped his head cloth so only one of his blue eyes could be seen. Very pleased with himself, he posed dramatically in costume for a photographer. His theatrical flair stood him in good stead, for when he dressed in ragged robes with a sheepskin flung over his shoulder, he was very much "Abd-el-Raheem el Soulimanie" — a Mograbi camel trader.[11]

His Arabic was passable and any peculiarities of speech or accent were explained by his claim to come from a town that anyone he encountered could not possibly know. If he met a native in the Western Desert, he would claim to be from Soulimanie in northeastern Iraq* and ask if they knew the town. Not wishing to appear ignorant or risk offending "Abd-el-Raheem," they would usually nod in agreement. He would riposte by saying, "Well if you know Soulimanie, then you'll know the house with the green door. That's where I live."[12] Good manners and this "proof" invariably ended any questions as to his authenticity, but as the need arose he would also pass himself off as a pilgrim from Persia or Afghanistan.

Jennings-Bramly occupied himself from May to August 1899 mapping portions of the inland area east of the road to Makkah and returned to Cairo barely able to walk because of dreadful sores on his legs. During this expedition, Jennings-Bramly had both a quarter-plate camera and a Kodak pocket camera which had been provided by the PEF. Jennings-Bramly's servant, Yunes, had been shown how to operate the shutter of the smaller camera, and somewhere in Sinai snapped a wonderful picture of Sheikh Suleyman and the smiling, bald and bearded Jennings-Bramly seated on a carpet in the desert.[†] Among the other photographs is a unique snapshot of a group of Bedouin, horse, and camel, with a white male Saluki in the foreground. It seems likely that he intended to send it back to Florence Amherst as she was always asking for pictures of Salukis in their native environment. It is the oldest-known photograph of a Saluki and certainly the first of one in its native habitat.[§]

Back in Cairo, he procrastinated terribly in delivering his promised reports but was bold enough to ask the PEF and RGS to employ him — this time permanently. They demurred and by December Jennings-Bramly had asked for an extension on completing the maps so that he could go to the Sudan and work under Colonel Milo George Talbot, the new direc-

---

*Located near Kirkuk in Iraq, it is now known as As Sulaymaniyah. There is an identically named town in central Saudi Arabia, but this does not seem to be the one that Jennings-Bramly used for his standard ruse.

†The location of the quarter-plate photographs, if they still exist, is uncertain, but a number of the snapshots remain with his grandson, Jasper Scovil, to whom I am greatly indebted for permission to reproduce his grandfather's photographs.

§Alois Musil, the Czech Arabist, took a blurry snapshot of a smooth grizzle in a Howeitat tent about 1900 (Arabia Petraea, 1908, p.37). Doubtless there were photos taken of the Salukis at Didlington after their arrival in 1895, but these have yet to surface.

Wilfred Jennings-Bramly in his Arab disguise, ca. 1896. With the kind permission of Jasper Scovil.

The oldest known photograph of a Saluki, taken in Lower Egypt or Sinai by Jennings-Bramly between 1898 and 1900. With the kind permission of Jasper Scovil.

tor of Sudan Surveys. Basil Thomson, one of the officers of the PEF, worried justifiably that if Jennings-Bramly left Cairo, the reports might never be done: "[H]e is such a casual creature that I'm afraid a good report can only be got from him while the journey is fresh in his memory, quite apart from the danger of continued procrastination."[13] Despite the misgivings of the PEF, Jennings-Bramly went to the desolate Sudan and lived there for nearly two years while a stream of entreaties for his overdue reports and maps poured out of London. While he did manage to get a brief version of his notes on Arab sport published in the October/December 1900 *Quarterly Statement* of the PEF, Amherst's private monograph on Arab hunting never materialized.

   In the summer of 1901, Jennings-Bramly wrote to the PEF and told them that he was to be married but they saw this as yet another delay and urged him to come to England to finish his work before the wedding.[14] He had fallen in love with Phyllis de Cosson, the daughter of a renowned scholar and collector of arms and armor, Baron de Cosson. After the relatives had all traveled to Florence, Italy, for the wedding, Jennings-Bramly, to the extreme annoyance of the two families, asked Phyllis to delay the marriage by one year.* He finally did complete the promised work on the Edom area late in 1902.[15] While the Fund and Society were less than thrilled with the accuracy of his maps, the PEF was admittedly impressed with the wealth of ethnographic material he collected. In 1904, five years after the RGS and PEF commissioned Jennings-Bramly for the Edom expedition, they were still after him to return their survey instruments.[16]

   Phyllis and Wilfred were finally married in July 1902 and that same year he accepted a post as inspector for the Sinai Desert. See Appendix 2 for a summary of his extraordinary life and career.

Keeping in mind Florence's interest in Salukis, Jennings-Bramly periodically sent tantalizing snippets to Didlington Hall about hunting in the desert. This account of a khedival hawking party near Cairo became a favorite story of Florence's and most likely came from one of his letters: "The princes ride out, 'with a gay retinue, with hawk on wrist, and Slughi in the leash.' When the gazelle is sighted, 'with a peculiar shrill cry' the prince lets his hawk fly, the Greyhounds following with their tails waving like banners, which are said to 'steer them over a breezy plain.'"[17]

Jennings-Bramly was never much of a dog person but did try to oblige Florence and her father as much as he was able. Salukis were mentioned in some of his writings — "*slughis*," "*slooges*," and "*sellages*" were his various phonetic renderings, but sometimes he just called them "Arabian greyhounds" or "gazelle hounds". In 1909, fifteen years after leaving the Giza Zoo, he listed a few memorable call names for the Bedouin greyhounds. Perhaps his tracker Dau's hounds were named Zarbuf, Farka, and Lissa, for these were the only Saluki names that Jennings-Bramly would ever record.[18]

On the cold evening of January 22, 1901, Queen Victoria died in her bed, having ruled three years longer than any other British monarch. Her death in the new century marked an end of a long and generally happy reign despite a constant peppering of colonial wars. The loss was felt keenly by her subjects and the entire country was plunged into mourning. Portraits of the Queen were draped in black, and black crepe was everywhere. Adults and children alike wore mourning clothes. Even people's personal stationery had somber black borders. The Amherst family went to London to prepare for the state funeral on February 4. There was to be a local service at St. Michael's and Lady Amherst stayed home at Didlington with the grandchildren to attend church. The boys wore black armbands on the left sleeves of their coats and the girls wore black sashes with their white frocks.[19]

Each village had sent a wreath for the London procession and these were used to decorate all the lampposts, along with black drapes, on the funeral route. As there had been for the Diamond Jubilee, a cinematographer recorded the procession on film. The streets were as crowded as for that happier celebration, but now there was a respectful hush. Albert Edward finally assumed the throne of England at the age of 59 and styled himself King Edward the VII. Only a handful of elderly Britons remembered when there had been a king on the throne.

It was a new century and Britain had a new king. Edward was not the reclusive monarch that his widowed mother had been and he and his wife, Alexandra, were very active in society. It was a national and cultural change that would affect Florence Amherst in an unexpected way. Queen Alexandra's enthusiasm for her Borzoi (Russian wolfhounds) had made the breed extremely popular with the nobility and upper classes. Astutely, Florence took notice and began to think about how to bring Salukis into the limelight.

PART II: THE CURTAIN RISES

5

Egyptology

*"Different breeds were employed in hunting, the largest species used being the "Slûghi,"
or Great Greyhound. They are exceedingly graceful and very swift, and their lineal
descendants are still employed to hunt the gazelle."*

Lady Margaret Amherst of Hackney[1]

Florence Amherst was jubilant when she received her copy of the May 28, 1904, edition
of *Country Life* magazine, for it contained the first published photograph of one of her Salukis.
It was an article on form and function of coursing hounds and she had been asked to write a
short paragraph about the antiquity of her breed. She sent along a photograph of Luman wearing a white leather collar with brass nameplate.* Although he had gone white in the face, he
looked very fit for his age of nine.

The photo was captioned, "The Honorable Florence Amherst's Assyrian Greyhound
Luman." Florence's interesting choice of nomenclature for the breed is likely derived from
the 19th-century travel accounts of Mrs. James Finn or Sir Henry Layard, but it was the first
and only time she ever called them "Assyrian greyhounds" in print. Egyptologists and family
friends Howard Carter and Percy Newberry referred to the hounds on Egyptian tomb walls
as "slughis or Nubian greyhounds" and to add to the confusion, Jennings-Bramly's dyslexic
renderings ("slughis," "slooges," and "sellages") made the question of their proper name still
more confusing.† As Florence's knowledge grew deeper and broader, she would cycle through
a number of names for the breed.

Lady Amherst published an impressive book in 1904 —*A Sketch of Egyptian History*—
and dedicated it to her husband, daughters, and grandchildren. Drawing on her own extensive experience, and with the resources of the Didlington library and Egyptian collection close
at hand, she produced a volume that gave a history of Egypt and its peoples from pharaonic
times up to the present day. She drew on the work of her Egyptologist friends, several of whom
provided assistance and suggestions. As with most Amherst activities, it was a family project.
Lord Amherst personally supervised the creation of a large foldout map of Northern Egypt
and the Nile. Their daughters were especially helpful: Alicia contributed photographs from
their 1895 trip up the Nile; Mary and her husband, William Cecil, provided others from their

---

*Regrettably, Florence was never consistent about citations (when she thought to include them) in her writings.
She noted in Leighton that early articles on Oriental Greyhounds and Salukis appeared in* Stock Keeper, *January 1902;* Exchange and Mart, *November 1904;* Lady's Pictorial, *February 1906; and* Country Gentleman, *September 1906. It is likely that Florence wrote these articles, but the author has been unable to locate these for
confirmation.*

†*Sir Terence Clark suggests that Jennings-Bramly's "sellages" may have been an attempt to write the colloquial
plural of "slughi"—silaagui—in an Anglicized form.*

own Nile expeditions; Sybil painted watercolors; and Cherry assisted with translations of hieroglyphics and cartouches. Howard Carter and Lord Amherst's uncle, Charles Fountaine, contributed watercolors, and there was an 1811 life portrait of Mohammed Ali Pasha* done by Lady Margaret's late father, Admiral Mitford. Finally, the Amherst's old friend Percy Newberry (who would publish his own book on Egyptian history later that year) vetted Lady Amherst's manuscript.

Of course Florence played an integral part in the book's creation, with her own watercolor illustrations of Egyptian monuments as well as the addition of her fund of Saluki lore to the book.[†] By the time it was published, nine years after the arrival of her first pair of Salukis at Didlington Hall, she had amassed a collection of historical references to the hounds. Egypt provided plenty of material pertaining to Salukis, such as the charms and amulets in Egyptian tombs inscribed with spells that enabled the dead to summon desired objects "swifter than greyhounds and quicker than light."[2] From the ample evidence she had seen in tomb paintings and on carved stelae[§], Florence was convinced that the lop-eared hounds depicted therein were the ancestors of modern sight-hound breeds and that the hieroglyphics for "greyhound" were generally synonymous with "Saluki."[**]

Lady Amherst made a particular point of referring to the depictions of certain hounds on tomb walls and stelae as "Slûghi" or "Great Greyhound." Guided by Florence, she cited the antiquity of the hounds by describing a 3,000-year-old rock carving at Hammamat in tribute to the last king of the Seventeenth Dynasty, Se-ankh-ka-ra, who is shown seated alongside his Saluki while servants hold captured gazelles. She also translates the names of four hounds from the Eleventh Dynasty stela of the Great Antef—"The Greyhound," "The Gazelle," "The Black," and "The Firepot."[3] Although she never gives details, Florence would later note that it was the appearance of the hound's name "The Gazelle" appearing in the famous Abbot Papyrus that actually led to the positive identification of Antef's tomb.[4] Lady Amherst had had firsthand experience with her daughter's Salukis at Didlington and Howard Carter confirmed in his published commentary on the Beni Hasan hounds that these "slughis" were still used in the desert for hunting.[5] She wrote authoritatively that they were elegant and fast hunters, and clearly the heirs of the Egyptian "Great Greyhound."

✧   ✧   ✧

There was no formal training for Egyptologists at the time and the Egypt Exploration Fund (EEF) recruited men with talent who they believed to be suited to the arduous work and who had a constitution that could stand up to the unhealthy climate. After intensive train-

---

*Mohammed Ali threw off Turkish rule in Egypt and became its first pasha in 1805. As a young captain, Lady Amherst's father had helped to build the pasha's navy. Coincidentally, Wilfred Jennings-Bramly's maternal great-grandfather, Pellegrino Tibaldi, Marquis of Valsolda, was one of Mohammed Ali's trusted counselors — until poisoned at the pasha's order for opposing the plan to exterminate the Mameluks in Egypt.

[†]A few years later, Florence also did several watercolor illustrations for The Herb-Garden by Frances A. Bardswell (1911). The book was dedicated to "Margaret, Lady Amherst of Hackney." Florence's illustration style was accurate, but delicate and lacking boldness.

[§]Upright stones or tablets carved with hieroglyphics or images.

[**]Egyptologists translate as "dog" and   as "hound"—which generally refers to a hunting dog. "Dog" is sometimes written with the first two signs repeated and this is thought to be an onomatopoeic representation of howling. I am grateful to James P. Allen, the former curator of the Department of Egyptian Art, Metropolitan Museum of Art, for his explanation and for referring me to Henry G. Fischer's definitive article "Hunde" in Lexicon de Ägyptologie III, ed. Wolfgang Heck, et al. (Wiesbaden: Harrassowitz 1980), 77–81).

ing at the British Museum, successful candidates continued their education in the field. Lady Amherst had noted young Howard Carter's exceptional artistic talents and his intense interest in the antiquities of Didlington Hall, and helped to arrange an EEF apprenticeship for him. He worked diligently in the museum, learning to produce accurate copies of paintings and wall carvings. In November 1890, Percy Newberry and George Fraser (Jennings-Bramly's former roommate from the Giza Zoo) had begun the seasonal work of photographing and surveying the thirty-nine tombs at Beni Hasan (named for the local Bedouin tribe) for the Egyptian Exploration Fund. With macabre practicality, the pair set up cozy living quarters and Fraser's darkroom in one of the empty and undecorated tombs — "our domestic tomb," as they called it.[6] Their work was part of the first systematic survey and documentation of the Nile monuments. Under Newberry's direction, Fraser did the surveying and photography of the tomb interiors while Marcus W. Blackden made watercolor copies of the murals. Howard Carter, now seventeen, had finished a hurried apprenticeship at the British Museum and was sent to join Newberry's team as assistant draftsman in October 1891.

Carter got on very well with Newberry but after being on site for only two months, became involved in a falling out between Newberry and the other two members of the team. Fraser and Blackden had "claim jumped" Newberry's discovery of the Hatnub quarry by rushing to publish their journal article first. The tension between the men did not make the work any easier. Shortly after Carter's arrival, in February 1892, Blackden fell ill and could not continue his work, so Carter took over and labored hard to finish copying the paintings through the end of the fieldwork in November of that year. Newberry, Carter, and a new team member, Percy Buckman, completed the colored facsimiles in England and prepared their findings for publication. A number of sight hounds were depicted on the tomb walls.

Tombs 2 and 3 had large murals on the north walls depicting hunting scenes with both lop-eared Salukis and prick-eared Pharaoh hounds. In Tomb 2, the resting place of Amenemhat, Great Chief of the Oryx Nome,* there was a painting of two lean and leggy hounds with wide collars — one lop-eared and one prick-eared — prominently placed next to their master, which Carter had copied and described. The lop-eared hound is clearly a Saluki.† Carter wrote of the painting, "In Pl.ii. is a greyhound, which may be compared with the Nubian greyhound or *slughi,* still used in the chase of the antelope. It is one of two greyhounds pictured in the tomb of Amenemhat."[7] Newberry had documented "Nubian greyhounds" in the tomb of Rekhmire — five years before the publication of the fourth and last Beni Hasan volume. Clearly, Carter was using both his supervisor's nomenclature and the local Arabic name for the breed.

Florence could have seen the Beni Hasan Saluki on the 1895 family tour, but curiously, she never mentions them in her writings. Her sister Alicia, who was generally meticulous about locations in her Nile journal, does not name Beni Hasan — although it was one of the usual tourist attractions at that time. The tombs are well documented in four volumes produced by the Egyptian Exploration Fund between 1893 and 1900. Lord Amherst had been a

---

*A "nome" was a district or province governed by a nobleman.
†The Beni Hasan prick-eared hound seemed to be a magnet for all manner of canine evolutionary theories. A decade after Carter's publication, an amateur dog scholar proposed that that hound was the progenitor of the Great Dane despite substantial differences in body type and lack of evidence that the Egyptians ever cropped their dogs' ears. Another self-proclaimed dog expert wrote that the Beni-Hasan prick-eared hound was evidence that the lack of erect ears in modern greyhounds was due to the atrophy of ear muscles over the centuries (Lillian C. Smythe, "The Greyhound of Antiquity," The Kennel, *May 1911*).

member of the Fund's committee in 1893 and had his own copies of the Beni Hasan volumes at Didlington. While Florence would have seen them in her father's library, the illustrations of domestic dogs, felines, fowl, and flora were not described or reproduced in detail until the last volume was published in 1900, five years after she acquired Luman and Ayesha as puppies from Wilfred Jennings-Bramly. It is possible that the Amhersts did not visit that site in 1895 but the explanation for the absence of the Beni Hasan Saluki in Florence's research may lie in the poor condition of the tomb painting and the lack of a good published illustration of the lop-eared hound.* In any case, Florence would find a better example to prove the breed's venerable lineage with Carter's help.

Ideally suited for his job, Carter had already made a name for himself by the time Florence had begun researching the ancient breed in the late 1890s. He resigned his position with the Egypt Exploration Fund in December 1899 to assume the prestigious post of Inspector of the Upper Nile area for the *Service des Antiquitiés de l'Egypte*. Carter made Luxor his base and would personally oversee the excavations and safekeeping of tombs, temples, and monuments. He loved his work and held that post until 1904 when he was transferred to serve as Inspector of the Lower Nile. Unfortunately he was fired one year later for his ill-advised handling of an incident involving drunken French tourists at Saqqara and his subsequent refusal to apologize. Apparently it was the end of a promising career for the country artist from Swaffham. Carter was reduced to eking out a living in Cairo selling watercolors and hiring himself out to wealthy tourists as a guide. His luck would not return until 1907 when he was hired to work on Lord Carnarvon's private excavations in Thebes.

Sometime after Carter's fall from grace in 1905 and before 1907, Florence commissioned a painting by him for her growing collection of historical material on Salukis. From Cairo, he had been in regular contact with the Amhersts and had wanted to help with the promotion of Lady Amherst's book, *A Sketch of Egyptian History*.[8] He was happy to have the income. Even when he was employed as inspector, Carter supplemented his income by selling his watercolors of Cairo bazaars, temple ruins, and desert scenes to tourists. His copies of tomb art typically sold for the healthy price of £15 each.[†] The Amhersts owned a number of his paintings and always found a way to help him when he was strapped for cash. In this time of hardship, Carter was both relieved to have the extra income and delighted to accommodate his patron's daughter.

By virtue of his former office and familiarity with the Salukis of Didlington Hall, Carter was in a unique position to oblige Florence. He knew of several sites that had representations of the narrow-waisted hounds — the Beni Hasan tomb and four more at Thebes: Queen Hatshepsut's temple at Deir el Bahari and the tombs of Ken-Amun, Rekhmire, and Nebamun. Salukis were frequently depicted in tomb paintings as smooth-coated or sparsely feathered, although the skill of the copyist, representational style, and importance of the tomb owner affected the amount of detail and fidelity of the paintings. The 15th-century-BCE tombs of Thebes can have great individual detail, while the Salukis, Pharaoh hounds, and domestic dogs depicted in Beni Hasan (2800–2500 BCE) are simpler line drawings filled in with color.[§]

---

*The Beni Hasan prick-eared hound from Newberry's book was reproduced in Lillian C. Smythe, "The Greyhound of Antiquity," The Kennel, May 1911, 59.

†In 2006 pounds, this is equivalent to income of £1,090.64. "Purchasing Power of British Pounds from 1264 to 2006." Measuring Worth.com, http://www.measuringworth.com/calculators/ppowerukl; accessed September 27, 2007.

§Interestingly, several of the "smooth" hounds in the hunting murals in Beni Hasan are shown with the same representation of tail feathering as used on foxes and jackals.

Carter himself had copied the paintings of Beni Hasan, Deir el Bahari, and Nebamun, and in his capacity as inspector, knew all the tombs from regular visits and examinations. Carter had to decide which tomb painting provided the best representation of Salukis for Florence.

Kenamun, the chief steward and cattle overseer to Pharaoh Amenhotep II, clearly had a favorite hound as it is variously portrayed hunting ibex, in the presentation of New Year's gifts, and attentively recumbent alongside his master's chair. While the hound has a slightly heavier muzzle than in later depictions, Kenamun's hound is consistent with other representations of Salukis from this period, with pendulous, smooth ears, greyhound body, and tail with feathering and thick plume at the end. Sadly, Kenamun's enemies later defaced the tomb and erased not only the noble's features, but in most cases that of his Saluki as well — denying both of them entrance to the afterlife. There was not enough remaining of any of the portraits to copy for Florence.

While employed by the EEF and under the eminent Egyptologist Edouard Naville's supervision, Carter had begun copying the temple reliefs and paintings at Deir el Bahari in Thebes in 1893. There were "white dogs with long hanging ears" captured by Queen Hatshepsut's naval expedition to the land of Punt* and taken as spoils of war to Egypt.[9] The partially intact paintings showed hounds that were rather heavy in body, resembling foxhounds more than Salukis and, as such, unsuitable for his patron's needs. The Beni Hasan lop-eared hound, while complete, was lacking in detail and badly deteriorated from the efforts of copyists who had soaked the walls in oil in unsuccessful attempts to restore the original colors.

At the Theban tomb of Nebamun, an Eighteenth Dynasty official, there was an interesting portrait of a feathered, white-and-red parti-color Saluki sitting beneath the chairs of her owners as they make grain offerings to the god Amun.† Called "La Chienne Favorite" (the favorite bitch) by French Egyptologists, she was tan and white with swollen teats, and wore a rich, wide collar.[10] Unfortunately the hound's pose was ungraceful and the head area had been badly damaged.

All of these paintings had a flaw of one kind or another and consequently would be unsuitable for Florence to illustrate the likeness between her Salukis and their Egyptian ancestors. Perhaps based on Newberry's recommendation or from Carter's own British Museum experience with the documentation of a particular tomb, Carter felt that the best painting of Salukis was in the tomb of Rekhmire — one of the tombs that Florence had visited in 1895.§

Newberry had worked on the 15th-century-BCE tomb of Rekhmire, Grand Vizier to Tuthmosis III, in 1895, and partially published his findings in 1900. The wall paintings had suffered from generations of bats and more recently the residence of an Arab family and their cattle. Rekhmire's tomb was a treasure trove of information about the ancient culture. Among the depictions of daily life, temple building, tax gathering, and foreign ambassadors from Nubia, Punt, Minos, and Syria, were men with a pack of Salukis and other tribute animals. Newberry translated the inscriptions and learned that the exotic animals were gifts from Nubia. The tribute Salukis were not the only ones in the vizier's tomb, for he was an avid

*Egyptologists suggest that Punt was most likely modern-day Eritrea or Southern Arabia.
†Tomb robbers had used Nebamun's tomb as a point of access to break into the subterranean chambers of Sebekemsauef's pyramid. A description of the latter's mummies and their funereal goods appeared in the famous Amherst Papyri kept at Didlington.
§Prior to Newberry's documentation of the tomb in 1900 there were few books that reproduced the Rekhmire paintings, but, coincidentally, Wilfred Jennings-Bramly's wife's maternal great-grandfather, Joseph Bonomi the Younger, had copied the tomb's paintings during the Robert Hay expedition of 1832. Carter had spent the summer of 1891 studying and copying the Hay manuscripts and Bonomi's illustrations at the British Museum.

hunter and there were murals of his Salukis hunting hare, gazelle, wild cattle, jackal, and even ostrich.

The animals from Nubia were quite intriguing to Egyptologists. Like Punt, there was little information on exactly what constituted the country of Nubia to the ancient Egyptians, but it was considered most likely to be the Sudan. Norman De Garis Davies wrote in 1944, "The group of hunting dogs is excellently rendered."[11] Percy Newberry had remarked that a master artist rendered the individual characteristics of the hounds with exquisite detail and care. The artistic skill behind the tribute animals contrasted greatly to the usual technique of tomb paintings, done by relays of painters who worked from templates. This was indeed a much finer representation of Salukis than the others Carter had seen.

The seven Rekhmire hounds are male and female, and one has the full teats of a nursing bitch. They have a thick brush on their tails and two are lightly feathered on the ears. The hounds are white, cream, and deep golden (the colors that Florence considered correct in her own hounds) and wear wide, decorated collars. Their attendants drive cattle, a giraffe, and a leopard. One man carries a monkey on his shoulder while a second monkey clings to the neck of the giraffe. Regrettably Newberry was never able to publish the other volumes of the tomb's documentation, which would have had illustrations of the Salukis and the rest of the tribute menagerie.

The standard technique of copying tomb paintings at the time involved making tracings on large sheets of thin paper, and then painting in the colors after the paper had been removed from the wall. Carter soon departed from this stilted method and his gifted eye and hand enabled him to make excellent freehand reproductions, which were not only precise, but captured the feel and spirit of the original. Francis Llewellyn Griffith, the Superintendent of the Archaeological Survey of Egypt, had no patience with artists who injected personal style or interpretation into their reproductions of tomb paintings and was quite happy with Carter's work. In the introduction to the third Beni Hasan volume, he pronounced the young man a "faithful copyist"—high praise indeed in those circles.

Carter copied tomb paintings in very much the same manner that they were made thousands of years before, with flickering candlelight or lantern, illuminating only a small section

Florence Amherst's copy of the Rekhmire tribute Salukis painted by Howard Carter. Edward C. Ash, *Dogs: Their History and Development* (1927).

of the painting at a time. For Florence, he reproduced only the left three-quarters of the scene, which included three of the hounds and a portion of the fourth — the right edge of the painting cutting off its head. For the sake of composition, the "faithful copyist" exercised some artistic latitude by omitting the fifth hound's seemingly disembodied head (which was within the borders of his copy) as well as the sixth and seventh hounds entirely.

Nonetheless, the painting was a great prize for Florence and she considered it to be definitive proof of the noble breed's antiquity and heritage. Carter's gift was nearly always mentioned whenever she wrote about Salukis and it must have greatly pleased her that the painting came from a tomb she had visited. Howard Carter would later come to play a key role in both the Amherst family fortunes and the history of the Saluki. In a way that neither of them could possibly have foreseen, his serendipitous discovery in 1922 would precipitate the long-awaited, formal recognition of the Saluki breed in England by the Kennel Club.

6

Foreign Dogs: Any Other Variety

"The wolfhound, Borzois, Scotch Deerhound, Persian or Arab greyhounds, are all evolved by careful selection from an original type which climate and conditions of life and sport have adapted to their surroundings."

Country Life, June 16, 1900[1]

While Florence was the preeminent advocate of the breed in England, she was not the first person to have shown Salukis in the ring. Kennel Club records indicate that Mr. H. Allen was exhibiting his two-year-old, fawn bitch Tierma in 1878. She stood only 22 or 23 inches at the shoulder, but was renowned for her elegance and beauty. She was a consistent prize winner whenever she was exhibited, but produced no offspring to carry on her line.[2]

During Florence's early years of interest in the breed there were three other identified Saluki fanciers in England. In the "Kennel Notes" column of *Country Life*, July 16, 1898, an illustrated section was devoted to a Persian Greyhound named Shah. The hound was the former property of a Persian prince who had traded him to one Colonel Mackenzie for the Englishman's Arab pony. The columnist recalled an earlier incident where a dog in the variety classes resembling Shah puzzled the judges, one of whom declared that no such dog had ever been in England before (much like Dalziel's assertion about Zillah). An older show catalog was produced with a description of a similar dog, a "Persian Greyhound, not unlike a broad-skulled Borzoi," and the dispute was settled.[3] Shah's head study was considered to be a fine visualization of that description. Indeed, to the modern eye, it is a typical Saluki head, although the shoulders appear to have more hair than usual, but certainly less than the Afghans of the period. Shah's gentle disposition, playfulness, and faraway look were particularly remarked upon — as was his slight tendency toward melancholia.

The second fancier was Captain J. P. T. Allen whose brace of white Persian Greyhounds, Persian Lightening [*sic*] and Persian Arrow, were imported around 1897 by a Mr. H. C. Brooke.* A photograph and description of the bitch Persian Arrow, as well as a few brief notes regarding Indian, Arabian, Persian, and Afghan hounds, appeared in *The Twentieth Century Dog,* by Herbert Compton, in 1904. The author declared that while the Oriental hounds were fine hunters, they had "very unreliable tempers, and are snappy and quarrelsome, and sometimes very treacherous and savage."[4] Obviously, Florence held the opposite opinion of her Salukis' temperaments and definitely considered Allen's hounds a distinctly different variety. She called them "Kirghiz Greyhounds" or "*Ak-tazeet,*" to indicate their origins, which she

---

*Brooke later introduced the Australian dingo to England.

ascribed to "Turkestan and Southern Siberia," a huge geographic region now consisting of Turkmenistan, Tajikistan, Uzbekistan, Kyrgyzstan, and Kazakhstan.

Captain Allen's wife exhibited Persian Lightening and his two-year-old offspring, Sharki and Gaffeer, in the "Foreign Dogs: Any Other Variety — Open Dogs and Bitches" class at Cruft's in 1906. Persian Lightening's age and pedigree were unknown, but that was common enough then for hounds imported from the desert. Lightening placed second and his offspring were rated as "Very Highly Commended"* (as were five other dogs in the class of nine). First and reserve went to Eskimo or Samoyed dogs and third place went to Afghan Bob. Mrs. Allen valued her hounds at £15 each, but does not seem to have bred any other litters. Two years later, she was back at Cruft's with Persian Lightening and Sharki, now valued at £12 12s and £15 15s respectively, and another import called Habibi, valued at £12 12s, whose age, breeder, and pedigree were also unknown. Florence thought much more highly of her hounds' worth, for by 1912 she had sold one of her adults for £50[†] and her puppies routinely went for twelve to twenty guineas each.[§]

Photographs of Persian Lightening and his two offspring show them to be good specimens that would be accepted in any Saluki show ring today. Florence, however, did not consider Capt. Allen's hounds to be true Salukis. His were decidedly larger than her hounds and came from beyond Egypt and Arabia and therefore were not suitable for her breeding program. She continued to call them "Kirghiz" rather than Persian Greyhounds. To Florence, adulteration of what she considered to be the pure strain was unthinkable. On this point she was adamant.

Florence's hounds were affectionate and had manners, but the Rev. H. W. Bush (along with Herbert Compton, another author who had spent years in the Middle East), felt that Saluki temperaments were unreliable and stated unequivocally that all eastern greyhounds were untrustworthy and had an aversion to white people.[5] William Youatt was the first to set this myth in print in 1886: "The Persian Greyhound, carried to Hindoostan, is not always to be depended upon, but, it is said, apt to console itself by hunting its own master, or any one else, when the game proves too fleet or escapes into the cover."[6]

While Bush did not precisely agree with Youatt's rumor regarding the traitorous nature of a frustrated Saluki, he did advocate that the only way for westerners to make them biddable, was to take them as puppies from the natives or acquire hounds bred by Europeans. He conceded that Salukis were excellent hunters and were better able to handle rougher ground than English Greyhounds.

Bush also believed that the strains should be kept pure, and in 1911 would advise against a scheme to cross English Greyhounds with Afghans in order to improve the former's feet, and increase their stamina and determination.[7] Bush had seen Rampur hounds in India crossed with greyhounds in an attempt to toughen the feet of the latter and add sufficient power to bring down a jackal. Even after several generations, these crosses were slow, ungraceful, and wholly unsatisfactory. Convinced that Afghans were too slow, Bush felt that if one *were* to mix the breeds, then the prepotent "smooth Persians" would be the ideal cross for greyhounds,

---

*Rankings given to dogs of merit after the usual first through fourth placements.

[†]*The equivalent of £3,491.39 in 2006. "Purchasing Power of British Pounds from 1264 to 2006." Measuring Worth.com, http://www.measuringworth.com/calculators/ppoweruk/; accessed September 27, 2007.*

[§]*The guinea (whose value was 21 shillings or one pound and one shilling) was replaced in 1816 by the sovereign (worth one pound) but continued to be an aristocratic monetary unit for transactions involving auctions, land, art, and horses until England converted to the decimal system in 1971.*

but that the offspring would have to be closely watched for signs of heaviness, lack of turning power, and reaching ability. Despite Bush's opinion of the Afghan's speed, a Mr. Dunn
of Alnmouth tried to improve greyhounds by breeding them with Afghans — and, surprisingly, the National Coursing Club allowed the offspring to be entered in the Greyhound Stud
Book.[8] Despite numerous offers of stud fees during a period of financial hardship, Florence
steadfastly refused to allow her males to be crossbred with greyhounds.*

But if Florence and Bush were adamant about crossbreeding Salukis, there was at least
one Bedu who had no objections to interbreeding his Salukis with greyhounds. After their
travels in Arabia, the Blunts had bought a house and compound called Sheykh Obeyd, a few
miles outside Cairo. They spent their time raising horses and a few English Greyhounds at
both Sheykh Obeyd and at Crabbet Park. In 1887, Wilfrid and Lady Anne Blunt gave their
greyhound bitch Manjustine to Prince Kamal Ahmed†, who later bred her to one of his Salukis.
Some sixteen years later, in 1903, the Blunts ran across a hunting party northeast of Cairo,
near the battlefield of Tel-El-Kebir (Tall al–Kabir)§ and met Abdallah Ibn Majelli of the Han-
nadi tribe, who was hunting with several hounds descended from that greyhound–Saluki litter. Ahmed had given the puppies to his kinsmen and friends — Arabs who had no objection
whatsoever to the outcross. Blunt remarked, "In spite of many crosses with Arab greyhounds
the English type is well preserved, though the dogs are smaller and lighter. Their master told
us they were quite acclimatized, retaining something of their English speed."[9] Wilfrid watched
the hawks and hounds course a hare over a plain scattered with brush, finally catching it after
what he estimated was at least forty evasive turns of direction.

The Blunts both left accounts of this meeting in their respective journals, but Wilfrid
edited his entries for publication years later, frequently adding a political spin or historical
revision. Lady Anne's entries are rather warmer and more personal and, as she was the real
dog lover of the two, her information about the hounds is a bit more reliable. Her description reads as follows:

> On first speaking, by H.F.** to the two nearest us, they seemed very suspicious of us but
> afterwards their chief was most amiable, he proved to be Mohammed Ibn Majello, owner
> of large lands near Karaim†† and a connection of Saoud el Tihawi [sic] between who and
> Majello there is a certain jealousy. 15 years ago we spent a night camped by Majello's place,
> the father of the man now met out hunting. He remembered that we had paid a visit there.
> He told us that all the beautiful greyhounds, 15 fawn and one much lighter, nearly white,
> of his pack were descended from the greyhound (Manjustine) we gave to Kamal Ahmad
> Pasha in 1887, through her son Jerboa. It is curious how marked the type was for they were
> all extremely like Manjustine and we had just seen them coursing a hare and turning in the
> most surprising way. Poor hare it had no chance. Majello's favourite hawk had killed a bus-
> tard just before we met them.[10]

It is interesting to contemplate the addition of English greyhound blood to the supposedly pure Saluki breed, but even more so to note certain coincidences. Lady Anne names two

---

*Saluki breeder Miss Helena I.H. Barr would later write that rumors of the day whispered that greyhounds had
been bred to Bulldogs and Bull Terriers in yet another unsuccessful attempt to improve stamina.
†Kamal Ahmad Pasha was Khedive Tawfiq's cousin.
§In 1882, after a night march, General Sir Garnet Wolseley's forces attacked the entrenched Egyptian Army at
Tel-el-Kebir (between Cairo and Ismailiya) and defeated them, ending Arabi Pasha's rebellion against the Dual
Control of Britain and France.
**H.F. ("Head of the Family") was Lady Anne's nickname for Wilfrid.
††This location is uncertain.

prominent men connected with these greyhound–Saluki crosses — Mohammed (called Abdul-lah in Wilfrid's journal), the father of Ibn Majello,* and Saoud el Tahawi. Both Blunts note that these men were from Abu Hammad, not far from the El Salhiya area. Florence Amherst's founding pair had come from brother sheikhs "Saud and Magelli" of the Tahawis of El Sal-hiya (Al Salhiyah). The Blunts' gift predates the birth of Luman and Ayesha by eight years and so it is perfectly possible for a fraction of English Greyhound blood to have been hiding in the lines of Florence's first imports.

With limited breeding stock in England, Florence was lucky to find the third Saluki fancier, for her imported Saluki was compatible with Florence's line. Around 1900, Miss Lucy Bethel had imported a bitch named Reish from the Wadi Sirhan region of Syria[†] to her home in the village of Newton Kyme, near York city. Florence and Lucy became friends and with well over a hundred miles between north Yorkshire and southern Norfolk, it seems likely that they must have met at one of the large dog shows in London or the Midlands. Without suit-able breeding stock in England, Florence had been inbreeding down from her original pair, Luman and Ayesha. Keenly aware of the need for fresh blood in her lines, she and Lucy agreed to breed Reish to Luman sometime between 1901 and 1903. As was customary in canine hus-bandry, when Reish came in season, Lucy took her by train to Didlington and left her with Florence for a couple of weeks until the mating was accomplished. Reish went back home afterward for her two months of gestation. Of the litter, a male called Reishan came to live at Didlington and was later bred to Sama in 1905.[§]

Florence also sent back to the desert to obtain an outcross to replenish the gene pool at Didlington. Friends in Alexandria — possibly Jennings-Bramly and his wife, Phyllis, acquired a bitch from the Beni Hasan tribe of the Western Desert and shipped her to Didlington. She was golden with white legs of unequal coloring. Florence named her Valda and in Septem-ber of 1905 the new brood bitch and Luman produced the second litter that year. Five male puppies were registered. There was a second litter sired by Luman that same year, this time with Zarifa — a dark golden bitch who suddenly appears in the Kennel Club records as the dam of one of the three 1905 litters. None of Zarifa's offspring seem to have been bred. Flo-rence would later import a pair from southern Syria and a male from Bethlehem, but these do not seem to have ever been registered. Lucy Bethel seems to have drifted out of Saluki breeding as there are no further references to her in Florence's notes.

Florence's appetite for information about Salukis was insatiable. Having scoured libraries and museums, her interest fueled by Jennings-Bramly's stories, she realized that she needed firsthand accounts of how the hounds were used by the Bedouin and describing their place in Arab culture. Her family's connections to Egyptologists and diplomats provided her with an entrée to people working in the Middle East who might be able to provide information. Florence began corresponding in 1905 with Major Percy Z. Cox (later Sir), Resident in the Persian Gulf and His Majesty's Consul-General for the Persian Province of Fars, Luristan, Khuzistan, the Persian coast and Gulf Islands from 1904 to 1913. Having soldiered in India and Africa, as a diplomat Cox was well suited to keeping British order in Mesopotamia. He was

*Ibn meaning "son of."
[†]Now along the border area between Jordan and Saudi Arabia.
[§]Sama was from her first litter in 1897.

a gifted administrator and would later play a key role in creating the modern Middle East after World War I. Looking more like a vicar than a soldier, the bespectacled Cox was a lean man with a long, thin face, high forehead, and neatly parted gray hair. Cox maintained an office in Bushehr on the eastern side of the Gulf but the majority of his work involved the Arabian coast and hinterlands. He kept a spouse-startling assortment of creatures in his homes, including an ill-tempered bear. Belle Cox was tolerant of much, but finally drew the line at keeping bats in the icebox to feed the eagle.[11]

Cox was a keen falconer both in Persia and in England.* He rode to hounds, and while he did not own Salukis, he was certainly familiar with them. One day, the weekly post bag brought a letter from Sir Edward Grey (later Lord Grey of Fallodon) who requested that he assist the Honorable Florence Amherst in her search for particulars about the breed. Her letter with several detailed questions about Salukis followed later. Cox wrote back that he had instructed his officers on the Arab coast and in Persia to collect information from their respective districts and to write directly to her. It is likely that one of these officers was Captain William Henry Irvine Shakespear, an extraordinary explorer, linguist, automobile enthusiast, and political agent who would later have Salukis of his own.† In addition to two reports from Cox's staff, Florence received a letter with a few snapshots of Salukis in Oman.§[12]

Now that the number of Salukis at Didlington was increasing, Florence started exhibiting at dog shows. Since the 1880s, breeding and showing dogs in England had become a fashionable hobby for well-to-do women. It could even provide a nice supplement to their income if their breed was in current vogue. While Florence does not seem to have shown her dogs before 1905, there is an intriguing reference to Salukis in a report on the Ranelagh Hound Show of 1900, held on the grounds of the Royal Hospital at Chelsea. Even if they were not being shown with the Borzoi, Bassets, Greyhounds, Beagles, Bloodhounds, and the newly popular Irish Wolfhounds,** Salukis were well known to the author of the article. He lists "Persian or Arab Greyhounds" along with the larger sight hounds in a statement about functionality and breed.†† The fact that Salukis are not listed in the prizes of Ranelagh but are mentioned along with the other breeds there, suggests that the hounds of Colonel Mackenzie, Captain Allen, Lucy Bethel, or Florence Amherst had been making appearances at the larger shows.

Florence seems to have avoided the local Norfolk shows and concentrated on prestigious events that were big enough to include the "Any Other Variety" section of the Foreign Dogs class. This permitted unusual and newly introduced breeds to be exhibited and it was only in that class that Salukis could be shown. She began showing at the Ladies Kennel Association (LKA) and Kennel Club shows in 1905 or 1906. The Kennel Club did not permit women

---

*In 1930 he became a member of the Saluki or Gazelle Hound Club.

†Shakespear became convinced that the sultan of the Najd, Abdul Aziz, would be the best ruler of an independent Arabian state, and worked ceaselessly to achieve that end, although he did not live to see it. He died in a Bedouin battle in 1915. For a fascinating account of his life, see H. V. F. Winstone, Captain Shakespear: A Portrait, London: J. Cape, 1976.

§These intriguing photographs have yet to come to light.

**The nearly extinct Irish Wolfhound breed had been carefully reconstructed in the mid-nineteenth century by Captain George Augustus Graham.

††A quote from him opens this chapter.

as members and so the Ladies Kennel Association had been formed in 1903, boasting Her Majesty, Queen Alexandra, as its patron. Two committee members, Mrs. Carlo F. Clarke and Miss Gertrude A. Desborough, would eventually take up the Saluki breed. Florence would become fast friends with the latter, who held the post of club secretary and was acknowledged as an expert in managing all the details of putting on a dog show. Florence's Salukis competed in the LKA shows against other canine novelties such as Elkhounds, Samoyedes [*sic*], Lhasa Terriers, Afghan hounds, Nyam-Nyam dogs (from the Congolese border of Sudan), German Sheepdogs, and Chow Chows.* Even dogs from the polar expeditions had made regular appearances in that class — the most notable being Farthest North, the sole surviving Eskimo dog of the Peary expedition and valued at the huge sum of £1,000.†

Traveling with good-sized dogs was quite a different experience for the Edwardians — it would be decades before the motorcar became commonplace at dog shows.§ Prior to the Great War, the motorcar was almost exclusively a toy for the rich and even by 1922, only one person out of 136 owned a private automobile.[13] Dogs were commonly taken to shows by foot, horse-drawn carriages, trains, and, in London, the underground or taxi. Traveling any distance to a show was a substantial ordeal for the dog. Prior to 1887, dogs traveled on trains in confined boxes or "boots" attached to the underside of the carriages. One can easily imagine the poor dog arriving at the show with nerves frayed by noise and coat dirty from dust and soot — hardly the best of condition in which to be handled by a judge.

The alternative was to confine the dog to a wicker hamper or specially made box and consign the dog to the baggage van — with the potential of rough handling or even suffocation below a mound of parcels and luggage. Of course, the affluent could commission their own carriage where owners and dogs could ride in comparative comfort together. In 1887, the line superintendent of the London and North-Western Railway, Mr. George P. Neele, saw the problem facing the average exhibitor and built six special dog carriages with interior kennels. Neele and his carriage superintendent, Mr. C. A. Park, had consulted with Charles Cruft, the great dog-show entrepreneur, and the result was an innovative carriage that included secure kennels arranged in top and bottom rows, zinc floors, water troughs, a galvanized drainage gutter, airy ventilation, and two seats for attendants. The trial idea caught on quickly and trains coming into London from the counties would have one or more of these carriages, depending on the bookings. These carriages were still being advertised in the Crufts Dog Show catalog eleven years after their introduction.[14]

For the Crystal Palace, Holland Park, and Crufts shows, Florence would take her luggage and Salukis by carriage or motorcar from Didlington to Brandon station and load them onto a train. In 1904, the forward-thinking Lord Amherst purchased a dark-blue touring motorcar. Like most technological innovations, internal combustion engines were still new enough that they were referred to by explanatory combinations of familiar terms — "horseless carriages" or "light locomotives on highways."** Presumably Florence's doting father would

Chow Chows were popular for more macabre reasons as well. In the American fashion and society magazine Dress and Vanity Fair, the December 1913 issue had an ad for floor and car rugs made out of Chinese Chow Dog skins (p. 4).

†*Farthest North participated in Peary's expedition to Greenland in 1892–95. He was shown in the Foreign Dogs class at Crufts in 1899 and 1900 and was about 12 years old when he died in 1902. His body is now preserved at the Natural History Museum at Tring. His last owner, Miss Ella Casella, was also a committee member of the LKA.*

§*Even by the mid–1930s, there were only a few members of the Saluki club who drove motorcars to dog shows.*

**A practice which continues in use today — "wireless cable," "electronic book," etc.*

have allowed his coachman to drive her and the hounds to the station.* Arriving in London, she could hire a "growler"—a large, enclosed cab, so-called because of the noise it made on macadam roads—to drive to their townhouse at Grosvenor Square. The train journey was direct and took less than three hours, but a full day had to be allotted in order to manage logistics on either end. Florence would arrive at least a day ahead of the show and take advantage of the opportunity to socialize, shop, or visit a museum or library.

The Amhersts had moved out of their town houses at number 88 Brook Street and Portman Square by 1888, and now occupied the more fashionable address of 8 Grosvenor Square on the corner of Brook and Duke Streets in Mayfair. The exclusive residential area was made up of solid blocks of town houses rising several stories above the street, with kitchens and pantries below ground level. Gardens were a precious commodity in the city, but the park in Grosvenor Square was enclosed by iron railings and afforded Florence ample opportunity to exercise her hounds and show them off to admiring Londoners.

Now that Florence was making regular appearances at the larger shows, she began to cast about for other ways of promoting the breed and couldn't help but notice that certain breeds, such as the Borzoi and Scottish Deerhound, were popular because they were owned by nobility—or even the army. The Irish Wolfhound gained respectability in 1900, when it became the official mascot of the newly formed Irish Guards.[†] Prince Edward's wife, Alexandra, had adopted Borzois in the 1880s and the breed enjoyed a sustained popularity. When she became queen in 1901, they were all the more in vogue.[§] The Borzoi Club had been in existence for many years and held its own shows as well as providing large entries at the all breed shows. The Queen and two duchesses showed their own Borzoi and were regularly mentioned in the newspapers. None of this escaped Florence's notice and in 1906 a unique opportunity for royal patronage of Salukis presented itself.

Alfonso XIII, King of Spain, had chosen to marry the beautiful Princess Victoria Eugenie of Battenburg, the daughter of Queen Victoria's youngest child, Beatrice. Florence's brother-in-law, Lord William Cecil, C.V.O., F.R.G.S.,** had been Groom in Waiting to Queen Victoria and Comptroller to the widowed Princess Beatrice. With these close ties, it was natural that his wife be appointed Lady in Waiting to the young princess on the occasion of her marriage. So Florence's eldest sister, Mary Cecil, would travel to Spain in Ena's entourage for the ceremony.

Princess Beatrice and Princess Victoria Eugenie (known fondly as Ena) had been frequent visitors at Didlington and under-gardener James Trimbee remembered one occasion when the estate's prize hothouse strawberries (inadvertently fertilized with imported London sewage) were served to the royal pair.[15] The guests complained of the taste and Trimbee was reprimanded, but fortunately the incident did not deter the princesses from their enjoyment of Didlington hospitality.

Needless to say, Florence was thrilled that Mary had the important honor of being Lady in Waiting to Ena. Mindful of this royal connection, she wished to mark the happy occasion

---

*It is possible that they drove all the way into London, but with irregularly paved, winding country roads, and the uncertain availability of petrol, it seems highly unlikely.

†In April 1900, Queen Victoria created the Irish Guards to honor the service of the Irish regiments who were fighting in the Boer War.

§Even the non-doggy Wilfred Jennings-Bramly had given his wife, Phyllis, a Borzoi named Cadi when they were married in 1902.

**C.V.O.—Commander of the Victorian Order (a personal award from the queen), F.R.G.S.—Fellow of the Royal Geographical Society.

with something other than the silver plate and jewelry that were usually given as wedding presents by the upper classes at that time. Florence saw that the gift of a rare Saluki could draw popular attention to the breed and in turn lead to formal recognition by the Kennel Club. After all, the popularity of Borzoi was enormous, not only due to Queen Alexandra's famous kennels at Sandringham (she and the King kept several other breeds as well), but those of the Duchess of Cleveland and the Duchess of Newcastle, where the latter had an astonishing fifty-four Borzoi in her kennels.

Florence chose from her kennel a striking white male with elegant feathering named Saädan, and arranged for him to be shipped to Spain — probably in Mary's care.* Florence would later take pains to see that the reporter for *Country Life Illustrated* noted her gift to the royal couple and included a photo of Saädan in an article about her hounds later that year.

Following Alfonso and Ena's wedding ceremony in Madrid on May 31, 1906, an anarchist's bomb exploded during the procession back to the palace. The screaming horses dragged the damaged carriage some yards through the dense smoke before Ena was thrown to the ground. One horse was killed and the others were wounded. Poor Ena was covered with horse blood and stunned, but otherwise uninjured. Alphonso quickly took charge and directed that they be transferred to another carriage and taken calmly to the palace.[16] It was a shock that Ena never quite recovered from and foreshadowed what was to be an unhappy marriage. Saädan's fate in Spain is not recorded.† Salukis would not catch the public's eye until seventeen years later.

*Sir Terence Clark notes that the spelling "Saädan" with an umlaut is highly perplexing. This may have been a printer's error or more likely, Florence's attempt to correctly transliterate an Arabic name. Sa'adan would be more usual.

†Curiously, Queen Ena seems to have acquired another Saluki later on. A. Goodrich-Freer, in her book Arabs in Tent & Town (p. 235), notes that she gave her Saluki to King Edward who in turn gave it to his niece when she was Queen of Spain. The Saluki gift would have occurred between her wedding in 1906 and Edward VII's death in 1910.

7

The Crash

"Didlington is in brown paper parcels and Lady Amherst is saving odd bits of string."
Howard Carter[1]

Just before dawn on the morning of April 15, 1906, a massive earthquake shattered the city of San Francisco. Fires from fractured gas lines could not be fought as the water pipes were also broken. Flames swept through wooden buildings not destroyed by the earthquake and the army crudely dynamited blocks of buildings to make a fire break — often starting new fires. In the days to come, the disaster would be huge news around the world, and a telegram announcing the quake, fire, and, inaccurately, a tidal wave even made its way to Jennings-Bramly's lonely outpost on the Gulf of Aqaba (Al Aqabah).* The year 1906 would also be a disastrous year for the Amhersts, and like the people of San Francisco, their lives would be dramatically altered by a single event.

Just after the Amhersts' golden wedding anniversary in June of that year, their trusted solicitor and estate agent, Charles Cheston, committed suicide. Shocked by the news, the Amhersts shortly discovered that he had embezzled over £250,000 of their money and a further £31,000 that Lord Amherst held in trust.† Seduced by the temptation of quick profit, the London solicitor had gambled and lost the money on the stock exchange. Broke and unable to face Lord Amherst, Cheston took the coward's way out.

The Amhersts were devastated by this betrayal and reversal of fortune. "The Crash," as it came to be known, would signal the decline of the great family. Lord Amherst was honor bound to make up the trust funds and despite an income of £100,000 a year it was no easy task to meet nearly £300,000 worth of immediate obligations.[2] Money had never been an obstacle for their pursuits and pleasures or the charities and scholarly organizations that they were so fond of supporting. The sale of a few properties and economizing on their lifestyle would not be enough and loans were not possible. Reaching a painful decision (and the only one possible) Lord Amherst sadly offered his prized collection of art and incunabula at auction. Fifty years of collecting had brought together the earliest, finest, or rarest examples of fine printing, engraving, and binding, travel in Palestine, the works of Shakespeare, herbals and gardening, the English Bible and Book of Common Prayer, and the literature of the Reformation and the Church of England.

The shelves of the Amherst private library were filled with the first examples of movable-type printing, illustration, and exquisite specimens of bookbinding. Even the earliest

---

*At the time, Jennings-Bramly was adding inadvertent fuel to a growing border dispute between England and Turkey. See Appendix 2.

†The trust established by a deceased Norfolk squire may have actually been as much as £70,000. £300,000 would be the 2006 equivalent of something over £22 million (Measuring Worth.com)

books printed in Norwich were included as well as leaves of medieval European, Persian, and Arabic manuscripts. Secret fireproof safes protected rare volumes such as a Gutenberg Bible, a prayer book with the finely embroidered arms of Charles II, and the heavy, crimson, velvet-covered bible on which George III took his coronation oath. There were also treasures of national importance — but no explanation was given as to how they came to Didlington. Safeguarded in the library were the gold frames of the crowns of Charles II, George IV, and Queen Adelaide which, as a biographer in 1887 wrote, "you and everybody else innocently believed to be safe in the Tower of London."[3]

The decision to sell the books was a hard one to bear. These were friends that Amherst had begun to collect while a student at Oxford. Just a year before, in 1905, Amherst had hired Seymour de Ricci, an antiquary and expert on manuscripts, to index and catalog his library of over 1,100 rare volumes and this bibliography was privately published in November 1906. Amherst's wife and daughters had cherished the library and relied upon it to research their own books. Had she not had access to the family's library and learned to translate the cramped script of monks and clerics, Alicia could not have written the *History of Gardening in England*. Initially, Bernard Quaritch's firm (Amherst's book dealer and publisher for over forty years) were going to handle the sale of some of the incunabula and de Ricci's serviceable handlist was to serve as the catalog.

But on Quaritch's advice, the sale was postponed in anticipation of bibliophiles coming from the continent and America who would be keen on bidding. Amherst had seventeen precious volumes by William Caxton — a 15th-century man of Kent who printed the first books in English. Eleven of the Caxtons were in perfect condition and were sure to realize the highest prices of the sale. Eventually Amherst transferred the sale of his entire library to Messrs. Sotheby, Wilkinson, & Hodge who produced a bound catalog — this time with much more detail than de Ricci's work. Included were the literary, historical, and sale provenances for each of the volumes and manuscripts. Amherst hoped that the library might be kept intact and sold to a national institution or wealthy collector. Two sympathetic articles describing the significance of the collection, its highlights, and the impending sale appeared in *Country Life Illustrated* in October of that year. But giving up the books was not the only indignity to the Amhersts. The antiquities and art of Didlington — paintings, violins, armor, limoges, majolica, and even the leather walls by Vernet would have to be sold as well.

Lord Amherst did not cope well with the aftermath of the Crash. Florence, Sybil and Maggie took their parents south to Valescure for the privacy and restful atmosphere of Lou Casteou. Lord and Lady Amherst would not return to Norfolk until the following spring. Two of the married daughters, Mary Cecil and Alicia Cecil, moved into Didlington and began to arrange the sale of the library, art, and antiquities. For some reason, the Amhersts' other married daughter, Geraldine "Cherry" Drummond, did not help with the sale and a distinct coolness settled between the two families.[4]

For Florence, there was a small bright spot in the gloom of 1906. The first article about her kennel was published in *Country Life* magazine on July 14. In addition to articles on gentlemanly pursuits of hunting and fishing, managing country estates, gardens, bird watching, country houses, antiques and curios, *Country Life* carried regular features and columns on dog shows and field trials. Although no author was listed, the promising dog writer, canine expert, and judge Arthur Croxton Smith* most likely wrote the piece on Florence's Salukis. He had become quite intrigued by the exotic hounds and would be a staunch supporter of Florence for many years.

*Also known as A.C. Smith.

Smith and a professional dog photographer, Thomas Fall, made the train journey to Didlington for the article and Fall shot eleven portraits of Florence's Salukis, including Saä-dan (who was about to be sent to Queen Ena in Spain) and Luman, who at eleven years was showing his age. His face had lightened considerably, most of his ear feathering was gone and his back was beginning to sag, but his coat still had the deep golden color that Florence preferred in her hounds. In the article she referred to them as "slughis or gazelle-hounds" and declared that they were principally to be found amongst the nomadic tribes of the Eastern Desert.* Florence described some of the lore that she had read in Layard, mentioned that intriguing khedival hawking party, and told of an Amherst or Bethel Saluki who was seen "to leap a deer park wire railing" from a standstill (presumably in pursuit of a deer or hare). Florence noted that they gave good sport with rabbits and hares, while their medium size of 22 to 24 inches made them "suitable as well as ornamental house pets." They were faithful, sensitive, good with children, reserved with strangers, and resented ill use. Their proper colors were gold, pale cream, or white. Saluki anatomy was specially adapted for the desert — the feet were "pressed open in order to give a greater hold on the sand" and the feathered tail was used as a rudder, helping them to turn at speed. With three pages of glowing prose and photographs, the article was quite a triumph for Florence.[5]

The following year was also bittersweet for Florence as it saw not only the publication of her first major work on Salukis but also the death of her beloved Luman. His health had remained reasonably good and at eleven and a half years, he had kept all his teeth except one premolar. The cause of Luman's death is not recorded but his longevity is impressive for a time when vaccinations did not exist. Distemper epidemics periodically swept through England and took a toll on purebreds and mongrels alike. Many owners who had lost show dogs in the prime of life altruistically donated the bodies to the Natural History Museum in London.[6] There, the museum had a growing collection of mounted domestic animals, with purebred dogs being the larger part. Although grieving over the loss of the grand old hound, Florence was still mindful enough of posterity to realize that Luman, as the original sire of her lines, had a very special place in canine history. She donated his body to the museum's collection of domestic dogs. Florence never recorded what happened to Ayesha — Luman's mate from the Al Salihah desert.

By the time the *Country Life* article was in print Florence was considered an eminent authority on the subject of Salukis and their eastern relatives. She had already been contacted by novelist Robert Leighton to produce a chapter on Middle Eastern hounds for a book that was to be the first scholarly work on the dog breeds, their origins, mythology, husbandry and care. Before Leighton, dog books tended to rehash content and apocryphal anecdotes from previous publications. This was particularly true in the case of Salukis, where brief thirdhand accounts of hunting technique were mostly what was available. New information does not seem to have been actively sought or thought necessary by authors until Leighton's advent. Florence was the perfect person to rectify some of these omissions and she wrote an extensive chapter for the *New Book of the Dog* entitled "Oriental Greyhounds" which focused primarily on the "*Slughi Tazi* or Gazelle Hound" (as she then called them), but also the Kirghiz greyhound, the North African or Saharan *Slughi*, Sudanese greyhounds, Barukhzy or Afghan hound, the Rampur hound of Northern India, and the Poligar hounds of Southern India.

*"Eastern Desert" refers to the Egyptian territory between the Nile and the Red Sea, but Florence well knew that they were native to other areas, so she may be using the term to mean the Middle East in general.

The briefest mention was also made of greyhounds of the Tartars and those of Crimea, Caucasus, Anatolia, Kurdistan, and Circassia.

Florence's chapter in Leighton was a rich tapestry of history, folklore, and cultural anthropology. A distinctive feature of her prose, Orientalist romanticism was woven throughout all her writings about Salukis. This is hardly surprising considering her background, nor is it unusual given the Victorian and Edwardian imaginings of chivalrous Bedouin knights and sultry, half-naked harems.

From her correspondent's information, she identified the four Saluki variations by geographic locations: the *Shami** (silky feathering on ears and tail) from Syria, *Omani* and *Yamani* (sparsely feathered) from Oman and Yemen, and *Nejdi* (unfeathered or "smooth") from the Nejd (Najd) desert in central Arabia. It is here that Florence first sets out a breed standard. To accomplish this, she borrowed language from the work of others. Comparison of her 1907 Saluki standard and other Victorian sighthound standards reveals that she drew heavily from these documents and their accepted nomenclature. Phrasing remarkably similar to that of certain passages in the standards of the Irish Wolfhound (1886), Borzoi (1892), Scottish Deerhound (1901), and Whippet (1900) appear in the Saluki standard.[7] Also evident is the influence of author Stonehenge's lengthy descriptions of greyhounds set down in the 1870s and 1880s. Mindful of the Borzoi's ever-popular standing with royalty, peers, and public, she derived much from the flowery descriptions of that breed. Significantly, Florence's standard of points remained unchanged for sixteen years.

Florence now called them "The *Slughi Shami*," but there were a variety of competing opinions as to the name's etymological origin. A line from a thousand-year-old Arabic poem — "My dog brought by kings from Saluk"— suggested the long-vanished town of Saluk in southern Arabia, traditionally famous for armor and hunting hounds. Mr. H. L. Powell, an Eastern traveler, held that it originated from the Turkish name for the hounds of the Seljuk tribe, and that Seljuki had been corrupted to *Saluki, Salaak, Saluk,* or even *Salag.* Others thought it might even be derived from the Turkish towns of Seleikeh or Saleuzia. Dr. Talcott Williams, an American who had also traveled in the Middle East, came closest to the mark when he wrote that Arab tradition held that hound's name is derived from Seleucus Nicator, Alexander the Great's general who later founded the Seleucid Empire."[†]

At the time there was no standard transliteration for Arabic in English and phonetic approximations were more usual. Florence's lexicon for the breed in 1907 was as follows:

Arabic
Masculine: *Slughi* (colloquial); *Saluki* (classical)
Feminine: *Slughiya* (colloquial); *Silaga* (classical)
Plural and genus: *Salag*

Persian
Tazi (meaning "Arabian")

---

*El Sham was the Arabic name for Damascus and the feathered Salukis from that region known as "Shami."
[†]There were several towns in the Greek Empire in Syria named after Seleucus. Professor G. Rex Smith in "The Saluqi in Islam," Saluqi: Coursing Hound of the East (1995), suggests that the name "Saluki" (in Arabic, Saluqi) was most likely not an Arabic word and may well have originated from the Seleucia (Saluqiyyah) southeast of Baghdad — which was better suited for hunting than the other Seleucias. Simply, the breed may have once been known as the "Seleucid" hound.

Coincidentally, the Rev. H. W. Bush would publish a similar but shorter article the following year, 1908, in *The Kennel Encyclopædia*. Bush had lived in India and wrote with authority on "Eastern Greyhounds," going into more descriptive detail on the obscure hound breeds from Persia, Afghanistan, and India than Florence had done in Leighton's book. His information was largely based on his own experience and those of his friends.* Bush gave physical descriptions and his opinions of their temperaments but presented no archaeological or literary provenance to complement the breed folklore as had Florence.

He asserted that the pronunciations "Slughi," "Sleughi," and "Sloughi" were incorrect and was the first to suggest that the proper transliteration should be "*Saluqi*— pronounced *Salooki*, the *a* being short."[9] His stance on the correct spelling of the breed's name does not seem to have influenced Florence (nor does he seem to have been aware of her). Indeed, she had already noted that "Saluki" was the classical pronunciation a year before Bush's article, but never did adopt his suggested spelling of *Saluqi*.[†]

To illustrate the Saluki section of the chapter in Leighton, Florence selected photos of a handsome but unidentified male of her breeding, a head study of Luman at eleven and a half, the engraving of Zillah, and a photo of seven Salukis and their three keepers in the Egyptian desert. She described the usual hunting styles, their speed of 21 to 32 yards per second,[§] their pampered life among the Bedouin, and how Salukis differed from the unclean *kalb*. She included information from Charles Doughty, Lady Anne Blunt, Lord Curzon, and Sophia Lane Poole.** The learned men and archaeologists on which she drew included Sir Henry Layard, Edward Lane, James H. Breasted, D. G. Hogarth, and three unidentified Muslim scholars. Florence tantalized readers with brief glimpses of Salukis in the presence of crusaders, khans, Renaissance artists, and even Alfonso de Albuquerque, the Portuguese viceroy of India, who sailed in the Persian Gulf in 1508. She quoted from Arab *tardiyyahs* (classical hunting poems) and the translation (considered inaccurate by current scholars) of Proverbs 30:29–31 from the King James Bible, and gives the first reliable description of the Rekhmire hounds based on Howard Carter's painstaking copy.[††]

The extent of Florence's fact gathering via library and museum research, and correspondence with scholars, soldiers, diplomats, and travelers may be appreciated when one looks at the geographic range she cites in Leighton.

> The *Slughi* (*Tazi*) is to be found in Arabia (including the Hedjaz), Syria, Mesopotamia, Valleys of the Euphrates and Tigris, Kurdistan, Persia, Turkestan, Sinai Peninsula, Egypt, the Nile Valley, Abyssinia, and Northern Africa. By examining the extent and position of the deserts inhabited by the great nomadic Arab tribes connected by pilgrim ways and caravan routes, the distribution of the Gazelle Hound can easily be followed.[10]

Despite this new wealth of information on Salukis and Oriental greyhounds, the popular (but less than scholarly) Stonehenge barely added to his twenty-two-year-old paragraph on Per-

One such was Captain Prideaux of the political service, who provided Bush with photographs of smooth and feathered Salukis belonging to a sheikh in Bahrain.

[†]*Considered now to be linguistically correct.*

[§]*An impossible 42–65 miles per hour. However an average of 30–33 mph has been recorded under controlled conditions (Dan Belkin, "A Functional Saluki: Lessons from the Coursing Field," Saluki International 2, no. 4 (Spring/Summer 1994), 33.*

**Sophia Lane Poole was the wife of Reginald Stuart Poole, a well-known Egyptologist and Orientalist. Her brother, Edward Lane, was the foremost scholar of Arabic studies in Europe.*

[††]*A crude, inaccurate rendering and garbled description of the Rekhmire hounds appeared in James Watson, The Dog Book (New York: Doubleday, Page and Company, 1906).*

sian Greyhounds when he published *The Dogs of Great Britain, America, and Other Countries* in 1909.

By April 1908, the liquidation of the Amherst treasures escalated. Sotheby, Wilkinson, and Hodge had published their detailed, hardbound catalog of 1,031 rare books and manuscripts that would be sold at auction in December and the following March. Some of his books had been already been sold privately but Lord Amherst still hoped fervently that the collection might kept intact and the auctioneers advertised that an offer for the entire collection en bloc would be strongly considered.

The measure of the family's desperation may be read in Carter's sympathetic comment to Percy Newberry: "Didlington is in brown paper parcels and Lady Amherst is saving odd bits of string."[11] The financial difficulties stemming from the Crash and the resulting loss of his beloved books and antiquities broke Amherst's health. At seventy-four, he was not well. He no longer had his lush beard but sparse, white side-whiskers, and his greatly thinned hair was almost completely white. He felt the cold now more than ever. In one of the last studio photographs he sat for, Amherst was still the model of a country gentleman — with high collar, cravat, polka-dotted waistcoat, and black frock coat and holding a small, shaggy dog on his lap. On the table beside him, his woolen deerstalker hat and two leather field cases. From the waist down he was draped in a heavy lap robe to keep the chill from his legs.

The hope that Amherst's library would be purchased by a national institution was not realized, even though the Chancellor of the Exchequer offered to contribute £30,000 towards the purchase of Amherst's books by the British Museum.[12] J. Pierpont Morgan's nephew, Junius Spencer Morgan, had seen the library at Didling-

Lord Amherst in the last years of his life. Courtesy of the Norfolk Record Office. MC84/198, 527X9.

ton and felt that some of the Amherst rarities would make fine additions to his uncle's library. Like Lord Amherst, the American millionaire was an enthusiastic collector of fine art, incunabula, and rare manuscripts. The Pierpont Morgan Library was to have the finest examples of the history of the written word, from cuneiform tablets to three Gutenberg bibles.

Morgan sent Belle da Costa Greene to London in December 1908 for the express purpose of obtaining the seventeen Amherst Caxtons. The sagacious young woman was Morgan's personal librarian and collection manager. He was willing to spend up to £32,500 for the volumes, but Greene submitted a private offer of £25,000 cash two days before the public sale.[13] Lord Amherst agreed to the offer and Greene bought the Caxtons and other precious volumes from under the nose of the British Museum.* James Trimbee, former under-gardener at Didlington, recalled hearing rumors that Morgan had paid $200,000 for a "hand-written bible."† On December 3, 1908, at one o'clock in the afternoon, bidding commenced at Sotheby's on Wellington Street in the Strand, and the magnificent library that had taken fifty years to build was sold piece by piece over three days. The rapping of the auctioneer's hammer would be Lord Amherst's death knell.

A little over a month later, on Friday, January 15, 1909, Lord and Lady Amherst arrived at their leased townhouse at 23 Queen's Gate Gardens, Kensington. It was and still is a fashionable neighborhood, dotted with embassies and just a few blocks away from the Royal Geographical Society, the Natural History and Victoria and Albert Museums, and Harrods, the fabulous department store that advertised they could get "Everything for Everybody Everywhere." The Amhersts had a choice corner address just across the street from a private park. The house featured an upper-level conservatory and had the usual servants' quarters on the sixth story under the roof. The journey from Didlington had been more than usually fatiguing and Lord Amherst retired early. He came downstairs the next morning looking quite well, but collapsed during breakfast. Doctors were immediately sent for, but there was little that could be done. Fardie never regained consciousness and died that evening.

Amherst's body was to be interred at Didlington. The funeral service was arranged for Wednesday the 20th at St. Michael's on the estate. A considerable number of people made the two-hour and forty-five-minute train ride from London to the small station at Brandon, and hired nearly every coach or motorcar in the district for the six-mile journey through the woods to Didlington. Florence, Margaret, Mary, Cherry, Lord Cecil, Capt. Drummond, and Evelyn Cecil served as the principal mourners for Lady Amherst; Sybil and Alicia were too ill to attend. Over a hundred floral tributes filled the church, including an impressive arrangement from Queen Alexandra. The King, the Prince of Wales, and Princess Henry of Battenburg sent their personal representatives to the service. Howard Carter was in Egypt but his family attended the service, as did a long list of dignitaries and the Amherst, Cecil, Drummond, Daniel, and Fountaine relatives. For friends who could not get away from London, a simultaneous service was held at St. George's in Hanover Square — the church where Alicia had been married.

Amherst's body was laid to rest in the family vault alongside daughter Bee, siblings Francis and Amelie, and his mother-in-law, Mrs. Mitford. As he had no sons, it was inevitable that Amherst's title would eventually pass to his eldest daughter, Mary Cecil. By special

---

*The catalog states that fourteen Caxtons had been sold prior to the auction, but this appears to be an error.
†Amherst's Gutenberg bible was for many years in the possession of Doheny Library in California, and was recently sold by Sotheby's. In addition to the Caxtons, Morgan did buy other items from the Amherst Library but not the Gutenberg Bible.

remainder in default of male heirs, Mary became Baroness Amherst of Hackney and the title would now pass to her eldest son and his heirs. Lord Amherst's widow was now distinguished as the Dowager Baroness Amherst.

Finances continued to be tight for the Amhersts. Knowing that the Sekhmet statues would most likely have to be sold, Florence posed a young bitch, Nafissah,* in front of the best preserved one for a photograph sometime between late 1909 and early 1910. The seven diorite or "black granite" Sekhmets were originally taken from the Temple of Mut at Karnak and date from Amenhotep III (approximately 1391–1354 BCE). On average, they were seven feet tall and weighed two tons each. Lord Amherst purchased them in 1864 or 1865 from the collection of Dr. John Lee of Hartwell House, Aylesbury. At Didlington Hall, Amherst placed them outside between the large windows of his museum and it was here that Florence posed the cream-colored, feathered Nafissah in contrast against the dark lion-headed goddess. Florence always demonstrated considerable artistic flair for staging photographs of her Salukis. Nafissah had also been photographed posing on a fancy cut-velvet settee at Didlington as an "elegant drawing room pet," but the image combining the ancient Sekhmet and the lineal descendant of the Rekhmire hounds became a signature of Florence's advertisements for many years. Today, it remains one of the most interesting images of an Amherst Saluki.

A. Croxton Smith continued to support Florence in her efforts to advance the breed. In his book *Everyman's Book of the Dog* (1909), he pointedly contradicted the Rev. Bush

Nafissah posed with the best of the Amherst Sekhmet statues before the sale of Didlington Hall in 1910. *Dress and Vanity Fair.*

*Like Luman, there were variant spellings of her name that seem to have been interchangeable.

by stating that Salukis made "excellent companions, the close communication with their native masters doing much to develop their intelligence. They are very docile with a great fondness for children."[14] Smith noted that "*Slughi* or Gazelle Hound" colors were rich gold, pale cream, or white. This naturally echoed Florence's opinion and the evidence of the Rekhmire hounds that these were the correct colors for the Saluki. She did know of other colors from her own citations — most notably the dark Zillah and the wolf-colored (grizzle) hounds from her desert correspondent's photographs. These other colors were not relevant to her "*Shami*" strain although she would occasionally note that black and tan specimens were sometimes found.

As she was the only active breeder of Salukis at that time (Lucy Bethel seems to have dropped out of sight), there was no one to gainsay her but the opinionated Rev. Bush. While breed popularity was just not progressing satisfactorily, one could purchase the occasional sentimental postcard featuring a Saluki — surely a hopeful portent of things to come.* In 1910, Smith would write that the enthusiasm for Borzois was understandable in light of their "handsome appearance and graceful lines," yet he noted that Afghan hounds (which he considered similar in build and equally striking) numbered fewer than ten in the country. Smith speculated that this might have been due to the rumors that they were treacherous in the East and mimicked their master's dispositions.[15] He goes on to discuss some of the other foreign dogs in vogue and being classified by the Kennel Club — Pekingese, Chow Chows, Great Danes, Elkhounds, Samoyedes, Pyrenean mountain dogs, Lhasa Spaniels, Tibetan Terriers, Mexican Hairless, and Chihuahuas. Smith did not mention royal patronage as one of the primary reasons for the popularity of the Borzoi and despite his enthusiasm for Florence's breed, Salukis were not included in his list.

On May 6, 1910, King Edward died, and for the second time in nine years, England went into national mourning and prepared to crown a new king. Money was still in short supply for the Dowager Baroness and her three unmarried daughters and even though the treasures of Didlington continued to be sold, there was not enough to pay the debts and run the estates. Funds would again come in from America, for J. P. Morgan would purchase the Amherst collection of cuneiform tablets for his own library in 1913.[16] Some of the Egyptian artifacts went to William and Mary Cecil and the pieces that were not auctioned off were put into storage. Portions of the Hackney and Norfolk properties had been sold and about that time, Howard Carter's family was able to purchase Sporle Road House in Swaffham from the estate.[17]

Finally, the sacrifice that the Amhersts had been dreading became inevitable. On November 29, 1910, the magnificent "freehold, manorial, residential, and sporting domain of Didlington, Norfolk," with 7,105 acres, was sold at auction along with much of the remaining furnishings.[18] Florence, Sybil, Margaret, and Florence's Salukis moved into Lady Amherst's dower house, Foulden Hall — the entitlement from her husband's estate. The golden years of Didlington were forever gone.

One such example published in New York in 1910 shows a pale Saluki affectionately interrupting his mistress at her piano practice.

8

Dear Miss Amherst ...
Yours Sincerely, T. E. Lawrence

"About getting another pair of dogs ... the cream ones as good as yours, are not in every village up here!"

T. E. Lawrence[1]

Their new residence was just down the road from the grand Didlington. It was a two-story house built of red brick with six chimneys and tall windows. But for All Saints Church, it was the largest building in the little village of Foulden. The dower's amenities and mere seven acres paled in comparison to the splendid Didlington. Lady Amherst still owned lease-hold interests in several family properties, grazing rights to Foulden Common, and sporting rights to Northwold Fen. The income from these and a small but lucrative floral business kept her, Florence, Sybil, and Margaret living in modest comfort, if not the style of Didlington. Florence continued breeding her Salukis and since 1908 had generally adopted the now common practice of giving each litter names beginning with a particular letter of the alphabet. In 1911 there were three litters at Foulden, one of which was of significance to American fanciers. Florence mated the photogenic Nafissah to Lucy Bethel's Sindbad to produce the "S" puppies.* Shadig was one of these and was shipped to Mrs. T. D. Murphy in San Francisco.[2] Nothing more is known of Shadig but he has the distinction of being the second documented Saluki in America.†

In 1912, the year of the *Titanic* disaster, the British Museum published the second edition of *A Guide to the Domesticated Animals (Other Than Horses)* and a photograph of the stuffed Luman was featured along with a descriptive paragraph. Florence contributed her standard breed lore and a brief history of Luman to the booklet which interchangeably used the terms "Slughi or Gazelle Hound," "Syrian or Persian Greyhound," and "Slughi or Arabian Lop-Eared Hound."[3] Describing Luman, Florence wrote, "In its prime it had bright golden-yellow hair, passing into deep cream-color on the face, limbs and underneath parts, and the middle of the tail. At the time of its death, the face had, however, turned white, and the ears had lost much of their fringe of long hair."[4]

Since 1909, Florence had been calling the breed "*Slughi* or Gazelle Hound." An article written by Florence for *Every Woman's Encyclopedia* between 1910 and 1912 is entitled simply "Salukis" and in it she uses "Saluki" and "Slughi" interchangeably.[5] She notes that "Slughi"

Sindbad had been purchased from Florence Amherst.
†*Hope and David Waters note in* The Saluki in History, Art, and Sport, *that Col. Horace N. Fisher of Boston imported a Saluki from Thebes in 1861.*

is the form adopted by French, Germans, and Dutch at their dog shows. Evidently, she was unaware of the elegant name "*sulkan*-hunde" used by the Czech Arabist, Professor Alois Musil, who had made extensive archaeological surveys of the Transjordan at the turn of the century.*

Florence's use of different names is an indicator of the progress of her research over the years. Between 1904 and 1915, in a search for a name that was both proper and descriptive, Florence experimented with a number of spellings for the breed name in classical Arabic, colloquial Arabic, Persian, and a variety of English transliterations — all suggested by her correspondents. She progressively called the breed *Slughi*, Assyrian Greyhound, *Slughi*/Gazelle-hound, *Slughi*/Gazelle hound/*Tazi*, Gazelle hound and Saluki *Shami*. Sometime between 1912 and 1915 she settled on a name that satisfactorily covered a range of possibilities, "Saluki Shamis or Arabian Gazelle Hounds," and that was the name that stuck until 1923.

Florence saw two more litters born at Foulden in 1912 and that year wrote the first publication exclusively on the breed. It was a modest four-page pamphlet that she had printed in nearby Swaffham. The romanticized prose was a highly condensed version of her chapter in Leighton's book. She now called the breed "the Gazelle Hound or Saluki Shami" and had reduced the varieties to two — feathered and smooth. There was increased interest in breeding by the small community who had imported Salukis and related breeds. Accidental matings and casual attitudes toward breed type and pedigree threatened to dilute pure bloodlines. Florence took this opportunity and many others to admonish against mixing the different Eastern greyhound strains and she particularly warned against breeding Salukis to the *Aktazeet* or Kirghiz greyhounds, despite their close physical resemblance.[6]

By 1913, Florence Amherst's hounds were making quite a splash at dog shows. At Crufts that year, there were eleven dogs shown in the "Any Other Variety" class and of the eleven, six were her Salukis. The Afghan hound Chuku took first, and five-year-old Sultan (Nafissah's litter brother) took third. Sultan was a light golden color with lovely feathering and did quite well in the ring — often being singled out for mention in the show reports. His dam, Nefer, was out of Luman and Valda — two of Florence's desert imports and his sire was an obscure hound named Marjan.[†] Florence commissioned an oil portrait of Sultan and would later attribute England's notice of the breed largely to his show career: "My Saluki Sultan, just before the War, was the one that drew people's special attention to the breed at shows as he used to take so many firsts in Foreign Classes."[7]

In England, showing dogs was considered a pleasurable hobby for women of quality, as witnessed by the popularity of the Ladies Kennel Association (the female adjunct to the gender-segregated Kennel Club). America had yet to catch up to this sophisticated view, for women who showed dogs in the land of *E Pluribus Unum* were considered fast and unladylike. Freeman Lloyd, an ex-cavalryman, expatriate Welshman, Borzoi breeder,[§] and dog judge, was doing his best to turn this attitude around by chronicling dog shows as sophisticated events for the New York magazine *Dress and Vanity Fair*. Lloyd, who would later write for *National Geographic* and edit the American magazine *Dogdom*, frequently took passage across the

---

Musil wrote his texts in German and hence the use of the word "hunde." "Sulkan" is a transliteration of the plural "Sulqan" in classical Arabic. Another Arabist, the German-born Arabian horse expert Carl Raswan, also used the term "the sulkan" for Salukis, but it would not appear until he published Drinkers of the Wind *in 1942.*

[†]*Either an import or one of her unregistered puppies.*

[§]*Lloyd's Elsie became the first Borzoi to be imported to America.*

Atlantic to report on shows such as Crufts and the Kennel Club event at Crystal Palace. On his visit in 1913, he met Florence Amherst and declared that Salukis would "very likely become a rage in England."

Lloyd interviewed Florence and she cited her usual Egyptian provenances indicating that the breed was between 3,000 to 6,000 years old. She noted that their ancient forebears were "Soudan coursing hounds"—a name doubtless derived from the Nubian greyhounds that Newberry had described at Rekhmire. The best specimens of Saluki *Shami* or Arabian Gazelle Hounds were found in Khartoum, Aswan, and Asyut, "where the *Saluki* tribe of Bedouins attends the fairs selling the hides of wild animals, ivory, ebony sticks, and various wild creatures are purchased by agents for European and American zoological collections."[8] Further, the article noted that the Saluki tribe roamed southern Darfur* with what they called "Syrian Hounds" or *Shami*—inexplicably proving that the hounds first came from the Holy Land. The finishing touch for the article was the photograph of elegant Nafissah and the Sekhmet statue.

Aside from Florence's conventional article in *Every Woman's Encyclopedia* (1910–1912) and her 1912 pamphlet, the only evidence of her thoughts on breed origin between 1912 and 1927 are contained in Lloyd's article. This singular and somewhat confusing account of marketplaces and Sudanese tribes is reminiscent of the Egyptian experiences of both the Amhersts and Jennings-Bramly (who did indeed purchase specimen animals). One is tempted to wonder if Florence had taken a new direction in her research or was just badly misquoted by Lloyd, for none of the Darfur, Saluki tribe, and marketplace references occur elsewhere in her writings. Nevertheless, it was good publicity for Florence. Lloyd was clearly enthusiastic about the breed and became one of Florence's regular correspondents.

Since 1905, Florence had been extending her search away from libraries and museums to acquire firsthand information from a variety of people in the Middle East, including Percy Cox's agents. A year before Freeman Lloyd's article was published, another potential source presented itself through David George Hogarth, whom Florence had cited in her chapter in Leighton. D. G. Hogarth had been a fellow and tutor at Magdalen College, Oxford, made several expeditions to Asia Minor, excavated at Alexandria and Al Faiyum, and published two archaeological papers. He was working on his third one, *A Wandering Scholar in the Levant*, at the same time the Amhersts had their Egyptian holiday. Naturally, he was well acquainted with the Didlington antiquities and in 1909 was honored with the post of Keeper of the Ashmolean Museum.

Hogarth and Laura, his bride of one year, had enjoyed socializing with the Amhersts while sailing up the Nile, so Florence wrote to her in September 1912 asking if she or her husband might know of someone in the Middle East with whom she could correspond about Salukis. As it happened, Hogarth had organized the British Museum's excavation of a Hittite palace of Carchemish on the banks of the Euphrates, some 200 miles northeast of Damascus.† In that lonely spot, one of Oxford University's more promising graduates was helping to catalog and photograph the dig. On her husband's advice, Laura suggested that Florence write to the young archaeologist. On September 28, Florence Amherst posted a letter to the young man who the world would remember as "Lawrence of Arabia."

*Darfur is located west of Khartoum.
†Near Karkamis, Turkey.

Young Thomas Edward Lawrence was an excellent scholar, gifted with languages, and possessed a mischievous sense of humor. At 5'5", he was slight of stature, but had amazing mental and physical stamina. "T. E." (as he was known to his friends) attended Jesus College at Oxford, where he studied classics and specialized in medieval history. He was also an accomplished photographer, avid cyclist, and reportedly a good shot with pistol or rifle. Lawrence had a pronounced aesthetic streak and during the Great War he dreamed of establishing a fine book press back in England. During the years 1906–1908 he made cycling tours of France, taking photographs and detailed notes of castle architecture. In preparation for writing his thesis comparing the development of European and Crusader castles, he made a walking tour of Syria in 1909. He was able to converse in Arabic dialect and demonstrated Spartan fortitude in a harsh land. At one point he was badly beaten and robbed, but, undaunted, continued his field studies in Syria. His thesis, *The Influence of the Crusades on European Military Architecture—to the End of the XIIth Century* would later be published as *Crusader Castles*. It is still considered an authoritative work on the subject, proving the design of castles had moved from west to east rather than the reverse, which had been the previously held assumption.

Hogarth was able to assist Lawrence in obtaining a small fellowship from Magdalen College to help with the excavation at Carchemish (Jerablus). Wishing to expand Lawrence's archaeological experience after the first season's work in 1911, Hogarth arranged for Lawrence to work for a brief period under the tutelage of the gruff Sir William Flinders Petrie, who had also instructed Howard Carter. The apprenticeship took place at the Kafr Ammar cemetery but Lawrence never liked Egyptian digging. The workmen's preoccupation with finding gold and callous treatment of the unearthed mummies soured Lawrence on that aspect of archaeology. He was very glad to return to the architectural remains of Carchemish.[9]

Beginning in the 1912 season, Hogarth had given oversight of the dig to Charles Leonard Woolley, whom Lawrence had known from Oxford. Woolley was eight years older than Lawrence, but by mutual agreement he shared many responsibilities with the young archaeologist. Lawrence's particular duties at the site included identifying pottery and ceramic fragments, photographic documentation and cataloging. His working knowledge of Arabic helped him to develop good relations with the locals employed at the excavation and he interacted easily with them. A deep friendship grew between him and a young tribesman, Dahoum. Both the seasonal nature of the task and the comparative freedom of the working conditions permitted Lawrence and Dahoum to wander and explore when their work was done, unlike other archaeologists who tended to live at their digs and then head for home when the season was finished. Lawrence's extracurricular travels gave him the opportunity to purchase small artifacts for the museum, as well as increase his intimate knowledge of the land, people, language, and customs.

A full two months after she posted it, Lawrence received Amherst's letter at Carchemish. The first Balkan War had begun in September of that year and the Turkish postal system was even more erratic than usual. The season's work had just been completed and there was much to be done before he and Woolley could return to England. Lawrence was not able to respond until he was back in Oxford.

Dec. 22 [1912]   2 Polstead Road, Oxford

Dear Madam,

You will have been astonished at my not replying to your letter of Sept. 28. The fact is that I have received it in the first week of December (the war has given the coup de grace to the tottering Ottoman post office) at Carchemish, and in the hurry of closing down excavations it was quite impossible for me to answer it. I am not particularly doggy — but some of our men own greyhounds, and no doubt can tell me *something* about them: — though they are villagers only, without nice ideas of breeding or pedigree.

We have only the feathery sort ... and they call them *Shami* because the great sporting centre is Damascus; Silogi (g=k in Bedouin Arabic) is the proper name for the species of dog, but there are as many family and tribal names for the dogs as there are for horses. Only a town sportsman or a rich Kurdish chief could tell one of these; and I am not likely to see any of these till the end of February.

The only trifle I know about them is that Arabs eat the flesh of the hares the dogs kill, (though not lawfully blooded) on the pretense that the iron collar of the dog has touched the wound, thus making the ceremonial slaughtering. Most dogs though don't bite their captures, but press them down until relieved.

I am going out to Syria again early in January, would information coming in the end of February or early March be of any use to you? I can ask some sporting Sheikhs for you ...

> With apologies for knowing nothing!
> Believe me,
> Yours sincerely
> T. E. Lawrence[10]

Despite Lawrence's protestations of only knowing a trifle about Salukis, he would have encountered at least few during his walking tour of Syria and had read about them in Doughty's *Travels in Arabia Deserta*. Lawrence admired Doughty greatly and in his introduction to the 1921 reprint noted that he had been studying the book for ten years and thought it a masterpiece. Still, Doughty does not dwell on the hounds and it is certainly easy to lose track of them amongst his hundreds of pages. While Lawrence professed to be "not particularly doggy," he did indeed have affection for certain of the canine species. He would later comment to his biographer Robert Graves that he disliked children, dogs, and elephants en masse, but that he did like "some children, some dogs, and some elephants."[11]

Less than two weeks after Lawrence's reply to Florence's inquiry, he and his youngest brother, Arnold, were invited to London to see Sultan and the rest of her Salukis. At Grosvenor Square, Florence and her kennel man, Mr. Harris, offered refreshments to their visitors and showed off the hounds that she had in town. "There was a golden dog and a team of four cream-colored Salukis which Lawrence thought quite beautiful."[12] In the years after the war, when Lawrence became famous, Florence would proudly mention that luncheon with "Colonel T. E. Lawrence — the Lawrence of Arabia."[13]

From Florence's point of view, Lawrence was ideally situated to provide her with information and possibly new stock for her bloodlines, and she continued to write to him. Lawrence believed that correspondence was very personal and having once been read, no longer served any purpose.* Typically, he burned letters after reading them, but the three surviving letters to Florence give a very good sense of what she must have asked of Lawrence. Indeed, they are the only surviving evidence of Florence's inquiries of her foreign correspondents.† Lawrence

---

*Lawrence was deliberately capricious when he translated Arabic names and places into English.
†While most of Florence Amherst's original research has been lost, the Lawrence letters (continued on page 82)

did make some efforts to assist her, including the request to locate a pair of hounds that might be shipped to England through Mr. R. Hensman, a Saluki expert that she knew in Jerusalem.* Both the time and exertion needed for the 200-mile trek to Damascus and the city's periodic epidemics of cholera prevented Lawrence from going south on her errands. Eight months later, at the beginning of the next season he replied to another of her letters.

Aleppo   August 26 1913

Dear Miss Amherst

I am sorry to have got your letter at this time of day as I was actually in England when you wrote it. I only came out here a few days ago, and found it [a]waiting me here in the Consulate. I'm also sorry that you haven't heard from me: I wrote, it must have been in January, to say that there was cholera (and consequently quarantine) in Damascus and that I had to pass it by unvisited on my way out.

I have not had a chance of going there since: in June we had to go to Alexandretta [Iskenderun] with our luggage:—just now coming out, I found no Beyrout [Beirut] steamer in Alexandria. So I have not done anything or found out anything for you, for we agreed that nothing was possible up here.

Digging here will begin soon now, for a three months autumn season. So Damascus is at any rate that far away.

We have been over-busy of late, with our more particular work, and I have not since I saw you, been able to do any traveling for myself.

About getting another pair of dogs ... the cream ones as good as yours, are not in every village up here! We have them much more brown yellow ... but tiny skinny looking things, that you would not consider them. Of late I saw one pure black, which was beautifully made, but would rather confuse your "stud." I'll enquire in Mesopotamia if there is anything to be got: they are not sold by their owners but given away. When we wanted a pair of wolf dogs (Kurdish) for the Counsel here, we had to have them taken for us by force. Of course in such a case one makes a judicious peace later.

I measured three dogs in a Turkoman 'effendi's house a few months back: two were 18½ inches high, one 18 inches: but this the sole information I gathered, was hardly enough for a special letter!

If I find a pleasant looking animal for disposal, I'll write to Mr. Hensman ... and if I can manage to get to Damascus (where I have all sorts of things I want to do), I can get you some decent information.

The smudges on the paper are not tears, but due to spilling water over my head. Likewise paper, pens and ink are beyond my bettering. Am very sorry to have been such a fraud.

Believe me
Yours Sincerely
T. E. Lawrence[14]

From her letters and his visit to Grosvenor Square, Lawrence knew of Florence's preference for golden and cream colors and hence his mention of the black Saluki "confusing" her breeding program. She must have immediately fired off another letter to Lawrence but getting no reply, wrote to D. G. Hogarth regarding Lawrence's delays in producing Salukis for

concerning Salukis were preserved by an odd twist of fate. After his death in 1935, historian David Garnett made a nation-wide call for Lawrence's letters to be published in book tribute. Two of his letters to Florence were published, but all three were copied and archived in the Bodleian Library. The originals were inadvertently thrown away after her death.

*Not much is known about Hensman, but he was a local aficionado of the Salukis and supplied Florence with a couple of her later imports. He owned a famous sire called Jack of Jerusalem and used him at stud in England in the 1920s.

export. Hogarth wrote to Lawrence to find out why Amherst was bothering him with this business of importing dogs. From Baron's Hotel in Aleppo (Halab), Lawrence explained the situation briefly in a letter to Hogarth on September 29, 1913 — just one month after his last letter to Florence. The very first paragraph of Lawrence's response reads "Greyhounds, as I have explained to Miss Amherst sundry times, must wait till I can pass out of Syria by way of Damascus: and as long as we are exporting material we are doomed to Alexandretta."[15]

Lawrence's frustration with her incessant requests and now bothering Hogarth is easy to understand. After all, why should he have to explain to his employer about a trivial matter completely unconnected with the dig? To Lawrence's credit, he was still willing to assist her as long as it was no great burden. In the next two months, he would receive two more letters from Florence. Lawrence's mention of a special hunting collar in his first letter had intrigued her, and she had asked him to try and obtain one or two.

> Carchemish
> Dec. 10, 1913
>
> Dear Miss Amherst,
>
> I got your two letters about a fortnight ago — and I am ashamed to say that I had forgotten all about the collars. However please accept my profound apologies ... and the assurance that I have written to a Syrian I know in Damascus to try and find me the thing required in the bazaar there, or among his friends. Aleppo has nothing of the sort, and I fear that I will not be able to go South to Damascus this year.
>
> Digs ended three days ago, and I only got back today from a visit I paid to a Kurd chief about 30 miles across the Euphrates. He had four Salugis, all hairless [smooth] ones, of a biscuit color, very large to my eyes. I measured them and they were from 22½–24 inches high, very ugly dogs, of the slinking type: not your sort at all. He knew nothing of pedigree dogs, and said that they did not keep them carefully enough for that, or of names for special breeds or colors: as he only spoke Turkish his knowledge, if any would not have been of any use to you.
>
> I ought to hear from Damascus almost at once: — at least I should get a collar, for I do not suppose my friend will write before. I will let you know (immediately, this time) as soon as anything happens.
>
> We have found masses of stuff this year in the digs: rows of sculptured priestesses, and men carrying gazelles: alas no dogs with them!
>
> More apologies for my neglect and rudeness,
> Believe me,
> Yrs sincerely
> T. E. Lawrence[16]

Carchemish is very near the Turkish border and the local tribesmen were predominately Kurds. The Euphrates runs north-south at that point and Lawrence traveled generally eastward on his visit to the Kurd sheikh — which was less than 200 miles from the area where Sir Austen Layard acquired Touar. Despite his lack of interest in dogs and his annoyance with Florence's persistence, Lawrence did think of her when he encountered Salukis in his travels. The fact that he specifically mentioned pedigree, size, names, coat color, and terminology, and measured the hounds, indicates that these were the points of interest that Florence had emphasized in her letters to both Lawrence and Major Percy Cox. Lawrence's comments about pedigree in the first and third letters (that neither the Carchemish villagers nor the Kurdish sheikh bothered to monitor their dogs' bloodlines and breeding) are an interesting counterpoint to Florence's image (and indeed the current lore) of the genetically select, desert-bred Saluki. His remarks about the hounds being of the "slinking type: not your sort at all," refer to the natural shyness of desert dogs unused to strangers, as compared with Florence's cosmopolitan Salukis.*

Having assured Florence in his letter that he had already written to his Syrian friend about the collars —"I ought to hear from Damascus almost at once," and promising to let her know immediately, Lawrence dashed off four letters that day, one to his Arabic tutor, Miss Fareedah el Akle.

> To Miss Faredah,   Carchemish Dec. 10, 1913
>
> An English Lady, Lady Florence Amherst, has written to me asking if I can get her from Syria one of the old iron collars which the Arab Sheikhs use to put round the necks of their dogs ساوغو — the sort that catch hares and gazelles — Silūgi, as we say it. They used to have iron collars so that the iron might touch the hare they killed and so it is lawful meat for a Mohammadan to eat.
>
> These collars used to have little blue beads also on them, to keep off the evil eye.
>
> Of course one cannot get such a collar in Aleppo. In that town there are no silugis, and no old collars to buy. But I wonder if you would find me something of the sort in Damascus? If you know of any sporting sheikhs they could find the thing, or perhaps some of the people in school. Pay anything you like for it (if it is a pretty one with gold or silver on it she would love it, and she has lots of money to spare) and I will send you a cheque exceedingly quickly!
>
> If you cannot make out from this letter *what* I want, ask Miss Hod to help you, wrap a cold wet towel around each of your heads, and parse every word in the letter. That is a great help.[17]

Miss Fareedah was a Syrian Christian school teacher at the American Mission in Jubayl, near Beirut.[18] Living in a city, she would have better access to collars in the souks and bazaars than he would at Carchemish or Aleppo (Halab). Perhaps he thought that if the hunting collars could be supplied that Florence would be satisfied and direct her inquiries elsewhere. The rest of the letter mentions the separate visits to Damascus by his brother Will and Miss Fareedah, and Dahoum's *salaams* to her. Lawrence remained polite and at least for a time continued to work on Florence's request. Miss Fareedah wrote back to Lawrence asking if a delay in obtaining the collars would be all right. On December 26, with a large slice of sarcasm, he replied:

> Dear Miss Fareedae,
>
> Certainly, I will wait, and Lady Amherst will wait for weeks and weeks and weeks for a dog collar. I hope you will find a beauty all over gold and silver, with diamonds stuck round about. I'm sure she would like it so.[19]

The "iron collars" mentioned by Lawrence were actually leather or fabric and ornamented with iron fittings much like Bedouin pistol belts and bandoleers which are decorated with brass studs and rivets. The Kurds that Lawrence knew believed that the iron ornaments substituted for the knife in the ritual killing prescribed by the Qur'an and technically satisfied

---

Lawrence's notes on the sizes of the dogs are worth considering for a moment. While there is no way of knowing exactly how Lawrence took the measurements (perhaps Amherst demonstrated this during Lawrence's visit to her kennels or described it in a letter), it seems safe to speculate that whatever method he used, it couldn't diverge more than an inch or two from the standard measurement to the top of the withers. That the dogs mentioned in the third letter were "very large" to his eyes suggests that other Salukis he had seen (Amherst's and those of the tribesmen) were of lesser size. The three that he described in the second letter at 18" and 18½" were obviously not worthy of any special remark as to their height. By 1912 Amherst would put the typical height of a Saluki at 23". Lawrence's measurements are interesting in light of both the English and American standards developed in the 1920s, which establish 23" to 28" as the size range for dogs and bitches "proportionally smaller."

Muslim religious requirements. The hare and gazelle caught in this fashion would provide a supplemental source of protein for the Bedouin aside from the slaughtering sheep for feasts (or camels in times of starvation). Despite Lawrence's good intentions, the collars never arrived in England and are not mentioned elsewhere in Saluki lore as she was unable to locate these or confirm their existence.*

For someone with his own work to do and no interest whatsoever in hounds and collars (however eastern they were) Lawrence remained gracious and made some efforts to help Florence. Despite his protestations of promptly attending to her requests, three months later the collars had not arrived from Damascus. One may imagine the stream of letters that Florence must have sent Lawrence as well as her other correspondents in her efforts to acquire as much knowledge about the breed as possible. He did continue searching for the hunting collars when time permitted. In January 1914, Lawrence and Woolley were hired to work with Captain Stewart F. Newcombe of the Royal Engineers on a surveying and photographic expedition into Sinai under the official auspices of the Palestine Exploration Fund.[20] It was during Newcombe's thinly veiled military survey (later published by Lawrence and Woolley as *The Wilderness of Zin*) that Lawrence saw the wondrous lost city of Petra. He and Newcombe also surveyed an area which would prove to be a keystone in the Arab Revolt — the small coastal town of Al Aqabah, where Jennings-Bramly had fomented the "Akaba Incident" in 1906 and nearly sent England and the Ottoman Empire to war.[†] Lawrence popped into Damascus briefly, but had no time to cut over to the coast to see Miss Fareedah. Returning to Carchemish, he wrote a long letter to her on March 8 and among the news of his recent travels, he asked about the collars again: "Any luck about those dog-collars? If you cannot find old ones please write to me, and I'll send you another letter asking you to have new ones made...."[21]

The delays between Lawrence's letters on the subject of Salukis are attributable to lack of interest, his extended treks into the desert, and the logistical problems of moving mail by camel, train, and steamship. In June 1914, he and Woolley were back in England for a rest, fully expecting to continue their work at Carchemish during the upcoming season. Indeed, there seemed to be at least four more years of work there. Florence doubtless anticipated another exchange of letters with Lawrence on the chance that he might get around to accommodating her requests. But events of a larger scale were to interrupt their lives and those of people all over the world. The Austrian Archduke Ferdinand was assassinated in Sarajevo on June 28 and European war broke out one week later. The "War to End All Wars" put a stop to Lawrence's archaeological career and his attempts to oblige the baron's daughter, but it was not the last that he would hear of Salukis or Florence.

In none of the standard works (The Saluki in History, Art & Sport; Saluki: Companion of Kings; The Complete Saluki; and Saluqi: Coursing Hound of the East) is this peculiar bit of folklore described. Nor do the Europeans who lived in the desert and wrote about Salukis (Jennings-Bramly, Cheesman, Dickson, Raswan, Musil, Blunt, Doughty, Burton, Digby, or Layard) mention them. Clearly the metal-ornamented collars are a regional custom that persists to this day for they are also described by author Sir Terence Clark, who has seen these worn by Salukis in Syria.

†Complicated in nature, the Aqaba Incident (also called the Tabah Crisis) resulted from a border dispute in Sinai over Turkish-Egyptian protection of Egyptians on their pilgrimage to Makkah. See Appendix 2.

9

The Foulden Home Front

"Very little is now available for dog owners beyond biscuits, horseflesh, sheep's paunches, or scraps from the butcher that are not suitable for sale in the ordinary course. Bread may not be given, nor barley or maize meal."

Editor, *Country Life*
September 29, 1917

Two pistol shots by a Serbian nationalist had finally touched off the Balkan powder train. Austria-Hungary issued an outrageous ultimatum and marched on the hapless Serbia on July 28, 1914. Czar Nicholas mobilized Russia's vast army to assist his hereditary ally and Germany demanded that France declare her intentions if Russia were to fight Austria-Hungary. Sensing the foregone conclusion, the French generals mobilized their armies and the Kaiser quickly declared war on Russia and France. German plans to invade France through the lowlands of Belgium had existed since 1905. On August 3, the German army crossed into neutral Belgium, ruthlessly punishing their resistance.

Both Britain and Germany had been guarantors of Belgium's neutrality since 1831, but in addition to Britain's altruistic duty to protect Belgium, there was a real strategic need to do so. Antwerp lay just across the English Channel and the idea of this major port and industrial city occupied by militaristic Germany was intolerable. On August 4, the day after Germany invaded Belgium, Britain declared war. With her new ally, France was now sure that Germany could be defeated in a few weeks. Ironically, Britain and her Allies were so sure that it would be a fast, mobile war that the entrenching tools, which had been so vital to the British soldier in the Boer War, were not issued until much later and after very costly lessons.

It was the first time England had fought in a European war since the defeat of Napoleon a hundred years before. The island was consumed with patriotic fervor and everyone was certain that the war would be over by Christmas. Colorful posters invoking nationalistic allegories of St. George fighting the dragon, the British lion, Britannia in armor, and even the Brotherhood of Empire, urged stalwart young men to enlist for the duration of the hostilities. Germans were now known as Prussians, Huns, Deutschers, or the Boche.

The conflict escalated to a magnitude that was previously inconceivable. Poland, Czechoslovakia, Hungary, Bulgaria, Romania, Turkey, Albania, Montenegro, and Bosnia-Herzegovina soon took sides. By the end of the war, Italy, Portugal, Greece, and the United States would be fighting as well.

England watched closely to see what the Ottoman Empire would do. With close ties to Germany, Turkey was in a position to seriously threaten the Suez Canal — Britain's lifeline to India. As it happens, Turkey's hand was forced. Prior to the war, Turkey had commissioned two warships to be built in England, but at the outbreak of hostilities, the Royal Navy confiscated them. A few days later, Turkey regained her loss when two German cruisers dashed into the Dardenelle Straits to escape pursuit by a British squadron. A fictitious sale to the government in Istanbul was arranged, the German crews donned Turkish uniforms and their commander was made an admiral in the Turkish Navy. On October 29, 1914, the Turkish fleet shelled the Russian port of Odessa on the Black Sea. Four days later Russia declared war and the Ottoman Empire joined the conflagration.

Foulden Manor was a pleasant place even if it did not have the splendor of Didlington. There was a Dutch garden, large reflecting pond with water lilies, rows of pleached lime trees, lavender hedges, and herb gardens. There were marshes, woods, and a small lake called Becket End. The brick residence was filled with oak furniture and such family treasures as they had been able to spare from the auction block. Lady Amherst still found the time to turn ivory carvings and the splendor of her voice was undiminished by the years. Sybil and Maggie kept busy with their respective hobbies and Florence continued to research and cultivate her Salukis.

Their reduced income and financial difficulties forced them to sell the Grosvenor Square townhouse and one of Lord Amherst's more spectacular Egyptian treasures. As a favor to the family, Howard Carter acted as an intermediary in the sale of the Sekhmet statues to Mr. Henry Walters, the second vice president of the Metropolitan Museum. The negotiations had actually been concluded in the summer of 1914, but due to the onset of war in August and the subsequent German U-boat ravages on shipping, they could not be sent to New York until 1919. At that time, Walters graciously gave them to the Metropolitan Museum and there they stand to this day.[1]

During the war, Saluki appearances at dog shows began to taper off. Charles Cruft continued to hold his premier event in the Royal Agricultural Hall until 1917, but well before then many smaller shows had difficulty finding venues.* Attendance and entries dropped off and "Kennel Notes" in *Country Life* was dropped and a replacement column on automobiles took its place. A. Croxton Smith continued to write features on the shows that did take place and he seems to have always had a good word for Florence's Salukis. She began exhibiting at Crufts in 1913 and in 1914 Sultan won the Foreign Section, beating the largest entry ever in that class, 24 dogs, including a German Sheepdog, Lhasa Terrier, and a Siberian sled dog which had formed part of the late Captain Robert Scott's team during his South Pole expedition.† *The Illustrated Kennel News* described the "Persian Greyhound" Sultan as a "big dog, lovely shaped head, fringed ears, good expression, true front, very nice body and stern."

In February 1915, Salukis were making an impact on the show scene and had been admitted as a distinct breed or variety at Crufts where the first breed-specific class was created for them. Florence guaranteed funds to support the prizes of £2, £1, and 10 shillings for the first, second, and third prizes. Ever mindful of promotion, she named the class "Saluki Shami Arabian Gazelle Hounds — Open Dogs and Bitches" and the catalog description noted their origin as Arabia, their purpose for coursing "Gazelles, Hares, etc.," and their speed as "20–30

---

*Crufts would not resume until 1921.

†*Scott and his four men reached the South Pole on January 18, 1912, only to discover that Roald Amundsen's Norwegian team with their well-trained sled dogs had already been there and left. Amundsen made it home but Scott and his men froze to death trying to reach one of their supply caches. Presumably the sled dog shown at Crufts came from one of ancillary research parties in Scott's expedition.*

yards a second."[2] Her dogs Sultan, Shubra, Durrat and Durra were the only entries. Despite having her very own class and no competition from other Salukis, Florence also entered them all in the "Foreign Dogs: Any Variety — Open Dogs and Bitches" for an additional chance to have them seen by the public. There they filled the class competing with a German Sheep-dog and three Lhasa Terriers. She won the team prize with her four Salukis, and Sultan and Durrat were highly complimented.

Four months later, at the Ladies Kennel Association show, Florence again had most of the entry in the class. A downpour of much-needed summer rain kept the public away from the Royal Botanic Gardens that day but fortunately for the exhibitors, the rings and bench-ing were sheltered under a large marquee. Queen Alexandra showed two of her Basset Hounds and made the rounds with Princess Victoria, a Russian duchess, another princess, dispensed biscuits to dogs on the benching. Florence's good friend and secretary of the Ladies Kennel Association, Miss Gertrude Desborough was disappointed at the lack of public attendance but quite pleased with the large entry. A. Croxton Smith wrote, "Foreign dogs afford no nov-elty, the Hon. Florence Amherst filling a picturesque class with her gazelle hounds."[3] That soggy show appears to be the last record of Florence showing her Salukis during the wartime privation.

Meat began to be rationed and due to the high cost of feeding foxhounds, many packs were sold and dispersed by 1917. It was reckoned that the cost of feeding meat and oatmeal to fifteen couple (thirty) foxhounds was £110 per year.* Naturally, this did not include expenses for veterinary care, bedding, kennelman, or the tax on all dogs older than six months.[†] Rice, bread, and grains were restricted to human consumption and the only meat available to dog owners were the local butcher shop scraps considered unfit for human consumption — sheep's paunches, joint trimmings, solidified blood, and fish and poultry heads. In 1917, "worn-out" horses were no longer exported to the Continent and their flesh became available for dog and human, but a year later, one lady who owned a St. Bernard was fined along with her butcher, for feeding the dog an astonishing ten pounds of meat every day. Letters appeared in maga-zines questioning the necessity of any nonessential dog. Working sheep dogs had value, but meat-consuming sporting packs were a pure luxury and many advocated that all but the best specimens of a breed be put down to reduce the drain on essential foodstuffs. One correspon-dent noted slyly that this would have the beneficial side effect of purifying the breed strains.

Florence had definite views on canine nutrition and described her preferred feeding pro-gram:

> Salukis need good food, nourishing food ... it is necessary to watch them almost daily as they may be off their food for no apparent reason and become visibly thinner. A good nourishing broth can be made of meat, onions, carrots and lentils or pearl barley and this poured over wholemeal bread is sustaining and appreciated. Rice boiled or baked rice pud-ding and boiled suet puddings are useful.[4]

During the war, this was necessarily restricted, but the wholesome ingredients and prepara-tion are an interesting insight into the attention that her Salukis received.

With rationing of essentials (including tea), reduced train and motorcar transport, increased demands by military authorities for war contributions from civilians, Florence's

*Equivalent to £4,235.86 in 2006 (MeasuringWorth.com).
†In June of 1917 rationing had become severe enough that a further dog tax was proposed for people who kept more than one dog.

breeding program, along with that of rest of England's dog fanciers, came to a virtual stand-still. She bred only two litters in early 1914 and the records do not show another until January 1917.

The Amhersts became involved in patriotic work, growing vegetables for the Royal Naval Reserve, making gift parcels for soldiers, and working with the British Red Cross Society. Many women signed up for war work, but Florence's 21-year-old niece, Victoria Drummond, defied social conventions by aspiring to break into the all-male domain of marine engineers. Victoria secured work as an apprentice mechanic in a Perth machine shop.* She frequently went south to Foulden to spend holidays with her grandmother and aunts and remembered that when the wind was blowing in the right direction, they could hear the massive siege guns in France.[5]

One of Florence's war efforts was to have an entirely beneficial effect for Norfolk poultrymen. In addition to her other avocations and interests, Florence was keenly interested in all aspects of poultry production.[†] When she learned that a dozen eggs in the Brandon market sold for sixpence and that same dozen in London fetched three shillings, a sixfold increase over the local market price, she developed a scheme to organize the poultry producers in Norfolk. Eggs were collected at depots, graded, dated, and marked with their distinctive rose stamp. The eggs were then packaged and shipped directly to London and the profits returned to Norfolk. The coalition of egg producers became the National Poultry Organization and Florence was the first president. She and Sybil traveled all over the county to lecture on poultry keeping and egg production.

In the intial year of the war, there were 250,000 British casualties, and for the first time, there would be civilian casualties in London from Zeppelin bombing raids. As it did to most families, the war quickly affected the Amhersts personally. The Honorable William Amherst Cecil, M.C., a captain in the Grenadier Guards and the eldest son of Mary Cecil (née Amherst), was killed at Aisne, in September during the opening gambits of the war. He was twenty-eight, and had been awarded one of the new Military Crosses — a medal for gallantry and distinguished service for army captains and junior officers. "Billy" Cecil had been one of the many nephews and nieces who scampered through Didlington on holidays and accompanied his parents on their archaeological work in Egypt. His mother had dedicated her book *Birds on the Nile* to him and he would have become the 3rd Baron Amherst of Hackney had she predeceased him. Billy was missed grievously by the Foulden women. Victoria noted that reading the casualty lists in the newspapers became "compulsive but dreadful."[6]

As the war dragged on far longer than anyone expected, the government asked for large homes with unused rooms to be made available for auxiliary hospitals. Two of these were established at the Amherst properties of Buckenham near Norwich and Mundford near Didlington and Margaret became a matron at the former. With characteristic Amherst enthusiasm, Florence, her mother, and sisters organized the local contributions for the Didlington and Foulden branches of the Norfolk Education Committee and produced 88 boxes of food and clothing in sixteen weeks.

Florence corresponded with soldiers overseas, passed along their news to friends and relatives and even visited their parents. She sent soldiers photographs, cocoa, woolen scarves, tobacco, golf balls and clubs, and in turn, they wrote back with news of their promotions and

---

Victoria became a marine engineer and was decorated for bravery at sea during World War II.
†*According to family tradition, she also raised white Arabian pigeons.*

doings. One poor fellow was grateful for the packet of cigarettes that she had sent but not having seen action, he could only tell her of the accidents that had befallen him. Florence responded to every letter she received and kept track of every soldier and his situation. She always asked about soldiers' war experiences — particularly those who were serving in Egypt.

Stationed at the Citadel military hospital in Cairo, Isaac Eagle of the Royal Army Medical Corps kept up a running correspondence with Florence. In a chatty letter dated October 11, 1915, Isaac described a camel ride and a visit to the pyramids, and sent along a photograph. In turn, Florence suggested that he look up her nephew, the Honorable John Francis Amherst Cecil who was also in Cairo at that time. Eight days after his October 11 letter, Isaac wrote to inform Florence that he was being transferred to Alexandria and that Jacky Cecil was going to try and secure for him a better and more permanent billet.

Known to the family as "Jacky," John was Billy Cecil's younger brother and a junior member of the Diplomatic Service in Cairo. He obviously had high regard for his aunt's opinion — even when she was recommending a comparative stranger. Cecil was an avid racing and shooting enthusiast, and well known for his sense of humor. According to family tradition, he was involved in some way in the transfer of gold to the sheikhs in the British efforts to encourage an uprising against the Ottoman Empire. Cecil kept a golden, lightly feathered Saluki and knew several officers who also fancied them. The well-mannered hound had the run of the house and accompanied his master on outings and treks to the local ruins. One particularly charming snapshot shows the Saluki accepting a tidbit from a lady.

Always hungry for firsthand details on Salukis in the Middle East, Florence and her nephew exchanged information about their hounds as well as the war news. She had asked him about the rarity of certain colors in the breed and evidently mentioned the pending sale of another puppy to America. In a reply to his mother, he wrote from Cairo on September 12, 1917:

> Tell Fluff I got her doggy letter. I hope that the coup with the U.S.A. will come off. Lots of fellows in the Sinai Desert have been seeing slughis and wanting to get them — some have managed to — but none so far as I know, have seen a golden one, which is immensely more valuable than creamy ones. So if she sells golden ones, make her stick the price up 100% at least.[7]

Throughout the war, Florence continued to correspond with her soldiers and as much as she was able, kept her little gifts flowing. All too often, there would be bad news in the post or newspaper. Painfully, she added notes to the names in her address book of those who had been killed, gassed, wounded or were missing in action. At the end of the war, she was reading in the papers about the exploits of another of her correspondents from the Middle East. It was none other than Colonel T. E. Lawrence of the Arab Revolt — the archaeologist who had once admired her Salukis — and it was the war in the Middle East that was to have the most unexpected and dramatic consequences for the breed in England.

PART III: SOLDIERS OF THE KING

10

From Wadi Rum to Damascus

"Of dogs there is never, in the British Army, any lack. They swarmed in every mess; they brought up litters in the ante-rooms; they yapped from every tent in the lines—dogs of all shapes, colors, and sizes ... among them, slim, mincing and disdainful, a few Selugis, Persian greyhounds of as ancient and pure a strain as our own."
"The Armageddon Hunt," *Blackwood's Magazine,*
January 1924

Just before Turkey began hostilities at the end of October, T. E. Lawrence decided to do his bit for King and country. With his detailed knowledge of the Middle East and Hogarth's influence, he secured a civilian post (later converted to military rank) at the Geographical Section of the War Office. Lawrence worked fervently on completing a report on Sinai that included the maps he had made with Captain Newcombe earlier that year.[1] In December 1914, he and Woolley embarked for Cairo to work for the Military Intelligence Department under Newcombe — which for the first time in the British Army, was a coordinated effort to gather, assess, and structure information needed to develop strategy and tactics.

Faced with securing the Suez Canal and protecting the oil fields of Mesopotamia, the British Army had immediate need of men who knew the land, the tribes, and the languages. Who better to gather intelligence in the desert regions than field archaeologists and surveyors? Lack of military training or fitness for combat was not necessarily an obstacle, and Jennings-Bramly, Lawrence, Hogarth, Woolley, and Howard Carter, all found work for the War Office.

Early in 1915, Carter became attached to the Intelligence Department of the War Office in Cairo in a nebulous capacity. In later years, Carter hinted that he was involved with decoding ciphers, but it might only have been tedious and sporadic office work. He still had time for his archaeological work and by the end of 1917 seems to have been no longer needed by the Intelligence Department. Nothing tangible exists about the nature of his war work but for one intriguing rumor.[2]

In November of 1917 an explosion awakened the sleeping hamlet of Qurna near Luxor. The startled inhabitants rushed outdoors to see German House burning to the ground. Little could be done to save it. The building had been the operational base for the German Archaeological Institute and stood near the Theban Ramesseum on the western riverbank. Supposedly fashioned after an Egyptian noble's villa, it was the center of German archaeology on the Upper Nile. The architect Sommers Clarke, Carter's old mentor, called it an "ugly ridiculous red abomination emblematical of German pushful vulgarity."[3] It seems certain that the strike was officially ordered by Cairo, but other than shady exportations of antiquities and

91

the possibility of being a conduit for German intelligence, one wonders what kind of threat it could have posed, 450 miles up the Nile from British Army Headquarters. The demolition may have even been a gesture or reminder of British military power, but who carried out the mission?

Carter and German Egyptologist Ludwig Borchardt were keen rivals in the competition for artifacts and detested each other heartily. Borchardt blamed Carter for the sabotage but could prove nothing. Carter certainly wouldn't have attracted any untoward attention had he shown up in Thebes leading one of his tour groups. In this case, he was with a small group of men who kept their luggage close to hand. Carter felt strongly about the war for he wrote to the curator of the Metropolitan Museum, "We must all do the best in the terrible struggle — to win we shall even if the last drop of blood is necessary ... I am glad as it is up to us all to do something."[4] Although there is no proof of his involvement, tradition still has it that Carter was either one of the planners or a participant in the destruction of the German presence in Luxor.[5]

Meanwhile, Lawrence's map work was proving to be very useful to the War Office in London and he was sent to Cairo with a promotion to captain in the Intelligence Department. In April 1916, he was given a letter of introduction to Sir Percy Cox at Basrah, who was now the Chief Political Officer in Mesopotamia. A force of 10,000 British and Indian troops had been sent to secure the oil fields of Mesopotamia and after some initial success they attempted to attack Baghdad but ended up besieged at Kut-al-Amara in December 1915. The British had underestimated the hostile land and climate, the incidence of disease, and the strength of the Turks, who were emboldened by their recent victory at Gallipoli. After months of siege and privation, there appeared to be little hope of relieving the British garrison. Lawrence was to go to Kut-al-Amara and if he could, either stir up the local Arabs to harass the Turks sufficiently to allow the siege to be broken or bribe senior Turkish officers to pull troops away from the siege lines.[6] By the time he arrived, relief was clearly impossible and at the end of April, the British garrison finally surrendered on the brink of starvation.

While his mission at Kut was unsuccessful, Lawrence's reputation grew and after his return to Cairo his superiors found other work for him. He managed to simultaneously annoy his immediate superiors while impressing them with his up-to-date knowledge of the Arab situation in the Hijaz. Lawrence was transferred to the Arab Bureau (which had been formed by Hogarth to collate intelligence for the expected fight in Arabia). He had conceived the idea of the *Arab Bulletin*, a periodic supplement to the Military Intelligence Bulletins.[7] The *Arab Bulletin* would become a rich and valued source of intelligence for Army staff and political agents about the work of the Arab Bureau and the embryonic war in the desert. Lawrence and others in the Bureau would eventually get the chance to help persuade the Bedouin to interrupt their tribal rivalries and redirect their aggression against the Turks.

Jennings-Bramly, "the Walking Englishman," had been given the rank of temporary captain when the war broke out and he worked in Sinai to secure Bedouin loyalties and gather information. When he was in the middle of the "Akaba Incident" of 1906, he had predicted fighting in Sinai, and conducted an informal poll of the Bedouin as to whether their loyalties would lie with Turkey or England in the event of a major-powers war. R. C. R. Owen, Acting Director of Intelligence, Cairo, wrote to him and took a predictably shortsighted view: "My Dear Bramly ... It matters very little to us which side they take in such a case, as if such a war took place (and no one expects it even will). There would be no fighting in Sinai — it would be somewhere else."[8] From his own experience, he knew that Al Aqabah was a key foothold and would later admire Lawrence for taking it. There was mutual admiration between the two men as Jennings-Bramly was one of the three intelligence staff officers working in the desert (the others being Philip Graves and Lawrence).[9] Once on a journey together, the impish Lawrence suggested that the two of them swap one half of their rank insignia and cause some confusion at their destination.[10] Jennings-Bramly declined the practical joke — perhaps having more to lose than Lawrence who was notorious for his casual disregard for military formalities such as rank and decorations.

When Hussein, the Sharif of Makkah, finally committed the Arabs to the Allied forces, Lawrence was sent to Jiddah in the fall of 1916, to assess the military capabilities of the Arabs for the fight in the Hijaz. Of Hussein's four sons, Ali, Abullah, Faisal, and Zeid, Lawrence was instinctively drawn to Faisal*, who he knew would be the best leader for the Arab Regular Army and the guerrilla bands of Bedouin.[11] Lawrence's reports were well received and he was detached from Cairo to be the British Liaison with Prince Faisal. The Arab Revolt had began in June 1916 with attacks at Al Madinah and Makkah and then moved north along the Red Sea coast through the towns of Jiddah, Rabigh, Yenbo, and Al Wajh, always striking inland at the Hijaz railway — the Turkish lifeline connecting Medina (Al Madinah), Damascus, and Istanbul.

In January 1917, the small town of Al Wajh on the Red Sea fell to a combined effort of Faisal's army and the British Navy. It became the new base of operations and support for the Hijaz campaign. Taking care of the supplies needed to sustain both British troops and Bedouin raiders was a headache beyond belief. But the Saluki owner who managed to keep food, fuel, and ammunition in readiness for the support staff at base camp as well as those who raided far into the desert was Captain Goslett, the supply wizard of Al Wajh and Al Aqabah.

Raymond Gwynne Goslett was a Londoner who worked at Alfred Goslett & Co., Sanitary Engineers — the family firm which sold building supplies, furniture, and household fittings. He had grown up in Stanmore, Berkshire, and attended Rugby School in the family's tradition. Goslett was well liked by his friends and had a reputation as a humorist, although he was shy about speaking in public. He was ruggedly handsome, sported a neatly trimmed mustache, and like most men of the time was a habitual smoker. Always well-groomed and impeccably dressed, Goslett was keen on shooting and fishing, and loved animals. His home in Regent's Park was just a short ride on the Underground from the firm's location on Charing Cross Road. It was at Goslett & Co. that he learned the organizational aspects of supply, inventory, and management that would be put to such good use in the Arab Revolt.

In September 1914, just three weeks before his twenty-ninth birthday, Goslett was swept up in the patriot fervor of the time and volunteered to fight. He joined as a private in the 2nd Battalion of the 28th Battalion London Regiment, also known poetically as the Artists' Rifles.[†] At that time, the Army did not maintain a standing corps of transport and supply. In

---

Faisal bin Al Hussein Bin Ali El-Hashemi.

†*The Artists' Rifles had originally been formed in 1860 by Edward Stearling as a volunteer group of his fellow art students and came to include musicians, actors, engravers, sculptors, and architects. Appropriately, their badge features representations of Mars, the God of War, and Minerva, the Goddess of Wisdom, symbolizing war and the fine arts.*

the event of war they would activate reserve officers that had been previously recruited from the business community and trained in the particulars of military supply. The Army Service Corps was the source of food, ammunition, tents, petrol, lanterns, lumber, and all the myriad items that are needed to keep soldiers fighting in the field. Eight months after joining the Artists' Rifles, Goslett was commissioned as a lieutenant in the Army Service Corps and posted to supply depots in Manchester and Aldershot.

In October 1915, Goslett was assigned to the one of the supply depots at Gallipoli and arrived in time to serve through the last three months of the disastrous and bloody attempt to establish a foothold on the Dardanelles. He was promoted to temporary captain three days before leaving Gallipoli on one of the last troop ships. He spent the next year at various depots in Egypt and on December 4, 1916, Goslett embarked on the El Kahira to join the Hijaz detachment of the army at Rabigh on the Red Sea. Goslett became the supply officer at Al Wajh in June 1917 and would be a key player in the Arab Revolt.

General Allenby assumed command of the Egyptian Expeditionary Force that month and set about moving east across Suez toward Turkish concentrations in Palestine. The Mediterranean was on their left but there was no flanking support on their right. Protecting the canal — Britain's access to India through the Persian Gulf— was of paramount importance. Allenby needed to push the Turks far away from it. In order for him to strike more effectively, he needed another prong of assault that could be easily supplied by ships. Throughout the first half of 1917, the Arab Army had been making paralyzing strikes at the Hijaz railway. Having slowly strangled the Turkish Army along the coastal region of the Red Sea, it was now time to move northward. Lawrence knew that the best possibility for a new base of operations was the sleepy town at the head of the Gulf of Al Aqabah. The Turks in the garrison were well prepared for an attack from the sea and periodically traded shots with warships or sniped at airplanes on reconnaissance missions. Taking Al Aqabah by sea would be difficult, but Lawrence surmised that a surprise strike from the land could be successful. It was territory he was well familiar with from his old days of surveying with Captain Newcombe. Once Turkish supremacy in Al Aqabah and Sinai was eliminated, British movements toward Damascus could begin in earnest. Lawrence felt that if properly motivated and equipped with arms, the independent Bedouin tribes could be persuaded or paid to rise up against the Turks and in their sweep northward to Damascus provide protection for the right flank of Allenby's regulars.

In July 1917, after a difficult journey of two months, Lawrence, Sheikh Auda abu Tayi, Sharif Nasir, and their force of Bedouin raiders captured Al Aqabah and the Turkish garrison. The Turkish forces consisted of a few hundred bored soldiers who were very glad of the opportunity to surrender to fellow Muslims. Once General Allenby was certain that Al Aqabah was no longer under Turkish control, he began to sweep through the towns of Gaza, Beersheba, Jaffa, and Jerusalem. The Hijaz campaign's supply base was moved from Al Wajh over 200 miles north to the head of the Gulf of Al Aqabah. Captain Goslett was given orders to oversee the supply of the new base camp and on August 31, 1917, he disembarked on the sandy shore that would be his home for the next twelve months. Al Aqabah would now supply the Arab Army's push north to Damascus.

Goslett served as base commandant, paymaster and supply officer until additional personnel could be spared. Lawrence called on him to provide raiding and demolition supplies — one request sent through his superior, Colonel Joyce, included 1,000 pounds of blasting gelatin, as much or more gun cotton, 100 yards of safety fuse, 2,000 yards of insulated cable,

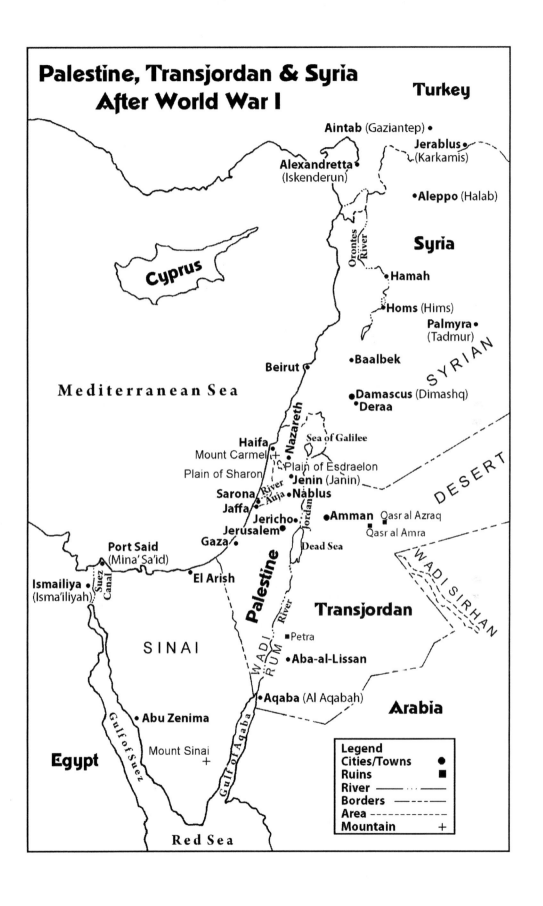

Palestine, Transjordan & Syria After World War I

Turkey

Aintab (Gaziantep) •

Jerablus •
(Karkamis)

Alexandretta
(Iskenderun)

•Aleppo (Halab)

Syria

Orontes River

•Hamah

Cyprus

Homs (Hims)

Palmyra •
(Tadmur)

•Baalbek

S Y R I A N

Beirut •

Mediterranean Sea

•Damascus (Dimashq)
•Deraa

Nazareth

Sea of Galilee

D E S E R T

Haifa
Mount Carmel +
Plain of Sharon

Plain of Esdraelon

•Jenin (Janin)

Sarona •
Jaffa •

River Auja

•Nablus

Jericho •

•Amman

Qasr al Azraq ■

Jerusalem •

Qasr al Amra ■

Gaza •

Jordan River

Dead Sea

W A D I S I R H A N

Port Said
(Mina' Sa'id)

Palestine

Ismailiya •
(Isma'iliyah)

Suez Canal

El Arish •

Jordan River

Transjordan

WADI RUM

■ Petra

S I N A I

•Aba-al-Lissan

•Aqaba (Al Aqabah)

Arabia

•Abu Zenima

Gulf of Aqaba

Gulf of Suez

Egypt

Mount Sinai
+

Legend
Cities/Towns	●
Ruins	■
River	——
Borders	- - - -
Area	- - - - -
Mountain	+

Red Sea

200 electric detonators, 31 pounds of adhesive tape, clasp knives, wire cutters, tenon saws, two Lewis guns, and rations and ammunition for two months.[12] Goslett was efficiently obliging — he and Lawrence came to regard each other highly and their friendship continued after the war. The London businessman was also an avid photographer and brought his box camera on campaign, taking numerous photographs of Lawrence and the military encampments.* Goslett's deft management of the supply difficulties at both Al Wajh and Al Aqabah earned him two mentions in *Official Despatches*— the publication devoted to campaign news and the promotions, awards, and honors of serving officers.

A little way beyond the gently curving beach, amidst a grove of small palms and bushes was Goslett's supply depot. Al Aqabah was a shallow water port and supplies had to be unloaded from the HMS *Humber* and HMS *Harding* by small boats until piers could be constructed. Once this was accomplished, the serious business of unloading supply and troop ships could begin in earnest. Goslett had his hands full in organizing and inventorying ammunition, explosives, water, food for British and Bedouin, medical supplies, petrol, oil, and spare parts for the Rolls Royce armored cars and their tenders, as well as fodder for horses, camels, mules, and donkeys. His experience at Al Wajh and organizational skill enabled him to sort out Al Aqabah in no time at all. He was a perfect man for the job and Goslett was highly praised by his comrades.

Supplying the forward advance of the Arab Revolt was no easy task. Once the supplies were off-loaded from the south pier, the crates, grain sacks, boxes, and the twelve-gallon water cans carried by camels were stacked in and around the sheds and bell tents of the army. Hundreds of "*barraked*† camels" of the Camel Transport Corps and Bedu tribes waited for loading. Soldiers coming and going on a hundred different errands were elbow to elbow with the natives of Al Aqabah and the Bedouin. There were colored and white *kaffiyehs*, pith helmets, blue glengarrys, khaki tam-o'-shanters, fezes, broad-brimmed slouch hats, trench caps, and all manner of turbans in the crowd. The camel groans and shouts of Bedouin competed with the accents of Cockney, Tyneside, Glasgow, Essex, and Oxford in a cacophony rivaling the Tower of Babel.

Goslett and his favorite Saluki, Snorter, moved serenely through the seeming chaos of Al Aqabah's main thoroughfare, nicknamed "Bond Street"§— seeing that the proper provisions went to their designated recipients, inventory and receipts were accurate, and the inevitable pilfering reduced to a minimum. He frequently took his camera along and his photographs provide an interesting glimpse into life in the Arab Revolt.

More officers arrived to increase their fighting capabilities, among them, two men who had known each other in the southern Sudan, Major Walter Francis Stirling (called Frank by his friends) was to be Lawrence's chief of staff, and Lawrence's nominal superior, Colonel Pierce Charles Joyce of the Connaught Rangers, a tall, unflappable Irishman with an easy laugh.** Goslett relinquished the post of base commandant to Major T. H. Scott of the Inniskilling Fusiliers and was able to direct his attentions on supply logistics for Lawrence's raids.

The British garrison at Al Aqabah would have seen little of the surrounding countryside. To the southeast was the long finger of the Gulf of Al Aqabah extending off the Red Sea.

Goslett's snapshot of Lawrence in his white robes with silver dagger was one of the inspirations for the iconic image in David Lean's film Lawrence of Arabia.

†*Apparently an Anglicized version of the Arabic "barraka"— which means to make a camel kneel.*

§*Bond Street in London was and still is a busy shopping district known particularly for its haberdashery shops.*

**Colonel Joyce would become a Saluki fancier in Baghdad after the war.*

On either side of the town were mountains and behind was the Wadi Araba—the long valley that led northeast to the Dead Sea. The soldiers lived in canvas bell tents and like soldiers everywhere, avoided work and officers whenever possible. When there was no loading or unloading to be supervised, the officers had a fair amount of time on their hands. Sports such as cricket, football, boxing, tug-of-war, sack races, camel races, camel wrestling, cock fighting, and gambling helped pass the time. While at Al Aqabah there was also the advantage of swimming and fishing. While in the Western Desert* the crews of the EEF's Armored Car Squadron found time to hunt gazelle with rifles and machine guns (albeit with limited success) and break into tombs.[13] S. C. Rolls, who would eventually serve as Lawrence's driver and mechanic after the Armored Car Squadron was transferred to Al Aqabah, noted in his memoirs, "Most of us tried to malinger in one way or another, but with little success."[14]

The comings and goings of Lawrence, armored cars, airplanes, and the exotic-looking Bedouin would certainly have been the main topics of conversation for British troops who were bored in much the same way that the Turkish garrison had been. The heat, dust, and flies of Al Aqabah must have made living conditions very difficult, but soldiers always manage to find small comforts and reminders of home no matter where they are. That comfort was often canine. Eric Barrass, general secretary for the Rolls-Royce Enthusiasts' Club, wrote, "In the Second World War in my own armored unit dogs, although officially banned, popped up everywhere. There was always room, even in a heavily loaded vehicle, for a dog."[15] At least two other officers had dogs. Major Scott, who as commandant disbursed the payments of gold that Lawrence made to the Bedouin, kept a small dog of indeterminate origin which the American journalist Lowell Thomas described as "about the size of a squirrel. Scott called the dog his Bulgarian weasel-hound."[16] Another officer had a sporting dog that traveled into the desert on missions. A Lowell Thomas photograph in the Bodleian Library shows a group of eight trucks on the Wadi Rum mudflats, and like dogs in cars everywhere, the black and white pointer hangs out over the door while his master scans the horizon with binoculars.[17]

Captain Goslett kept a small menagerie at the terrace of the headquarters tents. He had a black-and-white terrier named Bob, two Salukis, and a monkey known as "the Akaba Ape." The monkey perched on a wooden post and was tethered by a long chain. Despite the chain, the monkey would frequently come down to torment Bob the terrier. The Salukis were Snorter and Musa†—a grizzle and a cream, presumably a gift from one of Faisal's tribe at either Al Wajh or Al Aqabah.

One charming photograph shows Goslett in a relaxed moment with Musa standing on two legs to look his master in the eye—a pose familiar to all sighthound owners. Goslett is his usual dapper self, although he has substituted nonregulation knee socks for military puttees or boots. Musa wears a rope collar and lead, but Snorter (presumably named for some personal habit) has a proper leather collar but is unleashed. As he shows up in four photographs to Musa's one, it seems likely that Snorter was his master's favorite.

During his brief visit to the desert in 1917, Lowell Thomas and his photographer, Harry Chase, quickly saw that Lawrence was just the glamorous figure they needed to make a story for the American public. Thomas wore the uniform of an American officer (minus rank insignia) and knee-high, lace-up boots, but when he arrived in the desert, he quickly traded his "Montana peak" hat for the *kaffiyeh* and *'iqal,* which most of the British officers wore. For

---

*From Cairo west to the Libyan border.
†Arabic for Moses. Gebel Musa—"The Mountain of Moses" is also known as Mount Sinai.

Captain Raymond Goslett, M.C., receiving a typical Saluki greeting from Musa, with Snorter along-side. Aqabah, 1917. Photograph courtesy of the Imperial War Museum, London. Q59391.

the rest of his time there, Thomas and Chase shot moving pictures and dashing photos of Lawrence. Thomas had a healthy ego and made sure he was included in photos with Allenby in Jerusalem, and posed in costume with Lawrence. He was photographed with the bulky motion-picture camera in a biplane, and even posed on camels and a borrowed white Arab mare.

The two Americans shot numerous photographs in Al Aqabah and Goslett was very helpful to them.[18] During their stay at the base camp, they photographed Goslett and Snorter at least twice. One features the pair who had been out for a walk and stopped next to a small circle of squatting Bedouin, surrounded by an assortment of privates from different armies and a lone sergeant. Goslett has his ever-present cigarette and a walking stick, and is petting Snorter who stands very near the tribesmen (who clearly do not object to his proximity). The photo was mislabeled as a conference between Lawrence's special bodyguard and British officers.[19] Thomas later sent a copy to Goslett who noted on the back of the photo that he was wearing new shoes that had just arrived by boat.

The other photograph is unique as it is the only image of Lawrence with a Saluki.[20] It shows seven officers listening to a gramophone in front of the large staff marquee on the head-quarters terrace. Colonel Joyce and Major Scott sit cross-legged on the carpet and the latter holds his Bulgarian Weasel Hound. Lawrence wears full Arab dress and is seated on a camp chair in the middle of the group and Goslett rests on a camel saddle with Snorter alongside. The men are wearing a variety of uniforms and all but Goslett wear the Arab headdress — which he never did adopt. In characteristic, sartorial precision, Goslett wears shorts, puttees, necktie, and pith helmet. The men are in good humor and most of their attention is focused on Scott's dog, wiggling on its back in his lap and looking up at a smiling Lawrence. Snorter seems bored and his gaze wanders off past the photographer.

Goslett did quite a bit of traveling while on station, making several trips by ship back to Suez and going up-country past Aba al-Lissan and as far north as Tafileh near the Dead Sea. Snorter traveled with him on at least one occasion up the Wadi Ithm.* In November

The dapper Captain Goslett, Snorter, Arabs and soldiers at Aqabah, 1917. With the kind permission of Lowell Thomas Jr. Image courtesy of the Bodleian Library, University of Oxford (MS. Photogr. c. 123/1, fol. 84) and the Lowell Thomas Collection, James A. Cannavino Library, Archives & Special Collections, Marist College, Poughkeepsie, New York. © Lowell Thomas Jr. 2008.

*A narrow valley running northeast from Aqabah, and the main route for the army's raids on the Hijaz Railway.

Arab Revolt staff at Aqabah, 1917. Col. T.E. Lawrence (seated in center) admires Major Scott's "Bulgarian Weasel Hound" with Captain Goslett and Snorter on the right. With the kind permission of Lowell Thomas Jr. Image courtesy of the Harry Ransom Humanities Research Center, University of Texas, Austin (LR-P420) and Lowell Thomas Collection, James A. Cannavino Library, Archives & Special Collections, Marist College, Poughkeepsie, New York. © Lowell Thomas Jr. 1967.

1918, after the armistice, he was made Supply Officer for the Arab Army. During the military occupation, Goslett took command of the primary supply depot and rail station at Amman, northeast of the Dead Sea, and four months later, in February, he embarked at Port Said for England where he relinquished his commission.

For his service and extraordinary efforts, he had been awarded the Military Cross and the Order of El Nahda from King Hussein — a decoration bestowed on those who helped to free the Arabs from the Turks. He also received the usual medals that were the army's reward for making it through the war with pulse and skin intact. Unfortunately, Goslett has left no record of his hounds beyond the Al Aqabah photographs. Snorter and Musa did not come back to England with him.* Quarantine was both expensive and difficult so dogs acquired on campaign were generally left with friends still on service. Another officer who served with his mixed-breed dog, Richard, in Egypt and Palestine, describes the dilemma of any soldier wanting to bring a dog home from the desert.

*His son remembers that there was a kaffiyeh and 'iqal that had been brought home as a souvenir, but that the war and the Salukis were never talked about at home. I am very grateful to Mr. John H. Goslett for sharing information about his father with me.

He had no idea of traffic. The only time, in our company, he met a tram — lighted, in a dark suburban road — he fled before it up the track, terrorized by its headlamps, while we waited with our hearts in our mouths. As for motorcars, he lay asleep day after day in the centre of the road they most frequented; grinding brakes and Arabic curses announced that they had seen him just in time. He had never seen snow or felt cold. Would he survive a winter in England, or a week in the thronged streets of a town? To take him seemed impossible, to destroy him unthinkable.[21]

Richard was given to an admiring French man in Alexandria and knowing Goslett's fondness for his hounds, it is likely that Snorter and Musa found a home with a brother officer.

Goslett's story is fairly typical of soldiers and Salukis in the Middle Eastern campaigns. Horace White, an apprentice motor fitter who served in an Indian Army transport unit, tells a similar tale from the average soldier's experience. Owned by important tribesmen, the Salukis they saw in Persia frequently rode with the women on a howdah atop their camels. White was impressed with their cleanliness and on their ability to withstand the biting cold of Persian winters — when fires had to be kept burning underneath car engines to keep the oil liquid. "You'd be surprised how hardy those dogs were. There are hard night frosts. You could dust their coats at night and see the sparks from (static) electricity fly it was so dry."[22] Several Salukis were companions for him and his mates from 1916 to 1919 in eastern Persia. The hounds happily rode in army trucks and would occasionally disappear after Bedouin caravans that had bitches in season.*

Lawrence himself includes two fleeting mentions of the hounds in his brilliant narrative of the Arab Revolt, *Seven Pillars of Wisdom*. During the slow process of assembling Bedouin for the raid on Al Aqabah, he and his party were feasted by Ali abu Fitna of the Howeitat. While the food was being prepared, the wait was made more pleasant for the guests by polite small talk and displays of a prized hawk and Saluki.[23] At last, a great meal was served to the hungry guests. From the cooking area, two slaves carried a giant platter, sagging under a steaming mountain of rice, quarters of boiled lamb, and the heads of several sheep. The metal platter belonged to Sheikh Auda abu Tayi, who would loan it to his tribesmen on occasions of prodigious hospitality. Smaller bowls had intestines, fatty tails, and chunks of muscle floating in simmering fat. Seated around the platter, the normally loquacious Bedouin fell silent as conversation during a meal would dishonor the host and his generosity. Lawrence was careful to avoid burning his hand in the liquid fat, yet appear to eat quickly as was expected of an honored and hungry guest. Eating continued until the men were satiated. After the second and third seatings had finished, the children ate from the scraps, and "the master of the tent fed the choicest offal to his greyhound."[24]

Lawrence was admittedly not a doggy person and it is understandable that he would not dwell on Salukis as his mind was otherwise occupied with the business of war. Even though they did not interest him, one wonders if he ever thought of Florence Amherst and her hounds after seeing the Howeitat Salukis at Wadi Rum and Goslett's at Al Aqabah. Florence would have been quite keen to hear of them and she evidently missed the obscure reference in *Seven Pillars of Wisdom* when it was finally published.†

*In England after the Second World War, White acquired a couple of Salukis from Gwen Angel (Mazuri Salukis) and went in for coursing. He started his own kennels but had to give them up because of his wife's poor health.
†By private subscription in 1926 and for general circulation in 1935.

In August 1918, Lawrence and Colonel Robin Vere Buxton's Imperial Camel Corps spent the night at Qasr al Amra, a partially ruined hunting lodge and bath complex. Built by the Umayyad Caliph Walid I in the 8th century, it was an elegant refuge from the desert heat. Marvelous wall paintings depicted people and animals and hunting scenes, including Salukis coursing gazelle.[25] Lawrence and Buxton had much in common, as the latter had a master's degree with honors from Oxford, had been in the Sudanese Civil Service, and spoke Arabic. Buxton was also an avid foxhunter when not soldiering.* They set up headquarters inside and as Lawrence wrote, "we lay there gazing at the vault, and puzzling out the worn frescos of the wall, with more laughter than moral profit."[26] In addition to the frescoes of Qasr al Amra and the Howeitat hounds, Salukis make three more notable appearances in the war — at the castle Azraq, in a Turkish prison camp, and at the surrender of Damascus.

Edward Turnour, the 6th Earl Winterton, had served with Buxton's Imperial Camel Corps and for a time was detached to Lawerence's staff. He was a devoted hunting enthusiast, and had known both Joyce and Buxton in the Sudan before the war. While commanding a depot at Isma'iliyah in early 1918, Winterton hunted foxes both with hounds and a group of men armed with broken polo sticks and lances.[27] He held the rank of major and was known to his friends as "Legs Eleven" because of his 6' 2" height and his absent-minded habit of wearing his gaiters on the wrong legs.[28] In September 1918 and shortly after Lawrence's stay at Qasr al Amra, Winterton joined Lawrence and a *hamla* (baggage train) carrying petrol and spare tires for a new forward base at Qasr al Azraq, about 100 miles due east of Jericho (a day's march from al Amra).† They departed from Aba al-Lissan (60 miles northeast of Al Aqabah) for the 200-mile journey to Azraq. It took two days for the Model T Ford and Rolls-Royce tenders to make the journey.§ The English had not had a chance to wash since leaving Al Aqabah and Lawrence promised the men good bathing at the Azraq springs when they arrived.

From the surrounding lava rocks and pale-pink desert, the green tamarisk trees, palms, and bullrushes of the Azraq oasis beckoned to the men. On a hill above the oasis rose the empty castle where Romans as well as the Ghassanid Arabs had been garrisoned. Having once proved useful to ancient armies, it was again called into service and became a base and airfield for the strike at Damascus. Lawrence thought Azraq to be quite wonderful and despite the plague of ravenous insects, he dreamed idly about retiring there — until it became spoiled by overcrowding with troops, stores, and airplanes. Lawrence wrote in *Seven Pillars of Wisdom* how they listened to strange noises at night, which Ibn Bani of the Serahin proclaimed to be the ghostly hounds of the Beni Hilal, roaming the six towers of the castle in search of their ancient masters. Lawrence noted that whatever it was that made the eerie keening — jackals, wolves, hyena, or spectral Salukis — they did an effective job of keeping interlopers away from the castle at night.[29] Winterton was quite intrigued with this phenomenon and in an article for *Blackwood's* magazine, he wrote:

> This castle of Azrak [*sic*] was once the property of an Arab prince, so L. (Lawrence) informed me, famous for his love of hunting and pack of hunting-dogs, probably the local Selugi Greyhounds, who hunt by sight only, and there is a local tradition that their spirits

*Buxton would become the joint huntmaster for the Bicester and Warden Hill Hounds between 1939 and 1946.
†Lady Anne and Wilfrid Blunt acquired their second Saluki near Qasr al Azraq.
§It is interesting to note that the only two vehicles that could reliably handle the adverse conditions of the desert were the Model T Ford (known as "galloping bedsteads") and the Rolls-Royce — opposite ends of the existing automobile spectrum.

howl round the castle at nights. I must confess I never heard them, though it would have been most appropriate that I, who happen to be what the Arabs would call 'a keeper of hunting-dogs,' on another continent, should have heard these spirit-hounds acclaiming the haunts of their earthly existence.[30]

Despite what one might expect from a self-proclaimed sportsman, Lord Winterton later tried his hand at machine-gunning gazelles after he and Lawrence attempted a demolition raid near Mafrak. The swift and wary gazelles bested the sporting peer much as they had with Driver S. C. Rolls, and Winterton wrote about it with good humor.

> However, on this occasion, owing to a gun and a machine-gun post, we failed to reach the railway. We had to back out of action, and the cars sustained some minor damage from the bullets, and, so far as I know, we killed no Turks; moreover, with that brutal love that the Englishman has for killing *something* before breakfast, we tried to murder a gazelle or two on the way back by pursuing and machine-gunning a herd, and again failed to score a hit. I have never seen any buck go such a pace. Indeed they entirely outstripped us, and at last vanished into a mirage.[31]

The ghostly hounds of Azraq notwithstanding, it was to be "the Yozgat Hunt Club" which provided probably the most unusual appearance of Salukis in a military endeavor during the Great War.

Major Charles Hugh Stockley of the 66th Punjabis was taken prisoner when the besieged forces at Kut-al-Amara surrendered in April 1916. The men were brutally marched north out of Mesopotamia and subjected to beatings, starvation, and even murder on the road. Stockley and one group of officers survived the march to be sent through two prison camps, finally ending up at Yozgat, deep inside Turkey.* There, he found that the eighty British officers had four Salukis and the camp commander permitted thirty men at a time to hunt, as they had given their parole not to escape while out with the hounds. While they had pledged not to escape while hunting, the rest of their time was fair game. The "Yozgat Hunt Club" provided not only diversion for the prisoners, but helped to conceal a mass escape.

In the spring and summer of 1918, the hunters met from 4:00 A.M. to 9:00 A.M. on Mondays and Thursdays, and followed the hunt with a bath, breakfast, and endless discussion of the morning's escapades and game. The Turkish guards even allowed the prisoners to increase the pack, and the officers pooled their meager funds to purchase another dog and bitch — the female being a "lemon-pied" smooth. They hunted in the stony hills and valleys surrounding the camp for hares and, more rarely, foxes. The only occasion that they returned empty handed was the one time that the master wore a homemade, reddish coat — which allegedly so surprised the hounds that they could not concentrate on their business.[32]

Stockley was an experienced big-game hunter, but his experience with the Yozgat Salukis was unique.† The prison camp hounds were very much appreciated by the British inmates for they were good hunters, clean, and affectionate. Coursing was blessed relief from the tedium of prison life and, as Stockley wrote for *Dog World*, "The sport shown by these Salukis was a very great boon to the camp as a whole, and was of a much higher class than expected."[33] The hunters would form a walk-up line about 200 yards long and, moving forward, would generally slip the hounds in couples, sometimes four at a time. The smooth bitch excelled at

*About 100 miles east of Ankara.
†*Stockley was an expert on hunting in India and was an accomplished photographer. After the war, he wrote four books and contributed regularly on a variety of topics to weekly and monthly magazines in England, Africa, and India.*

coursing and was known for her speed and stamina on the hills, having once killed an Anatolian fox and a hare in two successive courses on one of her first hunts. On one occasion, a fox that she was chasing vanished from the sight of man and hound. Using her nose, she found the quarry by scent and eventually made the kill. As the rough ground frequently tore up the hounds' feet, it was rare that all six were fit for hunting at the same time. One area was so rugged and precipitous that the club dubbed it "Hades."[34] Stockley thought the Salukis were exceptionally keen and tough for they always finished a course despite badly cut up feet — frequently having to be carried home by the officers.

While the officer-prisoners of Yozgat had given their word of honor not to escape while hunting, other opportunities were fair game. A plan was devised for twenty-five officers and one orderly in six groups to break out and follow various routes out of Turkey. Knowing that they had anywhere from 100 to 450 miles to walk (depending on their route), for months before the escape, coursing provided a convenient cover for testing their boots and kit and building strength and endurance for the long walk before them. Additionally, it gave the men chances to map the immediate area and better plan their escape routes. The regular hunts with the Salukis provided one final cover for the escapees. The break was planned for a moonlit Wednesday night, for they knew that the usual early morning coursing on Thursday would further delay roll call and the eventual detection of their absence. They had in fact a six and a half hour head start before the Turks realized that one third of their prisoners were missing. Major Stockley and sixteen others were eventually recaptured, but after thirty-six days at large, eight officers made it to Cyprus and were home in another month. When Stockley finally returned to England at the end of the war, he brought the souvenir brush of the Anatolian fox killed by the smooth bitch.

Damascus was a jewel of cities. It is believed to be the oldest continuously occupied city in the world and gave its name to damask cloth and Damascus steel swords. A major caravan center, it had been occupied by nearly every army in the ancient world. In the mid–7th century, Damascus became the seat of the Arab Caliphate until it was moved to Baghdad. It was the most prominent city in Syria and Christians, Jews, and Muslims always managed to live reasonably amicably together there. For the last four hundred years, it had been ruled by the Ottoman Empire and it was in a sorry state when it finally surrendered.

Crumbling walls and houses dotted the streets and the fine old mosque was suffering from neglect and decay. The Turks and Germans had evacuated, leaving the wreckage of their army and those sick with malaria, typhus, dysentery, or smallpox behind. Human and animal corpses were intermingled with the dying — choking the filthy streets and river. Rats and mongrels boldly took to the streets in search of food, and the poorer inhabitants of the city were in rags and starving while children died in droves. The hospitals overflowed with the sick and municipal services were erratic at best.[35] Arab troops looted like there was no tomorrow and it took two days for the chaos to die down. With the Australian Mounted Division installed as a police force, order in Damascus was gradually restored.

As Lawrence's chief of staff, Major Stirling assisted in stirring up the Bedouin and waging guerrilla warfare against the Turks. Stirling's military experience (Boer War, Egypt, the Sudan, Gallipoli, and Palestine), fluency in Arabic, and consummate diplomatic skills made him ideally suited to the job, so much so that Lawrence called him "Stirling the Suave." On the day Damascus capitulated, October 1, 1918, Stirling and Lawrence had motored into

Damascus under a shower of petals and attar of roses. They quickly set up a provisional government, subdued a tremendous amount of looting and unrest, put down a pro–Algerian fracas, drove through the city to demonstrate the new authority, organized the restoration of electricity, sanitation, food, civil services, and the fire brigade.[36] They must have had a very busy time of it indeed, yet somewhere in that long day, Stirling, resplendent in his uniform and *kaffiyeh*, and holding a cigar, found time to have a steam bath and pose with a white Saluki bitch for a photograph.*

About the Saluki, there is no information other than that which the photo provides. She wears a wide leather collar and is in good weight and condition. Very typical of the breed, she would do well in the show ring today. It is curious that Stirling, a self-professed dog lover, does not mention either this Saluki or Goslett's pair (which he had seen at Al Aqabah) in his autobiography, where he does describe a gift Saklawi Jadran mare from Faisal, his batman's Springer Spaniels, and his wife Mary's dogs. He even writes how Mary could not abide his name "Frank" and for the rest of their lives together called him "Michael," after her favorite Sealyham Terrier. The ultimate validation to the importance of dogs in Stirling's life may be seen in his remark that it was widely known that "the Stirlings lived in their own house by kind consent of their animals."[37]

So, the white Saluki did not come with Stirling and Lawrence in their Rolls-Royce — it had to have belonged to someone in Damascus. With terrible living conditions before the surrender, such a fine specimen of the breed could only have been kept by one of the city's wealthy sportsmen. Stirling had posed with the borrowed hound in much the same way that tourists have posed on camels by the pyramids since the advent of Cook's Tours and portable cameras. The interlude lasted only a few minutes and Stirling went back to helping Lawrence setting up the provisional government and mopping up the last enemy resistance.

Regrouping near Damascus was an Indian cavalry division whose active strength had been severely reduced because of fever. Part of that division was the 19th Lancers Regiment (Fane's Horse). The 19th and several other Indian cavalry regiments had seen action at the front in Europe even though the effectiveness of mounted troops had been severely limited in the mire of shell-scarred No-Man's-Land. Among their officers was Major Frederick Fitzhugh Lance, a family man who had a distinguished Army career on the North-West Frontier. After three years in France, the 19th was sent to Palestine to join the Egyptian Expeditionary Force and lend strength to the capture of Damascus. This strategic decision would prove to have far-reaching consequences for the Saluki breed in England.

This photograph appeared in Stirling's autobiography Safety Last *and was sold at auction by Christie's along with his medals — two Distinguished Service Orders and Military Cross — and other material in 1989.*

11

The Bengal Lancer

"An exceptionally fast and clever coursing dog ... the fastest dog I ever struck."
Brigadier General Lance

In the same year that Luman and Ayesha first arrived at Didlington Hall, Frederick Fitzhugh Lance graduated from the Royal Military College at Sandhurst. Born on December 8, 1873, he was the second son of Lt. General Sir Frederick Lance, an old campaigner from India who had seen forty-eight years of hard service in both the infantry and cavalry. By the time he retired, Lt. General Lance had a chest full of medals and had the scars of two nearly fatal wounds — on one occasion, his horse being shot from under him during the Indian Mutiny.* Three of his four sons, Frederick, Henry William, and Charles Francis, chose military careers.

Young Lance had been at Clifton College, near Bristol, prior to Sandhurst and his education at the latter included military engineering and law, topography, tactics, languages, drill, fencing, riding, musketry, and gymnastics. Lance had grown up in the saddle and as a cadet was encouraged to ride with the local hunts. The horsemanship skills for hunting or waging war have much in common and any officer worth his salt rode to hounds. At Sandhurst, life could be very easy for the cadets and they could readily arrange Saturdays off to go hunting or partake of other amusements. After graduation, his father's connections helped to secure a post, which promised ample opportunity for advancement. In 1896 at the age of twenty-three, Frederick Lance joined the 19th Bengal Lancers, also known as Fane's Horse,† and packed his trunks for the long voyage to India and overland journey to wild Baluchistan on the North-West Frontier.

Lance was 5'7½" and had ramrod straight posture. He had an intense gaze and in his early army years sported the de rigueur cavalry mustache with waxed points, but later adopted a neatly trimmed, more natural style. His light-brown, wavy hair began receding at an early age and in a time when gentlemen nearly always wore hats, there are few photographs of him without one. Like many men of the period he smoked a pipe and cigarettes. His regiment had a handsome dress uniform of dark blue with French gray facings (light blue) and silver lace. Being an Indian regiment, the officers wore both the British uniform with cork

---

*From 1857 to 1858, large numbers of Sepoys or Indian troops rose in rebellion against the British Raj. Many factors are cited as cause for the initial mutiny, but it is generally accepted that British misunderstanding of religious and caste issues were the primary tinder. Many Sepoy troops remained loyal and fought with British regiments against the mutineers. The year long conflict was particularly bloody with both sides inflicting horrible retaliations on both soldier and civilian.
†Named after Lt. Fane, who raised the regiment in 1860.

helmet or the *kurta** with chain-mail epaulettes and blue, white, and gray *lungi* or turban, wound in Rajput style. Lance was a smart dresser and looked very dashing in all of his uniforms.

British cavalry tactics had changed little since the Crimean War or even Waterloo. Regiments such as the Horse Guards, Scots Greys, and various dragoons were heavy cavalry—large horses and large men (often wearing breastplates and helmets)—were shock troops used to break an infantry formation or roll up an enemy's flank. The dashing hussars, light dragoons, and lancers were light cavalry and specialized in scouting, probing, harassing flanks, and pursuing enemy over broken ground where roads cannot go. Only the more agile light cavalry could be effective in the rough terrain of the North-West Frontier.

During his time in India, the 19th had duty at several stations in the Baluchistan and Punjab border regions. The troopers were a tough mixture of the martial people of India—proud Sikhs, Dogras, Punjabi Muslims, and Pathans. In the 19th Lancers, all but one of the four squadrons (each composed of two troops of approximately 80 men each) were homogeneous with respect to ethnicity and religion. Ever since the Indian Mutiny forty years before, it was common practice to mix the ethnic composition of a native regiment under the theory that a mutiny would be that much more difficult to organize. Any officer who wanted to be a *pukka*† leader in his regiment needed to understand and respect the different religious and cultural practices of Hindus, Sikhs, and Muslims, as well as being able to speak their languages.

Urdu was the standard language of the military in India but the hill tribes spoke Pushtu, so officers had to pass tests in at least one of the two. Lance had passable Urdu, but quickly grew fluent in Pushtu, which not only helped gain him the respect of his men but gave him extra pay after passing the language examination. He also passed the exams for marks-

The dashing Captain Frederick Lance (ca. 1903) of the nineteenth Bengal Lancers, wearing both his Boer War medals. Published in *Saluki Heritage*, 1983.

**A comfortable native tunic.*
†*Good or genuine.*

manship, heliograph signaling, and proficiency with the new Maxim machine gun. Much time was spent polishing his riding and swordsmanship skills, as well as perfecting his technique with the 9-foot lance — the distinctive weapon of lancer regiments which had to be handled dexterously while riding at all speeds. Certain sports such as tent-pegging and pig sticking were considered to be viable forms of military training, so spearing tent pegs and wild boars served as both lance practice and entertainment.

The lancers were superb horsemen, good fighters, and, having sworn allegiance to the Raj, fiercely loyal. Despite three different religions, the men were respectful of each other and there was a genuine comradeship among them. During World War I, a patrol of Sikhs and Muslims were captured by Turks in Palestine, and the Sikhs would have been killed on the spot as unbelievers had it not been for the intervention of their Muslim corporal. Solemnly taking his oath on the Holy Qur'an, he explained that the odd-looking Sikhs were in fact from his country, as good as Muslims, and therefore should be treated as prisoners of war. The Sikhs were spared and the whole platoon managed to escape the following day.[1]

Like the American West in the 19th century, service on the North-West Frontier was a proving ground for the British Army. The Pathans, Baluchis, Afridis, and Afghanis were tough, self-reliant, and clever in whatever trade they turned their hands to. On the North-West Frontier, if they chose not to be soldiers, they made excellent bandits and guerrillas. Modern rifles like the magazine-equipped, Lee-Enfield cavalry carbine were great prizes and the tribesmen excelled at stealing them — even when chained or strapped to a sleeping solider. Hit-and-run raids on villages and towns were difficult to stop as the bandits could disappear into the steep and rocky terrain and wait to ambush the ponderous troop movements. Because the bandits were not often caught, British retribution was frequently limited to burning villages. The cavalry, being the fastest and most mobile portion of the army, was always in the thick of any pursuit and skirmish. Officers were constantly on the watch for signs of trouble, for a looted village or cut-up supply column might be an isolated incidence of brigandry — or the opening shots of a *jihad**, mutiny, or a Russian invasion with Afghans and hill tribesmen as the vanguard.

In 1899, hostilities broke out in South Africa between the British and the Boers. At that time, Indian regiments did not serve overseas and Lance and several officers who were "keen to get in on the show" asked to be temporarily detached from the 19th in order to serve with the Imperial Yeomanry in South Africa. Lance fought throughout the duration and earned both South Africa campaign medals (Queen Victoria's and King Edward's) with six clasps — each clasp representing a major engagement or period of service.[†] The British Army now wore khaki — having painfully learned the value of blending with the countryside in the dawning era of long-range rifles and smokeless powder. Of course, Lance and the soldiers on the North-West Frontier in India had been wearing khaki in the field since 1897, not only to better stand the heat, but to be less of a target for Afghan and Pathan snipers. The new art of camouflage took another step forward in South Africa as brass buttons and white equipment belts were begrimed or painted to avoid reflecting the sun. Even sources of regimental pride such as the colorful flashes on their pith helmets would become smaller and made of drab fabric by the end of the war. Officers learned to dispense with swords, Sam Browne belts, and other dis-

---

*Literally "struggle" but often used to mean a "holy war."

†As Queen Victoria died before the war ended, her son and successor, Edward VII, issued his South Africa medal for those serving in the last eighteen months of the war.

tinctive symbols of rank, for these would attract the attention of Boer snipers who always tried to kill the officers first.

Serving officers in South Africa continued to hunt despite the war, with or without official approval. Captain Gardyne of the 2nd Gordon Highlanders recalled making "wholly irregular" requests for leave to go hunting, and each time his commanding officer allowed him to go, with offers of help if needed.[2] While pursuing Boer commandos on long treks across the grassy veldt, there were lulls where officers could indulge themselves and put fresh meat in the pot. In the absence of hounds, the Yeomanry pursued springbok on horseback and shot them with revolvers.[3] It was not at all uncommon for mounted troops to acquire "long dogs"* and hunt whatever game was put up on their marches across the veldt. Purebred hounds and lurchers were both used — Lance himself hunted the Steenbok and springbok antelopes and other quarry with greyhounds during the war. He survived the war, apparently unscathed and evidently with a good deal of military glory and more hunting experience. At the end of hostilities in 1902 he was promoted to captain and returned to Ambala in the Punjab.

Officers' duties in peacetime were never arduous or time-consuming — even on the frontier. There was ample time for picnics, dances, theatricals, card games, and athletic competitions, including polo, gymkhanas, foxhunting, big-game hunting, paper chases, and the lancer specialties of spearing tent pegs at the gallop and hunting wild boar. Pig sticking was a rough-and-tumble sport which took great riding skill and supreme nerve, for there was always the risk of serious injury or death to horse and rider by a fall or a boar's tusks. All these were major attractions and excellent opportunities for personal glory as well as military training. According to family tradition, while at Sandhurst Lance had won "The Saddle," a pentathlon-style riding contest. While accounted a good horseman, he never managed to win any of the 19th's riding competitions.

The Englishmen's fondness for dogs came with them to India. Dog shows were a regular occurrence and held under the auspices of the Indian Kennel Club at Jullundur, near Lahore. The Rev. H. W. Bush (Florence Amherst's chief competition as an authority on eastern hounds) was quite active in dog affairs in India and wrote frequently for the *Indian Kennel Club Gazette*. The Lahore show in December was a large attraction and special prizes included the Dobson Trophy for Best Dog Imported into India and the Dholpur Challenge for Best Dog in Show. Both were prestigious awards and Rampur Hounds competed with Salukis, Greyhounds, Foxhounds, and Wire Fox Terriers for the prize. Showing dogs in India was a popular pastime, but riding to hounds was really the thing for men and women alike.

In the year of his promotion to captain, Lance accepted the prestigious post of Master and Huntsman for the Peshawar Vale Hunt (PVH). There had been hounds at Peshawar beginning with a hussar regiment's bobbery† pack in 1863 and the purebred Foxhounds of the 19th Regiment of Foot in 1865. When the 19th left for England two years later, the hounds took up permanent residence in Peshawar and a captain formally established the PVH in the Royal Horse Artillery regiment. The Peshawar hounds even accompanied soldiers through the campaigns of the second Afghan War, 1879–80. The army fought its way through the Khyber Pass with hounds in tow and after the occupation of Kabul hunting meets were held. The defeat of a British force at Maiwand signaled a serious turn to the campaign and put a halt

---

*Any type of sighthound or sighthound cross.
†A pack consisting of several breeds of dogs.

to hunting jackal and fox. In one perilous situation, the soldiers were on the verge of shooting their own hounds to prevent the pack from being captured by the Afghans.[4]

The PVH boasted of "twenty-three and one half couples of foxhounds"*— about half imported from England and the rest bred by the hunt. Organized hunting was both a social activity and entertainment — rarely was it ever done to put meat on the table. If food was wanted then hunting was done with a smaller group and without ceremony. In Lance's time, the PVH hunted jackal on Sundays and Thursdays from November through March and occasionally stag, fox, and wolf when they presented themselves. While hunting, Lance wore a white pith helmet with red *puggaree* and the club's scarlet coat[†], which happened to feature the same French gray facings as the 19th wore. Other hunters wore black tailcoats or everyday jackets and the obligatory pith helmet or topee.

There are always surprises when hunting — even for old hands who think they've seen it all. Riding to hounds in the twenty square miles around Peshawar could be a dangerous business — even for experienced horsemen. The ground was crisscrossed with irrigation ditches and streams and one fellow likened it to hunting in Ireland.[5] It was not unknown for crippling injuries to result from falls and in 1918 one PVH master drowned in a ditch in midhunt. During Lance's time as master and well into the 1930s, hostile tribesmen were known to take pot shots at officers going to and from hunts but, curiously, never interfered with the hunt itself. Revolvers were often carried and memsahibs[§] were required to stay at home when the frontier was restless.[6]

The Peshawar Vale Hunt with 42 Foxhounds about to ride out after jackal (twelve years prior to Captain Lance's tenure as master and huntsman). Note the four ladies riding sidesaddle. Circa 1890. *Army Navy Gazette* (1890) reprinted in David Clammer, *The Victorian Army in Photographs* (1975).

*Forty-seven hounds.
†Commonly referred to as "pinks" after the London manufacturer Thomas Pink — an 18th-century tailor who specialized in fine gentlemen's hunting coats.
§English ladies.

Rudyard Kipling recorded a Persian saying about jackals and Salukis in his novel *Kim*: "The jackal that lives in the wilds of Mazandaran can only be caught by the hounds of Mazandaran."[7] This echoed the feelings of the British who considered jackals to be "nasty tough beasts that took a lot of killing," and, as such, were considered by the PVH to be a better quarry than the fox. They were also known to give excellent sport when hunted with Salukis, which several members of the PVH owned.[8] One Englishman wrote of a plucky Saluki bitch in Egypt who "was run into by a more clumsy dog as she was turning a jack which had jinked,* and her foreleg was broken close to the shoulder, in spite of which she went on and killed the jackal single-handed."[9]

Lance owned Salukis in India and there seems to have been several men in his regiment who kept them. He had a large, smooth (featherless) Saluki that was fully capable of running down an adult black buck (common Indian antelope) as well as the Chinkara deer. At 30 to 34 inches at the shoulder and weighing in at 80 pounds, the black buck was bigger than the Steenboks and the larger springboks of South Africa. Lance considered bringing down one of these to be an impressive feat, as his greyhounds were never able to bring down a springbok in South Africa. Lance judged the large hound to be 29 to 30 inches at the shoulder and this Saluki was the only one he had ever heard of in India that could kill a black buck. The hound once accounted for at least fourteen black bucks in a winter's season at Ambala in the Punjab.[10] Lance had spent many years hunting in India and considered this Saluki's prowess unique — "I have seen him do it myself and know that he did it on many occasions, and that he killed full-grown males and not does in young."[11]

Lance's smooth Saluki was not unique in his ability to bring down black bucks. Baron Saltoun of Abernethy, writing in 1883, described his Saluki "Puggy" who had also brought down a black buck, unassisted, after a three-mile chase on the hard, rolling ground of Gujarat.† Lord Saltoun had never seen or heard of any hound being able to bring down an adult, unwounded black buck before. In his autobiography, *Scraps*, he describes Puggy's appearance and highly variable pain threshold:

> I have mentioned on a previous page a Persian greyhound that I received as a present from a friend. He was a very handsome dog, and as good as good-looking: about the size of an English greyhound, and of a red color with blackish ears and feet white from below the knees; speckled with red spots. The hair was short and smooth over his head and body, but on the ears as long and as silky as that of a spaniel; there was a fringe down the back part of his fore-legs, and his tail was feathered with long silky hair. He possessed extraordinary high courage, but at the same time was most delicate and tender. When lead along, if a rough bush or anything annoying touched his side, he would whimper piteously and shrink from the contact; but as soon as let loose in pursuit of game he would dash over the roughest ground, and through thorns that cut and scarred his skin in all directions without seeming to feel them or pausing an instant on account of them.[12]

Salukis or Persian Greyhounds were well-known as hunting hounds in India and believed to have been originally imported from Kuwait along with Arab horses.§ The hounds were used to hunt gazelle, deer, hare, and boar on the subcontinent, and often appear in Indian and

*"Jinked"— a hard, sharp turn at speed.
†*A state in Northwest India bordered by Pakistan and the Arabian Sea.*
§*"Gulf Arabs" & "Walers" from New South Wales were preferred by the British Army in India over local horses due to their hardiness, stamina, and ability to carry a trooper and the heavy load of equipment for both man and horse.*

Persian miniatures.* The Moghuls frequently dyed their Salukis' feet red with henna as both a protective charm and to toughen their pads. Like aristocratic hounds anywhere, they were held in high esteem and frequently given as gifts. His Royal Highness Albert, Prince of Wales, had toured India in 1875–76 and returned home with a staggering load of souvenirs and princely gifts crammed on board the HMS *Scorpion*. Full of big-game trophies, jewels, robes, and fine arms, it must have resembled the Ark, with a menagerie of gift animals which included a cheetah, bear, Arab horse, tigers, leopards, elephants, ostriches, and two Salukis. One of the Salukis died after arriving in England but the other lived on for several years at Sandringham.[13]

Indian Salukis also found a place in western literature. Rudyard Kipling, who wrote so much and so well about India and soldiering, was a great dog lover himself. In one of his best-known works, *Kim*, published in 1901, he mentioned two different Salukis owned by Muslim hunters. In the more interesting of the two passages, Mahbub Ali describes his missing partner, Lutuf Ullah, as "a tall man with a broken nose and a Persian greyhound."[14] Intriguing stuff, but that, as Kipling would say, "is another story."

After Lance retired as Master of the Peshawar Vale in 1909, he distinguished himself for gallantry in a rough-and-tumble skirmish with brigands. The ruthless bandit chief Multan was large, strong, and reputedly able to see in the dark. Making his appearance in 1907, Multan and his outlaws became extremely adept at robbing the train stations and banks around Peshawar. The British periodically tried to stop him over two years of depredations, and succeeded only partially by eliminating many of his men. Despite the price on his head, Multan acquired a new gang and began to terrorize the district again.

In January 1909, a squadron of the 19th moved against Multan. Acting on information that he was hiding in the village of Serozai Bala, Lance and two other officers took "C" squadron six miles out of Peshawar on the Phandu Plain. There were not enough troopers to cover all the bolt-holes around the ramshackle village and the bandits erupted like angry wasps. In the ensuing meleé, Lance's horse was wounded and he took a bullet in the knee. Despite heavy fire all around, Lance's unarmed trumpeter, Muzaffar Khan stood guard over him. Multan was killed and his men taken prisoner, tried, and summarily hanged. The bandit chief's rifle had been stolen from another Indian regiment and it became one of the 19th's prized trophies. Lance himself had three lasting mementos of the fight — a citation for "gallant leading," a slight limp for the rest of his days, and, when he retired from the regiment in 1921, Multan's rifle as a gift.[†]

On July 26, 1910, Lance married Gladys Maud Lutwyche Waterlow at the parish church of St. George's, Wrotham, Kent. She was the youngest daughter of Sir Philip Hickson Waterlow, second Baronet Waterlow of London, who was Chairman of Waterlow & Sons, Ltd. — the famous family of London politicians, bankers, and printers who specialized in bank notes and postage stamps. Sir Philip had wed Amy Grace Lutwyche in 1869 and they had two sons and four daughters. Gladys's mother, Amy, had died in 1897 and a year later Sir Philip married Laura Marie Jones. Gladys was a stocky woman with dark wavy hair and a partiality to

---

*There are many Moghul and Persian representations of Salukis in the British Museum and Victoria and Albert Museum, but Florence Amherst did not write about these until the 1930s.

†The regimental history does not record any official recognition of Muzaffar Kahn's bravery.

cloche hats. Her short stature, signature millinery, and round, dark-framed spectacles, made her an easy figure to recognize. She had a cheerful disposition and well-developed sense of humor that endeared her to everyone who met her. Gladys was very fond of dogs and, as a child, the worst punishment her parents and nurse could devise was threatening to oust her terrier Jock from the nursery at their home, Trosley Towers in Fairseat.*

Prior to his marriage, when Lance was in residence in England, he lived at his father's house, The Laurels, in Roehampton near Wimbledon, Surrey†— some twenty-five miles west of Trosley Towers, Fairseat. How he and Gladys had come to meet is not recorded; perhaps it was in town at a ball or a luncheon, or even riding to the hounds. It was not at all uncommon for an Indian officer to propose to a newly met, wifely prospect while home on leave, with the intention of bringing a bride back to India. In any case, Lance and Gladys agreed that the marriage was a good idea and if they were not in love to begin with, it certainly came to them later. The Waterlows were well-to-do and there was a large marriage settlement that came with their daughter's hand. Captain Lance was 37 and she was 24. The marriage came a tad early in his career — there was an only partially joking maxim which held that "lieutenants *must not* marry, captains *may* marry, majors *should* marry, and colonels *must* marry."

Because of the long periods of isolation within the Frontier garrisons and the time needed to travel between the frontier and England, officers were given three month's leave with pay each year. Many officers were not content with nine months of separation from their wives and brought them to India. There, life was more relaxed, the cost of living less than that of England, and there were servants to do everything. As a well-off, career officer, Lance was able to bring his bride to India, where in short order they produced a family. In June 1911, at Murree Hills, the British Army sanatorium and summer station in the Punjab, their first son Frederick Henry was born but died in infancy. In April 1912, their second son, John Waterlow Fitzhugh, was also born at Murree. The next year brought both sorrow and joy to the family, for Lance's father, Lt. General Sir Frederick Lance, died in January at seventy-six, but another son was born. Childbirth was always potentially dangerous and particularly so in India. This time, Gladys went home to Kent, for the birth of Geoffrey Charles Philip. It is not clear where the boys grew up (the family did live in Bromley, Kent for a while), but they must have spent some time in India. Following both the family tradition of military service and appreciation of good hunting hounds, John Lance would eventually join his father's regiment in 1935§ and took a breeding pair of his parent's Salukis to India for coursing.

In 1914, the officers of the 19th Lancers read about the shocking assassination at Sarajevo in the newspaper. Few had heard of Archduke Ferdinand or even knew where Serbia was — "Something to do with the Balkans?"[15] By the time it became apparent that the incident was more than a nine-day wonder, the officers began to worry about how a war in Europe would affect them. Previously, Indian troops had never been used against Europeans for reasons of prejudice and paranoia. The idea of "colored" troops fighting white men had been too close a parallel to the bloody Indian Mutiny of 1857–58 and was considered to be unconscionable. In short, it was the sort of thing that was just *not* done. But, since the army was perfectly prepared to send native soldiers against a Russian incursion on the North-West Frontier, then

---

The Waterlow family residence. I am indebted to Adrien Sturgeon of the Stansted and Fairseat Society for providing me with a wealth of information about the Lances in Wrotham and Fairseat.

†*Now southwest London.*

§*During the post–World War I army economies, the 19th Lancers (Fane's Horse) was amalgamated with the 18th King George's Own Lancers to form the 19th King George's Own Lancers.*

Gladys Lance with Kelb and another Sarona hound at Wentfield, Kent; ca. 1923.

what real objection could there be to having them fight Germans? The ethical difficulty was quickly resolved, for Indian Cavalry brigades were sent to France, the German colonies in East Africa, and to the oil fields in Persia. The transports carrying the 19th Lancers, their horses and gear, docked in Marseilles on November 10, 1914. Lance did not go with the first embarkation but arrived in France somewhat later.

Fighting with *"les Hindous"* in France made some interesting problems for their officers. Care had to be taken to see that the troopers had their religious and caste needs met. Food that was suitable for Sikhs, Hindus, and Muslims had to be organized by the Supply Department, but to the soldiers' credit, religious proscriptions were discreetly overlooked when starvation threatened in prolonged combat situations. The *lungi* or turban was a terribly impractical piece of headwear in the winter cold and storms of France—its wrapped folds were designed to give protection from the sun but became a great nuisance when soaked with rain. It was not until May 1915 that forage caps were issued and in 1916 steel helmets replaced the caps. The Indian troopers generally refused to wear the "tin hats" and after ongoing arguments, the helmets were eventually loaded into a baggage lorry and sent back to the quartermaster's warehouse.

The Indian trooper and his horse were loaded down with an amazing amount of gear that allowed them to operate independently of transport. Including the rider, the horse carried 280 pounds in all.* There was the standard saddlery, bridle, and reins, as well as a huge amount of gear, including cartridge bandoleer hung from the horse's neck, two blankets, pouches, rolled up greatcoat, a raincoat, waterproof sheet, nosebag, canvas bucket, forage, spare horseshoes, sword, and rifle in leather bucket. The trooper carried lance, bayonet, two Mills bombs, cartridge bandoleer, water bottle, helmet, gas mask, and a small store of rations. Even though there were few opportunities to use the lance in combat, they were carried whenever they rode and *les Hindous* discovered an ingenious use for them as fishing poles.

The 19th were one-third of the Sialkote Brigade (named after their headquarters in India), which in turn was one-third of the 1st Indian Cavalry Division. As it turned out, the cavalry could scarcely be effective in France for there was hardly any ground that was not obstructed by trenches, bomb craters, and barbed wire. A massed charge was simply impossible and there were no flanks to attack; yet the 19th gave their best service at every turn and won six battle honors while in France. When necessary, *les Hindous* left their horses safely behind and fought in the trenches. In January 1915, Lance, who was now a major, led a party of soldiers to extend a muddy trench under enemy fire and was shot in the shoulder and sent to hospital. When he was well enough to travel, he was sent from the field hospital back to England to be reunited with Gladys, John, and Geoffrey while he recuperated. The following year, Gladys purchased Wentfield Cottage (a much grander house than the name implies) in Fairseat, Kent, just 500 yards from her girlhood home at Trosley Towers, and the Lances exchanged their home life in the town of Bromley for that of the countryside.

When Lance was wounded carving out a few more feet of quagmire, it was ground they had been fighting over for two months. The stalemate and attrition in the trenches and ineffectiveness of cavalry sharply contrasted with the highly mobile campaigns of Allenby's Egyptian Expeditionary Force and the Arab Revolt. In the open country of the Middle East there was room to use massed cavalry to maximum effect against the Turks. Lance's regiment would finally see the sort of action that they had been trained for—three years later in Palestine.

In April 1918, the 19th landed in Egypt at Isma'iliyah, with orders to march to the great staging camp at Kantara (Al Qantarah). They were one of three Indian Cavalry regiments in the 12th Brigade. Combined with two more brigades and units of Royal Artillery and Royal Engineers, they became the 4th Cavalry Division under the command of Major-General Sir George Barrow. In joining the Egyptian Expeditionary Force, Lance and the 19th had exchanged cold, rain, mud, and trench foot for heat, dust storms, flies, malaria, and scorpion bites. The lancers did not mind—here there was room to really ride.

The 19th entrained at Kantara for their journey to the front. They made their initial camp

A typical racing horse of the period might carry anywhere from 130 to 168 pounds of rider and saddle.

in El Bela and would eventually march around the Dead Sea and through the Jordan Valley, Jerusalem, Jericho (Ariha), and Ludd — all Biblical names of wonder to the officers. The summer passed with only minor skirmishes with the Turks but in September, they moved north to Jaffa (modern-day Tel Aviv) and encamped in the nearby orange groves of Sarona, hidden from the view of enemy planes. Allenby was preparing for his "big push" on the Turkish right flank while Lt. Colonel Lawrence and the Arab army moved north toward Deraa, distracting the Turks on their left flank along the Hijaz Railway. The 4th and 5th Cavalry Divisions were to move northward along the coastal range.

On September 19, 1918, the attack began with an hour-and-a-half bombardment. Pioneers set to work clearing the Turkish barbwire and Lance's regiment rode swiftly through a gap and onto the Plain of Sharon. Riding hard and fast, they were to get behind the Turks and cut off their retreat and communication lines. Skirmishing and taking prisoners all the way, the 19th Lancers and the 4th Division covered sixty-eight miles in just under twenty-eight hours and at the end of that period, they could see the city of Nazareth. By September 26, Allenby's forces had destroyed the VIIth and VIIIth Turkish Armies. Lance's regiment along with the 4th Cavalry Division received orders to advance toward Damascus, attacking the IVth Turkish Army, which was retreating to Deraa.

By the time Deraa was in sight, Lance and his regiment had crossed the River Jordan and fought two engagements. On the night of September 27–28, it was apparent that Deraa had already been captured by Lawrence's force and the 19th was sent on toward Damascus. There they took up station south of the city. On the morning of October 1, Lawrence and Stirling were driving "Blue Mist" — a Rolls-Royce tender* — and heading north for Damascus with the 4th Cavalry Division on his left. Lawrence had spent the night at Kiswe and was now poised to enter Damascus with the Arab army. He was dressed in his usual Arab robes, Stirling in *kaffiyeh*, uniform, and native cloak, and their drivers in dusty khakis. They were washing up at a small stream when a patrol of Indian Lancers from an unidentified regiment rode up and, mistaking them for the enemy, took them prisoner. As neither Lawrence or Stirling spoke Urdu or Pushtu, it took a bit of doing to find a British officer and explain who they were before being allowed to drive on to Damascus.[16]

The great city surrendered to Allenby's forces and after a few days rest, the 4th Division (including the 19th) began to march northward to cover the 185-mile distance to Halab, this time in support of the 5th Division. In the first week of October, so many men from the 4th Division were sick with fever that a temporary field hospital was set up at Bar Elias, thirty miles northwest of Damascus. Extra rations of milk, tea, and sugar were set aside for the sick and the regiment borrowed cooks from other units and a captured German cooking wagon. The area had plenty of wheat, sheep, and goats but they needed to be collected. Lance was charged with requisitioning fodder, livestock, and supplies from the local population. With years of experience of creative foraging and making do on the North-West Frontier, he excelled at the task.

Years later, Lance would say that his foundation Arab mare was a "spoil of war" — captured from an Arab sniper during the advance on Halab. But in a conversation with a Dutch friend and Saluki owner, Han Jungeling, Lance confided that his troops had been suffering nighttime attacks by ostensibly friendly tribesmen and they put a stop to the raids by confiscating their goods and animals. As requisitioning officer, Major Lance had first crack at purchas-

A passenger model converted to a truck configuration and used for carrying supplies for the armored cars.

ing forfeit horses from the Provisional Army authorities.[17] The regimental history dryly records, "Major Lance of the 19th Lancers was appointed requisitioning officer; he soon had a going concern, and when the Division moved on he had charge of the brigade details as well."[18]

After some rest, the 4th Division was able to move forward to Baalbek, a Phoenician city that the Romans had renamed Heliopolis.* By then, fever had reduced the 19th to three squadrons and other regiments in the brigade were similarly affected. On October 15, the division arrived at Lebwe, sixty miles north of Damascus. It was readily apparent that their numbers were not sufficient to support the 5th Division which was rapidly outdistancing them. The 4th Division was undergoing a reorganization when the ceasefire was announced on October 31. With hostilities over, the British now turned to administering the captured territory and restoring order. During the demobilization of the regular army, it was decided that the Indian troops should stay on for the occupation. The 19th was sent to Beirut in December 1918 but Lance did not go with them, as he had been was given temporary command of another Indian Cavalry regiment. His new command carried a field promotion to Brevet Lieutenant-Colonel, effective January 1919.

Now that the war was over, Lance could once again indulge in his favorite recreation — coursing. In Halab, he found a black-and-tan Saluki that he considered to be one of the fittest hounds he had ever seen, but the owner refused to sell at any price. Undaunted, Lance acquired a small grizzle bitch from the *Kaimakam* of Baalbek — the Turkish officer formerly in command of the town and district who was now working with the British occupation. He never mentioned the identity of the *Kaimakam*† or the nature of their relationship, but as Lance and other officers only refer to this man by his title, he was certainly not English. Lance named the bitch Baalbek after the city and nicknamed her Beckie.§ From a Syrian sheikh near Damascus Lance acquired a white hound with black spots, pale tan markings, and sparse ear feathering. He was named Seleughi** and was a coursing hound of the first water — Lance always maintained that he was the fastest and cleverest hound he had ever seen. With 55 miles of bad road, mountain pass and river between Damascus and Baalbek, and the usual suspicion about outsiders, it is highly unlikely that the breeders of Seleughi and Beckie would have ever come together to mate these two. Lance did not care about these distinctions of type or region. He was interested in good, strong coursing hounds. One such youngster out of Seleughi and Beckie was to figure prominently in his and Gladys's lives.

*The Romans erected a spectacular temple to Jupiter and another to Bacchus — the ruins of which are still considered very impressive.

†A corruption of the Arabic qaimaqam, the Turkish title usually refers to the governor of a district— often the equivalent of a Lt. Colonel. The Egyptian Army also used kaimakam for the rank of a Lt. Colonel but it was always held by an English officer.

§Baalbek's sire and dam were Raak and Naya.

**Whose sire and dam were Kachkari and Selwah. Both Lance and his wife describe Seleughi's colors accurately in their early writings, but later it became easier to refer to him just as a black-and-white parti-color.

12

The Armageddon Hunt

"I have crossed the River Auger near Jaffa with eight or nine Salukis where the current is very swift, but the hounds were not distressed. They swam against the current diagonally and allowed themselves to drift down stream without any fear."

Gladys Lance[1]

Frederick Lance was in Damascus with his temporary command of the 36th Jacob's Horse when Baalbek was bred to Seleughi in early April 1919. On June 6, the same day that King Faisal convened a General Syrian Conference to solidify his authority as monarch and approve his position for the Cairo Peace Conference, Baalbek produced a whopping litter of tricolored puppies. Lance was on leave when the pups were born, and returned to find that his pick male puppies had been named Kelb and Torr in his absence. Torr seems to fit with Lance's preference for geographic locations as dog names as it was a tiny village just southeast of the Dead Sea (his former command, the 19th Lancers, had passed through there on their initial advance into Palestine). It is odd that the littermate was named Kelb, as that is the Arabic term for a common, and therefore unclean, dog.* It seems likely that one of Lance's Indian orderlies or friends must have made the mistake as no Bedouin or anyone familiar with Arab culture would have ever given that name to a Saluki.†

Naming the hound Kelb may have actually been something of a crude joke as it was quite common in those less enlightened days for black sporting dogs to be given the now offensive names of "Darkie," "Samboh," or "Nigger." As a Saluki enthusiast who had soldiered and hunted in the Middle East for over a year, Lance surely knew what it meant but the name stuck — and he even used it again for one of Kelb's offspring. He never offered any explanation as to why he kept the inappropriate name and he certainly had plenty of opportunity to change it. Lance was not very creative when it came to naming his hounds but Gladys would eventually make up for his lack of imagination. Baalbek was bred again to Seleughi and on February 3, 1920, her second litter was born at Tiberias§ on the western shore of the Sea of Galilee, making a total of twenty-one puppies between the two litters.**

---

*Today the word is more correctly spelled kalb. There is also a shark called Kalb al–Bahr (dog of the sea) and the Kalb River north of Beirut. At the outlet of the river there are two large rocks that resemble dog's heads which are said to bark and howl on stormy nights.

†Some Bedouin will refer to a particular male Saluki as kalb during informal conversation in the much the same way we might refer to a purebred as a "dog," but there is no evidence that Lance was ever that intimate with true Bedouin.

§Now called Teverya. Herod Antipas built Tiberias in the first century C.E. It became a center of Judaic scholarship and one of the four holy cities of Judaism.

**Eighteen of the twenty-one survived.

In December 1919, the 19th Bengal Lancers, after other relocations, were back at Sarona (now in the center of Tel Aviv-Yafo), where they had camped before Allenby's major push north and which had served for a time as brigade headquarters during the war. The transition from British occupation to French administration was progressing* and while British regiments were being sent home during the spring and summer of that year, several of the Indian cavalry regiments continued on to oversee the peacetime administration while local governments were reformed. Faisal was now the uneasy King of Syria, as he had to negotiate his monarchy with the French who maintained "oversight." Trouble was already brewing, for various Syrian factions felt that Faisal's non–Syrian origin made him unsuitable as a king, yet neither did they want French influence. Faisal would not stay much longer on the throne that had been pledged to him by the British, and to fulfill their promise, they gave him Iraq.

In February 1920, Lance was posted back to Sarona to take command of his old regiment, the 19th Bengal Lancers. It was a great honor for him to be their colonel. The journey was 130 miles from Damascus to Sarona by the most direct roads and even longer by train. When traveling by rail in the occupied country, a soldier's personal luggage was to be kept to a minimum, but colonels did have their privileges. With his baggage and horses in the separate cars, Selughi, Kelb, Torr, Baalbek and her unweaned puppies rode with Lance in the passenger compartment.[†]

But not all soldiers thought keeping dogs in the desert was a good idea. The extreme heat, dust, insects, and constant threat of rabies or distemper made a hard life for any dog. Scrapping pi-dogs (the outcasts found in every town and village) were regularly killed by shotgun-wielding vigilantes or poisoned to prevent the spread of rabies. When these scavengers fought with pet dogs, the pi-dog was immediately shot and the pet tied up for ten days until the incubation period was past and no sign of rabies present. A person being bitten by a hydrophobic dog had to undergo a painful series of inoculations over a period of twenty days.[2] Sgt. R. C. Richardson of the Army Service Corps was a Bull Terrier fancier and his wife had been forwarding dog publications to him somewhere in Upper Egypt. It was a miserable station and the temperature inside a canvas bell tent could reach as high as 130°F during the day. In October 1916, Richardson wrote to the editor of the *Illustrated Kennel News*, commenting on previous letters about Bull Terriers and deploring the local living conditions: "Since being in Egypt I have not seen a decent specimen of the canine race, and would not expect to here ... Personally, I should be very sorry to bring a dog of mine here. It is not a fit place for any living creature, and should be given over to the millions of flies and mosquitoes, who seem to thrive amazingly."[3]

Richardson's circumstances may have been unusually harsh (or his outlook particularly dour), for there were plenty of soldiers who kept dogs despite the heat and flies. Providing both companionship and aristocratic sport, hunting Salukis proved very popular among the soldiers stationed in the Middle East. The "Yozgat Hunt Club" was one peculiar example, but

---

The Sykes-Picot Agreement of January 1916 had already determined the new British and French spheres of influence in the postwar Ottoman Empire.

†A measure of how dogs were tolerated by the British Army may be seen in the regulations concerning their transport on trains. Dogs were prohibited from traveling alone in the luggage van for fear they would chew up the luggage. As people were not allowed to accompany the dogs in the baggage car, this meant that the hounds (however many of them there were) could only travel legally in the passenger compartment alongside their owners.

there are tantalizing glimpses of attempts at more traditional hunts throughout Egypt, Palestine, Syria, and Iraq. Whenever a town was occupied and permanently garrisoned, makeshift racecourses, polo grounds, cricket pitches and football fields sprang up in short order. Games and competitions were great diversions, and hunting and horseback sports were almost mandatory for officers. Their horse races had picturesque names like the Sinai Grand National, the Rafa Cup, the Promised Land Stakes, the Syrian Derby (for Arab horses only), the Anzac Champion Steeplechase, The Ubique Stakes,* and the Jerusalem Scurry — which were all held under the auspices of the Sinai Hunt Club.[4]

In the post-armistice calm, there was considerably more time for sport and diversion and it was even easier to keep dogs. E. V. Knox wrote, "My company used to have more than a dozen dogs parading with it every day. They had never seen so many men so willing to go for so many long walks before. They thought the Millennium had come. A proposal was made that they should be taught to form fours and march in the rear. But, like all great strategical plans, it was stiffed by red tape."[5]

Hunt packs were assembled from whatever canine resources were at hand. It was not uncommon to see packs consisting of "long dogs" (Salukis, Greyhounds, and sighthound crosses), pointers, foxhounds, and terriers. These mixed or bobbery packs would be used to hunt whatever presented itself for the chase — typically jackal, fox, wolf, and hare. Traditional scarlet hunting coats being impractical (not to mention hard to get) in the Middle East, the Masters of Fox Hounds (MFH) substituted loose, yellow cardigans as their badge of office.[6] Like Lance's old hunt club, the Peshawar Vale, many hound packs formed during the war continued afterward — often being converted to a purely foxhound constituency with exports from England.

As early as 1913, Major D. C. Pimm of the 110th company of Royal Indian Army Service Corps had gathered several Salukis and formed the Baghdad Hounds in Mesopotamia. They hunted jackal and foxes regularly and Pimm boasted that he was the only hunt master to have his entire "field" taken prisoner by the Arabs — although no further explanation is made about that intriguing incident.[7] In the early 1920s, the Salukis were gradually replaced with imported foxhounds, the kennel moved to Hinaidi near the RAF base at the southern side of Baghdad, and the club's name changed to the Royal Exodus Hunt — "Ex O Dus" being a phonetic rendering of the number 110 in Hindustani, and thus an excellent pun.[8]

Hunting was always good practice for soldierly skills and war always provided opportunities for soldiers to hunt. "Hounds Will Meet — War Permitting" advertised the notices for wartime hunts with foxhounds near Salonika in northern Greece, and the same notion served for the troops in the Middle East who hunted whenever possible.[9] There was the Aleppo Hunt in the rocky hills near Carchemish (where Lawrence had excavated before the war), the Ramleh Vale in Palestine, and even a hunt group styling itself the Lebanon Hounds that worked the flat coastal area around Tripoli.[10] The XXIst Corps in Jaffa (Tel Aviv) boasted Assistant Director of Supplies and Transport Lt. Col. W. W. Herring Cooper, D.S.O., and Assistant Provost Marshall Capt. W. P. Armitage as two of the best hunting men in the Middle East.[11] One of the Camel Transport Corps depots in Palestine kept a pack of Salukis which veteran huntsmen praised for their ability and stamina. More used to foxhounds that sniffed out the quarry's scent, the English frequently remarked upon the keen eyesight of the Salukis. Brevet

*Rather than an impractically long list of battle honors, the Royal Artillery simply uses the Latin Ubique — "Everywhere."

Lt. Colonel G. E. Badcock, C.B.E., D.S.O.* of the Royal Army Service Corps wrote, "These 'long' dogs — Seluggis they were — hunted entirely by view and not by nose; but they were almost uncanny the way they'd pick up the sight of a 'jack' barely visible to one on horseback, and off they'd go."[12] Apparently, twenty to thirty minutes of hard galloping after a jackal was typical and considered very good sport indeed.

Colonel Robin Buxton, D.S.O., M.A., the man who had been such an excellent leader in the Arab Revolt and a good friend of Lawrence, was the M.F.H. of the Imperial Camel Corps Hounds at Cairo. The bobbery pack consisted of ten or so assorted hounds, most of which were Salukis. His wife of three years, Irene Marguerite (Lady Levinge),[†] joined him in 1919 and rode sidesaddle along with the other officers on cross-country jackal hunts. Always the enthusiastic huntsman, after his retirement Buxton would serve as the joint Master of the Bicester and Warden Hill Hounds from 1939 to 1946.

Perhaps the most well-known pack in Egypt was that of Major H. A. Waddington of the Hertfordshire Yeomanry at Kantara. He was in his forties and having done his military service in the South African War, did not re-enlist until April of 1918. Kantara was "the biggest waiting-room in the world! Here men waited, eternally waited to go up the line, waited for orders, waited for leave. Spreading sands on which a city of tents had arisen and became Kantara, but after the war the city was not."[13]

Waddington was Assistant Provost Marshall for the "redcaps" or military police force. In the relative calm of peacetime army life, he kept a bobbery pack of seven couples that included several Salukis, foxhounds, pointer crosses, and mixed breeds. Friends, guests, and acquain-

Major H. A. Waddington (flanked by two corporals) and his celebrated bobbery pack at Al Kantara, 1921. *Country Life Magazine.*

*Commander of the British Empire and Distinguished Service Order.
†Irene was the widow of Sir Richard Levinge.

tances passing through Kantara were always welcome to hunt with the pack. As in most military hunts, the men rode in their tunics and peaked caps despite the heat. Fortunately, most hunting was done in the dawning hours of the day when it was cooler and the quarry most likely to be afoot.

In 1921, Major Waddington's pack was still going strong and several officers reminisced fondly after their retirement, about hunts in Kantara. Waddington was highly regarded for his hospitality and the excellent sport provided by his hounds. One of their hunts met eight miles outside of Kantara, where the hounds had been transported in traps and carts.

> We proceeded to draw the first covert at about 10:30, when suddenly a large wolf was sighted and away we went all out along the canal bank; the wolf broke left and as he was well ahead was abandoned. A large covert was then drawn which yielded another wolf, which was run and killed. Hounds then moved on and drew several other coverts, out of one of which two wolves broke; we ran one and again killed. After a brief halt, when light refreshment was partaken of, off we went again; a fox this time provided us with an excellent run and evaded us. Here the Master decided to pack up, and home we went, thoroughly satisfied with a real good morning.[14]

Despite the number of hunt clubs organized in the Middle East after the war, not all soldier-sportsmen were fortunate enough to have a pack of hounds. One group in the vicinity of Jerusalem met three mornings a week at 5:15 A.M. to hunt the wily jackal. Their master was described as a "hard riding cavalry officer whose recreation in life is to chase something to the destruction of himself or the quarry."[15] As the informal hunt club had no hounds, they armed themselves with polo mallets, lance shafts, sharpened tent poles, and a cavalry saber.

During the summer of 1920, officers' wives and families joined their husbands overseas, and Gladys Lance came to Sarona. It was a pleasant station with tidy bungalows and plenty of green orchards. The little hamlet had been founded in 1871 by a colony of German Christian millenarians — the *Templegesellschaft* (Temple Association) — who were devoted to purifying their faith away from what they believed to be the corrupting influence of cities and organized religion of Europe.[16] A central part of their philosophy involved self-sufficiency in the Holy Land by introducing new agricultural techniques. The colonists grew oranges, bananas, wine grapes, wheat, barley, vegetables, and spices, and raised barnyard animals. The occupants had been evacuated late in the war and now the British Army moved into the vacant cottages and bungalows. The neglected buildings were full of dirt and grime and needed a major cleaning before they were fit to occupy. There was no glass to be had for repairing broken windows but good use was made of transparent blueprint paper cadged off the Royal Signals' officers.[17] Furniture for the memsahib's domestic improvements was imported from catalogs, made locally, or taken as spoils of war.

Once the bungalows were fit for company, the customary social calling began. An officer of another regiment, described the welcoming ritual for the wives of the officers at Sarona.

> Clattering troops of "sirdars" rode into stable yards and straightened each other's Sam Browne's* and neckties punctiliously before calling, with gifts of silk handkerchiefs and fruit, to welcome a newly arrived memsahib in warm Hindustani (which, being sometimes a war bride, she did not always understand).[18]

---

*Waist belts with shoulder strap to support swords or pistols. Designed by General Sam Browne to help him overcome the loss of his arm during the Indian Mutiny, it was highly practical and would become a hallmark of the British Army, as well as being much imitated by other armies.

John and Geoffrey Lance were eight and seven years old then and as Gladys does not mention them in her writings, it seems that their sons must have stayed in Kent with her family. Nonetheless, with coursing country close by, it was an idyllic post for the Lances.

Gladys's stocky physique, bookish appearance, and round eyeglasses belied an adventurous spirit, for she took right away to the rough hunts with her husband and his Salukis. While many women were beginning to wear trousers or divided skirts to ride astride, respectable women in those days still rode sidesaddle. Riding astride for a woman was considered to be less secure than riding sidesaddle — although with the former it was easier to disentangle one's legs if the horse fell. The easier dismount notwithstanding, riding astride was thought to be unladylike and possibly damaging to delicate female organs.[19] Making riding even more difficult, women in the tropics frequently carried a parasol to fend off the sun. During Gladys's time in Palestine, it was just becoming acceptable for women to wear slacks or jodhpurs when riding. Several women in Sarona did ride with the scarce sidesaddles, and those who had none rode astride on whatever saddles were available. Of course, the topee or sun helmet was still mandatory even with the new fashion of informal riding dress. In Sarona, Gladys would have maintained the proprieties expected of the colonel's wife but was less formal in her dress while hunting on the Plains of Esdradaelon. She was a hardy memsahib and was as enthusiastic about hunting as her husband.

By the time Kelb and Torr were a year old — old enough to hunt — Lance and Gladys made hunting expeditions (perhaps combined with official business) far away from Sarona to the small town of Jenin (Janin), about 12 miles west of the River Jordan. It was the southernmost town on the Plain of Esdraelon and nestled in a gap in the hills of Samaria. It had no great distinguishing features, but is known as a garden in the Bible and variously referred to as En Gannim, Beth Haggan, and Ginoea of Josephus.[20] There were plenty of hare, gazelle, and jackal in the area and hunting was good. Since jackals were a tough and nasty quarry and they could pop up on any hunt, Lance put spiked collars on his Salukis to protect their throats. With the language of a tactician, Lance describes a fairly typical hunt in *The Cavalry Journal*:

> An early start at 4 A.M. in the grey dawn of a September morning, the field consisting of some half-dozen officers and about the same number of Indian officers and orderlies. A line is formed across the open plain of Esdraelon and the pack, consisting of six Selukis (the lop-eared greyhounds of Syria — Salak Sham') and two terriers take up their self allotted posts, one old dog on each flank and one with the master in the centre, each accompanied by a young dog....
>
> We proceed over broken stony ground, covered with thorny scrub, and though a couple of hares are sighted, we cannot get on to them, when suddenly, in the distance, a large jack is seen making from the high ground to a wadi, and some fruit gardens in the distance. We are all racing for him, but the dogs get a long lead over the rocky ground, and as we get down on the flat we can see Seluki, half a mile away, run into the jack and take him by the loins; this lets up the rest of the long dogs, a running fight ensues, the jack with his back arched like a cat and his head tucked into his chest to protect his throat. Then up comes Whiskey, an imported pedigree fox terrier; he does not wait a moment, but makes a frontal attack and, getting hold of the throat, the rest soon polish him off. After this, nothing is found for a long time, and it is decided to return home, as it is now after nine o'clock and the dogs and horses are feeling the heat. A patch of rank weed is drawn on the way home and a gazelle is put up; the pack is straggling in the open ground outside the patch, but seeing a horseman galloping puts new life into it and the gazelle breaks cover some 50 yards in front of Seluki, who is leading. Then for 200 yards there is a magnificent race and it looks as if the dog would win, as they disappear from view over the edge of a shallow wadi, but the next thing we see is Seluki and Dhole, an old red dog, some quarter of a mile

Colonel Lance after a successful gazelle hunt on the Plain of Esdraelon, 1920. Left to right, the dogs are Whiskey, Kelb, Torr, Dhole, and Seleughi. Courtesy of The Saluki or Gazelle Hound Club; image provided by the Kennel Club, London.

further down the wadi with their heads up. We gallop to them and see two saplings, 'Kelb' and 'Torr,' racing like mad further down the wadi. We cut off a bend to get up to them, and as we strike the wadi again we come on these two with the gazelle, which they had pulled down — a buck with good horns, which had been run down in about a mile. These gazelles are the Dorcas, and resemble very closely and are about the same size as the Chinkara of India.[21]

Littermates Kelb and Torr had grown up equally matched in speed and coursing ability. They were predominantly black with tan and white markings, very similar in appearance. Lance would put colored collars on them so that he could tell them apart while they were running. He could never make up his mind as to which was the faster of the two. Eventually, Kelb's personality, stamina, and coursing enthusiasm made him Lance's favorite. Despite Kelb's affection for his master, he was frequently seen roaming around the camp or out in the hills on his own mysterious errands — returning to headquarters when it was time for food or a snooze. The regiment cheerfully accommodated the Salukis and no one blinked at one or two napping in the regimental office.*

In India, Lt. Col. G. E. Hyde Cates was known for keeping half a dozen Greyhounds in his office.

✧ ✧ ✧

Horses were inseparable from every aspect of the life of a cavalryman and as a result, the subject of constant discussion and attention. Every officer in the Indian cavalry kept a string of horses for polo, hunting, and military duties. Even though "shop" was never talked in the officer's mess, horse topics were exempt from this restriction. Lance studied the breeding of the Gulf Arabs, Anglo-Arabs, and thoroughbreds that the Indian cavalry used as mounts, and after his retirement wrote a treatise on the 19th Lancer's stud farm.[22] His military and hunting background instinctively led him to look for the same kinds of characteristics in a hound that made a good cavalry or hunting mount — a strong neck, back, fore and rear quarters, speed, endurance, agility, and intelligence. Everything Lance understood about horses and hunting led him to choose larger hounds. Kelb was of fair size, and had the muscling, depth of chest, speed, and power that Lance considered necessary to bring down a gazelle. Interestingly enough, the Arabs also considered that many of the same qualities that made excellent hounds could also be found in excellent horses. He was not aware of this at the time, but Florence Amherst would later tell of an old story where a khalifa sent an attendant to choose a horse. The servant demurred as he did not know how to select a good horse. His master said to him, "You know a well-bred pedigree Saluki and its points that govern speed and endurance, well look for those points in the horse."[23]

Lance had kennels built for his hounds — nine or ten adult Salukis, assorted puppies, and two terriers.[24] As colonel, he could generally schedule his own leisure and activities, and would ride out as he wished with Gladys into the countryside along with the hounds and a few troopers to make a hunting camp. Gladys took photos of the Salukis and her husband on these expeditions. With a pipe clamped between his teeth, riding boots, jodhpurs, khaki shirt, necktie, and the inevitable pith helmet, he was the very picture of a sporting officer. The pack consisted of Seleughi, Beckie (Baalbek), Kelb, Torr, Echo (from Baalbek's second litter), Larry, Dhole, and a small black-and-white terrier named Whiskey.

Lance had been acquiring and breeding other Salukis, for Dhole and Larry were not of his original litters. Lance's friend and brother officer Major H. F. Whitby owned a couple of Salukis and they would sometimes hunt together. Whitby had joined the 19th Bengal Lancers in 1904 and had fought with Lance throughout the North-West Frontier, France (where he won the *Croix de Guerre*), and Palestine campaigns. He and the other officers occasionally left their hounds with Lance when on leave and the numbers of Salukis at the bungalow and kennels fluctuated. It was a good hunting pack and Lance would often later remark (as had many others) that Saluki feet were tough enough to handle any ground. Whiskey was a different matter and in order for him to keep up, he was probably carried on the saddle for much of the hunt. They hunted gazelle, jackal, fox, and the occasional hare. Kelb and Torr showed great promise as hunters and Lance would later brag about how the fourteen-month-old youngsters brought down that Dorcas gazelle on the Plain of Esdraelon after a "fair run" that lasted three miles.

In addition to hunting with their own Salukis, the Lances could also ride with the Armageddon Hunt.* This pack had become a formal hunt in Mount Carmel with the transfer of a Master of Fox Hounds and his four hounds from Alexandria in 1919. Shortly thereafter, a number of foxhounds from an Egyptian prince and a demobilized Australian officer

---

*The name "Armageddon" is believed to come from the battle site of Tel Megiddo in Israel.

were acquired, bringing the total up to eighteen hounds and two terriers. Like many of the hunts in the Middle East, the pack had been originally composed of Salukis, Fox Terriers, pointers, and any other camp dog fit for duty. The Armageddon Hunt had been stationed at Mount Carmel, Beirut, and desolate Homs (Hims). The hunt finally came to Sarona about the time that the wives did. Organized hunting meets provided welcome diversion for all — a hundred riders were a common turnout in "the Sarona Vale" and they once boasted of fielding 150 riders. Ladies frequently rode and their participation was noted in the hunt master's diary.

The surrounding lands were rolling hills of springy turf—likened by one hunter to the Sussex Downs, although more brilliant with spring wildflowers. As beautiful as it may have been, danger was always near. Hunters had to look out for cactus hedges with inch-long spines that could kill a dog, unexpected *wadis* or ravines full of thorny brush and deep enough to swallow horse and rider, and the wreckage of war — partially overgrown earthworks, rusted steel shards, and barbwire. As it was in India, rabies was endemic in Palestine in those days and jackal and fox were the most common carriers. Lance says nothing about rabies in his writings although others who hunted in Sarona noted that the month of May was marked by the abundance of mad jackals. Skin contact between a human and a dog that had been exposed to rabies was frequently all that was required to start the agonizing, three-week treatment of abdominal injections — and to kill the dog as a precaution.

The Lances and their Salukis regularly hunted the area around Sarona and made expeditions far afield to new hunting grounds. Lance went out of his way to meet sheikhs and soldiers who bred and kept Salukis. He took advantage of every opportunity to make connections and increase his store of practical breed knowledge and lore. He was on particularly good terms with Pasha Hussein Ibshi of Damascus. The pasha was a wealthy Damascene who bred Salukis and Arab horses. Hussein practiced the common, local technique of strapping his Salukis' waists to prevent them from over-eating and thus getting out of coursing trim. Lance prized a photograph of the stout pasha wearing a fez and a tightly buttoned suit, seated in a courtyard flanked by a black and tan and a white Saluki — both strapped. On Lance's nomination, the Pasha would later become an honorary member of the Saluki or Gazelle Hound Club.

Like soldiers who live and train together, Lance's Salukis became efficient hunters — each having a place in the pack and role when hunting. Gladys noted that they would spread out in a line of their own to work the terrain and always took their lead from Seleughi: "When a rocky mound or hill provided a point of vantage to scan the country, the opportunity was never missed by the scout of the party, who would leap to his position and stand like a statue, his beautiful ears and tail blowing in the wind, and only the head in keenest expectancy turning from side to side to catch the movement of his quarry."[25]

It was the rare occasion when they did not return with a trophy skin or haunch of meat hung from their saddles. The local tribesmen did not believe that Salukis could catch gazelle unassisted by hawks, but it was never a problem for Lance's hounds. On hunts near Janin and Sarona, they crossed the wide, powerful Jordan where it enters the Sea of Galilee and the swift-running River Auja.* Amazingly, the Salukis managed just fine, fearlessly swimming diagonally against the current and allowing themselves to drift down stream to reach the other

---

*Gladys's was the English version of the Arabic name — Nahr el–'Auja. Now called Nahal Yarqon, the river winds across Israel and flows into the sea at Tel Aviv.

bank.[26] On days when it was too hot to go long distances, the Lances would ride with the Salukis and terriers to the ocean just two miles away. Gladys wrote of those outings, "the dogs would sport about in the surf and roll about in the sand, emerging as if covered with a brown plaster. This was very interesting and amusing to watch."[27] Their time at Sarona was happy, and, as was the case for many fanciers who kept Salukis in the Middle East, the residence would later inspire their kennel name.

As leisure time was ample for Lance, like Jennings-Bramly and Major Stirling, he also collected specimens for the Giza Zoological Gardens on his hunting expeditions. It was a common enough pastime for British officers to collect wild animals — either live or wall-mounted, depending on the scientific inclination of the individual. A wagonload of crated specimens to be escorted to the zoo was always a good excuse for official leave. Jennings-Bramly's successor at the Giza Zoo, Major S. S. Flower, was still in charge and delighted to have Lance's contributions, as well as those of other officers who were serving in the Middle East.* In 1920, Lance crated and shipped to Major Flower a lesser spotted eagle, a mole rat from Sarona, and an impressive collection of twenty Palestinian snakes and lizards consisting of eight species — three of which were entirely new to the zoo.[28]

In January 1921, after six years soldiering overseas, the horses of the 19th were handed over to the 31st Lancers and the officers and men entrained for Egypt and the passage through Suez back to India. Lt. Col. Lance had decided to retire — he had been twenty-five years in the cavalry. At a farewell dinner, he was toasted and presented with Multan's rifle — the weapon of the Peshawar bandit whose career Lance had ended in 1909. Lance arranged passage to England for himself and Gladys, and, boarding the steamer at Port Said, left active duty behind. He retired with the scars of two wounds, the Military Cross for gallant and distinguished service, campaign medals from the Great War (three), and the Boer War (two with six clasps), the India General Service Medal, and the Order of the Nile from the Egyptian Government — with two mentions in *Despatches* and a field promotion to his credit. Old General Lance would have been proud of his son.

Dogs were everywhere among the army and *Punch* magazine once joked that there were more dogs on parade in the regiment than there were soldiers. During demobilization, soldiers who had adopted dogs while overseas were faced with a distressing dilemma. They either had to pay expensive shipping and quarantine costs (well beyond the reach of the average soldier) or leave the dog behind. It was a common enough practice to attempt the smuggling of regimental mascots and assorted cats and dogs onto troopships despite orders to the contrary and soldiers were quite ingenious in this regard. When shipping out from Canada in 1851, the Connaught Rangers chloroformed their pet bear and stuffed him in a cask in order to get him past their officers on deck.[29] Dogs were less difficult to conceal and it was easy enough to transport them with the regiment abroad, but trying to bring them back to England with the rabies quarantine in effect was quite a different matter. It tore the heart of many a soldier to leave a faithful companion who had followed his master into battle and shared his privations, victories, and defeats. Leaving the dog with a fellow soldier who was staying on was frequently the best option.

Those familiar with the Arab Revolt will recognize the names of two other prominent donors to the Giza Zoo in 1920 — Maj. W. F. Stirling, D.S.O., M.C., and Col. R. Meinertzhagen, D.S.O.

In 1919, many soldiers tried smuggling their dogs back home despite the stringent laws and watchful eyes of their own officers and customs officials. The British public was torn between sympathy for their veterans and the very real fear of rabies. England had enacted the quarantine law in 1897 and had been blessedly rabies free from 1902 to 1918.[30] It was the recent memory of a rabies outbreak from smuggled dogs that pushed the problem to the fore. Ads appeared in magazines and newspapers trumpeting that soldiers were compelled to leave dogs behind that had been often "cruelly treated by the enemy" and that the abandonment of their faithful dogs was "a Tragedy of Peace." The Society for the Prevention of Hydrophobia and the public clamored for the government to effect a solution for veterans and their dogs.

The Royal Society for the Prevention of Cruelty to Animals, the Army Council, and the Board of Agriculture combined to propose a compromise worthy of Solomon. They would pay the quarantine fees and repatriate dogs approved by the Royal Army Veterinary Corps.[31] The Battersea Home for Dogs supervised the construction of special kennels at Hackbridge with a capacity for 500 dogs, which the RAVC had certified in France as free from disease. Citizens helped the RSPCA raise £20,000 for the Soldiers' Dogs' Fund to pay for the quarantine of any dog that a soldier wished to bring home.[32]

There's an old saying, "There is no man so poor but what he can afford to keep one dog. And I have seen them so poor that they could afford to keep three."* Lieutenant Colonel Frederick F. Lance could certainly afford the shipping and quarantine of a dog. In fact, he could afford three. He brought their favorites, Kelb, Echo, and Whiskey, the terrier, back to England, intending to try his coursing Salukis against the English hare. Lance also paid for the shipping of his Arab mare Mejamieh (who happened to be in foal).† And that was how the famous Sarona Kelb came to England and became arguably the most significant sire of Salukis in the West.

---

*W. H. Shaw (writing as Josh Billings), On Poverty, 1865.
†Horses were exempt from quarantine, even though they are quite capable of carrying the rabies virus.

PART IV: APPROBATION

13

The Stage Is Set

"Exhibits attracting considerable attention were the Persian Greyhounds, a graceful breed gaining many new adherents."

Commentary on the 1922
Ladies Kennel Association Show[1]

On November 11, 1918, Germany capitulated and the armistice was signed. The English were ecstatic that the war had been won and looked forward to a return to normal life at home, but it would take some time for that to happen. The shortages and adversity of war had finally caused the suspension of Crufts Great International Dog Society Show in early 1918 and it would not resume until 1921. Florence Amherst had bred two litters in 1914, prior to the outbreak of the war, and with the exception of one in January 1917 did not breed for its duration. August of 1919 saw puppies again at Foulden Hall and Florence began to think about continuing her campaign to have the breed recognized by the Kennel Club. Help would come from an entirely unexpected quarter.

But Florence's efforts at publicity would not quite get off the ground just then. At the age of 84, her mother, the Dowager Baroness, died at home on November 2, 1919. She was laid to rest under a simple white stone cross in All Saints churchyard in Foulden. Her grave is in a place of honor — a quiet nook at the side of the church and very near the war memorial cross with the name of her grandson Captain William Cecil, M.C.*, and the other casualties of the locality. The daughters were utterly crushed at the loss of their beloved mother. Now Foulden Manor was home to only Florence, Sybil, and Margaret. In the midst of their grief, death struck again. Five days before Christmas, the eldest sister, Mary Rothes Margaret Cecil, Baroness Amherst of Hackney, O.B.E.,† died in London. She was 62. Her eldest son, Capt. William Cecil, would have been the successor to the title, but as he had been killed in 1914, the title of 3rd Baron Amherst of Hackney went to William's eldest son, William Alexander Evering Cecil, who was seven years old — and so the peerage passed into the Cecil line.

There is not much evidence of Florence's activities in the years immediately following the death of her mother and sister. She continued the work she had begun during the war on egg production and marketing for the National Utility Poultry Society — occasionally giving lectures and attending conferences. Between 1919 and 1924, she bred only one litter, which was whelped in March 1922. Florence normally had a fair number of Salukis at any given time, but records for this period are sketchy. Showing had come to a halt during the war and

---

Cecil had been a lieutenant but was promoted posthumously to captain.
†Officer of the Order of the British Empire.

it seems to have taken some time for her hobby to get started again. A. Croxton Smith, canine author, journalist, and her sympathetic friend, noted Florence's conspicuous absence from dog shows. In February 1922, he wrote, "I have not heard if Miss Amherst still has her strain, but I am hopeful that it may be so, as I saw a brace in Victoria Street a few weeks ago."[2] It is possible that it was Florence, but at that time she did not have a house in London and Victoria Street is far from her former neighborhood. Perhaps prompted by Smith's comment in *Country Life* magazine, two months later she put in an appearance at the Kensington show. Florence did not compete, but exhibited two eight-year-olds and their eleven-year-old mother.

Despite income from flower sales, grazing and sporting rights, rent from cottages in Northwold Fen, and leasehold interests in Hackney, money was tight at Foulden Manor. By February 1920 they had decided to sell the remaining Didlington antiquities, certain items of which had already been passed on to the Cecils. Howard Carter knew the collection intimately and as a family friend, was the best person to prepare the catalog for Sotheby's. The Amherst sale finally took place in June 1921 and the last of their treasures were sold.* The Metropolitan Museum of Art was very successful in bidding but the Cleveland Museum of Art (another institute with a major Egyptian collection) rather less so.[3] The 965 Amherst lots realized only £14,533.[4]

Lt. Col. Lance and Gladys returned home to England in January 1921 and Kelb, Echo, and Whiskey went into the isolation kennels for six months. Mejamieh, the pregnant mare, went straight away to Wentfield Cottage in Kent — the house and land that Gladys had purchased in 1916. It was an eminently suitable property for boys, hounds, terriers, and horses.

Wentfield Cottage was pleasantly situated above the hillside village of Wrotham in north Kent. The Lances did not have to ride very far for the stunning views of the surrounding countryside and, to the south, the English Channel. In 1921, the village had a population of just under 2,000 and the surrounding area, another 2,335.[5] There was a pub, two churches, and a memorial altar to the casualties of the Great War, and in 1923, a large stone cross would be erected to honor the war dead. Wrotham had been populated for centuries — the Romans had established a camp nearby and prior to the 14th century there was a bishop's palace at Wrotham. The village's name had come from William of Wrotham, the governor of Dover Castle. The area around the villages of Wrotham, Stansted, and Trottiscliffe† was home to Gladys, for her family had had their residences there since the mid–1870s. The Lances' new home was a two-story house with several bedrooms, and was situated on well-kept grounds complete with lawns, gardens, trees, paddocks, garage, and wooden outbuildings with metal roofs. There was plenty of land to go for a ramble with the hounds and the lovely tree-lined avenue became a favorite spot for a walk. Wheat, barley, oats, potatoes and fruit did well in the rich soil and Lance even tried to grow tobacco for a time.

Mejamieh took over a prime paddock, and Lance set about constructing quarters for the Salukis. Wood and wire mesh fencing enclosed a large paddock and one of the drafty outbuildings was converted into a kennel. Each dog had its own bed in a wine crate on a low bench up off the cold floor. Gladys had the crates coated with creosote for "hygienic reasons"

---

*Including a drawing identified 81 years later as an undiscovered Michelangelo. "Michelangelo Found Stashed, Forgotten," San Francisco Chronicle, July 10, 2002.
†Pronounced "Trosley."

and filled with plenty of fresh straw for bedding. As there was no electricity to the kennel or the other outbuildings, artificial heat would only be used when a hound was ill or the winter temperatures threatened to plummet. Dog owners commonly used oil heaters or lamps to take the chill off the air, and despite precautions, kennel fires in those days were relatively common. The Sarona Salukis had a good billet in their paddock and kennel, but a few favorites, like Kelb, were allowed to sleep in the house.

In June, Lance's hounds were released from quarantine with a clean bill of health and they came to live at Wentfield.* Three months later, Kelb was bred to his younger full sister, Echo, and the first English-bred Sarona litter was born on January 26, 1922. The litter had both tri and black-and-white parti-colors.[†] They would keep three puppies for themselves — Sheriff, Shawa, and Maluki. The Lances had two kennel maids and a groom that helped with the dogs, but each morning, Lance would dress in his day clothes — hat, tweed jacket, waistcoat, tie, knickerbockers, knee socks, and boots, and take a large bowl of food out to the puppy pen. After breakfast, it was time to play with the puppies and exercise the adults. From that first litter, the Lances sold Abdi to Miss Sybil Kerrison, of Shipton-under-Wychwood, in Oxfordshire — who later adopted the "Iraq" prefix for her kennel, and Shahin to Mrs. Evelyn Crouch, of Swanley Village, Kent (about eight miles from the Lances), who was a noted poodle breeder and would use "Orchard" as her prefix. The black-and-white parti bitch, Orchard Shahin, would later become the first Saluki champion.

In February, the *Kennel Gazette* published the registration for show competition of Sarona Kelb and Sarona Sarona[§] as "Persian Greyhounds."** Florence Amherst was still registering her hounds with the fulsome "Saluki Shami Gazelle Hounds." Both of these appellations fell under the impressively general category of "Any Other Breed or Variety of British, Colonial, or Foreign Dogs Not Classified" — where even crossbreeds were allowed to be registered. Lt. Col. Lance was listed as the breeder of Kelb and Echo and in a convention that the Lances would use for many years, Gladys was to be the official owner of the Sarona hounds. Already registering their dogs with the Sarona prefix, they did not formally apply to the Kennel Club for exclusive use of the name until November 1924.

In 1921, there were only a dozen or so Salukis in England — all but a couple of them belonged to Florence and the rest to the Lances.[6] A. Croxton Smith's comments about the Salukis in Victoria Street may have been the impetus for Florence to find others with the breed in England. Equally possible would be the registration of Kelb and Echo as "Persian Greyhounds" in the April *Kennel Gazette* as well as that of another imported bitch, Hama, owned by a Major Bayne-Jardine and named after the city (now called Hamah) north of Damascus. By May, Florence and the Lances certainly knew of each other's existence for that month the *Kennel Gazette* published the registrations of a pair of two-year-old littermates from Hama sold to the Lances and Miss Kerrison. They were listed as "Persian Greyhounds" alongside Florence's "Saluki Shami Gazelle Hound" eight-year-old bitch, Teira.[††] Florence would have been interested in the sudden activity reported in the *Gazette* but may have been wary that these "Persian Greyhounds" were the same sort as Mr. Allen's Kirghiz greyhounds and therefore unsuitable for breeding with her stock.

---

*At some point, the Lances dropped "Cottage" from the name of their home.
[†]Even though both parents were tricolor, the parti-color factor came through from their sire, Seleughi.
[§]An error in the Gazette had Echo's registered name as "Sarona Sarena."
**Dogs could not be registered with the Kennel Club until they had cleared the six-month quarantine.
[††]Teira was from her last prewar litter.

It is by no means certain how or when Florence and the Lances first met — their homes were separated by four counties. They did not move in the same social circles, and Lance still had some military duties. A chance meeting at a dog show in 1922 seems most likely or perhaps an article about one led the other to write a letter of introduction. Florence Amherst and Frederick Lance had very different outlooks on life. She was a nobleman's daughter — a scholar, an aesthete, an artist, and an Orientalist — but with no practical experience of the hounds in the desert. Lance was the pragmatic soldier who had hunted extensively with Salukis in the Middle East, and knew horses, combat, and organizational politics. Both Florence and the Lances came to realize that with their combined talents and the sudden influx of Saluki imports, recognition might now be achievable. The very next year would see five new owners and the beginning of the long-awaited popularity.

Major Christian West Bayne-Jardine D.S.O., M.C., Royal Regiment of Artillery, had returned from the Middle East some months before Lt. Colonel Lance. Taking up his post of Adjutant at the Royal Artillery Headquarters in Ipswich (about thirty miles from Foulden), he brought with him a beautiful white Saluki with cropped ears.* Hama of Homs had been born in Syria† in February 1919, and was shipped to England in late November 1920. Like Kelb, Hama would come to be a significant influence in the pedigrees of English Salukis as she had no fewer than eight litters during her breeding years.

Born on July 25, 1888, in the county of Dumfries in the Scottish borders, Christian West Bayne-Jardine was the third son of a Presbyterian minister. The family was descended from the Jardines, one of many border clans that made their living by stealing livestock or "cattle reiving."§ Christian's father enrolled him in Marlborough College as they had reduced fees for sons of the clergy. Surrounded by teachers and students with upper-class accents, he was eager to fit in, and the young Scot worked hard to lose as much of his brogue as possible. After graduation, he attended Woolwich Military Academy and was able to fulfill his lifelong ambition to be an officer. He joined the Royal Artillery as a second lieutenant in 1909. At twenty-one, the blue-eyed Bayne-Jardine was tall, good-looking, mustachioed, and prematurely balding — a defect which he later jokingly attributed to having to wear tight military hats. A very private man, he possessed a wry sense of humor and dearly loved the outdoors and dogs. In 1912, he served for two years with the 81st Battery of Royal Field Artillery at the Kirkee Arsenal, India, until the European war broke out. At the Western Front, Bayne-Jardine and his artillery battery saw active service in France and Belgium and he was wounded four times, the last time in April 1917. During a hellish bombardment, a shell fragment tore into the back of his right leg, just above the knee. It was a bad wound and when he was able to travel, the acting major was shipped home to recover.

It was not until October of that year that he was fit for duty — although the wound

---

*Certain breeders believed that cropping eliminated the possibility of torn ears in fights with jackal, foxes, or wolves. The practice of cropping one or both ears to varying degrees is prevalent among Kurds but also seen through Syria and Iraq. It may also serve as a method of identification. As England outlawed ear cropping in 1895, Hama was ineligible for the show ring.

†Named after the town where she lived with her owner. Homs (Hims), is located in western Syria, about 90 miles north of Damascus and Hama (Hamah) is just north of there.

§Cattle reiving was often the only way to make a living in the hard borderlands between England and Scotland. Practiced by poor and rich alike, the only stigma attached to reiving was not being clever at it. The Steel Bonnets by George MacDonald Fraser is an excellent history of the borders.

Major C.W. Bayne-Jardine, D.S.O., M.C., Royal Artillery, in full dress uniform, about 1921. With the kind permission of Dr. Colin C. Bayne-Jardine.

would trouble him all his life. He returned to the front that month and from March of 1918 served in Italy until the armistice. He had been mentioned in *Despatches* three times, and won the Distinguished Service Order and the Military Cross. Coinciding with the cessation of hostilities, Bayne-Jardine came down with a terrible case of flu and was incapacitated for days. To finish the war incapacitated by a microbe was somewhat ignominious. Major Bayne-Jardine took home leave in December and then rejoined his battery at Padua where he found the soldiers of his command restless, bored, and itching to be demobilized and sent home. In April 1918, his brigade was posted to Egypt, and in August to the occupying forces in Syria and Palestine.

In the Indian Horse Artillery Brigade, Major Bayne-Jardine served with the Brigade Artillery Column, commonly referred to as "The Column," which consisted of three subsections of transport for artillery ammunition and five for rifle ammunition, initially stationed at Aintab (Gaziantep), Syria near the Turkish border.* He was in charge of two subsections of each and was greatly disappointed at the state of his command. He wrote in his journal, "the battery is a mere skeleton, 37 other ranks, no specialists, and all drivers Indians, and a dreadful lot of horses."[7] Morale was low and nothing ever seemed to get accomplished. Aside from the occasional intact rail line, the transport of tons of ammunition through Syria was dependent entirely upon wagons drawn by mule teams. Life and work revolved around its four-legged recruits — "To know The Column, one had to know the dogs and the horses, everything else hung on these."[8]

In his journal, Bayne-Jardine gives an eloquent and insightful description of the officers' dogs.[†] There was Hardwicke, "a fox-hound of some girth and age often lame with rheumatism but as obstinate as a mule, and self opinionated to a degree"; Hopeless, a "Great Dane by reputation with about the smallest heart possible in a large body"; Moggs, "a blundering fat black and white pointer pup with all the qualities of a retriever"; and Daglio, "otherwise known as The Rat. A small long non-descript brown pup — who got his name from me as he so forcibly reminded me of an Italian Liaison Officer in Italy in earlier days." "[L]ast but not least, a tiny pup which belonged to K." — named Maggotts.[9] Hama had once been part of the pack, but she had been temporarily lost at Gaziantep, earlier in the year.

Hampered by sick horses, inadequate fodder, insufficient and indolent men, military duties for Bayne-Jardine were frustrating and depressing. He had taken great pride in his commands in India and Europe, but this was denied to him in Syria. Unable to take satisfaction in his work, he took what solace he could in sport. Recreations for the officers at their camp along the Orontes River included jackal hunts at dawn and polo in the afternoon. The hunts, Sunday afternoon paper chases, and pleasure rides were made all the more challenging by the large number of irrigation ditches and ponds, which added "gentle excitement to a pleasant outing."[10] Homs (Hims) was known for its abundant population of jackal and hare. It was also desolate and called "the last place that God ever made." [11] During the postwar period, the fledgling Armageddon Hunt was there for a while and years later, its hunters remembered that good sport had been had in the vicinity of Hims.

In September 1919, the battery was ordered to Halab and Hama appears in Bayne-Jardine's journal for the first time. In the confusion and delay in leaving, the seven-month-old

---

Now part of Turkey.
[†]*I owe much to Dr. Colin C. Bayne-Jardine who kindly gave me permission to quote his father's wonderful journal and reproduce family photographs.*

The Artillery Column in Syria, 1919. Major Bayne-Jardine stands in the center with the ill-fated Hopeless, and Hama. With the kind permission of Dr. Colin C. Bayne-Jardine.

Hama was left behind, and at the time, Bayne-Jardine did not elaborate as to the circumstances in his journal. As much as he worried about Hama, he could not leave his command to go and search for her. A month later, he and his men were at Hims, and with the arrival of the XIXth Machine Gun group on November 18, young Hama was restored to her owner after being missing for two months. Bayne-Jardine wrote sarcastically, "and I also collected a white Selugi which had been stolen from me earlier in the year at Gaziantep in Syria, which dog made a notable addition to our pack."[12] Three days later, they were ordered to turn what remained of their garrison over to the French, who were now to occupy Syria, and withdraw to the coastal town of Haifa, some 175 miles to south. During this march, Bayne-Jardine took steps to ensure that Hama would not go missing this time.

The long-anticipated secret orders had finally come for the British occupying forces to leave Syria. The orders and destination were officially hush-hush, yet it seemed that every *bazaar-wallah* knew all the details. The Column was to leave Hims and march through Baalbek to Beirut, and then down the coast to the port of Haifa. In what was considered by Bayne-Jardine and his brother officers to be a typical military foul-up, headquarters had delayed ordering the Column's movement until the beginning of the winter rains. What were once passable roads in dry weather rapidly turned into great rivers of sticky mud. Anthrax and attrition had reduced the number of mules to seventy (just under 200 being their usual strength) and the beasts had to haul far more ammunition than their normal capacity. Preparations for the march turned the camp into a beehive of activity and confusion. Not only did the ammunition have to be sorted out, but tents, stoves, stores, and personal baggage all had to be packed and stowed on wagons. When at last the command "Forward!" was given and the artillery train began to move, hooves, boots, paws, and wagon wheels sunk into the mire, making progress at a bare two and a half miles per hour.

Bayne-Jardine had placed Hama and Daglio in a baggage wagon in the care of Habib, a Syrian boy who knew that looking after the major's dogs meant a ride. Also in the wagon was an Indian soldier who held on to Moggs and Maggots. Even though the wagon stopped and started, lurched and bounced, it was preferable to slogging through the muck with "half of Syria clinging to your boots."[13] Hopeless, the black Great Dane cross, had been scrounging in the camp's garbage heaps and was almost left behind. Strictly speaking, it was not a retreat, but the whole atmosphere was as dismal as if the Column had been defeated in battle. The dogs were a bright spot in the whole operation and all made it to Beirut except one. At Baalbek, Daglio raced forward to investigate some attraction at the head of the moving column and fell headlong into a deep well. No sign of the poor dog could be seen or heard in the darkness, and a deeper gloom fell over the wet soldiers.

By the end of 1919, the Brigade Artillery Column had settled in at Sarona, and their regimental mess tent was brightly decorated with Oriental carpets and fabrics brought from Syria. Bayne-Jardine and Hama would spend most of 1920 in Sarona and Jaffa.* Riding down to the wide Jaffa beach to swim in the ocean and bask on the sand was a favorite pastime for both man and hound. Hama and Hopeless had coursed foxes together and she caught her first hare in February 1920 at the age of one. To Bayne-Jardine's chagrin, on one post-luncheon ride she even chased and bit a lamb, but did no serious damage. In March, Hopeless got into a dogfight and Bayne-Jardine reacted instantly, wading into the melee to separate the dogs. Entirely by accident, Hopeless bit him in the fury of the fight. Fearing the ever-present threat of rabies, the medical officer ordered Hopeless to be destroyed. Bayne-Jardine had little time to be upset about the loss for he was promptly packed off to the Pasteur Institute in Cairo for preventative treatment. There he was subjected to a series of twenty-one painful inoculations into the wall of his stomach — administered by a tipsy French physician and made even more excruciating by the use of a dull needle. During the course of the treatment, Bayne-Jardine did the usual tourist activities — visiting the Sphinx, climbing the Great Pyramid, and having his picture taken on camelback. In his wartime photo album, he would call this episode as "The Dog Bite Visit."

Happier memories of his time in Jaffa included outings with his brother officers, and, in particular, rambles with Assistant Provost Marshal Dudding who kept a male Saluki coincidentally named Jaffa. The men and hounds would frequently go down to the beach to bathe and relax in the sand. In the fall of 1920, Hama had taken quite a fancy to Dudding and his hound, and she would run off to join them. Bayne-Jardine had to frequently drag her home and noted dryly in early October, "Dudding has evidently been petting her considerable."[14] A week later, he had to tie up Hama to prevent her from running off to see Jaffa and Dudding. Bayne-Jardine received his demob orders to go home and on November 20, and he and Hama embarked for Al Iskandariyah. Gaskin, his orderly, had ensured that there were biscuits for Hama tucked away in Bayne-Jardine's kit. In December, they boarded ship for England. Poor Hama was miserable throughout the whole trip and at the end was consigned to quarantine. The cause of Hama's affection for Jaffa became obvious when her narrow waistline began to swell and her teats engorged with milk. She had mated with Jaffa in late October and produced a litter of seven puppies in quarantine on New Year's Eve 1920.†

---

*Jaffa had been a fortified seaport in the ancient world. It is now the southern part of Tel Aviv-Yafo in Israel.
†Arranging for a litter to be born in quarantine is still considered to be a cost-effective strategy for increasing the gene pool.

Hama in Syria, 1919. Her companionship made the retreat from Syria bearable for Major Bayne-Jardine. With the kind permission of Dr. Colin C. Bayne-Jardine.

Now the adjutant at the Ipswich headquarters of the Royal Artillery, Bayne-Jardine could not get down to see Hama at the Cox & Co. kennels as frequently as he would have liked. A month after the puppies were born, the isolation, lack of exercise, and physical drain of nursing her puppies had adversely affected her health. For a Saluki, normally lean to begin with, Hama had lost a frightening amount of weight. On February 19, the puppies were happily eating solid food and no longer needed to nurse — or be confined as they had been born in quarantine. So the puppies were taken to Ipswich where they invaded the officers' quarters and were watched over by Gaskin and Bayne-Jardine. Poor Hama remained in alone in quarantine until June. Bayne-Jardine had been very worried about her loss of weight, but after she was reunited with her puppies, he was thrilled to see her looking "more beautiful than ever."[15]

Used to army life, Hama's good manners made her welcome anywhere, although her propensity for escaping to run free would eventually cause problems for her master. Hama and her family settled into an easy life in Ipswich barracks with lots of admirers always willing to play and scratch their ears. The dashing major bought a late-model Bentley touring car and proudly drove around with Hama on the seat next to him. Bayne-Jardine even took her to a photographer's studio where she posed obligingly for a handsome portrait. He connected with the Saluki fanciers and was briefly interested in dog shows — however, more appealing than shows was coursing. The pair went hunting hare in the open land of Suffolk and Norfolk and their rambles reminded Bayne-Jardine of the happy times at Hims. Hama's devotion was a constant reminder that she was perhaps the best thing that happened to him in Syria. While in Jaffa, it had been his habit to go riding with Hama after lunch each day and these soothing rambles intensified the bond between them. One night after a particularly wonderful outing, he wrote of her in his journal in an uncharacteristic display of emotion, "My queen! my snake, my Agabey dog!"*

At the same time that Bayne-Jardine was in Sarona, Colonel Lance had resumed command of his old regiment stationed on the outskirts of that town, and it is possible that the two men first met at one of the Armageddon Hunts, or through the local Saluki fraternity. Being hound enthusiasts and both having served in India, the Western Front, and Syria and Palestine, the two men had much in common. Like Lance, Bayne-Jardine had acquired his Saluki on active service but knew little about her background other than the names of her sire and dam. When Bayne-Jardine finally registered her with the Kennel Club in April 1922, he could only note "pedigree and breeder unknown"—a common enough situation for postwar imports. Knowing that new blood would be required if the Sarona Kennels were to amount to anything, the Lances approved of Hama's bloodlines since she came from the same general area as had Kelb's parents. In addition to the necessity for an outcross, there was another equally, if not more, important reason for acquiring a bitch. Echo had gone missing from Wentfield and was never found.[16] As well as an emotional blow, the loss of their foundation bitch at the inception of their breeding program must have been a great setback for the Lances. They arranged to purchase one of Hama's puppies, a red bitch named Nurnisha. Bayne-Jardine also sold litter brothers Ispahan to Miss Kerrison and Yaffa to a Mrs. E. Renton.

When Nurnisha was mature, she was mated to Kelb and the second Sarona litter was born on August 20, 1922. It was evidently a successful match for the Lances did a rebreeding of the parents a year later and arranged for some of the pups to go to homes overseas. Other than Florence's early export to San Francisco, the Lances were the first breeders to send Salukis out of England. Of the third litter, born on Halloween 1923, Sarona Dhole would eventually be sent to Bermuda and then America, and Sarona Durra would go to Germany. During the 1920s the Saronas would also be exported to Holland, Belgium, Sweden, and Ceylon.

Using their combined organizational savvy, the Lances began a systematic campaign to gain recognition for the breed. In 1922, Lt. Col. Lance applied for and was elected to membership in the exclusive Kennel Club, where influential and sympathetic men like A. Croxton Smith and Robert Leighton were members. Years of socializing in the regimental mess, staff headquarters, and hunt clubs had taught Lance how to lead and influence people and organizations. He brought these skills to bear in the show ring, and the meeting rooms, lounge bar, and dining room of the Kennel Club.† The same year, Gladys joined the Ladies Kennel Association and created another base of support through meetings, luncheons, and teas. Dog-show ways and politics were not entirely unknown to Gladys, for her aunt, Mrs. Charles Waterlow, was a well-known breeder and exhibitor of French Bulldogs. Membership in the Kennel Club and LKA, and the networking that came with them, were important, timely steps in lobbying for the breed. Florence had not yet made this politically important move and did not join the LKA until 1924 or register her kennel prefix till 1925.

---

*Dr. Colin Bayne-Jardine suggests that his father may have been combining two Turkish words in his nickname for Hama—"Aga" meaning "distinguished chief or officer" and "Bey" meaning "governor"—to mean something like "Top Dog."

†At that time, the Kennel Club was located at 84 Piccadilly Street, a short distance from its current location at 1–5 Clarges Street.

Not only were the Lances good at "seeing and being seen" in doggy circles, they looked for other ways to bring the breed to the public eye, and, as Florence had, found an opportunity to present one to a member of the royal family. One of their puppies, Maluki (a black-and-white parti-color), was a wedding gift to Princess Mary, the Princess Royal,* who married the 6th Earl of Harewood on the last day of February 1922. Both were hunting enthusiasts, for Mary had ridden with the West Norfolk Foxhounds and the Earl was a Master of Fox Hounds for the Bramham Moor Hunt. Coursing became another of their pastimes and Gladys would later write that Maluki proved herself to be very good at catching hares.

In the April 22 edition of *Country Life*, A. Croxton Smith wrote a glowing article on the Saronas entitled "With Hawk and Hound." He noted the differences in type between Florence Amherst's hounds and the heavier, darker colored Saronas. At that time, Lance had adopted the name "Selughi" for the breed and pointed out the differences between the Afghan hound and the Arabian and Mesopotamian Salukis in the article. Illustrated with Thomas Fall portraits of Kelb and Echo, the article included a charming shot of the entire three-month-old litter with one of the apple-cheeked Lance boys hugging two puppies while another peeked over his shoulder.

In 1922, Florence began to resume activity in the breed and registered two Salukis while the Lances registered eight puppies from two litters. Another import appeared on the scene — a bitch called Tazi of Abbotsford (allegedly from Egypt, but breeder and pedigree were officially listed as unknown). As Tazi was registered to Mrs. L. Armstrong as a "Saluki Shami Gazelle Hound," a strong connection with Florence is likely for she was the only one who was using that carefully constructed breed name. Tazi was later sold to a fancier who lived near the Scottish Borders — Miss Aline Doxford (Ruritania Salukis[†]) of Silksworth House, Sunderland — and her name was changed to Tazi of Ruritania. The practice of transferring dogs to other fanciers became very common in the English Saluki circle. Frequently, as in Tazi's case, the kennel prefix was changed as well — making it sometimes difficult to keep track of individual hounds.

Gladys Lance entered her Salukis in several shows in 1922, and after Florence's extended absence from the ring, the dog fancy were glad to see the exotic hounds again. Bayne-Jardine seems to have shown Hama only once — at Kensington in April where Florence also put in an appearance. After the Ladies Kennel Association show in November at Tattersalls, *The Field* published a favorable write-up of the judging which contained a prominent mention of Salukis. Gladys won the dog and bitch classes with Kelb and Nurnisha. Also competing were Mrs. Foster Mitchell, who had imported Egyptian Harem and Egyptian Princess (the first smooth Saluki in England), and Sybil Kerrison, with Ispahan. The breed was now catching the public's eye and with more press, the Lances began to keep a large scrapbook of the articles and reports from papers and magazines.

The Lances' efforts to bring Salukis into the public eye were aided by the popular enthusiasm for all things Oriental and exotic. In 1919, Edith Maud Winstanley of Derbyshire, writing under the pen name of E. M. Hull, published her first novel, *The Sheik*.[17] It was the time-tested saga of the dashing savage ravishing an English beauty and then winning her heart. In this case, it was "Sheik Ahmed Ben Hassan" doing the ravishing and who, of course, turns out to be the son of an English peer. (Edgar Rice Burroughs had been using essentially the same story line in his *Tarzan* books since 1912.) Edith's romantic novel was a major hit in England and later in America. It was so popular that a Hollywood film was made of it in 1921 and a mania for desert fantasy swept the two countries.

The Italian-born Rudolph Valentino had been catapulted into stardom by his performance in *The Four Horsemen of the Apocalypse*, released earlier that year, and he was the perfect man to play the lead role in *The Sheik*. Smitten by the smoldering lovemaking of Valentino's on-screen characters, women worked themselves into a frenzy of worship for the star and other exotic lovers in general. The desert represented many things for Orientalist fantasies: the conventions of society left behind; the lack of prying eyes; sensual heat; the shedding of constricting clothing and the adoption of dramatic, flowing robes; the noble but lusty Arab chieftain; gentle captivity; the mysteries of the *harem;* and uninhibited lovemaking. All these were promised and delivered by *The Sheik*. The wild success of both film and novel inspired Edith to write several more books on much the same premise—*Shadow of the East* (1921), *The Desert Healer* (1922), *Sons of the Sheik* (1922), *Camping in the Sahara* (1926) and *The Lion Tamer* (1927).[18]

Motion pictures were fast becoming a popular entertainment for people of all classes and an easy way to get a dose of fantasy. In Liverpool some 40 percent of the population escaped to the cinema once in any given week, and 25 percent went twice.[19] In 1921, London had 266 cinemas where in 1911, there had only been 94.[20] Costume dramas were obviously what the public wanted on both sides of the Atlantic, and Valentino made another film in 1922 called *The Young Rajah*. That year also saw *Nero, Queen of Sheba*, and *The Shepherd King* (actually produced in Egypt and Palestine at great expense).[21] Films like *The Sheik of Araby* (1922) and *The Arab* (1924) were remakes of earlier works, given new titles to take advantage of the popular mania for "sun and sand" films.[22] Twice in 1923, screen heroine Norma Talmage was menaced in films, *Song of Love* (adapted from the novel *Dust of Desire*) and *Voice from the Minaret*. The latter's tagline summed up the general theme of the genre: "What is a vow to man or God when two sway in the desert's spell—where none know, none hear, where no prying eyes may see?"[23] That year there were also two biblical films—*Salome*, starring the exotic Russian actress Nazimova, and Cecil B. DeMille's *The Ten Commandments*.* Not only was there plenty of fiction about the Middle East available to the hungry public, there was also an increasing appetite for stories from the Arab Revolt and the war in Mesopotamia.

Since the armistice and the subsequent Peace Conference of 1919, interest in the Middle Eastern campaign had grown and articles, histories, and memoirs appeared regularly in newspapers and popular magazines of the day. *Blackwood's Magazine*, *The Times*, and *The Strand* were a few of the publications that carried pieces by soldiers, historians, the ever-sensational Lowell Thomas, and even Colonel T. E. Lawrence himself. Articles such as "The Rob Roy of the Desert," "Storm in the Desert," "Desert Blades," "An Adventure with Arabs," "A Journey in Arabia," "Arabian Nights and Days," "Rifle Thieves of Iraq," "Gun Running in the Gulf," and many similar titles were all published in *Blackwood's* magazine between 1920 and 1922. They also published Lord Winterton's two-part article about his adventures with Colonel Lawrence along with the ghost Salukis at Azraq.

DeMille would remake the film thirty-three years later in 1956.

Of course, not everyone interested in the Middle East cared about the adventures of British soldiers. The press was also full of film actresses photographed as dancing *harem* girls and bare-breasted beauties decked out in Egyptian and Arab costumes. Touring Ziegfeld girls performed in scanty Arabian finery and society ladies had their portraits taken wearing turbans and attended fancy dress balls draped in Middle Eastern robes. Scenes from the Arabian Nights were used to sell "Omar Khayyam Perfume" and "Shem-el-Nessim — The Scent of Araby," and Harvey Nichols of Knightsbridge offered genuine Persian rugs as ideal Christmas gifts. There were plenty of advertisements extolling the pleasures of wintering in Egypt, and Thomas Cook & Sons were always delighted to make arrangements tailored to any travel budget. The time was almost perfect for Salukis in England — the tinderbox was primed and ready — but it was to be a singular occurrence 2,500 miles away that would provide the necessary spark.

14

Tutmania and Breed Recognition

"The paintings on the casket's lid are wonderfully spirited. Here we have hunting scenes full of the sense of speed and movement. Incident and action are manifold, and in them all Tut-ankh-Amen is accompanied by his slughi hounds."

Howard Carter[1]

In the last days of October 1922, Howard Carter began a new (and almost the last) season of work for Lord Carnarvon in the Valley of the Kings. Like Carter's former patron, Lord Amherst, the Earl also had his own collection of important Egyptian artifacts at his family seat, Highclere Castle in Berkshire.* A motorcar accident was the quirk of fate that had led to his interest in archaeology. In 1902, the Earl had been seriously injured in a wreck on a country road in Germany and the subsequent English winter was very hard on his knitting bones. His doctor advised him that warm climate and dry air were what was needed for recovery and in 1903 Lord Carnarvon wintered in Egypt. Recuperating in Luxor, he took a fancy to semi-recreational excavating to help pass the time. Despite only a few finds from his energetic but undirected efforts over the years, Lord Carnarvon remained undaunted. In the 1908–09 digging season, he began to work with Howard Carter, who was still unemployed after the Saqqara Affair. Despite class differences, the combination of Carter's experience and Carnarvon's patronage was to make a good partnership for over nineteen years.

Earlier in 1922, Lord Carnarvon had in fact been considering relinquishing his concession to dig in the valley for there had been only modest results after eight seasons and an expenditure of £20,000.[2] Carter had met with him at Highclere that summer and urged that another season might bear fruit as there was one particular area that had been hitherto untouched. He wanted to remove the piles of excavation rubble from a spot near the tomb of Ramesses VI and systematically dig there—a strategy that had never been tried. Carter even offered to pay for the season's work if nothing significant was found. At last, he was able to persuade his patron to try one more season.[3] Despite other opinions that the Valley of the Kings had been exhausted of finds, Carter was sure there was more as he had made his own catalog of the known pharaohs and excavated tombs and knew that not all the pharaohs of the 18th Dynasty had been accounted for. Carter believed that at least one royal tomb, possibly that of a mysterious Tutankhamun, might be in the area, as promising artifacts with that pharaoh's name had been found in that area from time to time.[4]

Due to the brevity of his reign, very little was known about Tutankhamun.† Toward the

*George Edward Stanhope Molyneux Herbert was the 5th Earl Carnarvon.
†Lady Amherst noted on page 142 of her book A Sketch of Egyptian History (1904) that "few monuments of his reign have been discovered."

Red-and-black-painted limestone ostracon depicting a Pharaoh and his Saluki attacking a lion. Found in the vicinity of Tutankhamun's tomb. The Metropolitan Museum of Art, Purchase, Edward S. Harkness Gift, 1926 (26.7.1453). Image © The Metropolitan Museum of Art.

end of the First World War, Carter himself had turned up a small ostracon — a flake of limestone that had a lovely drawing in black and red of a crowned pharaoh armed with spear and arrows, and his male Saluki slaying a lion symbolic of Egypt's enemies.* Executed by a sure hand, it was almost certainly a sketch for a larger tomb painting — but nothing like it had yet been discovered in the Valley of the Kings. While the identity of the pharaoh was (and is) uncertain, Carter would later feel that the location of the find, the type of crown and the Saluki depicted were clues that could identify the king as Tutankhamun.[5]

Carter's workers methodically cleared tons of rock and sand in the last un-excavated plot in the Valley of the Kings. His strategy paid off far beyond imagination. Beneath the rubble from an area of ancient huts below the tomb of Ramesses VI, on November 4 the diggers found the top of a flight of steps. Two days of excited digging revealed sixteen steps and a

*Originally in Lord Carnavon's collection, the ostracon is now a prized highlight in the Egyptian Collection of the Metropolitan Museum of Art (26.7.1453).

door with the royal necropolis seal intact. The find was unprecedented. Carter reburied the entrance to secure it and sent a congratulatory telegram to Lord Carnarvon asking him to come at once to the Valley of the Kings.[6]

The find was an immediate sensation as this was the first time an apparently unrifled royal tomb had been discovered. Lord Carnarvon arrived in Luxor on the 23rd and saw that Carter had waited for him before proceeding further. The steps leading down to the sealed door were uncovered again and the necropolis seals and cartouches of Tutankhamun were removed. Beyond the meter-thick door was a rubble-choked passage over seven meters long. By the 26th, the corridor had been cleared to a second door — also intact with seals. Beyond this door lay a room, which would come to be called the Antechamber. As Carter flashed a light into a small hole, fantastic objects glinting with gold mesmerized him. When Carnarvon impatiently asked him if he could see anything, Carter is said to have uttered the words that caught the world's imagination — "Yes, wonderful things."*

The Antechamber was entered the following day and proved to be full of exquisite objects in haphazard piles from two ancient robberies. Clandestine glimpses into the Annex and Burial Chambers revealed other artifacts equally promising. Officials and dignitaries arrived on November 29 for the formal opening, and the next day the correspondent from *The Times* wired the first news of the discovery to the outside world.[7] There was an electric surge of interest around the globe, for which Carter could hardly have been prepared. With everyone claiming some privilege to get inside the tomb, Carter knew that with the jumble of fragile objects weak or decayed by the centuries, the handling of one might destroy another — resulting in valuable information forever lost.

Carter faced the almost insurmountable difficulty of preserving many of the delicate objects where they rested before they could be moved to their field laboratory — a nearby vacant tomb. Meticulous documentation and preservation were always his paramount considerations. Based on the finds in the Antechamber and his assessment of the robbers' damage, Carter knew that the other chambers must be equally full of delicate treasures and, with luck, an undisturbed royal sarcophagus. The demand for published details and personal tours of the tomb became staggering. Visitor interruptions and haste were the very things that would interfere with the methodical process of clearing and recording the delicate contents of the tomb. The world was impatient for details and images, but Carter's experience told him it would take many seasons to clear the tomb properly. In fact, it took nearly ten years.

At the end of the first season, the Antechamber's contents had been removed to the field laboratory for preservation before shipment to Cairo. As the Annex was known to contain only a further load of funerary goods, it could wait until after the Burial Chamber had been safely entered. The sanctum sanctorum of the Burial Chamber was where the real prize should lie. The excitement was tremendous. Was there a royal mummy? A small opening was carefully made in the painted wall. Carnarvon and Carter entered the chamber and saw that the royal shrine and necropolis seals were intact. Due to the growing summer heat, no more could be done that season. It was enough to end the work knowing that their hopes appeared to have been realized. The season of 1923–24 would reveal unimagined mysteries and cause a revision of much of what was known about the ancient Egyptians. In a supremely ironic quirk

---

*Prof. T. G. H. James notes that other eyewitness accounts have Carter saying, "There are some marvelous objects here" or "Yes, it is wonderful."

of fate, Lord Carnarvon would die of a septic mosquito bite seven weeks after the official entry of the Burial Chamber.*

The first object to be conserved and removed from the Antechamber was a spectacular wooden chest, covered with gesso and delicately painted with scenes of Tutankhamun and his Salukis vanquishing Syrian and Nubian enemies and lions and gazelles. Eight gold and red hounds, male and female, are seen singly, or in pairs and trios on the lid and sides of the chest. As was characteristic for representations of Salukis, they had no feathering on their ears, a modest tail brush, and all but one wore a decorated, wide collar. Alongside the king's chariot, the hounds attack their master's foe, whether two-or four-footed. Even at that early stage of the clearance, Carter considered the chest to be one of the tomb's greatest treasures. The skill in rendering the images was masterful and he commented that photography was inadequate to reproduce the detail of the scenes, which were appreciated best with a magnifying glass. It was only with close inspection that details such as the stippling of the lion's fur or the ornaments on the horse trappings became apparent.[8] Two of the Salukis are portrayed running, with heads turned toward the viewer as they bite their prey — an unusual pose within the profile conventions of Egyptian art.

From another chest in the Antechamber came an open-worked, gold buckle depicting the king on his chariot returning from battle with his Saluki. To further enhance the embossed figures, the king's ceremonial wig, collar, horses' trappings, and hound's collar are all decorated with tiny gold beads. Evidence from the artifacts in the Antechamber made it clear that this king was passionately fond of sport. Eventually they would find slings, bows, arrows, throwing sticks, model boats and many depictions of the king hunting fowl or wild game. In fact, there were more representations of sport than in any other royal tomb.[9] Carter had seen wall paintings of Salukis in other tombs before and even a few sculptural artifacts. While digging for Carnarvon at Thebes, he had identified a board game with ten delicate, carved ivory jackal and Saluki heads from the Twelfth Dynasty tomb of Ammenemes IV.[10] He named the game "Hounds contra Jackals" and even worked out a set of rules.†

And there were many more Salukis represented in Tutankhamun's burial goods. As the rest of the chambers (Burial Chamber, Treasury, and Annex) were cleared over the next nine years, several other items decorated with broad-collared, hunting Salukis would be revealed. There was the golden fan that had been fitted with feathers from ostriches killed by his hounds near Heliopolis, a sheathed dagger from within the mummy's wrappings, a magnificent bow case, and another painted chest — this one of carved wood and ivory. Lord Carnarvon was quite struck by a calcite cosmetic jar with intact contents, decorated with Salukis and their prey, topped by a pink-tongued lion-figure lid. Carter himself would comment on the many depictions of the young king's hounds, "His slughi hounds are especially included in scenes suggesting fondness of field sport and of an open-air life."[11]

On November 30, 1922, Britons read the first detailed story about "the Egyptian find" in *The Times*. The hunting scenes on the painted chest were mentioned twice on the same page, and while no specifics were given, the scenes were described as "entrancing" and "beautifully painted."[12] The painted chest was briefly described in both *Country Life* (February 3) and *National Geographic* (May). Each time it was referred to in *The Times*, the marvelous hunting

---

*Carnarvon's death sparked rumors of a curse, which would in turn fuel a horror movie genre based on resurrected mummies stealing beautiful women and revenging themselves on hapless archaeologists.

†*Metropolitan Museum of Art 26.7.1287.* A replica of this game is played by the Pharaoh Seti and his daughter Nefretiri in the film The Ten Commandments (1956).

scenes were mentioned and the quarry described. Florence and the Lances would have read this and doubtless wondered if Salukis were depicted in these.

Photographs of the tomb entrance and descriptions of the treasures in the Antechamber had begun to be published in *The Times* in December 1922 and steadily increased in frequency and quality as the clearance progressed. Tutmania infected the world. People who had never written poetry in their lives were suddenly compelled to compose odes to Tutankhamun and editors felt equally compelled to publish them. Women's dresses developed along a markedly Egyptian style and furniture and jewelry followed the Egyptian trend.* Actresses and leading beauties posed for photographs in scanty costumes, and at the Chesham House Ball in February a socialite came dressed in her handmade Tutankhamun costume. Popular dances mimicked poses from tomb paintings and music halls abounded with topical jokes. Cinemas and office buildings began to be designed with Egyptian style and flourish. Absolutely everyone was talking about the discovery, and *Tatler* parodied the craze with a cartoon of a Cockney man inquiring of his friend, "What's all this about a treasure of a tootin' carman?"[13] Carter's fabulous discovery was the catalyst of a chain reaction, for there was a sudden enthusiasm for Salukis that Florence Amherst had never been able to generate.

As a tip of the hat to his years of service, in January 1923 Lance was promoted to brigadier and entitled to wear the crossed-sword-and-baton badge of a general. Brigadier General Lance would be one of the most visible Saluki fanciers, and the breed folklore would eventually come to include the mistaken belief that Lance had commanded a brigade in Palestine.[†] Bayne-Jardine would breed Hama to Kelb twice and the puppies from the first litter were born on February 23, 1922. The Lances bought another Hama puppy, this time a red male, naming it Sarona Sha Gee, but later sold him to Miss Beryl Thynne in early 1923. At the time of the transfer, the papers were full of news of the "Wonderful Carnarvon Egyptian Treasure." Beryl promptly changed her hound's name to "Tut-ankh-Amen."[§] Interest in the breed continued to grow. In several magazines and newspapers, Florence and the Lances made the public aware of their efforts to form a club. On February 1, 1923, *The Field* printed this announcement:

> It is many years since Miss Amherst introduced a specimen of the Selughi or Persian greyhound to the attention of fanciers here, and very little has been done towards furthering the breed until last year when Brig. Gen. F. F. Lance exhibited a handsome brace at Crufts, where they proved a great attraction and aroused considerable interest. Of late the variety has gained many adherents, and it is now proposed to inaugurate a Selughi Club. A meeting for this purpose will be held at Crufts show on February 8th in Room No. 1 at 2 pm. All interested are invited to attend.[14]

The notice paid off for at Crufts, a gratifying number of fanciers arrived for the meeting.

Foreign dogs at the show included Major Bell-Murray's team of Afghans** and a litter of Papillons, and while they attracted quite a bit of notice, it was the Salukis that received the lion's share of attention. Mr. Robert Leighton, the eminent dog expert and author, judged

---

*America was equally obsessed by the mania and one could even purchase oddities such as "Pyramid Suppositories" and a nut-roll candy bar produced by the Sifers Candy Company called "The Old King Tut."
†An impression that Lance does not seem to have corrected.
§The transliteration of the boy king's name is now rendered as "Tutankhamun."
**Bell-Murray's foundation Afghan stock and other early imports resembled slightly shaggy Salukis. The extreme coat that is seen today is a product of genetic selection by western breeders in the 1950s.

the "Persian Greyhound" entry of five hounds. In descending order, the prizes went to Mrs. R. L. Armstrong's import Tazi of Abbotsford, Miss S. Kerrison's Ispahan, and Mrs. L. Foster Mitchell's Egyptian Eve, with her younger, full sister Egyptian Priestess taking reserve.* After Leighton had made his decision and handed out placement cards, there was some sort of upset for Egyptian Eve was disqualified and Egyptian Princess was moved up to third place.[15] Leighton's critique noted politely that she was overweight and needed a deeper chest.[16] Perhaps the disqualification was due to some irregularity in her papers, for when Mrs. Mitchell changed her kennel prefix from "Egyptian" to "Fresco" the next month, Eve was registered as "not for competition."

Away from the crowds and noise, fourteen people met in Crufts Agricultural Hall at the appointed hour. Florence brought her sister. Margaret Amherst, and Brigadier General Lance brought his elder brother, Captain Henry William Lance, O.B.E.[†] Besides the Lance brothers there were only four other men, Major Bayne-Jardine, Robert Leighton, Mr. L. Crouch, and a Lt. A. R. Spurgin of an Indian Regiment — the 12th Pioneers.[17] The LKA was amply represented with Gladys Lance, Gertrude Desborough, and Evelyn Crouch.[18]

The most pressing item for the first meeting's agenda was deciding the official breed name. There was a debate on the various names with the Amherst faction wanting "Saluki Shami Gazelle Hound" and the Lance side advocating "Persian Greyhound." It was here that Florence's vast knowledge of the breed came to the fore. She had been researching Salukis for nearly three decades and had been published numerous times. She would write of her researches and correspondents, "The cult of the Saluki leads you into paths and bye-paths of history and geography that probably would never be trodden in literature and art. I employ my 'wanders' in search of Saluki lore — and these 'wanders' never fail to bring fresh interest of some sort."[19]

Even the renowned A. Croxton Smith would later acknowledge her scholarship with characteristic English reserve: "Miss Amherst, who has gone into the subject...."[20] With the exception of Lance, the rest of the members were comparatively new to the breed. But none of them could trump her scholarship. Florence spoke with authority and cited from classical Arabic literature that "Saluki" was the proper term and "gazelle hound" the best English description (to further help breed recognition). She was convincing and persuasive. They agreed to drop the "*shami*" designation from the Florence's old terminology as there were also *yamani*, *omani*, and *nejdi* types owned by the members. In the end, they compromised with "Saluki or Gazelle Hound" noting that "Saluki" was the universal name for the breed in the East.[21]

With that hurdle behind, they agreed upon a subscription rate of one guinea and a five-shilling entrance fee for the club.[§] Foreign members who resided abroad for twelve months consecutively could subscribe for just five shillings.[22] The next agenda item was the election of officers and a steering committee. With an eye toward internal and external politics, Brigadier Lance diplomatically proposed the Honorable Florence Amherst for President and Mrs. Crouch seconded the motion. Lance himself was elected Vice President. In turn, Mrs.

*Egyptian Eve and Priestess were bred and born in 1918 and 1922 respectively — their sire and dam were Tickford Darkie and Ebony Lady.
†Lance's brother lived at Barnham — which was very close to Foulden Hall.
§A guinea (twenty-one shillings) was an older monetary unit that persisted in certain transactions, such as luxury items, solicitor's fees, and horse-race prizes. Clearly, the club was trying to set a certain tone by choosing that denomination. The membership fee would be £50.96 in 2006.

Crouch became the Honorable Treasurer, and Gladys elected as Honorable Secretary.[23] The steering committee was composed of Mrs. L. Armstrong, Mrs. Crouch, Miss. M. Grey, Miss Kerrison, Mrs. Foster Mitchell, Lt. Spurgin, and Major Bayne-Jardine.[24] Next, the membership debated the standard of points, but due to the myriad of opinions and the fleeting time, that vexing topic was postponed until the next meeting. As President, Florence duly signed Gladys' minutes in her small, careful signature. It was an act that betokened the beginning of a deep and lasting friendship between the two women.

In preparation for the next club meeting in two weeks time, Florence, the Lances, Miss Kerrison, and presumably one or two other committee members met in London, most likely at the LKA offices, to draw up a breed standard. They used Florence's 1907 standard as a starting point. While the club's minutes are rather sparse on this point, the revision was actually quite a task. With the influx of hounds from several other regions in the Middle East, they now had to include a much wider range of body types than Florence had originally specified for her "*shamis.*" In 1923, there were Salukis, feathered and smooth, in a range of colors imported from the regions where their officers had served — Syria, Palestine, and Mesopotamia (Iraq) as well as Egypt and Transjordan.* Clearly a collaborative effort to include the variety of hounds owned by the members, Miss Kerrison and the Lances were Florence's primary coauthors on the document. Her flowery, Victorian text — which had become a bit dated by Kennel Club standards — was transformed into a more practical document. The new standard was concise in language but broader in scope — being reduced from 677 words to 265.† Despite the reduction, Florence's original concepts of conformation remained essentially unchanged. Specific measurements for head, chest girth, and weight were dropped and only shoulder height retained. Noteworthy additions allowed for a broader range of type and colors, increased upper limit for height, and the inclusion of smooths.[25] The success of their collaborative effort is witnessed by the fact that at the club meeting on February 22, there was no heated debate about the revised standard, although heights were discussed in some detail. A proposal was made to judge smooths and feathereds separately, but the motion failed to pass and the members approved the standard.

In May 1923, A. Croxton Smith wrote another article about Salukis, this time for *The Field,* a well-known sporting publication. In discussing breed history, he suggested that there might well be representations of Salukis to be found in Tutankhamun's tomb, which Carter was methodically clearing. "It would not have surprised me to learn that a presentment of one of its representatives had been found in the tomb of Tut-ankh-Amen, because Pharaohs were in the habit of keeping up considerable establishments of hounds several thousands of years before the Christian era."[26] He was in fact correct about Tutankhamun's Salukis, but none would be published that year. Smith discoursed on the differences between the Lance and Amherst hounds and the surprising lack of popularity to date. He described the formation of the club, the development of the Saluki standard, and the Lance's endeavors to gain breed recognition. The article was illustrated with photos of the Sarona hounds. One shot of Kelb was captioned "Sarona Kelb, the Best Saluki in England" and Smith noted that he was the sire of a puppy presented to King George's only daughter, Princess Mary. Such glowing praise for the Saronas must surely have annoyed Florence somewhat.

---

*Lucy Bethel's "Reish" can be considered to be the first documented Saluki from Arabia brought to England. It would not be until after 1925 that Salukis from the Arabian states would be added to the English gene pool.

†With the exception of the Whippet standard at 128 words, other contemporary sighthound standards used more descriptive words than the Saluki standard (Scottish Deerhound: 742, Irish Wolfhound: 414, and Borzoi: 313).

The first year of the club's existence would see a number of military men sign on for membership, including Mrs Foster Mitchell's husband who was a captain in the 5th/6th Dragoon Guards, his friend Lt. Kaye of the same regiment, one Col. F. N. Radcliffe, C.M.G., C.I.E., C.B.E., and Major Bentinck of the Coldstream Guards. Officer-members on foreign service were Colonel Pierce Joyce of the Ministry of Defense, Baghdad; Captain A. V. Cooper of the Basrah Police, Squadron Leader J. H. D'Albraic of the Royal Air Force; Major F. W. Blacker of the Scinde Horse (another Northwest Frontier regiment); and, in Dehli, Major H.F. Whitby, Lance's brother officer from the 19th Lancers.* There were members in Sweden, Germany, Palestine, India, and the Punjab. Honorary membership was conferred upon A. Croxton Smith, veterinary surgeon Miss M. Cust, Mrs. Carlo Clarke, and Lance's old friend and Saluki fancier from Damascus, Hussein Ibshi Pasha.

Just after the inception of the club, Major Bayne-Jardine resigned his membership as he was being posted to Colchester in Essex and knew he would not be able to keep Hama. In October and November of 1922, Hama would escape from the Ipswich barracks and roam the countryside, sometimes going missing for days at a time. On October 19, 1922, two days after she and her puppies escaped, Bayne-Jardine noted in his journal, "Writing apologies for Hama all day." Quite possibly she interfered with game on the big estates, for on one occasion, a gamekeeper had to lock her up. Bayne-Jardine began to spend a lot of time looking for her.

It was usual to relocate officers about every two years and Bayne-Jardine knew there would be more moves to come in his career with no guarantee of Saluki-friendly quarters. His career was taking a different turn and rather than see Hama restricted to a progression of stuffy offices and unable to go for rambles or course hares, he made the hard decision to give her up before going to Colchester. At the end of November, he offered to sell her to Florence Amherst, but she declined.† Bayne-Jardine and Hama still went for their treasured daily walks and he would note these and her escapes in his journal. On December 11, just a few days after another lengthy disappearance, a transfer of ownership was arranged and in his journal Bayne-Jardine wrote only that "Hama left early."

She had been given or sold to a Miss M. Grey (Greyhill Salukis)—a recent breed enthusiast who had previously bred Shetland Sheepdogs.[27] Her new owner exhibited her at Cruft's that year but she did not place because of her cropped ears. In the class of five bitches, she was not even given reserve when one of Mrs. Foster-Mitchell's bitches was disqualified and Leighton's original reserve placement moved up to third place. In March 1923, the Kennel Club registered Hama's transfer to Miss Grey, but she only kept Hama for one year before passing her on to Miss Sybil Kerrison (Iraq Salukis) who in turn sold the "great brood bitch" to Mrs. A. S. O'Brien of Richmond.[28] Hama would be transferred to her fifth and final owner, Miss H. I. H. Barr (Grevel Salukis & Irish Wolfhounds) in 1926. The registered name of Bayne-Jardine's "Agabey dog" was never changed and she can be found in most English and American Saluki pedigrees for she produced a total of eight litters during the club's formative years. As far as it is recorded, Bayne-Jardine did not own Salukis again. In his eyes, Hama was irreplaceable.

Already amalgamated as the 19th King George's Own Lancers.
†*She was actually the type of Saluki that Florence should have liked. Hama's inability to be shown because of her cropped ears would most likely have been the objection.*

The club's petition for recognition was published in March 1923 *Gazette* but a clerical error listed them as the "Saluki *and* Gazelle Hound Club." This was corrected the following month after a note from Gladys Lance. On April 5, the same day that Lord Carnarvon died in Cairo, Salukis made their first show appearance under their new official name at the Kensington Canine Society's show in Holland Park. The club was formally recognized nineteen days later. By June 1923, it was reported at the club's meeting at the LKA Office in Regent Street that England could now boast of about eighteen owners, sixty hounds (not counting forthcoming litters) and nine imports in quarantine.[29] It was a far cry from the two owners and dozen hounds of 1921.

A petition from the club that Salukis be placed on the register of breeds was granted by the Kennel Club Committee on July 17. The committee ruled, "As a breed, the Saluki includes both Persian and Arabian Hounds, but excludes Afghan Greyhounds."[30] That month, all dogs who had been formerly registered as Persian and Arabian greyhounds were brought under the new, but redundant classification of "Saluki Hound." On July 31, the committee agreed that Salukis should be placed in the Hound Section of the Sporting Dogs group.[31] By October, the breed had been upgraded from the "Any Other Breed or Variety of British, Colonial, or Foreign Dogs Not Classified" to their own category — "Saluki Hounds." *The Kennel Gazette* had been periodically listing their registrations under the "Saluki Hound" misnomer and another letter from Gladys Lance pointed out that the membership was adamant that that name was in fact redundant as "Saluki" actually meant "hound or running dog" in Arabic. The Kennel Club acquiesced and the official designation was altered to "Saluki" in November. It was not quite the long-hoped-for sanction of Florence's elite "*shami*" strain, but a very acceptable compromise. She was 63 years old and breed recognition had come 28 years after her first imports.

15

Gains and Losses

"It is earnestly to be hoped that this encouragement will have the result of bringing the Saluki into the wide popularity it deserves. Thanks to the untiring energies of General and Mrs. Lance, a substantial foundation has been laid."

Robert Leighton[1]
(on the recent breed recognition)

Increasing membership was a high priority for the club in their inaugural year and one expeditious way of achieving this was to bring in relatives. Whether or not they ever owned Salukis is uncertain, but Florence's sister Margaret became a member (at least she lived with Florence's hounds) as did Lance's sister-in-law, Mrs. H. W. Lance, as well as Gladys's father, Sir Philip Waterlow, who was retiring from the family firm that year.*

Saluki owners showed great flair and imagination in naming their hounds. Inspiration was drawn from the Bible, the Arabian Nights, and history. The expected Cleopatras, Fatimahs, Sinbads, Kismets, Samsons, Sheikhs, Saladins, and Pharaohs were in evidence along with Jeshimon of Judea, Ali Baba and Sheherazade of Iraq, Saladin Sag Ma Mohomet of Kayenne, Egyptian Eve and Priestess, Princess of Amer Road, Sheik of Darwin and, of course, Tut-ankh-Amen. Then there were names that had little if anything to do with the Middle East whatsoever — Tarzan of Ruritania, Rushford Piastre, Cheetah of Greyhill, Wild Rose, Hilda of Yeldersley, and, improbably, Christopher Robin and Winnie-Ther-Pooh [*sic*].

Early in the year, the Lances had commissioned a large oil portrait of Kelb and three other hounds set in the fields of Wentfield. It was reproduced in the April 12 edition of *The Field*, providing invaluable publicity for the breed. In August 1923, the first Saluki breed column appeared in the weekly newspaper *The Dog World*. F. B. Fowler noted show results, SGHC activities, new members, and imported Salukis in quarantine, and published the breed standard in several consecutive parts. At the end of every year, the *Dog World* published their annual issue full of special features and advertisements for breeders. The Lances were the first to seize upon this opportunity and in later years their ads frequently had pictures of John and Geoffrey walking up to ten hounds down the lane at Wentfield. The Sarona Kennels ad of 1923 featured a photograph of Kelb, a list of his wins to date, the names of three dogs available at stud† and advertised that "young stock and puppies" were for sale.

In addition to their work to bring Salukis into the limelight, Brigadier General Lance and Gladys had established the Wentfield Stud with his imported Arab mare and other horses acquired in England. He showed Mejamieh's foal at the National Pony Society in March 1923,

*Gladys's father was living in Wrotham at the time.
†Kelb, Najib, and Kataf.

151

and was lauded as an importer and exhibitor of Salukis in the subsequent show write-up.[2] Horses were an important part of life at Wentfield, and when young John Lance was old enough to take responsibility for the care of several Salukis, his parents bought him a Dartmoor Cob.[*] Geoffrey would have a pony of his own later on, and the Salukis and Whiskey the terrier would accompany them on rides. Lance would occasionally don the Arab robes he brought back from Syria and ride Mejamieh (also wearing Arab trappings) with a brace of Salukis on a long lead. On one occasion they posed on a windy hilltop and Gladys snapped a photo, labeling it "A Mock Arab on a Real Arab Mare with Arab Dogs."[†]

The eminent authority, author, and judge, Robert Leighton had evaluated the Saluki entry at Crufts in 1923 and reprised his judging in October of that year at the Kennel Club Show. It was their third show as a recognized breed (Kensington Canine Society in April, and Maidstone, Kent, in September, being the others) and the first one where championship certificates were awarded. At the Kennel Club show he also judged a litter of Papillon puppies, and a team of Barukhzy hounds, three Afghan hounds, and a brace of Lhasa Terriers. Leighton had a great drooping mustache, narrow eyes and prominent cheekbones and ears, and was a commanding presence in the ring. In his critique, Leighton had no hesitation criticizing the dark and drafty exhibition hall at the Crystal Palace and pointed out that the ring was too small to allow the proper evaluation of the Saluki gait.[§] There was a good-sized entry and to no one's surprise Leighton singled out Sarona Kelb. He was lavish in his praise and considered the Saluki faultless. He made a special point of acknowledging the acceptability of his coloring and size as well as the Brigadier's skilled handling — and admonished the other exhibitors to take note of the latter for their own benefit. Leighton was likewise impressed with Orchard Shahin, a black-and-white parti-color daughter from Kelb and Echo's first litter. Kelb and Shahin were awarded the first Challenge Certificates for the breed and Shahin would become the first Saluki champion by the end of the year.[**]

Despite the Lances' strong presence in show circles, Florence still had a lingering influence. In both of Leighton's critiques that year, he used her classical terminology of *saluki/silaga* for male and female, and referred to Mrs. Foster Mitchell's smooth as a *nejdi*.[††] Interestingly enough, in his October critique Leighton also gave the first hint of a controversy that was beginning to surface in the club. He referred to Nedjim-el-Zobair (bred from an Iraqi pair imported by Mrs. A. Vereker Cowley) as "a promising little cream-colored hound of Mesopotamian type."[3]

In creating a standard to include Saluki types from the wide geographic range of Egypt through Iraq, there needed to be a great deal of latitude lacking in Florence's original 1907 standard for the *Shami*. What quickly evolved in 1923 were two different sides to the breed type debate. Confusingly, the hounds were labeled as either the "Syrian" or "Mesopotamian" type. "Syrian" denoted the larger hounds with darker and/or parti-colors — such as the Saronas and their descendants, the Orchards and Ruritanias. The Amherst Salukis were typical of the

[*]*A regional variety of a sturdy, short-legged horse.*
[†]*This and other Lance photos are part of the Sarona Album and archived at the Kennel Club library.*
[§]*A complaint that is still heard at dog shows today.*
[**]*Challenge Certificates (also known as "CCs" or "tickets") indicate judgment of championship quality. It takes three CCs to win champion status in England.*
[††]*Not speaking Arabic and dependent on her various correspondents (who frequently disagreed on the terminology) Florence never did get the Arabic correct. For classical/colloquial Male is Saluqi/Slougui, Female is Saluqiyyah/Slougiyya, and the plural would be Salaq or Sulqan/Salag, Sulgan, or Silagui. E-mail to the author from Sir Terence Clark, August 3, 2007.*

"Mesopotamian" type — lighter in color and smaller in size. The terminology is decidedly odd, for Florence had always insisted that her *Shami* Salukis' ancestors had come from Damascus (El Shams), Syria, and yet Lance's original pair had also come from that general area. The explanation suggests a shift in her belief about the origins of the breed (in her early years she thought they came from Upper Egypt and the Sudan) and recognition that in ancient times, Mesopotamia was a much larger territory and included parts of Syria, northern Arabia, and the Transjordan within its nebulous borders.

Judges' critiques frequently mentioned whether or not a hound was of the Syrian or Mesopotamian type, and certain breeders still used the old terminology of "Saluki or Persian Gazelle Hound." In the first years after breed recognition, the Syrian types tended to do most of the winning. Brigadier Lance judged the Saluki entry at the Kennel Club show in October 1924 and he reinforced the division by identifying his placements as either the Syrian or Mesopotamian types. Gladys displayed Kelb for exhibition only that day and the Brigadier made a point of noting in his critique that Kelb was "representative of the black and tan Syrian type."[4] That the Syrian types tended to do more winning in the early years was clearly due to the influence of the Lances and a discouragement to those with the smaller and lighter hounds. At many of the early shows, there would not be a single hound of Mesopotamian type to give the Syrians competition, and this further solidified the impression that Syrians were the correct type.

Despite having been ostensibly settled in the breed standard, the question of proper size for the two varieties raised its head again. There was even debate on whether or not the two types should be interbred and, if so, whether they would then produce medium-sized hounds with the qualities of both types. The Syrian-versus-Mesopotamian-type schism continued at least through 1925, for in May of that year, Gladys noted in her write-up of the Ranelagh show, "It was a disappointment to many that the Mesopotamian variety were not put up to Syrian types for high placements."[5]

At the end of 1923, the club published their first annual report — a slim pamphlet that listed the officers, members, and their addresses. It was the only Saluki or Gazelle Hound Club publication that would list Margaret Amherst as a member. She passed away on December 19 at the age of fifty-nine. Her health had never been robust and she had been stricken with heart failure and pleurisy. She had been staying with her sister Alicia in Dorset, and a few days before her death, she said, "there comes a time when one's number is up, and I think my number is up now."[6] Florence was greatly affected by her sister's death and did not speak to anyone in the club for nearly two months. When the club finally learned of Margaret's death in mid–February, the membership voted to send a note of sympathy to their president. The holiday season must have been an increasingly harder time for Florence and her remaining sisters as every family death so far had been in November, December, and January — usually within a month of Christmas or New Year's Day. No matter how happy the gathering, there was always sadness for their dear ones that had died during the holidays. There were now four of the family left: Alicia Cecil in Lytchett Heath, Dorset; Geraldine Drummond at Megginch Castle, Perth; and Florence and Sybil at Foulden Manor.

In the spring, a happier family occasion demanded Florence's attention. Eleven days out of Liverpool, the S.S. *Baltic* docked in New York harbor on April 21, 1924, and she set foot in America for the first time. The customs official on Ellis Island took down her declaration that she had at least $50 in cash, was in good health, had no occupation or profession, and was neither an anarchist nor a polygamist. Florence had come to attend her nephew Jacky's wedding. In September 1923, the Honorable John Francis Amherst Cecil accepted a post with the British Embassy in Washington, D.C. He had fallen in love with and proposed to Cornelia Stuyvesant Vanderbilt who had inheritd the family estate and fortune with the death of her father in 1914. The wedding took place in 1924 at the magnificent Biltmore in Asheville, North Carolina. John's widowed father, Colonel Lord William Cecil, had come over two weeks earlier, and together with Florence, represented the English side of the family. Florence stayed for a month and it is possible she met with some of the fledgling Saluki fancy in the States. Florence sailed from America to Barcelona to attend a poultry conference, and then returned to England.

The first Salukis in England were pets brought in by their owners. While soldiering, working, or traveling in the desert, there had been no thought of bringing Salukis back to establish a breeding program. Once in England and connected with other fanciers with similar interests, breeding seemed to be the thing to do. The breed had been recognized by the Kennel Club and achieved some fame. Puppies were wanted and new breeding stock was needed. Pets were still being brought in by newly returning owners, but there began a great movement by the SGHC members to import a second wave of Salukis from the desert. With the widespread network of military men it was comparatively easy to find someone who would assist with a Saluki transfer — but often one might have to write to three or four intermediaries before finding someone who could actually lay his hands on a desert-bred puppy or young adult. Getting photographs of sire, dam, and puppies or selecting a particular puppy from the litter was impossible. Negotiations and arrangements were done entirely by letter, so the importer had to take potluck. In many cases, the imported Saluki might fall short of the quality hoped for or did not match the type wanted. In these cases, the imported dog might be bred only once or not at all.

As the French now controlled Syria, that avenue for importation was closed — even to Lance who was known for having the "Syrian" type hounds. Transjordan and Iraq had become British mandates after the war and now offered the easiest access to desert Salukis.* In June 1923, the Lances imported a pair of two-year-olds to enhance their breeding stock. In December, the dog and bitch cleared quarantine and were registered with the Kennel Club. Sarona Kataf, a red male with white socks and throat, had come from Daoud Bey Daghestani, a well-known breeder of horses and hounds.

On the Caspian Sea, Daghestan is a thin strip of coastal plane that rises sharply to the steep mountain ridges of the Caucasus, which are pockmarked by isolated valleys. The population was predominately Muslim, and a virtual Tower of Babel with over thirty languages and dialects — the more cosmopolitan people speaking Arabic. Prince Daoud Bey was in fact a descendent of the Circassian rulers of Daghestan. His great uncle was the famous Shamil who had fought the invading Russian Army for years. After the conquest of Daghestan in the mid–1800s, the Russians split up the ruling family and relocated them to St. Petersburg and Istanbul to minimize trouble.[7] Daoud's father, Field Marshal Muhammad Fadhil Pasha al Daghestani had been commander of the Sultan's Caucasian Bodyguard, commander in chief

*Interestingly, the English would not consider importing Salukis from the continent. At that time, Germany had a sizable population of Salukis that came from postwar imports from Turkey, Iraq, and Iran. Later in the decade, the Netherlands and Sweden had significant populations, with Belgium, Finland, Switzerland, France, and Italy having smaller numbers.

of Mesopotamia and acting governor of Baghdad. The tough old soldier was killed at an advanced age of over seventy during the siege of Kut-al-Amara.[8]

Muhammad Pasha's eldest son Daoud Bey was a countryman by inclination with an estate at Al Amarah in the southern Iraq marshlands. While it had the usual crowded streets of any Arab town, it also had fine brick houses with orchards and gardens along the banks of the Tigris River.* Adam and Eve were said to have fled from Eden at that spot and so Al Amarah was known as the "Garden of Tears."[9] When in residence in Baghdad, Daoud Bey Daghestani was considered the leader of the Circassian circle and the darling of the British racing and polo cliques. His horses were considered to be among the best in Iraq. Something of a wastrel, he spent his money on dancing girls and deprived his mother and nine handsome sisters of their lawful inheritance.[10] In addition to horse breeding, he was an avid hunter, with perfectly trained falcons and Salukis, and liked nothing better than to take guests on hunts in the hills along the Persian border.[11] Kataf, the good coursing dog that Daoud Bey presented to the Lances, was of the Shammar Bedouin — a confederation of three great tribes who were famous for their horses.

The Lances' second import of 1923 was a golden bitch, Sarona Reshan, from Reza Gholi Kahn, the Vali of Pusht-i-Kuh.[†] He was the hereditary governor of a mountainous province — this one in Persia just east of the Mesopotamian border.[§] The Vali was not only a governor, but also a major general in the Persian army and, at the turn of the century, he was said to have an army of 30,000 nomadic, mountain men.[12] The capital, Husseinabad (known today as Ilam), was named after the first vali, and being a tent city, actually moved from time to time.[13] The few buildings belonged to the Vali whose family (reputedly of Arab origin) had been governing the Pusht-i-Kuh for three hundred years.

The Vali was a powerful, semi-autonomous ruler who only tacitly acknowledged his vassal status to the Qajar Shah in Tehran with annual tribute. He was reputed to be considerably less murderous than his father who had the terrifying appellation of *Abu Kadareh* or "Father of the Sword."[14] With a title worthy of a Gilbert and Sullivan character, the slender, fifty-nine-year-old Vali of Pusht-i-Kuh had an enormous, drooping black mustache and wore the cylindrical, black-felt Pahlavi hat, common to Persians. He had been handsome in his youth and by 1923 had ten wives and nine sons. Fond of ceremony, the Vali had once visited Baghdad with an entourage of over 200 people, having allowed a further 250 to return to Husseinabad when obliged to use a train that could not accommodate the full retinue.[15] Throughout his mountainous lands east of the border, there were wide plains teeming with gazelle, which were hunted with Salukis. The Vali was known as a sportsman and kept a kennel that was much admired.

Notorious both for its inaccessibility and merciless brigands, Pusht-i-Kuh was a part of Luristan and populated primarily by the native Fayli Lurs and a small number of Kurds. No outsider traveled there lightly. The tribesmen frequently raided into Turkey but spared Mesopotamia so that they might continue to trade with Baghdad. This Vali had ruled west-

---

Both the Tigris and Euphrates flow to the Hawr al Hammar basin through the marshy delta that once hosted both the ancient kingdom of Sumer and more recently, the Marsh Arab population. After the Gulf War in 1991, Saddam Hussein retaliated against the Marsh Arabs who had opposed him, by systematically draining the region on a vast scale — destroying wildlife, grazing, agriculture, and the ability of the population to survive there.

†*Written then as Push-ti-Kuh. Meaning literally, "Behind the Mountains," it referred to the Zagros range that separated Pusht-i-Kuh from central Persia. Its lesser neighbor is Pisht-i-Kuh — "Before the mountains."*

§*The term for the governor of a province, "vali" is the Turkish variant and "wali" the Arabic.*

ern Luristan since 1909 and despite his leanings toward Germany and Turkey, he managed to neatly fence-sit through the Mesopotamian campaign until the British occupied his domain in 1917. About the time that Lance imported Reshan in 1923, the rebellious Vali became embroiled in a struggle for power not only with some of his sons, but with the Persian government.[16] The man who was charged with stopping the rebellion in Pusht-i-Kuh was none other than the minister of war and future shah, Reza Khan of Mazandaran.* Reza's army began to hammer the rebellious Pusht-i-Kuh and other western provinces in 1922.[17] Hounded by his sons and one step ahead of Reza's army, the old Vali went into exile in Baghdad at the year's end of 1924.[18]

There are only about 75 miles between Daoud Bey's stud farm in Al-Amarah and the Pusht-i-Kuh mountains, but how Lance came in contact with either of these two men is not recorded. As a fellow horse breeder, Lance's friend Hussein Ibshi of Damascus may have known Daoud Bey, but the distance between Damascus and Al-Amarah is well over 600 miles. Lance had many military contacts but the most likely nexus was fellow SGHC member Colonel Pierce Joyce, who had fought in the Arab Revolt and was now an advisor to the Iraqi Minister of Defense. Joyce was a Saluki fancier himself and had connections with both the Vali of Pusht-i-Kuh and Daoud Bey Daghestani. He could have easily made the arrangements for Lance. For reasons which will be seen, neither Kataf nor Reshan would figure prominently in the Sarona breeding program. However, there were other Iraqi Salukis that would be a significant influence on the breed in England.

On the banks of the Tigris River in northern Iraq, Major Arthur Bentinck's Salukis had just caught a hare and it was a good time for the party to rest. The horses grazed on the sparse forage while the men sat down and relaxed in the noonday sun. Lying happily alongside them were three Salukis, and hovering in the distance, a local herd-dog. Bentinck had short, dark hair, an oval face, slightly drooping eyes, and a thin mustache. He was a proper Victorian gentleman — unflappable, straitlaced, and meticulously organized. Brought up to conceal his emotions, he could be brusque but was good-natured and affectionate with his family. Bentinck was comfortable with desert life and respected by his native servants and friends. In the days when native servants would kiss the boot of their English masters as sign of respect, it was said in his family that Arthur would at least lift his boot half way up.

While they were resting, Bentinck snapped a picture of one of his party in tattered tribal robes resting with the Salukis. Bentinck had seen the local Kurds hunt on horseback with their hounds on long slip leads — ready to be unleashed at the first sight of game. They rode in a wide line or, in Bentinck's army terminology, "extended order," across the plain around Mosul (Al Mawsil), and as Gladys Lance had noted about her hounds, they stopped at any rise to scan the horizon for the subtle movements that meant live game. Bentinck would come home in the summer of 1923, and the Salukis he brought with him would make an important addition to the gene pool in England.

Arthur William Douglas Bentinck and two of his brothers were officers in the prestigious Coldstream Guards. Arthur's grandfather, granduncle, and father had all been colonels of the regiment. In the British infantry, the Coldstream was second in precedence only to the

---

*Reza Khan was proclaimed Shah Reza Pahlavi in 1926 and it was his son who was forced into exile by the fundamentalist revolution in 1979.

Major Count Arthur Bentinck, D.S.O., and Rishan at home in Baghdad, about 1926. With the kind permission of the Earl of Portland.

Grenadier Guards. Like all Guard officers, Arthur Bentinck was tall, financially comfortable, and of a good family. His ancestors were in fact Dutch nobility, one of whom, Hans Willem Bentinck, had come to England as a supporter of William of Orange when Parliament invited him to become king in 1689.* In recognition of his friendship and support, William III made Bentinck the first Earl of Portland. That title passed into the line of his first son, William. After Bentinck's wife died, he remarried and fathered another son, Henry, who would become a Count of the Holy Roman Empire. This title was passed down through Henry's male heirs to the Coldstream Guard Bentincks, so Arthur and his brothers were entitled to style themselves "Count Bentinck."†

Arthur Bentinck and his twin sister, Naomi Mechtild Henrietta, were born on July 24, 1887. He was the youngest of four sons in a family of seven children. The Bentincks had houses in Dartmoor, Hampshire, and in London near Grosvenor Square, at 53 Green Street. The children were all raised with horses, pets, and an enthusiasm for country life and outdoor sports. Arthur learned to box in school and loved any sport that involved horses — polo, fox-hunting, and riding his own horses in military races were particular favorites. He was a patient man, a trait that would serve him well in numerous colonial postings throughout his career. They were very close-knit and deeply religious. After their father's example, Bible study, discourse, and daily prayers were a way of life for the family. After meditation, careful study of scripture, and a close watch on current events, Arthur (twenty-one at the time) and his elder sister Renira became convinced that the second coming of Jesus was imminent. The whole family knew about their theory and gave it absolute credence. When the event did not come to pass, there were no recriminations or laughter — life just went on for the Bentincks.

After earning a baccalaureate at Cambridge, Arthur spent some years in Egypt with his older brother Henry prior to joining the Coldstream Guards as a second lieutenant in 1909. He was promoted to lieutenant a year later at the age of twenty-three. From 1913 to 1914, he served with the King's African Rifles in British East Africa and when the war broke out in August 1914, Lt. Bentinck went to France with the 3rd Battalion of the Coldstream Guards. His battalion was part of the 4th Guards Brigade, which also had elements of the Irish Guards, the Connaught Rangers and the 2nd Battalion of the Grenadier Guards. The latter's machine-gun section was skillfully commanded by Florence Amherst's ill-fated nephew, the Honorable Lt. William Cecil.

Bentinck and "Stag" Cecil (as he was known in the Grenadiers) knew each other, as the latter's machine guns provided close support to Bentinck's company of Coldstreamers in the first month of the war. At the battle of Aisne, both men would become casualties on the same day. Cecil was shot in the throat and killed while reconnoitering a change of position for their machine gun. Bentinck himself was seriously wounded in the leg by a lyddite§ shell fragment while his company was being relieved after two days of bombardment in foxholes that had yet to become trenches. The walnut-sized, ragged piece of steel was removed but soil-born bacteria infected Bentinck's leg and he contracted tetanus. It was his second campaign wound that year, the first having occurred while campaigning in Africa — but this one nearly killed him.

*In 1690, William III defeated exiled Catholic king James II and his Jacobite army at the Battle of the Boyne and firmly established Protestantism and the roots of lasting religious conflict in Ireland.
†This unusual title was allowed by Queen Victoria's special dispensation to three families who had rendered exceptional services to the country. After the Great War, the title was revoked.
§A high-powered explosive, first used against the British in the Boer War.

Bentinck's jaws clamped tightly shut with the paroxysms of muscle contractions that characterize lockjaw and he was unable to eat or drink. The painful spasms affected other muscle groups in his body and movement would have been sheer agony — if possible at all. Dehydration and starvation were the primary dangers of lockjaw, although the diaphragm could also undergo spasms, causing suffocation. Bentinck lost weight and the paralysis caused his muscles to atrophy. Careful nursing by the hospital matrons was about all that could be done for him. His entire family prayed daily for his recovery. Surviving the crisis, the weakened Bentinck was shipped home to Brighton to the care and further prayers of his mother and sisters. He was over a year in recovering from the usually fatal disease and his right leg was no longer straight. Bentinck's bootmaker had to add a special set of laces on one riding boot in order for it to fit properly. Like Lance and Bayne-Jardine, he would have trouble with his wounded leg for the rest of his life.*

When at last Bentinck had his strength back and was again riding to hounds, he reported himself fit for duty at regimental headquarters. He was occupied with light duties in England and was promoted to captain in September of 1915. One year later, he was posted to the Imperial Camel Corps in Egypt and added camel riding to his repertoire of skills. His brother Henry had finally managed to get a transfer from Africa to the Western Front. On September 16, 1916, exactly two years to the day that the shell burst had injured Arthur, Henry was fatally wounded in an infantry charge at Ginchy, part of the great battle of the Somme. Like thousands of other British soldiers, he managed to get only a few yards out of the trench before being hit by machine-gun fire. He took slugs in his shoulder and both legs and a piece of shrapnel in his head. He lay in the mud for hours before being hauled back to the lines. His shattered leg was amputated but he died of gangrene two weeks later. Henry Bentinck became one of 60,000 British casualties on the first day of the Somme.

Arthur Bentinck's service in the Middle East is not well recorded, but about a year after he left for Egypt, he was back as staff to the Coldstream's 3rd Battalion. In 1917, he was posted to Abyssinia where he served through the last year of the war and was finally demobilized with the rank of captain in April 1920. He was promoted to major the following February and once again his movements become uncertain. By November 1922, Bentinck was working out of Baghdad with the local rank of lieutenant colonel. There was unrest in northern Iraq around Al Mawsil by Kurdistan tribes who were rebelling against King Faisal's new government. Now that their hereditary enemy, Turkey, was no longer in control of Iraq, they were bent on establishing their own country. It was a dangerous place to soldier — and was considered by the Turks to be their equivalent of the British North-West Frontier in India. Kurds killed four British officers and three soldiers in one eight-month period.[19]

Al Mawsil has always been a dangerous place, even before the Great War. After her visit in 1909, Gertrude Bell wrote, "It lies upon the frontier of the Arab and Kurdish populations, and the meeting between those two is seldom accompanied by cordiality or good-will on either side. Upon the unhappy province of Môsul hatred and lust of slaughter weigh like inherited evils.... The organization of discord is carried to high pitch of perfection in Môsul. The town is full of bravos who live by outrage, and live well."[20]

Bentinck worked at becoming friends with the local Kurdish tribes in the course of cementing alliances and gathering intelligence. There, on the Plain of Al Mawsil, as had Sir

---

Arthur had the shell fragment mounted in a glass case and it is still preserved by his great nephew, the 12th Earl of Portland — to whom I am grateful for sharing his family information.

Henry Layard, some seventy years before, Bentinck acquired a pair of Salukis that would become his favorites. A Kurdish sheikh from a small village between Al Mawsil and Zakhu* had given him a black-and-white parti-color brace — one feathered and one crop-eared smooth.† The feathered was named Rishan and the smooth Feena. Major Bentinck would note later that the Salukis of the area were not always as fine as his pair.[21]

Shipping the Salukis home was no easy proposition. Rather than go by ship from Basrah through the Straits of Hormuz and around Arabia to the Suez Canal, Bentinck went overland. In the late spring of 1923, they traveled with him through Baghdad, Halab, Jerusalem, Athens, Istanbul, and Paris. Then came the Channel crossing and six months of quarantine. Coming from the high plains of Kurdistan, just below the northern edge of the Zagros Mountains, Rishan and Feena were used to drastic extremes of temperature and the cold of the English climate did not affect them at all. They were the first parti-color Salukis imported to England. Like Major Bayne-Jardine, Bentinck had bred his pair sometime before taking the Channel crossing and Feena produced a litter in quarantine on October 1, 1923. In November, Major Bentinck§ joined the SGHC and was promptly recruited to judge the Saluki entry at the Ladies Kennel Association show that month.**

The next year, 1924, saw a marked rise in breed popularity. That year there were eighty-one Salukis registered compared to ten the year before. Crufts was very well attended in 1924 — there were 40,000 dogs on exhibit, more than twice the average for the years 1911–13.[22] A. Croxton Smith gave the usual post–Crufts account in *Country Life* and a photograph by Thomas Fall of "Mrs. Lance's Saluki, Sarona Kelb" was featured along with several other popular breeds.[23] Smith took pains to devote several glowing lines to the Saluki exhibits and newly formed club, and mentioned Florence, the Lances, and Mrs. Crouch.

Interest in the breed was growing internationally as well. The Saluki or Gazelle Hound Club was made an associate member of the Belgium dog club (possibly the Société Royale Saint-Hubert, which was founded in 1882 and was re-established in 1921 after the war). Salukis, while very rare in America, were being noticed and were finally classified as a breed by the American Kennel Club, although it was stipulated that a three-generation pedigree was necessary for registration and exhibition. As a new breed, where imports did not have pedigrees, this was going to be a bit difficult for the Americans. However, it was hinted that the AKC would be willing to forgo the three-generation requirement if three separate breeders in the United States announced their intentions to import, exhibit and breed. With the growing numbers of Salukis in England, Gladys knew that there should be no shortage of hounds to export to America and that breed recognition there was only a matter of time. That year, the Lances would send puppies from an April litter to America, Germany, France, and Sweden.

Only two breeders formally adopted kennel names in 1924. The Lances registered their kennel prefix and became entitled to the exclusive use of "Sarona" and their protégée Mrs. Crouch did the same with "Orchard." Florence finally got around to joining the Ladies Kennel Association that year and Robert Leighton judged the breed again in July. Bentinck eventually registered his pair as Feena and Rishan of Kurdistan in April 1924. He had kept at least three of Feena and Rishan's first litter, and was interested in getting another puppy. The

*Situated between the borders of Syria and Turkey and Iran.
†That one had cropped ears and the other didn't suggests that they were actually from two different breeders.
§After completing his service in Iraq, the local rank of lieutenant colonel reverted to his British Army rank of major.
**Flying Officer H. O. Fellowes would also import a Saluki from Kurdistan in 1926.

THE SALUKI CLUB MEMBER'S SHOW. TATTERSALLS. 1926.

Members of the Saluki or Gazelle Hound Club in Arab costume at the club show, Tattersalls horse auction hall, Knightsbridge, London, 1926. The gentleman on the left and two ladies on the right have dyed their skin for full effect. Courtesy of the Saluki or Gazelle Hound Club, image provided by the Kennel Club, London.

Lances had bred their new Daghestani Saluki, Kataf, to their bitch Nada, and Bentinck thought well enough of the breeding to take a bitch puppy from that April litter.* As they had taken a dog, Haroun, out of Feena and Rishan, a close relationship developed between the Lances and Major Bentinck. The Lances were very interested in his experiences in Iraq, and he presented them with a photograph showing his Salukis and a dead hare on the banks of the Tigris, as well as a portrait of Feena. The photos were added to the Sarona album and placed alongside the pictures of the crop-eared Hama and Hussein Ibshi Pasha and his belted Salukis.

In June, Bentinck bred Rishan to the Lances' Sarona Shawa (a bitch from Kelb and Echo's first and only litter). The Kurdistan pair was much in demand and Mrs. Crouch approached Major Bentinck about breeding Rishan to her Orchard Shahin. He obliged and the first Orchard litter was born on September 1, 1924. Shahin must have made a good recovery from whelping and nursing six puppies for when Bentinck judged the sizeable entry at the Ladies Kennel Association show on November 21, the prizes for Open Class Dog and Bitch went to Sarona Najib and Orchard Shahin. Smooths were shown separately and Miss Thynne's Pharaoh (another import) won in that classification.

Major Bentinck showed occasionally (with no great success), was quite active in the club and would serve in various capacities. He and the Lances continued interbreeding their hounds and would exchange the occasional puppy. The club membership was greatly saddened when Bentinck announced that he was leaving England late in the fall of 1925 to accept another

*Evidently the imported Kataf did not live up to the Lance's expectations as he was later sent to America, having sired only one litter in England. Another possibility is that Lance altruistically felt that the fledgling Saluki community in America could benefit from direct access to an imported stud dog. Sarona Kataf did figure prominently in early Saluki pedigrees in America.

advisory post in Iraq. Bentinck placed his Saluki puppies and youngsters in good homes, but could not bear to be parted from his favorites, Feena and Rishan. He made arrangements to take the pair with him — presumably on an easier route than the one that brought the three of them to England. Late in 1926, the loss was still felt, as Gladys lamented, "Major Bentinck's pair unfortunately is now lost to breeders in England as on his return to Iraq, he took his dogs with him."[24] Bentinck has the distinction of becoming the first person to export imported Salukis back to the land of their birth.

Ever mindful of the need for fresh blood in the English gene pool, Florence Amherst purchased two young Salukis of the Mesopotamian type from a friend and club member, Mrs. C. A. Vereker-Cowley. She and her husband had imported a dog and bitch obtained from two different sheikhs in the area around Basrah in southern Iraq* and their litter was whelped on February 9, 1923, the day after the club's first meeting at Crufts. Florence bought two litter brothers that were shaping well. Zobeid and Farhan were registered in her name in February and July 1924, respectively. She had had them for some time before registering them as they sired two of the three litters born at Foulden that summer.

Zobeid was an affectionate, handsome, deep-gold hound, and Florence was very fond of him and his lighter-colored brother. She had several portraits of the pair taken by Thomas

Florence Amherst with her only champion Zobeid (left) and his brother Farhan, 1924. The Mary Evans Picture Library/Thomas Fall Collection.

*Malik-el-Zobair and Zobeida-el-Zobair.

Fall, and for years they would feature in her advertisements as her Saluki beau ideal. The studio portrait of her seated on a bench, looking lovingly down at the two brothers would become the most familiar image of Florence to later generations of Saluki fanciers. Another Fall portrait of Zobeid with Farhan's head resting across his shoulders, would gradually become one of her signature ads, replacing that of Nafissah and the statue of Sekhmet. The two brothers were the only two Mesopotamian types to do any winning in the early years and Zobeid would become the third champion Saluki and Florence's one and only champion. He was responsible for restoring some of her former status in the show ring.

Another significant breeding pair cleared quarantine and was registered in July 1924. Binte El Nablous and Ebni El Nablous belonged to Miss Joan Mitchell, a nurse who had spent many years in Egypt and Nablus, Palestine. While there, she had had the loan of a bitch named Sheila of Amman* and bred her to Jack of Jerusalem, a famous sire owned by Mr. R. Hensman (the Saluki expert in Palestine who had tried to help Florence Amherst obtain imports before the war).[†]

Frances Joan Mitchell's parents were Stephen and Mary Ann Mitchell, and they brought her into the world at 12 Manor Road, in the north London borough of Stoke Newington, on June 18, 1874. There were four Mitchell daughters, Marie, Ernestine, Louie, and Frances Joan. All but Louie were tall and very slender. Joan, as she was known in the family, was nearly six feet in height, had blue eyes, brown hair, a longish face and thin lips. She wore wire-rimmed, round glasses and tended to wear severe suits. She was kind and generous in disposition, and a bit casual in her habits.

Her father was a middle-class merchant, and all the Mitchell daughters would work for a living. Joan had chosen nursing as a career and was a staff nurse (the lowest rank) at Albemarle Hospital at Stockwell, south of London, while she was in her twenties. As did many nurses from Albemarle when they reached their late twenties, she applied to the Westminster Hospital Training School and in 1902 she was accepted as a probationer. Joan spent four years in their rigorous program achieved satisfactory marks and did very well on her exams. In a time when nurse trainees were not supposed to be frivolous or too fond of the opposite sex, Joan's conduct was considered to be "very good" by the teaching staff. Upon completion of her term at Westminster, her instructor, Mabel H. Cave said, "Nurse Joan Mitchell is a good nurse and she is most kind and attentive to her patients. She is not very tidy in her work, and does not inspire confidence, but is conscientious and may be relied upon to do her duty. She is anxious to join the Army Nursing Service and there is no reason why she should not succeed in this capacity. Certificate received."[25]

Apparently army nursing had a less stringent standard than that of hospitals in England. Mabel Cave's recommendation seems to have been good enough for the military, for in 1906 at the age of thirty-two her pupil went to Egypt to wear the starched white aprons, collars, and caps of an army nurse. Sister Joan attended to soldiers with bullet and shrapnel wounds, broken bones and concussions from accidents, and a myriad of tropical afflictions such as sunstroke, malaria, dysentery, and parasitical infestations. Little is known about her career in the

---

Amman became the capital of Transjordan in 1921.
[†]*Jack had been bred by one Captain Jelf and would be imported to England at the age of ten in 1930, when Hensman retired from whatever occupation he had in Syria.*

Francis Joan Mitchell and her foundation Salukis, Ebni and Binte el Nablous, ca. 1924. Unknown, republished in *Saluki Heritage*, 1981.

Middle East except that after the armistice she accepted a post in Nablus at the Christian Missionary Hospital.*

A little over thirty miles north of Jerusalem, nestled between the mountains of Ebal and Gerizim, was Nablus — the Biblical city of Shechem, originally founded by the Romans as Flavia Neapolis.† A mountain oasis at 1,900 feet above sea level, the surrounding countryside is dry and full of scrub brush and thorns. A well said to have belonged to Jacob lay just to the south, and plenty of natural springs supported citrus and fruit trees, along with some of the largest olive groves in the country. There were also local industries, most notably fabric and sack weaving, and soap, manufactured from olive oil. Built out of local stone, the city was a compact, hodgepodge of eastern and western architecture and was dotted with minarets and the occasional cedar tree. Roads to Jerusalem, Nazareth, and Janin ran through Nablus. Prior to 1914, it could only be reached on foot or by donkey, but during the war, the Turks built a windy, narrow-gauge railway with a telegraph line alongside.

Occupied by the Germans and Turks during the war, the population of Nablus declined from 25,000 (prewar estimate) to 15,947 at the 1922 census.[26] Despite this, it was still the sixth-largest population center in Palestine. For the most part, the inhabitants were Muslims and Christians who lived together amicably (two of the three mosques had once been Crusader churches but there was still a church that dated from the Emperor Justinian).[27] Despite acceptance of their Christian neighbors, only a small number of Jews were tolerated by the staunch Muslims of Nablus.

Forward-thinking ideas about drainage of irrigation canals made Nablus one of the few places in Palestine that was not afflicted with malaria, despite the fact that the surrounding villages were plagued by the disease. The patients that Joan treated would have had the ailments that the country was known for at the time — typhoid fever, dysentery, tuberculosis, venereal disease, rabies, and a variety of eye diseases.§ Evidently her standard of nursing had improved considerably for she was eventually promoted to matron. As an act of solidarity with her sister nurses back in England who were struggling for professional recognition and state registration, in 1920 Joan joined the prestigious Royal College of Nursing.[28]

Somewhere along the line, she met a Captain J. Graham Ross who loaned her a Saluki bitch named Sheila. In the spring of 1922, Hensman sent Jack of Jerusalem to stay with Joan in Nablus and she bred the pair. On July 8, 1922, her first litter was born. There were seven puppies, and a deer grizzle, male and female — Ebni and Binte — would become her favorites.[29] Joan was in her late forties at the time, still slender and active. Fond of excursions with the hounds, she would go hiking in the surrounding countryside with a water bottle, sandwiches and her camera. Her hiking costume consisted of a narrow-brimmed, low-crowned hat, a short, fitted coat; long skirts; and sturdy shoes. Accompanied by her servant, a friend or two, and several hounds, they would climb the slopes of Mount Ebal, a thousand feet about the city. It was a taste of things to come, for in England she would become enthusiastic about the rugged exercise of coursing.

After eighteen years in the Middle East, Joan retired from nursing in February 1924. She had enough money saved for the shipping and quarantine, so Ebni and Binte went to England. Florence rented a house called Wyuna in Wendover. Near Aylesbury, Wendover was a mar-

---

One of five hospitals in Nablus at that time, it is now called the Evangelical Hospital.
†*The West Bank now surrounds Nablus.*
§*The Ophthalmic Hospital in Palestine was funded and run by the Knights of St. John of Jerusalem, the order to which Lord Amherst and his daughters belonged.*

ket town at the foot of the Chiltern Hills with a direct rail line to London and a connection to the Grand Union Canal.* Joan adjusted to her new life and made acquaintances in the SGHC. Eager to establish her line of grizzle Salukis, a month after her hounds cleared quarantine Joan bred Binte to Mrs. Crouch's Yaffa. At Wyuna, she hired a young woman to help out with grooming, feeding, and cleanup. A particularly good snapshot of the kennel maid combing two Salukis entitled "Preparation" was judged "Very Highly Commended" in a dog photo contest.[30] That summer, Joan moved some 40 miles away from Wendover to a modest house in Charlbury, a small market town northwest of Oxford. She took Ebni in the ring under Brigadier Lance at the SGHC show on the first of October, and while Lance thought that he had a good head and shoulders, he pronounced Ebni "dead out of condition" and did not award him a placement.[31] Less than a week afterward, Binte's litter was whelped on October 6 at the new house, which she had named "Nablous"—the same name that she would choose for her prefix, and which she would give to each of her subsequent residences.[†]

After his brief tour of the war efforts in Egypt, Arabia, and Palestine, the journalist Lowell Thomas returned to America and created an extraordinary lecture entitled, "With Allenby in Palestine, including The Capture of Jerusalem and The Liberation of Holy Arabia." After his initial run in New York, he was persuaded to bring the show to London in August 1919, and the crowds packed into Covent Garden for two performances per day during a two-week run.[32] With overtones of the Crusades, the show was so popular with the war-weary public, that it was extended to six months and moved several times to larger venues. It is estimated that over a million people saw it in London.[33] Colonel Lawrence was initially only a part of the performance, but as public interest in him grew, the savvy Thomas adapted the show accordingly and retitled it, "With Allenby in Palestine and Lawrence in Arabia." Lawrence considered the show to be entirely fictional and was greatly dismayed by the notoriety.[34]

Today the lecture would have been called a multimedia event, for Thomas combined hand-colored lantern slides, film,[§] live music, and even dance into his dramatic and highly embellished lecture. He was a spellbinding storyteller and gifted with improvisation, relying often on memory rather than a script. While some of his photographs, footage, and script notes have been preserved, no complete record of the performance exists but it is likely that one of the photographs of Goslett and Snorter was included in the show. After his run in London, Thomas took the show around England and then on a world tour that lasted until 1924.[35] That year, he published his sensational and wildly popular *With Lawrence in Arabia*. Interest in Colonel Lawrence grew even stronger.

Having once corresponded with Lawrence, Florence now saw a way to capitalize on the public clamor for things Arabian, and she began writing to him again. She may have even

---

*Until railroad efficiency, speed, and lower costs pulled business away from the canal boat trade, England's canal system was the primary method for transporting food and manufactured goods. The Grand Union Canal connected London and industrial Birmingham.

† "Nablous" was the accepted spelling in Joan's time.

§ There was always a certain element of danger in attending the cinema in the days before nonflammable, safety motion-picture film was invented. Nitrate film was highly volatile and if accidentally ignited by the heat of the arc lamps, it produced toxic fumes and fire that frequently took the lives of the projectionist and the audience.

seen the Goslett/Snorter photos in Thomas's stage lecture. She certainly hoped that Lawrence might have some stories of Salukis in the Arab Revolt that she could add to her collection of lore or perhaps provide her with contacts for additional imports. Lawrence felt he had been betrayed by the British government in their treatment of the Arabs after the war, and was sick of the publicity and stream of letters asking for lectures, favors, or even marriage. Once again, his lack of response to her letters caused Florence to write to D. G. Hogarth, who had long since ceased to be Lawrence's employer. She implored him to influence Lawrence (now going by the name T. E. Shaw to preserve some measure of anonymity) for a reply. This was the last straw. In early 1924, from his home at Clouds Hill, Lawrence wrote to Hogarth about the forthcoming special edition of his book, *Seven Pillars of Wisdom*. In his letter, he talks about his friends Gertrude Bell and Robin Buxton (the latter retired from the Imperial Camel Corps and now a London banker managing Lawrence's financial affairs). In his opening lines he writes testily; "I'll write to the greyhound fancier ... but she will get nothing out of me. I've finished with the East; & forgotten it."[36] What Lawrence said in his final letter to Florence is unknown for it does not survive, but she would still boast of her association with Colonel Lawrence from his days at Carchemish and his afternoon visit to see her Salukis.

Ironically, two years before Lawrence's death in a motorcycle accident in 1935, the Saluki would make an odd and final mark on his image. On August 26, 1933, while still serving in the Air Force as Aircraftsman Shaw, Lawrence attended a luncheon at Lympne, the home of Sir Philip Sassoon, the Undersecretary of State for Air. Harold Nicolson, an author and historian who had been His Majesty's Counselor at Tehran, was lunching there as well. Nicolson had known Lawrence from the Peace Conference of 1919, and in his diary that night, commented on how the man had changed physically since returning from Arabia. "After luncheon at Lympne Colonel T. E. Lawrence, the Uncrowned King of Arabia, arrives. He is dressed in Air Force uniform which is very hot. Unlike other privates in the Air Force, he wears his heavy uniform when he goes out to tea. He has become stockier and squarer. The sliding, lurcher effect is gone. A bull terrier in place of a saluki."[37]

16

The Limelight and a Broken Heart

"It is with the deepest regret that I relinquish the post of Honorary Secretary, especially as the Club has been very dear to me owing to its having been formed in embryo in my mind before its inauguration in 1923, with the sole object of benefiting the breed."

Gladys Lance[1]

In late November 1924, a harrowing accident occurred at Wentfield. The Brigadier was out for a morning ride on one of his Arabs and had brought along the Sarona Labrador and two frisky, thirteen-month-old Salukis. While riding over a bridge with a 30-inch parapet, Sarona Dhole suddenly leapt over the edge of the bridge and disappeared from sight. As the macadam road was thirty feet below, Lance held his breath while waiting for the sound of the inevitable and awful thud. "I would not have given sixpence for the dog at that moment," said Lance.[2] But the dreaded sound never came. He summoned a passing gamekeeper to hold his horse and anxiously scrambled down the bank. There was the dazed hound — on his feet and staggering toward home. Luckily, Wentfield was not far away and Lance led the injured Saluki home.

All morning Kelb's son lay as dead but toward evening he revived and took a little milk. Dhole slept in the house that night and the next morning was able to trot out into the garden, albeit stiff and limping. Three days later, he was almost completely normal except for tenderness in one shoulder and a slight limp in his foreleg. A week later, he was running and jumping, and Gladys believed that the inherent vitality of the breed would ensure a full recovery.[3] Dhole did indeed recover, for he was eventually sent to Bermuda and then to the United States in 1927. He coursed and killed a fox shortly after his arrival, and would become the first American champion.

In late 1924 or early 1925, Florence rented a small flat near the former Amherst properties in Queen's Gate Gardens and Grosvenor Square. Number 6 William Street, off Kensington Road in Knightsbridge, provided her with easier access to the London shows and club events. Here she hosted club meetings and always offered her guests tea, sandwiches, and cigarettes. Letters were read from Saluki owners abroad and discussed, as were requests for information and photographs of the breed. Florence still kept Salukis at Foulden but for the first time not all of her hounds lived with her. Zobeid and Farhan now stayed with a veterinary surgeon, Captain Widden M.R.C.V.S.,* who ran a quarantine kennel at 131 Lancaster Road in the Notting Hill district.

This arrangement made showing her winning brace easier as she would meet Captain

---

Member Royal College of Veterinary Surgeons.

Widden with the hounds at ringside and he would often exhibit for her. The brothers were also offered at stud and having them in London was convenient for arranged matings. Florence evidently trusted Widden with her instructions in these matters, for he was allowed to make breeding arrangements for the hounds, provided the stud fee of £10, 10 shillings was paid. At this stage in her life, Florence seems to have often been a beat behind everyone else — although in 1926, the year that the signature red British telephone kiosk debuted, she did have a telephone installed in William Street at a time when only 36 Britons in 1,000 had private telephones.* She had not joined the LKA until after the political moment had come and gone. As Florence had been for so many years the only person registering Salukis, she saw no need for a kennel name, and it was not until September 1925, that she finally followed suit with the other Saluki breeders and registered the now famous kennel name "Amherstia." Her devotion to the breed could be trying for her relatives (who fondly considered her an eccentric) for when she came visiting it was with a hound or two, and they were not always well-behaved guests.

Although Joan Mitchell did not exhibit very much, she usually attended dog shows and was an active member of the club. Coursing meets were just beginning to be organized by some of the members and Joan was particularly enthusiastic about them. The Nablous Salukis would become another significant addition to the gene pool in England and Florence and Joan became fast friends. Gladys and Joan interbred the Saronas and Nablousi, and Florence allowed Amherstia males to be bred to both kennels. But in order to keep her strain pure, Florence never used their stud dogs on Amherstia bitches.

Joan's hounds were quite popular in her neighborhood and she was continually refusing the offers of tradesmen wanting to buy puppies. She did sell them to suitable homes, exported at least one to Ireland, and at one point gave her sister, Ernestine, a pair. Late in the summer of 1925, she sent in advertising copy to the Kennel Club Show catalog stating that there were "some young stock for sale at present" — youngsters from her litter a year earlier. Joan noted further that she and her hounds were taking up temporary residence for the fall and winter, forty miles southeast of London in the town of Fleet.† The ad photo showed the overgrown Nablous garden outside her back door, and in it, a small girl in a summer frock holding the leashes of Ebni, Binte and two of their yearling daughters.

About the same time, Joan asked Gladys to mention in *Dog World* (Gladys had taken over the Saluki column from Mr. F. B. Fowler late in 1924) that Nablous Ebal and Gezirim (named after the mountains outside Nablus) were for sale. They were described as prize-winners, good coursers, and both "over distemper" for sale at 30 and 25 guineas, or 50 guineas the pair.§ There was still no vaccine against the periodic outbreaks of distemper and whole kennels could perish. In 1925, Miss Helena I. H. Barr's kennels (Grevel) were infected by a newly acquired Irish Wolfhound, and she quarantined herself and her smooth Salukis from shows and travel while she nursed her hounds and waited for the disease to run its course. Any dog that had survived the illness had immunity, and was consequently more valuable as show or breeding stock.

With the growing number of puppies in the country, prospective owners no longer had

---

*Great Britain was at the bottom of the list of major countries with telephones in 1927. America led with 160 telephones per 1,000 people (Charles Loch Mowat, Britain Between the Wars: 1918–1940 (Chicago: University of Chicago Press, 1955) 349.)

†Northeast Hampshire.

§50 guineas (£52 10s) would be worth £2,057.99 in 2006. MeasuringWorth.com.

to pay for import and quarantine costs and prices dropped to an affordable range. At that time, three-to five-month-old Saluki puppies were selling for around 15 guineas, but for an experienced coursing and show hound, such as Mrs. Foster Mitchell's Sheik of Egypt, the asking price was a startling 100 guineas. Prices for average-quality adults were generally slightly higher than those for puppies. In September 1925, when the Lances needed to decrease their kennel numbers, Gladys took out a special classified ad in the *Dog World* that advertised three bitches for sale at £25–£30 — "Owing to reduction before the winter."[4] She would run a similar ad again in August 1926 as the Sarona kennels were "overstocked."[5]

Joan seems to have led something of a nomadic life, for she moved six times between 1924 and 1930, and from the evidence one is tempted to suspect that it was because of her hounds. Evidently her temporary move from Charlbury turned into something rather more than she expected. In April 1926, the year that she registered her prefix "Nablous," instead of going back to Charlbury she moved her Salukis to Gertrude Desborough's kennels at Clarence Lodge, Earlswood Common, Redhill, Surrey, and took up residence with Gertrude. The Desborough Boarding Kennels were a full-service facility on five acres just off the London-Brighton road and offered training, handling at shows, weekly collection of dogs in London, litter whelping, and "Young Stock for Sale, and Dogs of any Breed obtainable at short notice."[6] Gladys reported in *Dog World* that Joan's yearlings were still for sale, and that at the new location at Miss Desborough's she "would have "plenty of scope to increase her kennel and specialize in the color that she terms 'deer-colored.'" This seems to imply that Joan either had insufficient room for her Salukis or that her landlord was unhappy with the number that she did have — or perhaps both.[7] Ending up with a few too many older Salukis was a common enough occurrence for breeders given the limited market for puppies. A year later, in 1927, Joan relocated "Nablous" to Pendall's Homestead, Hampstead-Norris, near Newberry, Berkshire, where again she would have "ample room for rearing."[8] Joan became relatively settled there and it would be three years before her next move.

Despite what Brigadier Lance had said about Ebni's lack of conditioning at the club show in 1924, Joan exercised him regularly, took him coursing during the season, and considered him quite fit indeed. Ebni had sired one litter to a Sarona bitch and Joan thought he held great promise as a stud dog. No sooner had she moved to Desborough's when there was a tragic incident. On Wednesday, April 21, Ebni had been out running free and was shot dead by a farmer or gamekeeper. Joan was crushed at the loss of one of her original pair, and telephoned Florence in London immediately with the sad news. Her friend offered condolences and seems to have persuaded Joan that the Natural History Museum would be interested in another Saluki import for their collection. Joan tried to telephone the museum the day after Ebni died, but the line was so bad that she could not be heard. Grief stricken, she would do nothing more for two days.

On Saturday, she wrote in her elegant hand to the curator and offered Ebni's body for their collection and a photograph of the hound in life to help with the mounting. Gertrude's kennels must have had some limited cold storage for Joan wrote, "Kindly send me an immediate reply as I must have him buried should you decide not to have him."[9] Two days later, the museum received her letter and already having Luman and Lance of Anatolia, politely declined the offer of the hound's body. A week after his death, Joan buried her Ebni at Clarence Lodge.

Interest in preserving the breed's original function led several members to form a coursing section in 1925. Specifically conceived to prove the functionality of their Salukis, the hunts were organized much like the Greyhound meets of the day, only without bookmakers or turf accountants. The hounds and owners (some on horseback) would systematically walk through an obliging landowner's field in search of hares. A professional slipper would release two hounds at the sight of healthy quarry speeding away and the mounted judge would gallop after the hounds. A winner was declared based on the judge's opinion of the comparative merits of speed, agility, and ability to force the hare to turn. As the hares were on their home ground and knew all the bolt-holes, they were not always caught by the Salukis, but those that were became a main dish at someone's table, for the English brown hare is excellent fare indeed.

As the hunting season coincided with late fall and winter, the fields were frequently wet and muddy. Clothing for hounds and hunters was always a mixed bag, depending on what was thought to be serviceable for the ground and the anticipated weather that day. Women tended to wear tight-fitting berets, belted overcoats over a suit jacket and skirt or jodhpurs, and knee boots. The men wore caps or fedoras, tweed jackets, vests, neckties, and knickerbockers. Footwear consisted of wool socks with ankle boots (sometimes with the addition of gaiters) or rubber boots known as "Wellies."* If rain was expected (and it usually was), trench coats and mackintoshes were worn. The Salukis had coats made of plaid wool, waxed cloth, or heavy quilting to keep them warm before their runs.

The first coursing meet was held in October 1925 at a farm near Chipping Norton, Oxfordshire, and one of Kelb's daughters, Sarona Nada, and Mrs. Foster Mitchell's Egyptian

The Saluki Coursing Club meet at Cleve Farm, Kent, 1933. Gladys Lance talks to Mrs. Cleve on horseback. Courtesy of the Saluki or Gazelle Hound Club, image provided by the Kennel Club, London.

Named after a style of boot that the Duke of Wellington popularized.

Bey won the day.[10] Joan Mitchell was an active participant in the sport as was Miss Kerrison, who served as secretary for the Coursing Section. Naturally, the Brigadier and Gladys were great coursing enthusiasts and frequently officiated at the meets. They made an interesting couple — the thin Brigadier in his tweeds and cap, and his stocky wife, wearing leather jacket, sturdy leggings, skirt, and her signature cloche hat.

For those not interested in open-field coursing or without the stamina to walk the field, but who still wanted to test their hounds, the Saluki Racing Club was formed two years after the Coursing Section. Also taking their lead from the Greyhound and Whippet races, the Salukis were run on tracks after a mechanical lure known as "Fluffy Herbert — the electric hare."[11] The organized chasing of mechanical hares had begun in Manchester, in 1926, and to regulate the new version of an ancient sport, the National Greyhound Racing Society was formed the following year.[12] Greyhound racing and the associated betting became phenomenally popular. In London, attendance at greyhound tracks increased from three million per year in 1927 to eight million in 1929.[13] In November 1927, Arthur Craven of Manchester proposed to establish a training kennel and racetrack to board, condition, train, and rank greyhounds, Borzois, and Salukis for track racing.[14] The scheme never materialized and owners were left to their own devices to train sighthounds to chase Fluffy Herbert.

That year there were four Saluki clubs in England, the SGHC, two coursing clubs — the Coursing Section of the SGHC and the Cleve Saluki Coursing Club, and the Saluki Racing Club. On December 14, 1927, Florence hosted a meeting of racing enthusiasts at her London flat, and naturally she was elected president of the Saluki Racing Club. The committee consisted of Mrs. Carlo Clarke (chair), Gertrude Desborough (secretary), Mr. W. E. C. Greenwood (treasurer), Gladys Lance, Mrs. Crouch, Mr. A. V. Cowley, Mr. Quinn, Lady Katherine McNeile, Miss Kerrision, and Major Bentinck, who had just returned from Iraq.[15] The first race took place at Wembley Stadium on Saturday afternoon, March 22, 1928. The following week, Gladys noted in *Dog World* that Florence Amherst's and Joan Mitchell's Salukis ran well but had been distracted during their races. This would tend to be a common occurrence for Salukis. They competed at the Staines Racing Track in London and as far north as Blackpool, Lancashire. At the racing meets, Mrs. Crouch frequently gave demonstrations of her Salukis' hurdle-jumping abilities.

The Lances' home at Wentfield was a popular stop for visiting Saluki fanciers and Arabists. Lady Anne Blunt's daughter, Lady Wentworth, had been there to see the Sarona horses and hounds.[16] Captain Cooper of the Iraq Police Force had come to Wentfield for tea in 1924 and described Iraqi breed type and the organized hunting in Basrah. In 1925, Miss Vivian Bonander visited from Sweden (she had imported two Saronas the year before) and reported on Saluki activities, which, as coursing was illegal in Sweden, were confined to showing, obedience, and agility.* Dutch Saluki enthusiasts Mrs. Jüngeling and her son Han (Barukhzy Kennel) were frequent visitors to Wentfield. Probably the most significant visitor in 1925 was Sheikh Hamad bin 'Isa al Khalifa, the ruler of Bahrein, who brought with him his wife, son, and brother and sister-in-law. The Sheikh's brother, Prince Abdullah, had been to England once before in 1919, but it was the first trip for Sheikh Hamad and his family. One of their goals

---

*In March 1928, a film of four Salukis in harness (complete with sleighbells) pulling Miss Vivan Bonander in her sleigh was a great hit in the Stockholm cinema.

was to purchase furniture and plumbing fixtures for his new residence, Sakhir Palace, and of course, to take in the sights — one of these being the Sarona hounds at Wentfield.

Sheikh Hamad was well-known in the Middle East as a hunting enthusiast and breeder of quality Salukis.* At home, Hamad's favorite bitch, Hosha, came with him daily to his office in the palace, and was hand-fed the choicest joint at the end of a meal.[†] At Wentfield on a gray day, the royal party, along with Major Robert Ernest Cheesman O.B.E.,[§] visited the Lances. Cheesman had met Sheikh Hamad four years earlier in Bahrein, and had discussed the Sheikh's preference for certain colors — Chessman recalled the Sheik believed "Pale Salukis withstand the summer heat better than blacks."[17] Sheikh Hamad was particularly interested in Lance's horses and Salukis. After seeing the animals, he gathered his family to pose with the brigadier, Major Cheesman, and Kelb, while Gladys snapped a photo. The picture was placed in the Sarona album underneath the shot of Lance as a "mock Arab" and titled, "The Real Thing at Wentfield."

Like Lance, Cheesman was from Kent and had also soldiered in the Middle East for many years. Cheesman had spent little time in his home county since enlisting in 1914. He had soldiered in India and Iraq, explored in Arabia, and was now living at Tilsden Farm, in Cran-

Major Robert Cheesman, Brigadier Lance, and Sheikh Hamad bin 'Isa al Khalifa of Bahrein (second from right), his wife, son, brother, and sister-in-law posing with Sarona Kelb at Wentfield, 1925. Courtesy of the Saluki or Gazelle Hound Club, image provided by the Kennel Club, London.

Noted Arabists such as Major Dickson and Carl Raswan have commented upon Sheikh Hamad's famous kennels. In 1977 Bahrein would issue a set of stamps depicting Salukis.

[†]*When Sheikh Hamad died, Hosha was given to his advisor, Sir Charles Belgrave, K.B.E., also a Saluki enthusiast.*

[§]*Later colonel and C.B.E.*

brook, about 20 miles southeast of the Lances' home at Wentfield. In March 1924, Cheesman had returned to England after eleven weeks mapping some of the Eastern Najd desert. He had brought home a young grizzle Saluki from the Jabrin oasis in Arabia*. In April 1925, the registration of Najman of Jabrin was published in the Kennel Club's *Gazette*. Najman was shown that month at Holland Park, and he took second place in his class — a fact that Cheesman proudly noted alongside a photo of the hound in his book *In Unknown Arabia*.

In December 1924, the Lances bought and imported a bitch from Peake Pasha, a high-ranking official and Saluki breeder in Transjordan. Four years old when she cleared quarantine in May 1925, Safedi was immediately mated to Kelb. Colonel Frederick Gerard Peake, C.M.G., O.B.E., and founder of the Arab Legion, was another of those officers who had been in India, Egypt, and the Sudan. As a poor officer in India he supplemented his meager income with the extra pay that was offered upon mastery of a language and became fluent in Hindustani, Urdu, Pushtu, Persian, and Arabic. During the war, he commanded 160 men of the Egyptian Camel Corps under Lawrence and Joyce. Peake's soldiers took quickly to Lawrence's guerrilla tactics and were so effective at blowing up trains and railways that his men were known as "the Peake Demolition Company, Ltd."[18]

After the war, he was commandant of Al Aqabah and in 1921 was promoted to inspector general of the Gendarmerie. He was given the title of "Pasha" and Peake moved his headquarters to Amman. The following year, he raised the Arab Legion as a peacekeeping force to quell Bedouin brigandry and rebellion on the contradictory borders of the newly created mandate of Transjordan and the Hedjaz State (later Saudi Arabia). Only sharp trackers and hard riders could catch Bedouin raiders after they disappeared into the desert. Peake and his Arab Legion were just the men for the job and happened to be keen Saluki enthusiasts — and not above kidnapping to obtain a good specimen.[†]

Peake Pasha was eventually promoted to Director of Public Security. Like many other British officers, he had taken up breeding and hunting with Salukis for a brief time in the years after the war, as did his second in command and eventual successor, Major John Baggot Glubb, O.B.E., M.C.[§] On the Arab Legion camel patrols, it was common enough for a Saluki or two to come along. Peake's good friend and biographer, Major C. S. Jarvis, described hunting while on camel patrol:

> Excellent fun can be had with hares if one is on camel patrol, as one is always accompanied by Salukis who thoroughly understand their business. On arriving at a likely piece of country the patrol extends to fifty paces, thus covering a wide expanse of desert, and the Salukis post themselves at different points along the line, running up to every small rise to scan the country in front. Immediately a hare gets up, the policeman nearest him gives a wild yell, which is a very good imitation of a 'view hallo,' and in a moment, as if they had telegraphed themselves to the spot, the whole pack of Salukis are all out after the quarry.

Approximately 150 miles southeast of Riyadh.

†*Bill Fraser, managing director of the first desert freight service from Damascus to Baghdad, had a Saluki stolen by one of the Arab Legion's armored-car patrols. Malek escaped from Amman months later and walked home to Rutbah Wells — a journey of over 250 miles. Fraser married Dorothy Lees and they founded the Rualla Saluki kennels based on Iraqi stock (Dorothy Lees, "The Rualla," in* The Saluqi: Coursing Hound of the East, *edited by Gail Goodman, Apache Junction, AZ: Midbar 1995), 561.*

§*Later lieutenant general and K.C.B., C.M.G., D.S.O., and during World War II, founder of the famed Desert Patrol.*

From the back of one's mount one gets an excellent view, but as the camel — normally a disgruntled, uninteresting beast — has apparently a sporting strain hidden in him somewhere, and takes charge on these occasions, going off at a lumbering gallop, one is usually too much occupied in trying to avoid coming unstuck to follow the hunt properly. The Salukis must have a very poor field of vision owing to the mass of scrub brushes that obscures their view, but their eyesight is phenomenal, and, unless the hare reaches a rocky hill early in the chase, his doom is sealed. He is not rolled over, however, until he has performed some marvelous right-angled turns that send the Salukis sprawling over each other in the dust, and one way and another a Saluki hunt on camel-back is a sport not to be despised.[19]

Forty years later, the Jordanian Frontier Patrols did not look much different than those of their Arab Legion predecessors. A typical Arab soldier wore red and white *Kaffiyeh*, khaki uniform, ammunition bandoleer, and the ubiquitous Short Magazine Lee-Enfield rifle slung across his back. Trotting alongside the camels, Salukis still went on patrol.[20]

Two Hijaz princes who had played key roles in the Arab Revolt exported Salukis to England. Colonel J. Dalton White was the proud owner of a bitch presented to him by King Faisal of Iraq.[21] She whelped seven puppies in quarantine and in August 1925 the pack was released to their owner. Faisal's brother, the Emir Abdullah ibn Hussein,* ruled Transjordan and evidently bred Salukis for four of his breeding were sent to England. In 1926 Florence Amherst received a pair of yearling bitches† who traveled to England partly by airplane. The Emir sent a fine, red male to Miss F. M. Cook of the Darwin kennels,§ and Joan Mitchell's friend, Captain Graham Ross, brought Sheila of Amman (bred by the Emir and the mother of the founding Nablous hounds), to England at the age of five, registering her in February 1926.

Salukis were slowly catching on in popularity and several members of the nobility had developed an appreciation for them. Princess Mary still coursed Sarona Maluki in Yorkshire (a fact which Gladys frequently pointed out in her breed publicity) and Lady Hervey Bathurst, Lord and Lady Ashburton,** Lady Katherine McNeile, and the Marchioness Tweeddale all owned Salukis, and did a bit of showing as well. The half brother of the deceased Lord Carnarvon, the Honorable Mervyn Herbert and his wife Mary Elizabeth, had acquired Salukis in Egypt and brought them back to Tetton House near Taunton, Somerset, when he retired from the Foreign Office in 1926. Herbert had been an attaché in the Diplomatic Service and served as First Secretary in Rome, Lisbon, and in Madrid, where he met his future wife, Mary Elizabeth, the daughter of Joseph Willard, the American ambassador. He was also First Secretary in Cairo at the end of the Great War. Herbert was still in Egypt when Tutankhamun's tomb was being cleared and had joined Carter and Lord Carnarvon on many forays into the tomb.[22]

Under British authority, Abdullah had been ruling the newly created country of Transjordan since 1921. It became the independent Hashemite Kingdom of Jordan, with Abdullah its monarch in 1946. He ruled for just five more years and was assassinated in 1951.

†*Zobeid was bred to both of them. Mr. Hensman may have arranged the importation of the two bitches for Florence.*

§*At the time that Sheikh of Darwin was released, Miss Cook had two more bitches in quarantine.*

**Emir Shaker of the Rualla tribe from the area near Amman, had given Lord Ashburton a red male. Prince Habib Lotfallah and the manager of the Ghezirah Palace acted as intermediaries in the arrangement.*

About the time Mervyn was thinking of retirement from the Foreign Office, he and Mary imported a ten-year-old male, Nimroud, and a five-year-old bitch, Sheba, who was bred to Kelb in 1925. The Herberts chose Tetton as their kennel name and joined the SGHC in 1928, but do not seem to have been very interested in showing or coursing. Mervyn Herbert died in 1929 but Mary remained semi-active in the club through 1932. Several of the Tetton hounds were brought to America but only casually registered.[23] It was in fact a family connection, for it was Mary's mother who imported the Tetton Salukis.

Mrs. Frank Holmes was certainly the only Saluki club member to have imported both a Saluki and an Arabian fox cub to England. Hosha the Saluki was from Bahrain and the orphan cub from Kuwait.* As was almost obligatory in the fraternity of Saluki bitch importers, Hosha was bred to Kelb. Mrs. Holmes did a bit of showing but having hunted with their hounds in the Arabian Gulf states, she and her husband really went in for coursing.

Major Frank Holmes, a native New Zealander, was one of those extraordinary colonial characters whose description could define the stereotype. Holmes was a stout man with a sunburned face, and who wore topee, vest, and coat at all times — even in the hottest weather. He liked to prod his servants with his walking stick and allegedly paid them extra for the privilege of doing so. All this was noted by Charles Belgrave, the British advisor to Sheikh Hamad, who described the tall New Zealander as a "Somerset Maugham" character, with a "varied fund of knowledge of literature, the Bible, astronomy, geology, and a great appreciation for Oriental antiques, especially china."[24] Holmes had been drilling artesian wells in Bahrain and had won oil concessions in Bahrain, Kuwait, and the Saudi-Kuwait Neutral Zone — beating out British Petroleum. He was in fact responsible for the discovery of oil in the Persian Gulf. His concessions were eventually transferred to the newly formed American company, Gulf Oil, and later to Standard Oil of California.[25]

When they returned to England in 1925, the Holmeses settled down in Sandon, near Chelmsford in Essex County, and started breeding Salukis. Hosha of Bahrein [sic] (bred by His Excellency Abdul Mohsin Al Mushari) cleared quarantine and was registered in July 1925. The following month they arranged for another import and in February 1926, Lady of Sherjah (bred by the Sheikh of Shammar), emerged from the six-month confinement at the Hackbridge Kennels. Hosha had her litter of five puppies in June 1926 and at that time they had three more hounds in quarantine. Getting back in shape after the litter, Hosha was both showing and coursing in the fall, although the Holmeses would always prefer the latter to the former.

Gladys and the Brigadier used to periodically visit the Hackbridge Kennels to evaluate the Salukis that were being brought into England. She would note in her column the progress of the Salukis in quarantine, their country of origin, and which ones seemed the most promising. Some were made available for sale immediately upon clearing quarantine. Salukis continued to flood into England from the men and women who were finishing their military or political service in the Middle East.

Iraq provided most of the imports in this period, as RAF officers who had been quelling the tribal rebellions with biplanes and armored cars brought their hounds back with them. With the influx of soldiers' dogs, there was again public concern that the government might relax the quarantine laws in order to enable "garrison dogs" to more easily come home with

---

*This was a different Hosha from the one that Sheikh Hamad owned. The fox cub was presented in her name to the London Zoological Gardens.

their soldiers.[26] From 1924 to 1928 there were at least 35 imports, but not all of them were registered with the Kennel Club or bred from. They came from Transjordan, Egypt, Iraq, and the Persian Gulf, but surprisingly only one actually came from Arabia — Cheesman's Najman. In 1927, Florence imported an excellent representative of the breed but it did not come from the Middle East. This Saluki came from Italy and was cast in bronze.

Benvenuto Cellini (1500–1571) was a brilliant goldsmith and sculptor who designed the fortifications for the city of Paris, seduced both men and women, committed several murders, and recorded all this in a very earthy memoir.[*] In 1545, he returned from Paris to Florence to work under the patronage of Grand Duke Cosimo de Medici. Cellini was commissioned to make a life-size bronze of the Greek hero Perseus and the beheaded Gorgon. The Duke wanted the sculpture for the Piazza della Signoria as both public art and a demonstration of his good taste and wealth. Sculpting and casting a monumental bronze requires a very different set of skills than those of the traditional goldsmith, who worked on much smaller scales. To practice his casting technique for the Perseus, Cellini sculpted an 18 x 27.8cm bas-relief of a Saluki[†] owned by his patron.[27] It was finished in August 1545 and so pleased the duke that he immediately bought it for his personal collection.[28]

The standing hound is instantly recognizable as a Saluki and very lifelike in appearance.[§] The work is stunning, and despite its apparent simplicity, it is a tour de force of modeling skill. In *Cellini*, John Pope Hennessy would write of the Saluki plaque, "The relief system is one of extreme subtlety — its poles are established by the head, which is fully modeled, and the back, which is in the lowest possible relief— and the technique is that of a goldsmith not of a bronze caster."[29] Florence had seen this sculpture in the Museo Nationale Bargello[**] in Florence, Italy, and was so taken with it that she commissioned an exact copy, by a local Italian sculptor. As a demonstration of her belief in the significance of new blood for the gene pool, she presented it to her club in 1927 as the Amherstia Perpetual Trophy, to be awarded to the "Best Imported Dog or Bitch."[††]

There was club fad for perpetual trophy donations — prizes for a specific class or type and which had to be won a certain number of times by the same dog or exhibitor in order to be permanently retired.[§§] Perpetual trophies donated by and awarded only to members of the SGHC included the Ch.[***] Zobeid Perpetual Trophy for best debutante, the Tut-Ankh-Amen Cup for best dog or bitch, the Lotus Flower for best black and tan, the Ch. Orchard Shahin Perpetual Trophy for best bitch, and the Ch. Sarona Kelb Perpetual Trophy for best dog. With the variety of trophies for these and other categories, it was perfectly possible for the best of breed to win several of the perpetuals. In 1927, Miss Aline Doxford who bred Salukis, Deerhounds, Afghans, and Cavalier King Charles Spaniels under her prefix, donated what must

---

[*]*Vita di Benvenuto Cellini.*

[†]*During the Renaissance, they were known as levrieri Turchi or Turkish Greyhounds.*

[§]*An excellent color photograph of this sculpture may be seen in plate 122 of Sir John Pope-Hennessy's 1985 book,* Cellini.

[**]*"Cane levriero," Bargello Inventory #19-B.*

[††]*That year it was awarded at the Ladies Kennel Association show and the National Dog Show in Birmingham. Still in the club's possession, it is now awarded annually by the SGHC.*

[§§]*The criteria of some perpetual trophies often pushed the donor's agenda or favorite cause.*

[***]*Ch. denotes a champion dog or bitch. In the English system, a dog that has won the Challenge competition against both champion and non-champion dogs of the same sex at three different shows is awarded champion status. Championship requirements vary from country to country.*

have been the white elephant of perpetuals — the Ruritania Trophy. It was awarded to the best Bloodhound, Borzoi, Greyhound, Deerhound, Irish Wolfhound, or Saluki to be retired after five wins or three in succession by the same dog. In this round of competition, the best of breed of all six of the breeds would be brought into the main ring and a judge would select the best representative of its breed as the winner. No Saluki ever won it and it was withdrawn after three years.

In May 1927, Florence's kennel manager, Captain Widden, died suddenly and she had to make new boarding and handling arrangements. It is not clear how many Salukis she kept at the house in William Street and she may have shuttled them back and forth between Foulden, keeping the best of her show and breeding prospects (such as Zobeid and Farhan) in London. Later that year, she left the Amherstias in care of her kennel man at Foulden when she took passage to New York for the second time. It must have been a poignant moment for Florence when she visited the Metropolitan Museum of Art to see the seven statues of Sekhmet that used to watch over Didlington.[30] There are no clear indications of her itinerary or the purpose of the trip, but she did tour America and Canada and presumably met with some members of the newly formed Saluki Club of America. The SCOA had just been organized in July and had less than ten members and even fewer Salukis. Florence did go to Biltmore House to visit John and Cornelia Cecil and their two-year-old son George.* John kept at least one Saluki at Biltmore and would become a member of the American club. In October 1927, she returned from America in time to exhibit at the Royal Veterinary College Dog Show at Crystal Palace on the 27th and 28th. Gladys noted her return from abroad in the *Dog World* and that the "popular president brought three exhibits from her large kennel."[31] At the age of 67, it was the last time she would go to America.

Most of the serious breeders in the club were asked to judge at least once, although it is interesting to note that the two chief advocates of the "Mesopotamian" type, Florence Amherst and Joan Mitchell, do not seem to have ever judged at a show. A. Croxton Smith O.B.E. (now on the Kennel Club Committee and an Honorary Member of the SGHC), Robert Leighton, and the Brigadier himself had repeat judging assignments in the Saluki ring during the decade. When exhibiting, Lance was always correctly attired in a three-piece suit, with his entry's number card tucked neatly in the hatband of his fedora. But occasionally for fun and to attract attention, he and some of the members and their guests would dress in Middle Eastern costume for their annual show at the exhibition hall at Tattersalls Yard. The Brigadier even persuaded Reverend F. W. Fisher to don *kaffiyeh*, *thaub*, *'aba'*, and curved dagger to pose with the rest of the members in costume at the third club show in July 1926. A stall set up by the members sold Middle Eastern trinkets and did a fair business. Gladys had organized the event that year and it was such a success that the members presented her with a dainty, silver-and-enamel cigarette case.

Public interest in things Middle Eastern continued to be fueled by the cinema. In 1924, Douglas Fairbanks Sr. wrote and starred in *The Thief of Baghdad*, an Arabian fantasy full of action, stunning special effects, and lavish sets. Union Army general and author Lew Wallace's chariot-racing hero Ben Hur was played in the 1925 film version by another Latin lover, Ramon Novarro. A Mexican national, Novarro had starred in *The Arab* in 1924 and would play other such exotic roles, including one in an improbable 1937 musical, *The Sheikh Steps*

George Henry Vanderbilt Cecil, the current patriarch of the family and chairman of Biltmore Farms, has been very generous with information about his father John Cecil and the Amhersts.

Out. And Valentino was back again after the success of *The Sheikh*. In 1926, Hollywood made a sequel by paring down the characters of Edith Maud Winstanley's sequel, *Sons of the Sheikh*. Rudolph Valentino did double duty in *Son of the Sheikh*—reprising his role as the now mature and happily married Sheikh Ahmed Ben Hassan and also playing his hot-blooded son, who, like his father, was also out to win an English rose. Female hearts on both sides of the Atlantic fluttered again and the film raked in huge profits.* The Saluki grapevine had it that Valentino had tried to purchase an entire litter in England but that his offers were refused. A dog lover with several different breeds, Valentino did acquire one Saluki and supposedly was going to establish a breeding kennel.[32] One scene in *Son of the Sheikh* shows Sheikh Ahmed Ben Hassan returning from a hunt with a pack of Greyhounds, which Hollywood had used as stand-ins, as Salukis were still very rare in "Dollar Land."

On the literary front, T. E. Lawrence had published *Revolt in the Desert* (a reduced version of his lavish and limited subscriber's edition of *Seven Pillars of Wisdom*) in both America and England in 1927 and it enjoyed outstanding reviews and sales.[33] Another Oxford graduate (this one a cavalryman, Legionnaire, Indian Army officer, world traveler, and prolific author), Percival Christopher Wren, published three well-received novels about the French Foreign Legion in the desert—*Beau Geste* (1924), *Beau Sabreur* (1926) and *Beau Ideal* (1928). Just when Wren's books were hitting their mark in both England and America, Ronald Colman captured the dashing title role of *Beau Geste* in 1926. Wren gives us a sample of the female enthusiasm for the Oriental romanticism of the day in *Beau Sabreur*. Maudie Atkinson signs on as maid-companion to a traveling English lady and upon being quizzed about her feelings about going to North Africa, Maudie says, "Oh miss! I'd give anything in the world to be carried off by a Sheikh! They *are* such lovely men. I *adores* Sheikhs!" and then gets carried away by rapturous descriptions of suave, passionate, desert Lochinvars.[34]

Salukis were now well-known enough to be the subject of cartoons in the dog newspapers. "Saucy Sirens" or nervous thoroughbreds frightened by toy breeds were the usual good-natured characterizations. Throughout the decade, there were numerous letters and articles in *Dog World, Our Dogs, The Field*, and *Country Life* about Salukis and the current breeders — mostly focusing on the Amherstias, the Saronas and their branch kennels. Kelb, well-known from his photograph, was frequently pictured, and Gladys was once called "our leading light" in an interview.[35] Lt. Col. Stockley's article about hunting with Salukis in the Turkish prison camp was published, as well as accounts of other officers who had owned the hounds during the war and occupation.

Florence and Gladys were the usual authors of the breed articles but Brigadier Lance wrote a brief chapter on the breed for *Pedigree Dog Breeding* by Captain Jocelyn Lucas, M.C. Various reporters, including the bastion of canine journalism, A. Croxton Smith, wrote still more on the breed. These followed the usual form of delineating the breed's romantic history, the Saluki's suitability as both a companion and a coursing hound, and the contribution of Gladys and Florence to the breed in England. Regrettably, Joan Mitchell missed the attention of the popular press and has left scant traces of her history with the breed.

Florence was to gain another canine literary triumph in early 1927. For several years, Edward Cecil Ash had been writing what would prove to be a seminal work on dogs and he relied heavily upon Florence's knowledge of the ancient breed. In the massive two-volume set *Dogs: Their History and Development*, Ash covered everything from the domestication of dogs

---

Valentino died suddenly in August, not long after the premiere of Son of the Sheikh.

and the evolution of the various breeds, to world mythologies and superstitions. Where Leighton had asked Florence to write a chapter, this time Ash asked her to provide extensive reference material on the breed for several sections of the book. In 1925 or 1926, she essentially wrote the "Saluki or Gazelle-Hound" section of the "Varieties of the Greyhound Family" chapter.

In her usual romantic style, she described some of the desert lore, hunting techniques, the history of the breed in England, and the formation of the club and the principal importers. There was no shortage of Saluki images in both volumes. Florence had directed Ash to Persian miniatures, Moghul art, Egyptian tomb paintings, and various artifacts from the British Museum that illustrated the antiquity of the breed. The Maharajah of Jaipur gave permission to reproduce selections from his collection of illuminated manuscripts depicting hunting Salukis. Florence also furnished Ash with a number of illustrations, including photographs of Nefissah, Zobeid, and Farhan, and her prized copy of Carter's painting from the tomb of Rekhmire. Obviously, these images favored the Amherstia type, and the exclusion of the Saronas and their descendants must have rankled the Lances and the other owners of the "Syrian" types at least slightly. By the time Ash finished the book, it had 778 pages and 108 plates containing some 700 illustrations. The Duchess of Newcastle, who was Britain's most eminent Borzoi fancier,* wrote the introduction to the book and it debuted in March 1927, selling for £5 and 5 shillings. In August of that year it was published in America.

The book was well received on both sides of the Atlantic and Ash was encouraged to tap into the doggy market again. Four years later, he published a somewhat smaller work, entitled *The Practical Dog Book*. This volume covered more in the way of canine husbandry, but also re-capped much of his breed histories from before. As before, there were an astonishing number of illustrations — often as many as thirty-eight diminutive pictures per plate. Florence's material once again filled the chapter on Salukis and Ash included one full page of seven comparatively large photographs of her hounds. This time, Ash honored Florence by inviting her to write the introduction. Clearly he thought highly of her for she is the second person thanked in a long list of acknowledgements.

In the course of preparing her first material for Ash in 1926, Florence had suffered yet another family loss. The Honorable Sybil Margaret Amherst's health had been delicate ever since her illness in Jerusalem in 1897, but she had always had her younger sister Florence to care for her. The last of the unmarried Amherst sisters, Florence and Sybil were extremely close. Gladys described Sybil as "a great sufferer."[36] She did have occasional periods of robustness — in 1907 she climbed Mount Blanc and apparently drove cars, for she was a member of the Ladies Automobile Club. Sybil, like several of the Amherst women, held the rank of Lady Justice of the Order of St. John of Jerusalem. She was interested in airplanes and once lectured to the Flighty Society on the intriguing, but mysterious topic of "Lightman Airy."[37] Sybil had shared Florence's interest in poultry and methods of increasing egg production. She died on June 21, 1926. She was 68 and left an estate of £12,417 and possessions worth a further £9,354.[38] With Sybil's death, Florence became the eldest of the three remaining sisters. She was now living alone at Foulden Manor.

At Wentfield, on a chilly night in late August or early September of 1928, the Lances were worried about an ailing bitch. To keep her warm, they left an oil stove burning in the

---

Queen Alexandra, who had popularized the breed in the 1890s, had died in 1925.

kennel sick bay/whelping room. Using safety lamps or stoves to keep a portion of the unheated kennel buildings warm was a common practice by breeders, and the newspapers frequently reported kennel fires caused by upset lamps or candles. Sometime in the middle of the night, a fire broke out in the Sarona sick bay. With plenty of straw bedding, creosote-soaked wine cases, and wooden walls, the fire caught instantly and quickly spread to the adjacent buildings of wood and corrugated tin. As the kennels were in the dog paddock, dozens of yards from the house, it was some time before the Lances became aware of the fire. They raced out in their nightclothes, but by then no garden hose or buckets could put out the blaze. The nearest fire brigade was at West Malling, six miles and a steep uphill climb away, and the transit time would have been substantial.[39] By morning, the kennel building was a smoldering ruin and amidst the ashes were the charred bodies of the Sarona hounds that had been trapped within, dead of smoke inhalation.

At the time, the Sarona Kennels had some thirty Salukis and a few terriers, but fortunately, Kelb and several favorites had been in the house or separate kennel. The loss of so many (including Reshan, their brood bitch from Persia) was a tremendous shock to the Lances, occurring just when things were so promising for them. They had exported Salukis to America, Belgium, Bermuda, Ceylon, France, Germany, India, British Malaya, the Netherlands, Spain, Sweden, and West Africa. The Lances had visited the El Saluk kennels in Germany and even attended a few dog shows there. In addition to showing Salukis, Gladys had been showing Cairn Terriers and Lance occasionally took the Sarona Labrador into the ring. Kelb, whose feathering had grown more luxurious, was winning the veteran class and the other Saronas were regularly in the ribbons. One of their two kennel maids often came along to shows in their Austin 20 touring car to help manage the hounds. The car had an external trunk mounted on the rear bumper for clothes and paraphernalia, and Lance had rigged a rope net over the rear seat to keep the Salukis in the car when the top was down.* The brigadier was moving high in doggy circles, for that year he had been elected a committee member of the Kennel Club and was serving on both the General Committee and the Shows Regulation Sub-Committee.

At Crufts several years before, Gladys and several Saronas (mostly Kelb) had won the Tut-Ankh-Amen Cup[†] for the third time, which entitled her to retire the trophy. She gave the cup back to the club with the new stipulation that it now be won four times in order to be retired. After four wins, Gladys retired it a second time and gave it back a second time with the same conditions. In February 1928, she retired the trophy for the third and last time (having won the cup a total eleven times) and finally elected to keep the silver cup. This sort of sportsmanship endeared her to the club members and she was held in the highest regard — even being honored by the members who asked her to judge the Saluki entry at the Ladies Kennel Association show in May that year.

The loss of so many of her beloved Salukis broke Gladys's heart and she could not begin to face the thought of club activities. She missed the debut show of the Shrewsbury Canine Association on September 29 and 30 but did manage to take five Salukis to the Kennel Club Show at the Crystal Palace two weeks later, and a few entries to the Metropolitan and Essex Show in November. The Brigadier judged the Saluki entry at the Birmingham show in December, but from that point on with the Lances' prior show commitments fulfilled, exhibiting slowed to a trickle.

---

*At that time, there were only four SGHC members who owned automobiles and drove to dog shows.
[†]Awarded to the best dog or bitch.

Writing about breed activities became very painful and for seven weeks, Gladys's column was absent from *Dog World*. She began to transfer the remaining Saronas to her husband's name and one or two to her eldest son, John. After the judging at the Crystal Palace on the weekend October 10–11, she announced at the committee meeting that for private reasons she would resign as of the Annual General Meeting in February. News of the catastrophe and pending resignation were published the following week in the *Our Dogs* "Saluki Subjects" column by correspondent Will Hally.* Gladys and the Brigadier had been intimately involved in the club, from its conception onward, and resigning was a hard thing to do. Her formal letter to that effect was published in the annual report of January 1929. By April she had found someone else to take over her column in *Dog World*. She maintained her membership in the club and would one day go coursing and show again. A little over a year after the fire, she was persuaded to judge, but Gladys would never have the same enthusiasm as before the tragedy. This was the first setback for the club.

---

*Dog World *and* Our Dogs *were weekly papers devoted to canine activities. Both are still published today.*

PART V: FURRIN' PARTS

17

A Wet Nose and a Velvet Ear

"The English speaking world may be divided roughly into two classes—those that love dogs and understand them, and those that merely like them. There is a third and very insignificant minority who dislike dogs and prefer cats, but they do not count in the general scheme of things."

Major C. S. Jarvis, C.M.G., O.B.E.[1]

There are many brief accounts of Salukis in their native land and not all of these were known to Florence Amherst. Usually they were written by explorers, travelers, anthropologists, and naturalists. Most record facts devoid of sentiment or colorful folklore and these tend to repeat the standard lore of Saluki hunting technique, athletic stamina, and privileged status, with the odd variation here and there. Owners who wrote with feeling or humor about the hounds were rare—Major Bayne-Jardine being a notable exception—but fortunately two extraordinary men have left charming insights into the human-hound relationship. Neither was a significant influence on the breed in England, but their humorous prose is a long-forgotten delight.

Brigadier Lance's friend and neighbor, Major R. E. Cheesman, O.B.E.,* had only the briefest of interludes with Salukis in England. A desert explorer, he is perhaps less well-known today than the more famous names of the period—Captain W. H. I. Shakespear, Harry St. John Bridger Philby, Bertram Thomas, and Douglas Carruthers—but Cheesman was nonetheless a celebrity in his time. He left a magnificent book, *In Unknown Arabia,* as a record of nearly three months of mapping the Eastern Najd desert. It is a well-written and appropriately humorous compendium of his journal notes on geography, natural history, archaeology, cultural anthropology, and the contemporary politics of the regions he visited. In his book, Cheesman committed to paper several amusing experiences with his Saluki, Najman.

Robert Earnest Cheesman was the son of Robert and Florence Maud Cheesman, and born in Westwell, Kent, in 1878. He was the second of five children and the eldest son. Natural history was a passion for the whole family and the Kentish countryside afforded them ample opportunities to observe animal life. Robert's younger sister, Evelyn, would become an eminent entomologist and, like himself, a world traveler. Birds held a special fascination for young Robert and he once tried to raise wood-pigeon chicks by eating clover and regurgitating for them as he had seen the mother birds do for their young.[2] He graduated from the

Later colonel and C.B.E.

South Eastern Agricultural College at Wye, Kent, and his first job was at the Sharpe and Winch brewery in Cranbrook. Catherine Winch, the daughter of one of the owners, made a great impression on him and he would marry her in 1927. In his time off from the brewery, he continued his own bird studies and became a member of the British Ornithologists' Union, making contributions to *British Birds*, a standard textbook of the day. When war was declared in August 1914, at one stroke, a contingent of over two hundred men from his alma mater joined the 5th Battalion of The Buffs to form the Wye College Contingent.[3] At 36, Robert Cheesman was beyond the age of enlistment and adjusted his age downward in order to serve with the Contingent.

After their training in England, the 800 men of the 1st/5th Battalion of the Buffs were shipped to India for a year of garrison duty and more intensive training. At the end of 1915, they were dispatched to Mesopotamia where they joined several Indian regiments to form the 35th Brigade, part of the 7th Division under General L. N. Younghusband. The division unsuccessfully attempted to relieve the besieged garrison at Kut-al-Amarna and fought in several bloody battles against the Turks. The casualties were terrible, for by January 1916 the strength of the 1st/5th Battalion of the Buffs had been reduced to two officers and sixty-five other ranks, with Lance Corporal Cheesman among the latter. He estimated that there were now only two of the Wye College Contingent remaining in the battalion, some having been scattered to other regiments and hospitals, but that the vast majority had been killed in action or died from wounds, colitis, or dysentery. Surprisingly, scurvy also took a heavy toll on the British Army. At that time, the German submarine campaign was sinking supply ships bound for the Middle East, and Mesopotamia could well have been left without adequate food to feed the Expeditionary Force. Cheesman would soon play an important role in enabling the army to feed itself.

At Basrah, Lance Corporal Cheesman, in the capacity of orderly room sergeant, had the tedious responsibility for keeping the regimental records. A mutual friend gave him a letter of introduction to a man who would change his life — Sir Percy Cox, the Chief Political Officer to the Mesopotamian Expeditionary Force D. Cox shared Cheesman's passion for birds and they began collecting specimens together. The two got on famously. Worried about the lack of local produce and a further tightening of the submarine noose, Cox and his assistant, Captain Arnold Wilson,* had been trying to devise a scheme to make fresh vegetables available to the troops in Iraq and their Arab allies. Cheesman the agronomist was just the man for the job. He was commissioned as a second lieutenant in the Indian Army Reserve, told to learn Arabic, and regroup a few men of the Wye Contingent to help him produce vegetables on a large scale.[4]

After a brief probationary period, Cheesman was appointed "Assistant to the Deputy Director of Agriculture of the Mesopotamia Expeditionary Force." He ordered irrigation pumps and seed from India and his small group set about establishing a large, experimental irrigated farm and set up a garden at every hospital. By the end of the war, hospitals were growing melons, lettuce, and cabbage. Cheesman's unit grew wheat, established four varieties of Indian cotton, taught tribesmen how to grow corn and hay, and grew enough surplus produce to provide the Veterinary Department with alfalfa for ailing horses and mules. His work was mentioned in *Despatches* and his monograph for the army, *Notes on Vegetable Growing in Mesopotamia in 1917*, was published in 1918.[5] Throughout all this, he continued his research on birds, and in 1919 he was honored by election to the British Ornithologists' Club. After

---

*Later Acting High Commissioner in Iraq.

the war, he chose to stay on in Iraq as an agricultural officer and was stationed at Kadhimain, just north of Baghdad.*

While Cheesman was sorting out agriculture for the MEF, Sir Percy Cox served in turn as Political Resident in the Persian Gulf and H.M. Consul General for Fars and Khuzistan. In 1920, when Sir Percy was made High Commissioner in Iraq, he asked his friend Cheesman to be his private secretary. Cheesman served in this capacity until his chief's retirement three years later. In 1921 Sir Percy granted him an extended leave of absence and Cheesman went off to map the Arabian Coast from Al Uqayr to the head of the Gulf of As Salwa.† With Sir Percy's blessing, there was also plenty of time for field studies and Cheesman's work in natural history drew notice in scientific circles. He was made a fellow of the Royal Geographical Society in 1920, a member of the Zoological Society of London in 1921, and the following year appointed officer of the British Empire in 1923. That he was held in high regard by all who knew him is evident from this quote by his friend, C.F. Beckingham: "In temperament and tastes he was a countryman, deliberate, patient, thorough, kind, and personally frugal. Never pretending to expertise he did not possess, he did whatever was possible to ensure that his travels should benefit every branch of knowledge."[6]

On Sir Percy Cox's retirement in May 1923, Cheesman returned to England but in October sailed for Basrah. For nearly a year, he had been arranging a specimen-collecting expedition in the Great Southern Desert of Arabia (now known as the Empty Quarter or Ar Rub al Khali). With consent and assistance of the future king of Saudi Arabia, His Highness Abdul Aziz ibn Abdul Rahman ibn Saud, C.G.I.E., Sultan of Najd and its Dependencies, Cheesman's safe passage was assured. Other Europeans had mapped the area previously, but heretofore there had been no scientific study of the local fauna. Cheesman would be the first and his work would later win the Royal Geographical Society's Gill Memorial Award.

Deep inland from the Gulf of Bahrain, lies the oasis of Jabrin. Cheesman, Mehdi (his servant), and their local guide had started at Al Uqayr on the coast and stopped at Al Hufuf in November to pay respects to the sultan and waited to hear about the feasibility of continuing. There had been a drought the year before and vegetation for the camels to feed upon had been almost nonexistent. It was 150 miles of hard trekking to Jabrin, and without forage, it was impossible to go. Word finally came in the beginning of February that recent rains in the interior had caused new leaves to appear and Cheesman's journey could continue. After two months of Abdul Aziz ibn Saud's hospitality, hawking parties, and specimen collecting, Cheesman set out for Jabrin, this time reinforced by two of the Sultan's soldiers (as a precaution against the bandits in the south), a guide, and another man to help manage the camels and their loads. Cheesman adopted Arab dress but rather than sandals, he wore sneakers.

Their path took them south of Al Hufuf along the edge of the great sand desert Al Jafurah, and there Cheesman took to wearing his kaffiyeh over his soft felt hat in order to get both shade and air circulation around his neck. After seven days, he was mightily glad to arrive at the oasis of Jabrin with its cluster of tents and prospect of a bath. Soon after setting up camp, the Amir Hamad ibn Maradvath§ visited Cheesman and made it clear that he would

---

*Now a part of Baghdad, the district is famous for the Al-Kadhimain mosque, targeted by suicide bombers in 2005.

†The Gulf of As Salwa lies between Saudi Arabia and Qatar, and contains the island of Bahrain.

§The name Maradvath is unusual, as "v" is not used in the Arabic alphabet, yet Cheesman is consistent in his spelling of the Amir's name.

only tolerate the Englishman by the will of the sultan. Soon after that disconcerting audience Cheesman had another visitor.

Strolling with dignity through a pack of snapping mongrels from a nearby Bedouin encampment, an underweight yearling Saluki made his first appearance in Cheesman's life. Unlike the pack of gray smooths belonging to the acting governor of Hasa, at Hufuf, this Saluki was a feathered grizzle. The coat and color was unusual in Cheesman's experience. Ravenous, the youngster eagerly ate the date stones that were discarded from the men's dinner. The Saluki seemed to like the company and hovered close. Later, Cheesman was told by one of his soliders, Muhammad Hasan, that the Saluki belonged to Sheikh Rashid ibn Daleh,* but could be presented to the Englishman if he would accept. A reciprocal gift, such as a large sack of rice (the standard measure was 168 pounds), would satisfy etiquette.[7]

Pragmatically, Cheesman wanted to see if the hound was any good on hares before committing himself to the gift. Not having suitable presents with him, he planned on arranging at Bahrain to send a sack of rice to Sheikh Rashid as the exchange gift. By the end of the expedition, the greedy Muhammad tried to persuade Cheesman to give money for the gift of the Saluki, with the intention of extracting his own healthy fee in the course of delivering it to Sheikh Rashid. He knew what Muhammad was trying to pull and beat him at his own game. The Englishman bluffed and said that he did not really want the Saluki in the first place and pointed out that it was Muhammad himself who had suggested the hound-rice exchange. The extortion failed when Cheesman said firmly that if money was the only exchange for the hound, perhaps Muhammad had better take the hound all the way back to Sheikh Rashid.[8] Muhammed demurred and the Saluki stayed.

The Saluki was named Najman and his aristocratic bearing and manners — particularly his habit of discreetly watching the men eat their meals — greatly impressed Cheesman, who wrote, "Behind Saud with the rice comes the Saluki, Najman (Two Stars, a most appropriate name), with quiet dignity; it stalks into the tent and sits down at a respectful distance; there is none of the vulgar familiarity an ordinary dog would show when begging for a meal."[9]

With great dignity, Najman exhibited the Saluki's characteristic "play bow," rear legs standing while the forelegs stretched out forward on the ground, and Cheesman thought this highly unusual for a dog. "The air of supplication is perfect and the appeal irresistible. When I did not feed it, it quietly left the tent, following the tray with the same dignified air."[10]

However, Najman's manners were not always quite so perfect and he revealed a streak of characteristic Saluki thievery that might well have cost him his life. On February 23, 1924, Cheesman's party had collected a number of *jirds* — a type of desert rodent — and the skins were given a chemical field dressing to preserve them for study back in England.

> One of them had been finished and well dosed with arsenical soap, and I had written the particulars and measurements on the label and tied it on, when, with the same dignified air that characterised his every movement, the Saluki swallowed the whole thing. Strange to say, neither the arsenical soap, the label, nor the string seemed to disagree with him, although we gave him up for lost.[11]

None the worse for his potentially harmful snack, Najman caught hares and proved to be a staunch companion. One day, after a fifteen-mile trek in the harsh sun, Najman was looking very worn and Mehdi, Cheesman's long-time servant, suggested that he be hauled up

---

Harry St. John Philby disagrees with Cheesman's transliteration and says that the name was more correctly Rashid ibn Andaila or Nudaila.

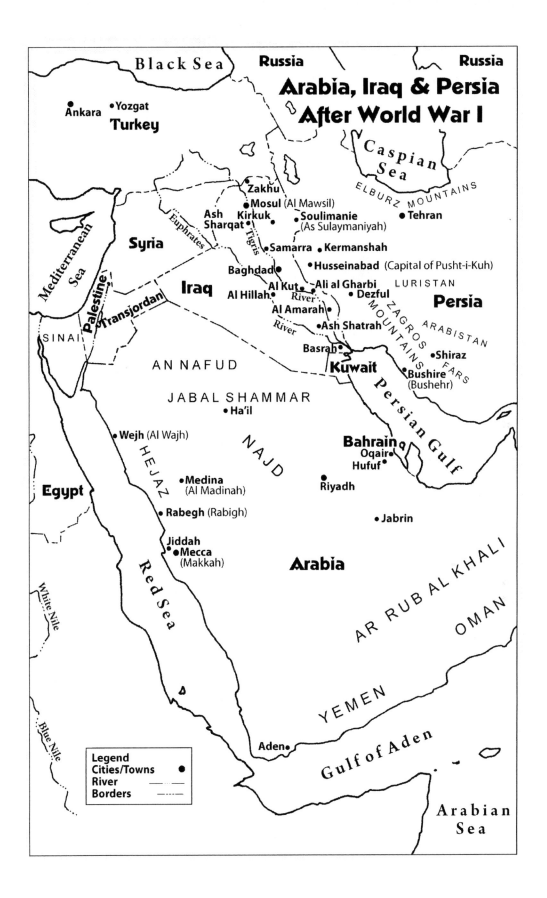

Arabia, Iraq & Persia After World War I

Black Sea

Russia

Russia

Ankara
Yozgat
Turkey

Caspian Sea

ELBURZ MOUNTAINS

Zakhu

Mosul (Al Mawsil)

Ash Sharqat
Kirkuk
Soulimanie (As Sulaymaniyah)

Tehran

Syria

Euphrates

Tigris

Samarra
Kermanshah

Baghdad

Husseinabad (Capital of Pusht-i-Kuh)

LURISTAN

Mediterranean Sea

Iraq

Al Hillah

Al Kut

River

Ali al Gharbi

Dezful

Persia

Palestine

Transjordan

Al Amarah

River

ARABISTAN

ZAGROS MOUNTAINS

SINAI

Ash Shatrah

Basrah

Kuwait

Shiraz

FARS

Bushire (Bushehr)

AN NAFUD

JABAL SHAMMAR

Ha'il

Persian Gulf

Wejh (Al Wajh)

NAJD

HEJAZ

Bahrain
Oqair
Hufuf

Egypt

Medina (Al Madinah)

Riyadh

Rabegh (Rabigh)

Jabrin

Jiddah
Mecca (Makkah)

Arabia

White Nile

AR RUB AL KHALI

OMAN

Blue Nile

YEMEN

Red Sea

Aden

Gulf of Aden

Legend
Cities/Towns ●
River ———
Borders - - - -

Arabian Sea

Major Cheesman, guides, and Najman with hare in the Al Jafurah desert between Hufuf and Jabrin, 1926. Note Cheesman's gym shoes and *kaffiyeh* draped over his felt hat. *In Unknown Arabia.*

onto a camel and given the chance to rest. Saleh, their *rafiq,* insisted that a Saluki's pride would never allow him to take rest or water until camp had been reached. Poor Najman had been trotting ahead to find shade and when there was a bit of brush, he would bury himself in the sand underneath to cool off. After the camels had passed by, Najman would emerge and catch up to them, a half-mile ahead. Finally, the Saluki could bear the heat no longer, and he sat down in the sand in front of the *rafiq* and pointing his muzzle upwards, let out a heart-rending howl. This was too much for even Saleh, who dismounted and scooping a depression in the sand, laid down a leather sheet to make a bowl for water. Najman licked up every drop and when they rode off again, Saleh picked up the Saluki and gave him to one of the men with a baggage camel. Thereafter, Najman rode for a portion of every day.[12]

Najman provided some great sport during Cheesman's expedition, some of the best coursing that he had ever seen. Najman's efforts to chase darting jerboas were as fruitless as they were amusing, but on larger quarry he had more success. He would tear after hares while the men futilely galloped after on camel. Once, during a course, the entire contents of a water skin were lost when the neck-string came loose and the precious liquid was scattered over the sands as the rider galloped after Saluki and hare. Usually they had a decent view of the hunt from camelback and could see the hound dodging in and out of the brush or tearing across the wide plain. On one frustrating occasion, the hare had a 400-yard head start before Najman was pushed off the camel, but despite a very long tail chase, the Saluki forced three turns and caught the hare on the last one. Being low to the ground, Najman was too far away to see his master and, much to the annoyance of the men who watched from camelback, the Saluki buried the hare in the sand. The hare was never found and their meal was rather plain that evening.[13] Even had they found the buried hare, Cheesman's *rafiqs* almost certainly would not have considered it lawful meat for consumption.

Early Muslim scholars had debated whether or not it was lawful to eat meat taken in the chase when no ritual slaughter was possible. Commentary in the *Hadith* literature (interpretations of the Qur'an) clearly stated that meat from an animal caught by either a trained or untrained hound could be eaten, as long as it had been slipped with the invocation (*bismallah*) "In the name of God" and the quarry was not mutilated. However, if someone else's hound should assist in the kill, then the meat was not lawful. "You mentioned God's name only over your hound, not any other."[14]

Cheesman debated with his Muslim companions about whether or not a hare caught and killed without the carefully specified *dhabh* (sacrificial throat cutting) was *halal* (lawful) meat. They cited a passage in the Qur'an stating that game killed in the chase need not have its throat cut in the name of Allah. Cheesman thought the quote somewhat dubious, but was content if they were.* Western scientific practice required that skins be removed from the animal by a single ventral slit from jaw to anus. This was completely at odds with Muslim practice where the throat was slit under the jaw, severing blood vessels, trachea, and esophagus in one stroke. The lack of proper *dhabh* on an animal destined for a scientific collection did not seem to bother Cheesman's *rafiqs*.†

On their return to Hufuf, Najman's acrobatics prompted his master to remark on the hound's nimbleness and he noted dryly: "He was also rescued from perilous positions on top of walls, for he ran along them with the agility of a cat."[15] Najman's misbehavior was a momentous occasion, for Cheesman had been given a parting gift by the sultan through Fahad ibn Jiluwi, the acting governor of the Hasa, the area surrounding Al Hufuf. It was a spirited bay stallion with black points. At the village of Jisha, Najman again caused a great deal of consternation by assaulting the pet rabbits and cats. He had never seen felines before and Cheesman wrote amusingly of the encounter, "He got his first education in the classification of animals, which he thought were all Hares. Having cornered a cat, he went in like a lion, only to experience the difference in the matter of toe-nails, and came downstairs howling, to be tied up in the stable."[16]

Like all desert-bred Salukis, Najman hated being confined indoors and escaped through any door left ajar. At sunrise the next day, they were about to depart when Cheesman heard a commotion: "[T]he Saluki, just liberated from the stable, was tearing madly round the narrow streets of the town, upsetting the composure of the stallion, who wanted to do likewise. When I arrived on the square, a few early risers were watching the scene. Every few seconds the dog crossed the square like a flash issuing from one street and disappearing down another."[17]

Cheesman told Mehdi to soothe the struggling horse (who was being ridden bareback) and catch up later with the party, which was to move out of town. Najman continued his solitary race and at each pass incited the stallion further. Cheesman knew that Najman would follow when they left and that the horse could then be calmed in the hound's absence. Mehdi and the horse would then be able to catch up. At least that was Cheesman's plan — but nobody told Najman. The party started out but only got as far as the town walls when they heard

---

*St. John Philby noted a similar example of this flexibility: "In matters of religious prejudice, public opinion is all-powerful, yet the meat of the chase may be hallowed with the knife after death, if the trigger is pressed 'in the Name of God, the Merciful, the Compassionate.'" The Heart of Arabia: A Record of Travel and Exploration (New York: G. P. Putnam's Sons, 1923), 14.

†Bertram Thomas was able to satisfy both collecting needs and his rafiqs by cleverly first opening the skin with the vertical cut and then slitting the windpipe in the ritual fashion so the meat could be lawfully eaten (Arabia Felix, New York: C. Scribner's Sons, 1932 62–63. I am grateful to Sir Terence Clark for clarification on the various Arabic terms connected with this practice.

pounding paws and hoofs, and looked behind to see the Saluki tearing after them at full
speed, pursued by the riderless stallion.[18]

The last we learn of Najman before Cheesman took him to England is in March 1924 at
the end of their journey. As with his first appearance in Cheesman's life, on approaching Al
Uqayr Fort, Najman was attacked by the local pariah dogs. Mehdi rescued his beloved Najman by grabbing him and kicking the snarling curs. Barring a few nips, he was able to keep
them at bay until the Saluki could be dragged into the fort. From there, Cheesman would
embark upon a *baghala* (native boat or ship) first for Bahrain and then Basrah, where the crates
of specimens, the stallion, and Najman were loaded aboard a steamer bound for England.

Later that month, Najman went into quarantine and Cheesman returned to his home in
Kent and began to transform his voluminous notes into a book which would not be published until 1926. Three of the photographs used to illustrate *In Unknown Arabia* featured
Najman* and one showed the favorite Saluki of the acting governor of Hasa — a pampered
white smooth. The expedition had been a particular success, for in addition to acquiring data
for new maps and a few archaeological finds along the way, he had returned with 343 preserved specimens of mammals, birds, fish, reptiles, insects, and plants representing 125 different species, of which Cheesman had identified fourteen new species and eight new
subspecies. The Arabian jerboa (*Jaculus florentiae*) he named after his mother and Cheesman
himself was honored with two — the leopard moth (*Cossus cheesmani*) and fittingly, Cheesman's
hare (*Lepus omanensis cheesmani*).[†] In his penultimate chapter, "Desert Colour," he discourses
on color adaptation in the desert, cross-species fertility, natural selection, and selective breeding, using the purity of the "Saluki or Gazelle Hound" as an example of the latter.[19]

The book was still in progress when Najman was registered with the Kennel Club in
April 1925. Cheesman got to know the Lances and visited Wentfield, to renew his acquaintance with Sheikh Hamad of Bahrein. Despite Cheesman's fondness for Najman, just three
weeks after his debut at Holland Park that month (where Gladys Lance had described the two
year-old hound as a "taking grizzle"), Major Cheesman was compelled to sell him. Gladys
mentioned his desire to find a home for Najman in the May 7 *Dog World* column, and noted
"no reasonable offer refused." Presumably a suitable home was found, for in August 1925
Major Cheesman was posted to Africa as His Majesty's consul for Northwest Ethiopia, a place
not at all suited to Salukis. He was to live at Dangila, in the Choke Mountains near the source
of the Blue Nile, and his official charge was to put a stop to the elephant poachers that crossed
the border into the Sudan. It was an exciting position and he knew there would be many
opportunities for his own passion for natural history. Cheesman later admitted that at the
time he accepted the post, he was not exactly sure where Ethiopia was, having only known it
by the old name of Abyssinia.[20] Cheesman's Saluki disappeared from notice, but it is interesting to note that while Najman was the first registered Arabian Saluki in England he was
never used at stud and so did not contribute to the gene pool.

While Florence Amherst was certainly the most prolific author on the topic of Salukis,
her writing is a Victorian blend of fact, history, folklore, and Orientalist fancy — which, con-

---

*Cheesman even mentioned Najman's one show win.
†And earlier, a species of gerbil in Iraq — Gerbillus cheesmani. The protocol of scientific classification proscribes
naming a species after oneself.

sidering the breed, is oddly fitting. Her articles and letters lack genuine emotion and we may only hypothesize about her feelings. Not so Major C. S. Jarvis, colonial administrator and raconteur, with an equal appreciation for the breed but an entirely different outlook. Close behind Florence in literary volume on the breed, he wrote several books about gardening, sport, and life in the desert, and the cultural clash between the Arabs and the English. In many of them, he writes movingly about his dogs, and his charming stories give clear insight into the English attraction for the Saluki temperament.

Major C. S. Jarvis, C.M.G., O.B.E.,* was an author, painter, sportsman, naturalist, historian, philosopher, and colonial administrator with an untarnished service record in one of the most desolate places that God created. He saw service in three deserts and capped his career as governor of Sinai from 1922 to 1936 and during most of that time he had Salukis and Scotties by his side.

Claude Scudamore Jarvis (or Jarvis Bey as he was known in the Sinai) was born in 1879 and led a life that might have been that of a hero in a Victorian novel for boys. The son of John Bradford Jarvis, a London insurance clerk, he had no formal education and with three brothers there was no assurance of a profession. His godfather arranged for him the beginnings of a career in the Merchant Navy. At seventeen, he signed on as a midshipman on the *Port Jackson*, an iron four-masted barque. Despite the lofty title of "midshipman," Jarvis on his first voyage was no better than a common sailor, and in fact rather worse because he was small and weedy, and had no experience whatsoever. As such, he became a target for abuse but Jarvis's school lessons in boxing stood him in good stead. He held his own in a fight with the ship's bully and true to the form of boys' books, the fellow left Jarvis alone afterward.

The life of a sailor was no easy one. From 5:30 A.M. until 5:30 P.M., Jarvis and the other hands were kept busy with the myriad and continual tasks that are necessary to keep a sailing ship in trim. The officers and crew of the *Port Jackson* were not a happy lot, and the two-year circumnavigation was a hard time in Jarvis's young life. Outbound, they sailed with a cargo of Rotterdam coke, destined for the furnaces of the Broken Hill mines of South Australia, and they returned with bales of wool filling every square foot of the hold.

On the *Port Jackson's* arrival London, news of the Boer War had the country in a patriotic frenzy for khaki.[†] Jarvis, fed up with the sailor's life, declared that he could ride, shoot, and was twenty-one years of age (he was nineteen), and so joined the Montgomeryshire Yeomanry. Trooper Jarvis and his fellow volunteers were given speedy training in military basics and shortly he found himself once again on a ship, this time crowded with troops, horses, and supplies bound for South Africa.

His regiment saw considerable service but other than occasional sniping and skirmishes, experienced little combat. The trooper's chief preoccupations were lack of sleep, exhausted horses, and hunger. The capture of a chicken was cause for greater celebration than the news of Mafeking's relief or Pretoria's surrender. Soldiers everywhere have a great affinity for canines and the dogs that take to soldiering seem to relish the carefree life of wandering with the regiment and having several hundred masters, all with kind words and pats. Two brindle hounds were acquired in the Cape Colony.

---

*Also *Orders of the Nile and Qaddara (Egypt), Phoenix (Greece), and Istikal (Trans-Jordan),* and the *Lawrence Memorial Medal* by the Royal Central Asian Society.
[†]At that time, khaki uniforms were only worn in India or Africa and never seen in England.

**Major C.S. Jarvis, C.M.G., O.B.E., inspecting an honor guard of Sudanese Camel Troopers, Sinai, 1931.
C.S. Jarvis,** *Yesterday and Today in Sinai* **(1931).**

> Our two lurchers saw the South African War as one long glorious hunting expedition, for
> almost every day of their lives they trotted along with a line of beaters across the veldt, and
> it was a dull day indeed when neither a hare or a springbok got up in front of the scouts.
> The springbok were usually too fast for them, but the hares, of which there were a great
> number in some parts of the Free State, were usually run down, and the wild rush to secure
> the body by a swarm of hungry Yeoman was not the least exciting part of the hunt.[21]

After 18 months (just 48 hours shy of the service needed to qualify for the King's South
Africa campaign medal), Jarvis was back in England and commissioned as a second lieutenant in the 3rd Dorset Militia. After a brief stint on the Isle of Guernsey, he was posted again
to the mainland. He met his future wife by the purest chance at a punting picnic that neither had wanted to attend. The two confessed to each other their original intentions of avoid-
ing the party altogether and instantly developed a mutual attraction. Her name was Mabel
Jane and she was the daughter of Charles Hodson of the American Embassy in London. Jane
was a slim, dark-haired beauty, just eighteen years old. Despite the lack of any firm prospects
and the semi-official proscription against marriage for very junior officers, in 1903 they were
married. Jarvis was posted to Ireland that year and his bride accompanied him. Their only
child, Elaine, was born in 1904.

Army discipline was more relaxed across the Irish Sea — particularly in Kilkenny where
the detachment had six officers and only three privates. There was not much work to do and
so the officers hunted constantly. The commanding officer lived in Clonmel, some twenty-

five miles away in Tipperary, the next county over. As automobiles were a rarity and Irish roads narrow and windy, surprise visits happened only when he took the train. With ample warning from collaborators at the telegraph office, hunting gear was quickly put away (to the extreme disappointment of the gun dogs) and a military appearance was created for the inspection.[22] Army duties only required Jarvis to be on parade for three days of the week, so he took full advantage of every opportunity to enjoy the local camping, shooting, fishing, and fox hunting. The combination of love for the outdoors, insight on animal behavior, and gift for humor led to an unanticipated source of income which was most welcome to the new family. He began to write under the name "Scudamore Jarvis"* and regularly sold articles on the sporting life to several English magazines as well as becoming an official sport correspondent to *Land and Water*, which would later become *The Field*. This status allowed him free rail travel and hotel rooms when he sampled regional sport attractions for his column.[†] For a man with a three-figure income and army duties, by the time he was thirty, he had enjoyed more hunting, shooting, and fishing than had many people with five-figure incomes and unlimited leisure time.[23] There was not much in the way of blood sport in Britain that he had not experienced. Jarvis knew he was a fortunate man and enjoyed every minute of it.

In 1914 when the war in France broke out Jarvis was called to rejoin the Dorsetshire regulars. There are few details about his service in France, but in 1916 he was transferred to the Middle East and took part in the Light Car Patrols[§] against the Senussi tribes in the Libyan desert and the campaign against the Turks in Palestine. Throughout his war service in the desert, he brought along a wire crate with his rooster and six hens that provided fresh eggs without Jarvis having to pay the exorbitant prices resulting from war shortages.[24] Somewhere during the war, he suffered an injury that seriously affected his hearing (most likely from an explosion's near miss) and in later years Jarvis was compelled to wear "aural-aid phones."

At the end of the war, law and order in the Egyptian frontiers had to be established. It was the military buccaneers who did well in war but were unsuited to the tedium of civilian life that took on this sort of task — at least until the excitement dried up. Jarvis, being acutely aware of the bleak prospects for a partially deaf soldier in peacetime England, began a new career with the Egyptian government on Armistice Day 1918. He was to be the police commandant for the district west of the Nile and stationed at Al Amiriya** (Al Amiriyah) on the coast just west of Alexandria. Primarily composed of English officers, the Frontier District Administration was responsible for enforcing laws in the outlying Egyptian deserts. Jarvis learned to speak and read Arabic and quickly showed a talent for this sort of work and eventually would be made commandant of Eastern Libya and acting governor of Luxor.[††]

By the fall of 1919, most of the soldiers had been sent home, leaving minimal garrisons here and there in the Middle East, except in Egypt. Up to that year, there were over 1,000 civil servants in Egypt striving for an impossibly western bureaucratic standard of "the full hundred per cent."[25] It was eventually realized that the country could actually be run with considerably fewer English, and that obtaining rigid British standards of efficiency and moral integrity were not likely to happen in Egypt and Sinai. Rising nationalism and self-rule

---

It was common at that time for magazine and newspaper columnists and contributors to use their initials or pen names such as Crixus, Bravida, Lochinvar, Beagle, etc. Jarvis would also write under the pen name Rameses.
[†] *Jarvis even attended the better ratting meets and cockfights as an observer.*
[§] *The ubiquitous "Galloping Bedsteads" Ford trucks, with engine covers removed to assist cooling.*
**Jarvis uses "Amria."*
[††] *In Luxor, Jarvis spent a good deal of time studying the hunting scenes depicted in the local tombs.*

demonstrations finally forced the issue of independence in 1922. Egypt became a sovereign nation with Britain retaining control of Suez Canal Zone and continuing to provide advice and assistance in key areas of the government. Finally, the massive dumps of British ammunition and ordnance left over from the war were removed.[26] Between 1927 and 1936 the number of English was to be reduced to a sprinkling of officials on "loan" to Egypt as civil administrators. This of course, had turned into an apparently permanent arrangement with the employment of British civil servants preventing deserving Egyptians from jobs. Jarvis felt that this actually contributed heavily to the constant civil unrest of that period. Between 1919 and 1936 there were only five peaceful years and the Egyptian government was kept busy quelling civil disturbances in the cities while the Frontier Districts Administration dealt with Bedouin feuds, land disputes, brigandry, and hashish smuggling in the Western Desert and Sinai. Jarvis, as a frontier administrator, excelled at placating litigious sheikhs, enforcing customs, appeasing wronged merchants, and outwitting desert bandits.

After establishing himself in Al Amiriya, he sent for Jane to join him. The climate was pleasant and there were urban amenities in nearby Alexandria—a fairly good setting in which to resume their married life. Shortly after she arrived in the spring of 1920, he was promoted to district commander and posted 600 miles south to the forsaken oasis of Kharga. Jane resolutely accompanied Jarvis along with dog and poultry. Curiously, he does not mention their daughter Elaine, who would have been about sixteen at the time that her mother came to Egypt. Yet Jarvis's written attention to all the other aspects of their desert life would seem to indicate that Elaine remained in England with relatives and her parents saw her during their annual summer leaves. Prior to the war, the Jarvises had always had some combination of terriers, setters, and spaniels (with Scotties being his perennial favorite) and Jane had brought their Scottie bitch to Al Amiriya. They would have to take her to Kharga. Jarvis knew he was tempting fate, for with hazards such as extreme heat, parasites, vipers, monitor lizards, wolves, and rabies, he considered the East to be "a place of sudden canine tragedies."[27]

Jarvis's initial impressions of the area surrounding Kharga reminded him of Milton and Omar Khayyam and their descriptions of "Dante's Inferno" and "Annihilation's Waste."[28] Some 130 miles southwest of Luxor, the village at Kharga was in a great depression with the hottest weather and worst anopheles mosquito infestation in Egypt. It consisted of houses made of mud, which after the rare rainstorm would dissolve entirely. The inhabitants would then rebuild them on top of the melted foundation, with the result that over the ages, the houses grew taller and taller and now resembled small fortresses. In winter the temperature was never lower than 80°F and the heat of summer typically hovered from 110° to 115°—with the only relief occurring when it reached 98° for short time around dawn. Jarvis made an underground cellar and fitted the ventilation port with a pipe that dripped water over poultry netting frames to cool the incoming breeze—making a bearable temperature of 70°.[29] From time to time, he and Jane would be startled by a loud crack—and it took them a while to realize that it was the wooden furniture splitting open due to the extreme dryness and heat.

Jarvis was promoted to sub-governor of Sinai in 1922 (and governor the following year) and they packed up and moved to another desert. He succeeded Lt. Col. Walter F. Stirling, who had just accepted a position as governor of the Jaffa district (Tel Aviv Yafo) in Palestine.* Stirling, in his autobiography, would write little about his time in El Arish for, "Jarvis Bey,

---

*In addition to being friends with Stirling, Jarvis also knew Wilfred Jennings-Bramly, who was then commandant of the Wadi Natrun District district, west of Cairo.

who succeeded me as Governor, has written so much and so amusingly on the subject of Sinai that he has left little for me to say."[30]

During the war, an Australian Light Horse trooper whom Jarvis knew called desolate Sinai 35,000 miles of "Sweet Fanny Adams"—a polite version of "Sweet F**k All" to be used in front of officers.[31] Fortunately for the Jarvises, El Arish was on the edge of that desolation being situated on the Mediterranean, between Port Said and Gaza—about 30 miles from the Palestinian frontier at that time. The ancient town, dominated by the mosque's minaret, was composed of narrow streets and flat square buildings—each one story in height and with a ten-foot walled garden. The Greeks called it Rhinocolura ("deprived of noses") for it was said that criminals who had had their noses cut off were all sent there. Romans, Crusaders, French, Bosnians, Turks, and even Australians had passed through and left their mark on El Arish and its population. In Jarvis Bey's time, the population was 7,000 souls of mixed ancestries. Law and order was maintained with the Sinai Police for local matters, Light Car Patrols where there were roads, and where the cars could not go, the elite Sudanese Camel Corps.

Located in the sands outside of El Arish was the governor's house. During his brief tenure, Stirling had planted eucalyptus trees for a windbreak, dug a well, and installed a noisy but functional camel-powered waterwheel. With constant hard work and persistence, the well provided sufficient water for the governor's garden and its population of chameleons to flourish. Jarvis would note dryly that water was a continual problem in both England and the desert—in one place you could not get rid of it quickly enough and in the other, you could not get enough of it. So that none of the precious liquid was wasted, Jarvis rigged the plumbing so that the water from his morning bath was piped into the garden.[32] During the war, Turkish cavalry had quartered their horses in the garden and the huge layer of manure helped transform the sand into something with the consistency of soil. Hollyhocks, oleanders, sweet peas, larkspurs, alyssum, cabbage, peas, carrots, artichokes, parsnips, tomatoes, limes, and asparagus thrived amidst the surrounding sand and gave Jarvis his "little corner of England."

Aesthetics aside, maintaining a garden and keeping poultry and livestock were nutritional necessities in the desert. Without fresh produce or meat, the only alternative was tinned food which was typically watery and anemic, and expensive to import. Jarvis once shipped a crate of two dozen Rhode Island Reds and an English bull to El Arish and upon receiving the heart-stopping bill, he was certain that the chickens each had their own cabin and that the bull had been lodged in the viceroy's suite and had taken his meals at the captain's table.[33]

Jarvis became a skilled horticulturalist and under his hand the governor's house at El Arish became the showplace of the region. It had fruit trees and plants, colorful flowers, sunken rock gardens, herbaceous borders, green lawns—and dogs to enjoy those lawns.

> It is a very satisfying sight when the lawn, having been well and truly rolled, is sown thickly with £5's worth of seed, raked over, and left in all its stark barrenness in anticipation of the delicate mist of pale green that will show in ten days time. The trouble is, however, that an unbroken smooth surface of yellow sand has a fatal attraction for dogs. Apparently the canine nature rebels against vistas of unbroken surfaces and something has to be done about it. There is the type of man we all know who walks into the breakfast room on a morning when we are none of us at our best, rubs his hands together vigorously, gives them a loud clap that shatters our nerves, and says, "It's a lovely morning." Dogs are just the same, and the trouble is that, as they do not have that extra glass of port at night, they all—and not a small minority—have that boisterous "early morning" feeling; but instead of clapping their hands they scratch and kick vigorously with their hind legs, and with each terrific kick they mutter to themselves, "By God—what a dog I am." And all

this, to get a really satisfactory result, takes place on any smooth — and what gardeners call "friable"— surface available, which in El Arish invariably took the form of a seed bed. Tinker, our Saluki, who had an enormous reach and spreading toes, ably assisted by the Scottie, who made up for his lack of stretch by the vigour of his footwork, apparently spent two minutes every morning on lawn destruction, telling each other how good they felt, and their physical jerks alone cost me £2 for repairs each year.[34]

The Jarvis home in El Arish was furnished with oriental carpets and cleverly constructed chairs, tables, and cabinets made out of acacia wood by a carpenter in Luxor.* These horizontal targets attracted yellow dust of the locality and it was a continual battle to keep the furniture clean. They would refer to their eclectic furniture collection as Amira 1919, Kharga 1921, Early R.A.F., and Early or Late El Arish.[35] Jarvis bought a three-horsepower generator and storage batteries and there was enough electricity to power his electric lights and a Frigidaire, quite probably the only refrigerator in Sinai.[36] Jarvis used to surprise tired and parched guests with iced, dry Martinis at cocktail hour. Geckos crawled up the walls inside the house, but as they reduced the mosquito population, the lizards were welcome houseguests. It was a comfortable home — but a trifle lonely.

Outside of the infrequent inspector or visitor, there were not many people with whom to socialize. There was, however, the occasional dinner party with a local sheikh, tea with the local officials and their wives, or the periodic inspection by a high-level administrator, the type of which was derisively referred to as the "Big Noise," in both English and Arabic. In those days a colonial administrator did not freely mix with the local inhabitants and the Jarvises would have limited themselves to socializing with the few English officers of the police force or the rare traveler.

Their Scottie bitch appears to have died in Kharga or soon after the move and they acquired another one — this time a male called Wattie — from a friend who was going home to England. The Jarvises' Saluki came to them in a similar manner. Lieutenant J. H. C. Lawlor of the Camel Corps owned a young male named Tinker, who had been given to him as a puppy by an officer who owned a family of Salukis. Tinker's sire, Smiler, became famous in the Camel Corps for a remarkable feat of endurance and navigation in 1922. Near the Libyan border, Smiler had once become lost after chasing a herd of gazelle on a Wednesday evening and despite a concerted search by his owner and the patrol, and bonfires at night, he could not be found. Eventually, the Camel Patrol had to give up the search and continue on to their destination at Sollum. Realizing he was lost, Smiler trekked south 130 miles back to the base at the Siwa oasis. He woke Lawlor in his quarters by nuzzling his wrist at 2:00 A.M. on Friday.† Smiler suffered terribly from the journey — his pads were bloody and his strength was nearly gone. It took ten days of nursing to bring the hound back to normal. Lawlor reckoned that Smiler's average of four miles per hour within thirty hours of the trek was some sort of a record.[37] Jarvis would inherit the hardy Smiler's son two years later.

In 1924 Lieutenant Lawlor was transferred from El Arish to the Sudan and asked Jarvis if he would look after Tinker for a few weeks while he settled into his new quarters. Apparently, the Sudanese quarantine regulations presented an impossible obstacle and Tinker's stay was extended while Lawlor went on leave to England to make arrangements for his parents

*One could also mail order furniture made not only from the mahogany and teak wreckage of sailing ships sunk by German submarines, but dismantled British ships of the line from the Napoleonic Wars.
†This area of the Western Desert was the same waterless furnace that had killed one of Wilfred Jennnings-Bramly's Salukis during his expedition to Siwa in 1896.

to take the hound. The plans came to naught and Tinker continued to be "looked after" by the Jarvises until he died at the age of fourteen in 1934. The governor of Sinai would comment dryly that this was "probably a record for accommodating another man's dog."[38] In the isolation of El Arish, their adopted dogs, Tinker and Wattie, would become an important part of their lives. Jarvis wrote:

> It is impossible to write about our life in the deserts without a description of the dog friends who have shared our exile and whose wonderful companionship and sympathy have made the somewhat monotonous and empty round endurable. Living the queer isolated existence we do, our dogs have figured far more in our lives than would have been the case if we dwelt and had our being in an ordinary community. We have so few social ties and so little to amuse us that it became a habit to order our day more or less on the lines that would suit the dogs, and the walks we took in the evening were along the routes that held attractions for the canine fraternity rather than for us; for instance a wadi full of scrub where five years ago a hare had been flushed and chased, and a dog never forgets a spot in which he has once located game; or the road down to the station where the telegraph poles and lampposts offer the best that Sinai can produce in the way of intriguing smells — a very different and uninteresting assortment, I believe, judging by the enthusiasm they showed for the scents of Port Said and Cairo. The result of this was that we were inseparable, and wherever one happened to be there was always a friendly wet nose or velvet ear never more than a foot away from one's hand — and this is neither fair to the dog nor the human. There was the question of leave home — a longed-for and wonderful event, but spoilt utterly for us because of the small friends who would be broken-hearted — and there was the other and final parting when the little dog had lived his allotted span and went out, leaving a blank that hurt most damnably, and an empty house that nothing could fill.[39]

Daily walks with the dogs would become a ritual, just like Jarvis's after breakfast pipe, and his six o'clock whiskey and soda. Like parents who do not want their children to get excited when certain words are used in conversation, the Jarvises spoke Arabic when they had to say "cat" or "rabbit" in front of the dogs. They were doted on like children and Tinker and Wattie had their special accommodations in the house: "All our dogs have beds — i.e. small wooden frameworks with sheep-skins tacked over them; we find it much more convenient and economical to do this as otherwise the most comfortable chairs are always occupied by the dogs, and we belong to that special brand of idiot that cannot turn a dog out of a chair even if we require it ourselves."[40]

Tinker and Wattie would go along on their motor excursions to Cairo and Jerusalem and the ancient castles, monasteries, and biblical sites in Sinai. Their master would avail himself of the fishing at Al Aqabah, shooting hoofed mammals or gamebirds, or even just bird-watching opportunities. Jarvis and "Herself" (as he called Jane) once circumnavigated Sinai by motorcar in nine days with their servant, Osman, a cook, a guide and the two dogs.[41] Leaving his khaki uniform and red fez behind on these outings, Jarvis was still correctly dressed for a holiday, wearing his shooting clothes — fedora, tweed jacket, tie, and riding pants with knee socks. He would take notes on the geography and ruins and develop his own theories regarding the Exodus and the different civilizations that passed back and forth across the deserts since recorded history began. Wattie and Tinker would find their own special interest in the vertical surfaces of these venerable and historic monuments.

> [W]e were driving along the desert road from Abu Zeneima to Suez, and as I have already stated I was feeling sleepy or drugged with metallic, synthetic beer when I saw trotting by the side of an old Arab a wonderful copper-colored Saluki. As Salukis go he was not very remarkable, for, to be exact, he had the merest hint of this breed in his general make-up,

his slim boyish figure being entirely due to lack of food; but this, owing to the beer, was not apparent. His color, however, was undoubtedly marvelous and, with visions of copper-colored Salukis sweeping the board at Cruft's and bringing in £50 a pup, I stopped the car and bought the dog for five shillings. On arrival at the house I handed the dog over to Osman and told him to remove the attendant ticks and camel flies that swarm on every Arab dog, and give him a thorough bath in hot water. I had by this time noticed that most of the Saluki points were conspicuous by their absence, but the wonderful Irish Setter copper color of his coat, with its metallic sheen, made up for any other failings. Imagine my surprise, therefore, when Osman turned up an hour later with a very ordinary looking cream-colored pi with its tail between its legs.

"But where is the dog I bought?" I asked.

"Here, effendim," said Osman.

"But the color — he was red when I gave him to you."

"Of course," replied Osman with conviction, "and so was the Arab you bought him from and the camel as well. They had all been working in the manganese mine at Abu Zeneima. But, thanks be to God, water and soap will remove it, and here is the dog quite clean and the proper color."[42]

The poor pi-dog was nonetheless adopted and given the distinction of being named after its birthplace — Mangam (Arabic for mine). Mangam proved himself to be a thorough cad with a weak stomach. He would seek out the foulest camel corpses and offal. "Although entirely devoid of culture in any form, he was one of the best judges of carpets I have met as he never by any chance was sick on anything but two valuable Kurdistans and a priceless old Turkish *kleam* — and we had quite a range from which to choose."[43]

They were driven to distraction by his indifferent attitude and indoor toilet habits. Mangam solved the problem himself by developing a sudden affection for one of the camel policemen. The dog moved out of the governor's house and never gave any indication of recognizing the Jarvises on subsequent meetings. Tinker and Wattie were glad to see the last of him and have the house back to normal.

Tinker, the Saluki — a most inappropriate name for a stately and immaculate pure white Oriental gentleman — was the direct antithesis of Wattie, for he came from a long line of aristocratic hunting dogs who, although bred with the greatest care by their Arab owners and respected for their speed, have never been admitted by them to an equal footing in the human circle. Their position in the Bedouin encampments has always been on a very much higher plane than that of the ordinary pi-dog on account of their ability to provide gazelles and hares for the pot, and because a well-bred Saluki is as much an adjunct to the dignity of an Arab as a blood horse. The Saluki, therefore, knows that he comes of good stock and his deportment at all times is definitely exclusive, not to say haughty, so far as other dogs are concerned. With human beings he is at a disadvantage, as it is very difficult for him to understand that he is expected to be anything but a dog, and that the human, whose sovereignty he admits, desires to make a friend of him is quite beyond his ken. It was rather hard on Tinker, therefore, that he had to share our companionship with a Scottie — a breed that beyond all others is definitely certain of his place in the family circle and insistent on the right to be treated as an equal entity on all occasions. Wattie was all this and more, with the result that in the house Tinker suffered from an inferiority complex and, beyond demanding his right to his dinner and the best chair in the room — till we provided him with a bed of his own — he was content to live his own life. This consisted of lying in a sheltered spot in the full blaze of the sun most of the day and, if the weather was cold and the house chilly, he would frequently refuse to come in for lunch but would order it to be taken out to him in the yard. In the evening when warmth had gone out of the sun he would race into the house, with an air of someone engaged on the most important and urgent business, shoot across the room and throw himself on to his bed with a deep sigh.

These beds (which I have already described) with which the dogs were provided were most popular — after a year's hard wear and tear the wool of the sheep skin became conspicuous by its absence and the bed less and less inviting, so on Christmas day the accumulated sheep-skins, representing twelve months' supply of home-fed mutton, were brought in and laid out for Wattie's and Tinker's inspection. They understood the arrangement thoroughly and were fully aware that they were being invited to choose a suitable skin as their own private property, and they were just as finicky over the selection as women are over the ordering of the material for their wedding dresses. Wattie would try them all in turn, an if Tinker showed a preference for any particular skin and lay on it to test its quality, Wattie would at once order him off and hurl himself on it with a thump as if to say, "I had my eye on this from the first and as senior dog I claim it." The selection having been made, the old skins were ripped off their wooden frameworks and burnt, the new ones tacked on, and for the next week it was difficult to get the dogs off them even to go for the evening walk. The sheep-skin bed idea was an excellent institution, for the dog is sufficiently humanized to appreciate absolute ownership of anything, and the provision of private beds prevents one from being ordered or pushed out of one's favorite chair by a dog.[44]

Wattie and Tinker were well-known to the population in El Arish. The Saluki would generally accompany Jarvis to the office during the standard working hours of 8:30 to 1:30 even though in all other respects, he considered himself Jane's dog, as did Wattie. Tinker was evidently a premier Casanova, as the local mongrel bitches were irresistibly attracted to this noble hound with "his ears cocked, his tail quivering, his muscles shimmering through the satin of his white coat ... and what chance had the poor drab, tick-ridden pi's who had born the heat and burden of the day?"[45] In addition to increasing the pi-dog population in the locality, Tinker also sired purebred litters for the Sinai Police and Sudanese Camel Corps. Jarvis had seen few Salukis in Sinai before Tinker's arrival, but after witnessing Tinker's prowess with hares while on patrol, nothing would do but for the local detachment of the Camel Corps to have Salukis of their own.* They acquired a bitch named Risha and eventually every police outpost and encampment had its own mascot. Each bore a distinct resemblance to their prepotent sire. Jarvis claimed to be unaware of how the matings were arranged and suspected that his servants accepted *baksheesh* of five piastres for a brief honeymoon at the back door. Naturally, the increase in the Saluki population resulted in a corresponding decrease of hares in Sinai.

As a representative for the Frontiers Administration and as was typical for most colonial types, Jarvis was responsible for all the functions of a full-fledged government: police, public health, public works, maintenance of roads, education, agriculture, customs, and justice. With almost no funding and nearly unlimited freedom from the government, he fought locust plagues, irrigated hundreds of acres of land, enforced customs regulations, built roads, dug wells, constructed buildings, put an end to Bedouin banditry, adjudicated court cases and land disputes, halted Arab blood feuds, and fairly settled the never-ending swindles, thefts, and chicanery that the Arishys and Bedouin were always trying to pull on one another.

The Arabs that Jarvis knew were a litigious lot and he would say that while a poor Arishy would avoid an hour's work with a pick to cut a water channel to his plot of land, the same fellow would happily walk 200 miles to appear in a court case regarding a goat worth eight shillings that was supposedly stolen four or five years before. Land disputes were of much the same character. The hard-working man who happened to cultivate a barren patch of land that might not have been entirely his own would suddenly find himself the target of a lawsuit by

*Jarvis was a good friend and biographer of Arab Legion's Peake Pasha.

the alleged owner of the newly productive land, whereas before cultivation no interest on the part of the owner had existed at all. There were frustrating tribal disputes where the area involved was vaguely described as being bounded by "north the sea, south a sandy area, west a sandy area with bushes, and east the land of Said Abdulla."[46] Pity the poor magistrate trying to make sense out of that, especially when Said Abdulla was probably involved in his own boundary dispute. Jarvis noted wryly that generally the more worthless the land, the greater the wrong claimed by the injured party and the larger the bribes to ensure victory in court.

There were no roads in Sinai prior to Jarvis Bey. Motorcar navigation was by landmarks and visiting motorists were required to carry a basket of messenger pigeons in case of breakdown. Despite Cairo's glowing opinion of the idea, the "Pigeon Post" failed, as the pigeons were contrary and rarely performed as the government expected. Road building became a major occupation during Jarvis's years in Sinai. In 1925 he built the first road between El Arish and Aqabah, enabling regular patrols in six-wheeled Morris cars armed with machine guns to put a stop to Howeitat raiding. More roads were built, not only enabling police patrols and speedy retaliation, but making visits by tourists and government officials much easier. The motorcar journey from El Arish to Cairo took eleven hours and covered 250 circuitous miles around mountains and sand dunes.[47] In 1926 there were a total of five tourist cars on the road but the traffic increased to the point where in 1935, Jarvis counted fifty cars in one day.[48]

This improved access encouraged official nosiness, which, in turn brought more frequent tours of inspection. Elaborate strategies and ruses were frequently necessary to convince a "Big Noise" that the Sinai administration operated just the way the government did in Cairo or London. The strategy behind passing any high-level inspection was to carefully arrange what the "Big Noise" would see — and what he would not see. The new Sinai roads and their attendant traffic necessitated the establishment of rest houses (with inspections thereof) at intervals of a day's motoring to accommodate pesky "travel-mongers" who would show up demanding to see the sights and real Arab "sheeks." The houses were stocked with essentials and maintained by a *farrash* (literally "bed maker") who was supposed to keep them clean and orderly, but who usually neglected the house in favor of his other interests. On one inspection tour, the assistant district commissioner entered a rest house and was highly irritated to discover antique sardines fermenting quietly in the teakettle and a newly whelped litter of Saluki puppies in one of the beds.[49] Both items had to be explained and apologized for by the exasperated Jarvis.

The Jarvises traveled extensively on automobile trips in Sinai — both for pleasure and business. Wattie would assume his rightful place as the governor's dog on Herself's lap in the front seat of the lead car. If she ever rode in another car, he would desert her and take his customary place of honor. From this prestigious position, he would bark at camels until they got off the road, and should a gazelle or hare be flushed, the cars would be stopped to allow the small terrier to join the chase. This was actually a matter of practical necessity, for if he was restrained in the car while the Salukis were coursing, he would yelp frantically and "run in place," clawing his mistress's skirt to shreds. The sight of the short-legged terrier barking and scrambling after the disappearing Salukis was laughable and one of the Sudanese drivers said that it "looked as if he were going in reverse."[50]

Wattie also loved going on camel patrol with the police and their Salukis — which could last easily a week. Each man and his camel were self-contained and could go five to seven days without fresh provisions and water, and sometimes ten days if needed. Because Wattie's enthusiasm would cause him to waste all his energy at the start of the trek, he would never make the full day's march of thirty-two miles. Also, his pads were more used to the soft sand of El Arish than to the granite of Southern Sinai. Exhausted and with sore pads, he would approach his camel and beg to be taken on board. Jarvis's orderly, Osman, would place him into a special saddlebag which allowed him to cradle his rear quarters while bracing his forelegs on the saddle. In this way he could still oversee the patrol like a mounted general.

The Scottie was a good rider and perfectly safe in this arrangement unless Tinker flushed a hare. Furiously eager, Wattie would have to be restrained to prevent him from leaping after the chase from a height of seven feet. The camel was *barraked* on the ground as quickly as possible to allow Wattie to join the hunt (he could tackle cats and jackals but was smart enough to leave monitor lizards alone). Even though hopelessly outclassed by the long-legged Salukis, he actually caught hares on three occasions. Twice he guessed correctly by cutting a corner and intercepted the hares that the Salukis had unwittingly driven straight at him. The third time, his terrier blood came to the fore and after five minutes of fast digging, he unearthed a hare that had gone to ground. On that particular occasion, the hare was welcome provender. The motorcars had been thoroughly stuck in Sinai mud resulting from three days of unexpected rain, and while waiting for the ground to dry out, Jarvis Bey's patrol had run out of food. Wattie and Tinker's catch made a very satisfactory jugged hare which alleviated hunger pangs until further supplies arrived by camel. Jarvis and his Sudanese policemen never forgot that when in desperate need, it was the dogs who had come to their rescue.

Even though Tinker was a "cast iron snob" and disdainful of terriers and other common canines, Wattie certainly appreciated Salukis. While he assisted in Tinker's hare coursing, the Saluki was not permitted to assist in Wattie's cat hunts.

> The most important part of Wattie's routine—and, like all dogs of character, he had his day's schedule worked out to the minute—was the evening cat-hunt. Immediately after sunset, when the cats of the village came into the garden seeking what they might devour, he sallied forth and put the tribe to flight, treeing a suitable animal and yelping beneath till loss of voice and a sense of approaching dinner brought him back to the house. Tinker, the Saluki, used to consider this a rather vulgar pastime, most unsuitable for an Oriental gentleman bred exclusively for running down patrician game such as hares and gazelle, and would look at Wattie when he came in after a hunt in much the same way that the polo fraternity in the Cairo Gezira Club look at the bowls players. One day, however, Tinker went out with Wattie and asked him what this cat-hunting business was he made such a song about, and was there anything in it? Wattie was delighted at having enlisted a recruit, and, rushing in amongst the tomato plants, flushed a fine ginger Tom that Tinker promptly ran down in the open and killed in true Saluki fashion, and he followed this up by finishing off three more before they had a chance to reach a tree. This completely spoilt the evening's amusement, for the whole technique of cat-hunting consists in not killing the gentleman who provides the sport, but merely the chasing of him with exceeding ferocity—taking great care not to get involved in a rough-and-tumble—to the foot of a tree and then to yell bloodthirsty threats till one is exhausted. If one kills off all the cats there is no fun to be had afterwards at the tree, which is the best part of the game, and besides although the cat is a pretty rotten sort of fellow addicted to eye-scratching and yowling by night, one does not wish to kill him actually. Wattie had a very dull time for a month after this till a fresh stock of cats began to occupy the garden, and he was very careful in future not to invite Tinker to accompany him. Tinker was a very fine fellow when hares were afoot, but he was not sufficiently intelligent to grasp the finer technique of cat-hunting.[51]

Time in the desert weighed heavily on Jarvis and his wife. They busied themselves with horticulture, animal husbandry, and charitable works. Jane established a knitting school for the young women of the village. She was affectionately called *Sa'adat al-Sitt*—"Her Excellency, the Lady." Jarvis in his leisure hours painted water colors and wrote about the desert, local history, shooting and fishing. During the war, he had written articles about impromptu quail shooting in the Libyan desert, partridge shooting in Sinai, and fishing in the Gulf of Al Aqabah. Now he began to write again with an eye toward the sporting publication using both his real name and "Rameses." Rudyard Kipling (also a great dog lover) visited Jarvis in El Arish and encouraged him to persevere in his writing. They became good friends and during summer leaves to England Jarvis would motor through two counties for lunch at Kipling's home, Bateman's, in East Sussex.[52] Kipling's poems and prose were favorites and quoted frequently in Jarvis's writings.

The dogs meant the world to them. Jarvis was about to go on his much-anticipated summer leave to England and had brought Wattie along to Port Said to be left with a friend.* On the morning that Jarvis's ship was sailing, the Scottie got into a fight with a pi-dog on his morning ramble and got two nasty wounds. When advised by the Egyptian army vet that Wattie's age and the likelihood of sepsis, combined with the absence of his owner, were indeed serious factors and that the little dog might not survive. Jarvis called the shipping company and rebooked his passage for two weeks later "on account of the political situation" (an always convenient and plausible excuse).[53] In the hotel room, Jarvis stayed by Wattie's side and the Scottie healed faster than anticipated. One morning a menacing pi-dog entered the garden and Jarvis could tell by Wattie's snarling reaction that this was the culprit. Jarvis shot the pi-dog with his revolver and took satisfaction in believing he had meted out justice to the cur that was both Wattie's attacker and the cause of his postponed home leave.

Jarvis would write movingly about the deaths of Wattie and Tinker. The Scottie had developed an attachment for a small black Saluki bitch that belonged to the Sudanese Camel Corps post in El Arish and while he would visit her twice a day, she never came over to the Jarvis home. The gallant Wattie died at twelve years of a heart attack after a successful mouse hunt. Within ten minutes of his passing, the Saluki bitch appeared and frantically searched the garden and house for her terrier friend. She had never visited the house before and after her fruitless search, left with despondent whimpers.[54] Wattie's quick end spared the Jarvises from having to make the decision that every dog owner dreads.

Tinker's death was not so easy for his master. At the age of fourteen (quite advanced for a desert dog in an age of no vaccinations) the iron-constitutioned Saluki's health suddenly plummeted. The "wonderful old gentleman" suddenly lost his sight and the use of his limbs within three days, possibly due to a brain tumor. Euthanasia by injection or "lethal chamber" was not available in El Arish and an Egyptian Army Veterinary Surgeon was days away. Jarvis used his large-bore shotgun at close range to put an end to Tinker's misery. The method was gruesome, but at least had the redeeming virtue of being quicker than anything else available. Even though Jarvis knew it was the only choice, there can have been few things harder for him than ending the life of a favorite hound with his own hand.

> I often think that the real dog-lover — the man who makes a friend of his dog — is rather a fool in the way he stores up sorrow for himself. He has the advantage of from ten to twelve years' wonderful companionship and sympathy, but he pays a heavy and inevitable price for it in the end. The gods are not unjust, but they exact a payment for all things, and possibly the man to whom a dog is just a dog is better off in the long run; but some of us are born to be that sort of fool, and nothing will alter it. Immediately the feeling of utter emptiness when the old friend goes out is blunted to some degree by the passage of time, another

Annual leaves typically began in April so as to miss the hottest months of the Egyptian summer.

small person is found who, from instinct or what you will, adopts many of the ways of his predecessor. The funny little half-human soul that one creates in a dog companion seems to fall upon his successor like the mantle of Elijah, particularly if he is of the same breed, and when we pass over ourselves to the other side—wherever that may be—possibly we shall not be greeted by all the little people that shared our lives but by one who embodies each individual. In any case, if the future life does not provide for meeting again one's dog friends as well as the human who have gone on before, it will be a very incomplete existence for some of us who have invested too heavily in canine companionship in this world.[55]

One of Kipling's poems affected Jarvis deeply and he quoted the first and last verses in the chapter on his dogs in *Three Deserts*:

> There is sorrow enough in the natural way
> From men and women to fill our day;
> And when we are certain of sorrow in store,
> Why do we always arrange for more?
> Brothers and Sisters, I bid you beware
> Of giving your heart to a dog to tear....
> When the body that lived at your single will,
>
> With its whimper of welcome is stilled (how still!)
> When the spirit that answered your every mood
> Is gone—wherever it goes—for good,
> You will discover how much you care,
> And will give your heart to a dog to tear.

After his retirement in 1936 and return to England, Jarvis joined the staff of *Country Life* and his regular column was popular with sportsmen, agriculturists, and naturalists. He would publish ten books in the years after his retirement—most of them about the desert. Gwen Angel (Mazuri Salukis) discovered the Saluki passages in *Three Deserts* and made the Saluki Club aware of him, but there is no evidence that Jarvis was ever involved with them. He and Mabel Jane would always have Scotties, but they never owned a Saluki after Tinker.

In the postwar years while Jarvis was working and writing in Sinai, and Florence Amherst and the Lances were enjoying the long-awaited breed popularity, Great Britain was trying to impose some form of order in the areas of the Middle East that it was responsible for after the fall of the Ottoman Empire. The amorphous area that had been Mesopotamia was divided into various functional territories or mandates, each with their own unique problems. One particularly thorny area was Baghdad, where a community of Saluki fanciers was helping to shape what would become a new nation—Iraq.

18

The Baghdad Crowd

.

"Some weeks passed, when suddenly one day the Saluki walked into the barracks; he was
thin and obviously suffering from his long and lonely journey of over 100 miles on an
unknown route and over mountains, plains, and even flooded rivers; he had found his
way back absolutely on his own."

Mrs. Colin Joyce writing to Florence Amherst[1]

Florence's Saluki imports from Emir Abdullah were not the only ones to have flown in
airplanes. Flying Officer D. A. W. Sugden was a stores officer with the 55th (Bomber) RAF
Squadron at Hinaidi airfield on the southern outskirts of Baghdad. He was with the No. 6
Armored Car Company and obtained a male puppy in August 1926 from Captain Growden.
Growden's litter was born on June 26 to Nesiba I and Lady while he was stationed at Kirkuk,
some 140 miles to the northeast of Baghdad.*

Local Iraqi tribesmen had been rebelling against the British postwar mandate and its
attempts to prevent the various tribal and religious factions from killing each other. The vast
and comfortless distances in Iraq† made the work of subduing the insurrections nearly impossible for the Army, but the mobility of the Royal Air Force was perfectly suited to the job.
With airplanes and armored cars, they could scout, pursue, and strike rapidly over hostile
ground. Bedouin armed only with rifles and mounted on horses and camels were no match
for the technology of modern warfare. The British strategy was to be vigilant and then find
and punish the offenders quickly. Aerial bombing raids were the tactics of choice.

The Hinaidi air field§ cantonment was a decent enough place to be stationed. There were
churches to accommodate three different religious denominations, hospital, school, and a
"hairdressing saloon." Most men had their afternoons largely free and sport kept boredom at
a distance. There were polo grounds, a point-to-point racecourse, an athletic stadium and
swimming pool. Shooting and hunting were also popular pastimes and there were plenty of
dogs for all purposes. A photograph (circa 1933–35) of the Hinaidi Motor Transport Pool
shows nineteen soldiers posing with as many dogs — puppies in arms, leggy Salukis, feisty
terriers, and mongrels or "Mosul Spaniels — the British Army's local term for mongrels.

Nesiba the Saluki was constantly with Sugden** — and frequently going on flights. The

---

*Growden also sent a litter sister to a Mr. & Mrs. P. L. Gerrard in England.
†After the war, the term "Mesopotamia" (literally "land between two rivers") was replaced by both "Irak" and
"Iraq"— the Arab name for the region. British soldiers called it "Mespot."
§On the southern edge of Baghdad, now the Rasheed Airbase.
**Coincidentally, there were two Sugdens at Hinaidi. The other was Flight Lieutenant R. A. Sugden, AFC.
Nesiba has been also spelled "Nasibe."

The RAF Motor Transport Pool's collection of "Mosul Spaniels," terriers, and Salukis at Hinaidi Base, Baghdad, Iraq, taken by Wing Commander A.R.M. Rickards, O.B.E., A.F.C., about 1934. With the kind permission of James Offer.

biplanes that were used for reconnaissance, supply and equipment transport, as well as bombing runs on rebel tribesmen, were the Bristol 2Fb and De Havilland DH-9A. Both planes had two crew compartments, one for the pilot and one for the observer/gunner.[2] Sugden's base was equipped with the DH-9A. Like the Bristol fighter, it was constructed of wood, wire, and doped canvas but designed for bombing and transport, so it was larger and could carry bombs, supplies, and spare parts. Slow but reliable, it was a good plane for British operations in the desert and remained in service from 1918 to 1931. To go flying, Nesiba would have been hoisted up to Sugden standing in the observer/gunner's cockpit and then stuffed down past his master and back behind the elevated seat onto a small platform with the supplies. Sheltered from the wind, the Saluki quickly learned to curl up tightly in his bedding and go to sleep — waking up when he heard the engine revs drop in preparation for landing. By the time he was imported to England, Nesiba had flown "thousands of miles by air."[3]

When Sugden retired to England in 1927, Nesiba went into quarantine and his master settled down with his wife in Buckinghamshire. Nesiba was registered in February 1928 and he and his owner made their ring debut at Crufts. He and his wife did a bit of showing, he with the Saluki and she with a French Bulldog. At the Kensington show in April 1928, Nesiba took the Graduate Dog prize. Florence was very taken with the fawn-colored import and purchased him in August. She would breed two litters from Nesiba and boast about his hours of flying time. Always looking to improve the Amherstia gene pool, she made a similar bargain with Flight Lieutenant Rickards a month later.

Aubrey Robert Maxwell Rickards ("Rick," as he was known to his brother officers), was born in Fairford, Gloucestershire, in 1898, and when the Great War began he was a student at the Royal Agricultural College. In 1915 he entered the Officer Training Corps but, seeing little chance of the action he craved, transferred to the Royal Flying Corps in August 1916. After eight months of training and fighting zeppelins on bombing raids, he joined the 100

Squadron and flew to the Western Front. Flying in the two-seater, "pusher" type F.E.2b, on bombing missions, Rickards lasted twelve days before his plane was shot down on April 6, 1917, and he was taken prisoner. He recovered from a wound to his cheek and spent the rest of the war in Germany.[4]

Repatriated in December 1918, he resumed his RFC duties and was eventually posted to Egypt in February 1921. That year he was awarded the Air Force Cross* for rescuing two downed airmen in the Transjordan. For the next five years he moved several times and had flying duties, as well as variously serving as a pilot instructor, and adjutant. In addition to Egypt, he served in the Aden Protectorates and Palestine. In Somaliland, he met Ras Tafari, and, after taking him aloft, Rickards explained to the future emperor of Abyssinia† why airplanes were very useful things indeed. While on safari in Somaliland in 1923, Rickards did a bit of big-game hunting and bagged kudu, gazelle, and lion. Always accompanying him were a few large-boned, leggy hounds that slept in his hut and participated in the hunts. It was dangerous work — a hound was dragged from the hut one night and killed by a leopard.[5]

In March 1924, Rickards left Abyssinia and the Sudan and was posted to Palestine with an RAF company of armored cars fighting Wahhabi raiders from the Najd desert. It was later that year at Sarafand (near Haifa) that he acquired three Salukis.[6] They were Barum, Amara, and Joan. Barum and Amara parented a litter in October and Joan, having been impregnated by an unknown sire, produced another litter the following month. Rickards kept a dog and a bitch puppy out of Barum and Amara and a dog from Joan's litter. The others he gave away to fellow officers. Keenly interested in horses, hounds, and hunting, in his leisure he practiced falcony and spent considerable time with friendly tribesmen learning hunting lore. Hunting from camelback, he would wear either a fedora or *kaffiyeh*, open-collared white shirt, khaki riding breeches, knee socks and low boots.

Presumably leaving his Salukis in Palestine, he was back in Africa in 1925 on a six-month safari through Western Abyssinia and the Sudan with Varges, an American photojournalist. Disappointed by the lack of good trophies, Rickards set out on his own into the Dinder region of the Sudan. He had been determined to photograph elephants rather than hunt them and did not carry a large-caliber rifle. Probably the most terrifying event of his life was being trapped with his shikaris in the middle of an elephant stampede sparked by lightning storms. Rickards likened it to a night bombardment in No-Man's-Land, saying "Hell itself was let loose."[7] The morning after the stampede, a maddened bull charged him and his shikaris from a distance of one hundred yards. Not having a clear shot at the heart or brain, Rickards waited patiently for the bull to expose the one spot on his chest and the small area behind the great ear that could be penetrated by a bullet. Methodically, he pumped five rounds into both targets as they opened up, and the elephant finally crashed to the ground a narrow fifteen yards in front of him. "How I wished the cinema man had been behind me, but perhaps he would have done the same thing as my two men, ran for dear life. I had been too scared to run, as if in a nightmare rooted to the ground, but thank God the rifle did not jam, and I remained quite cool enough to rattle back the bolt of the 375, which was a rather foolish toy to use against elephant."[8]

Rickards eventually went back in Palestine with his hounds and was posted home to England in April 1926. He took the Salukis with him, but his falcon died on the trip.

---

*Awarded for outstanding courage or service in the air when not on active service against an enemy.
†Tafari was made emperor in 1930 and changed his name to Haile Selassie.

When Gladys Lance had gone east to be with her husband in 1910, she was introduced to both military life in the tropics and his Salukis. In much the same manner, Mrs. Violet Dickson and Mrs. Colin Joyce were introduced to the same aspects of their new husbands' lives in Iraq. Like Gladys, they both married into the breed and would become life-long enthusiasts.

At the age of 23, Violet Penelope Lucas-Calcraft of Lincolnshire was working in Cox's Bank in Marseilles when she met Captain Harold Dickson, who was returning to Bahrain from leave in England. He was about to embark for the Persian Gulf via India and stopped in to pick up his letters. While there was no mail, he was intrigued by the slender, good-looking brunette who assisted him. Violet struck up a pleasant conversation with the fair-haired, handsome officer in khaki, with neat mustache and the chain-mail epaulettes of the Indian cavalry. Something obviously clicked, for a week later, Dickson cabled her from Port Said proposing marriage. She accepted and they were married on December 10, 1920, in St. Thomas Cathedral in Bombay. Twelve days later Dickson received a telegram from his new chief, Sir Percy Cox, the High Commissioner in Baghdad. He was instructed to report to Basrah for further orders. Dickson wired his servants in Bahrain and told them to pack up the household. The horses and other animals would come later, but on the ship along with the Dicksons' most important belongings were his two Salukis.

The dashing officer that had proposed to Violet was Captain Harold Richard Patrick Dickson C.I.E., F.R.G.S., late of the Connaught Rangers and Indian Army 29th Lancers (Deccan Horse). He would have a long and distinguished career, soldiering in Ireland, India, Kashmir, and Iraq, and serving variously as District Political Officer, Political Agent in Bahrain, Private Secretary to the Persian Gulf Political Resident, and finally as Political Agent in Kuwait and chief local representative of the Kuwait Oil Company. Dickson had the strongest ties to the Middle East for he was born in Beirut in 1881 and grew up in Jerusalem where his father, John Dickson, was His Britannic Majesty's Consul-General. By Harold's own account, his mother's milk dried up and a Bedouin wet nurse in Damascus was found by Sheikh Medjuel (Mijwal) al Mazrab, a sub-tribe of the Anizah. Drinking the milk of a Bedouin woman gave him the status of a foster son among the tribesmen and Dickson later found this to be enormously useful in his political work. The sheikh who arranged the wet nurse for infant Harold was in fact the same man that had married Lady Jane Digby. She died the year Harold was born and later his family would rent the late Lady Digby's house in Damascus. Sheikh Medjuel's son gave Dickson his first camel ride.[9]

At the outbreak of war, Dickson had been employed as guardian to the Maharajah Kumar of Bikaner when his regiment, the 29th Lancers, was sent from India to Europe. Because he had grown up speaking Arabic, he was transferred to the 33rd Queen Victoria's Own Light Cavalry where he would be more useful in the Mesopotamian campaign. There he fought in several battles and afterward was made intelligence officer for the little marsh town of Suq Ash Shuyukh, located on the southern Euphrates in the middle of Muntafiq tribal territory. The only Englishman in the area, it was his job to acquire useful military information and keep the locals satisfied with their British alliance.

Dickson acquired two Salukis there and they accompanied him everywhere. As Major Bentinck had discovered, Dickson learned that hounds were a good conversation starter with potentially hostile tribesmen and the resulting hunting stories easily led to more serious mat-

Violet and Major H.R.P. Dickson wearing Arab dress for a visit to King 'Abd al-'Aziz Al Sa'ud in Riyadh, Saudi Arabia, 1949. With the kind permission of Mrs. Zahra Freeth.

ters of allegiances and treaties.* One day while riding alone with his hounds, he was confronted by a masked Bedouin,[†] who turned out to be Hajji Nasir Al-Ajail, a well-known rascal with a blood price on his head. At the moment, he was in the employ of the Turks and bent on personal vengeance against Dickson for previous retributions. While the hounds looked on, Hajji pointed his loaded carbine at the Englishman's stomach and intended to kill him. The quick-thinking "Daksan" not only managed to talk his way out of being murdered, but devised a complicated face-saving scheme to satisfy all parties and patch up the blood feuds with fines. Even the Chief Political Officer, Sir Percy Cox, was ultimately satisfied with the solution, albeit grudgingly.[10] Dickson would be appointed Companion of the Indian Empire in 1917 for his political services in Mesopotamia, and Salukis would always be a part of his life in the desert.

    Violet would come to love the desert and the Bedouin as much as her husband but during a brief period in Baghdad before Dickson's final posting, she found life rather a trial. The idea of climbing up to the roof in the middle of the Iraqi winter to use the portable toilets or "thunder boxes" went against all the etiquette she knew. Once the Indian sweeper went missing and for days, while the level in the thunder box continued to rise alarmingly. Violet caught a bad cold and suffered alone while Dickson was at his office working with Sir Percy and his politicals, "Jack" Philby and Bertram Thomas.[§] Dickson's Salukis were used to roam-

---

*John Steinbeck, in his narrative about a trek across America, Travels with Charley (1961), also remarked upon the eagerness of country folk to talk with a stranger about his unusual dog, a large French Poodle.

[†]While on a raid or blood-feud revenge, Bedouins would cover their face with their kaffiyeh so that they could not positively be identified, thereby preventing another round of revenge.

[§]Harry St. John "Jack" Philby was an Arabist, explorer, and author, who played a key role in the Arab Revolt and later was an intelligence operative and adviser to Ibn Saud. Bertram Thomas was an assistant political officer and explorer who later held government posts in Jordan and Oman.

ing in the open desert but they could only have restricted exercise within the city. It was Violet's job to see that they were walked daily and she would take them through the narrow streets with overhanging second stories and heavily latticed windows. Outward signs of ostentation tended to attract the notice of tax collectors and robbers, so plain and unkempt facades might equally conceal a pauper's hovel or a princely dwelling with an elegant courtyard, a cool garden, and stables for the horses. Those first forays into the streets and boulevards of Baghdad with the hounds remained a vivid memory for her. She later wrote: "Our two salukis had to be taken out for walks, and I would venture out along New Street with them. They chased every cat they saw and I had much difficulty getting them back to the house. There was usually somebody to help me and produce a bit of string with which to hold them, but, as I did not know one word of Arabic, it was really a rather foolhardy undertaking."[11]

All this was capped off by a chilly reception from Gertrude Bell, archaeological expert and the Oriental Secretary to Sir Percy. Bell, who also owned Salukis, was at the center of much of the social and political activities in Baghdad. She had extraordinary political savvy and would eventually help to put Prince Faisal on the throne of Iraq. At the dinner party where Violet met her, Gertrude was clearly not impressed and remarked how disappointing it was for one of her promising officers to have married such a foolish woman.[12]

In due course, Dickson was appointed political officer at Al Hillah,* where Violet found herself rather isolated from the British community. While Dickson was at work or away on business, the Salukis became a great comfort to Violet, as did the pet mongoose. When their Arab horses arrived from Bahrain, life became a little more pleasant. Now their leisure would include riding, hawking, hunting, and, for Dickson, polo. When the railway line to Hillah was completed, his pair of Arabian oryx and a Persian wild sheep arrived one day with no notice. Violet had been raised with animals and had no problem with these after proper enclosures were constructed to keep them out of the house and garden. Their menagerie would continue to grow as Dickson was given presents from his tribal friends. In two years they added a wild boar, two gazelles, chickens, turkeys, geese, and a coot.[13] By the end of 1922 they were posted back to Bahrain and had to move their household and animals, and once again, along with the first of the household possessions, went the horses and Salukis.

Dickson accepted an offer from the 2nd Punjabis (2nd Battalion) and the household was off again, this time to Brigadier Lance's old stomping grounds at Quetta on the mountainous Afghan frontier. It took longer this time for the Salukis and horses to arrive at their new residence but once they were settled the Dicksons rode with the foxhounds of the Quetta Hunt after jackal. In 1924 Harold's old connections at Bikaner had resulted in the offer to tutor the maharajah's second son (he would eventually become private secretary to the maharajah). Bikaner was an independent state in the Indian Desert, northwest of Jaipur — which meant a move of over 400 miles for the Dicksons. They had moved their horses and Salukis much greater distances before, but for some compelling reason, they sold two of their horses and both of their Salukis to the Khan of Kalat (one of Quetta's neighboring states) who was known for his superior racehorses and hunting Salukis.

They were not to have Salukis again until 1929, when Dickson, by now a lieutenant colonel, accepted the prestigious post of Political Agent in Kuwait. There, they would spend the rest of their lives comfortably moving between Bedouin society and that of the drawing room, dressing appropriately for each. Dickson began making copious notes and illustrations about

South of Baghdad on the Euphrates River.

every aspect of Bedouin life and in 1936 he finished writing his manuscript and had it typed by his clerk or Violet. Due to various delays and the Second World War, he would not see *The Arab of the Desert** published until 1949. The book was well over 600 pages and contained a short but excellent chapter on the Saluki, in which he covered hunting techniques, rearing practices, breeding, and social customs concerning the hound. He noted that the late ruler of Bahrain, His Highness Sheikh Sir Hamad bin 'Isa al Khalifah, K.C.I.E., C.S.I., had been an eminent breeder of feathered Salukis. Sheikh Hamad's hounds were much-sought by fanciers, despite Dickson's opinion that they were larger and heavier than those seen in the rest of the Persian Gulf. This he attributed to the Sheikh's indulgence in overfeeding and lack of conditioning.[14]

While he and Violet never imported any Salukis to England, Dickson did manage to attend a few dog shows during his leaves home and would comment on the larger size of Salukis in England. On his leave in 1934, an unidentified "lady fancier and very well-known breeder of *saluqis* in London" asked if the Arabs kept separate breeds of Salukis the way they do with horses.[15] Dickson researched the question back in Kuwait and only confirmed tribal preferences for smooth or feathered. He could find no evidence for separate Saluki breeds other than hearsay of a very fine strain of feathered Salukis in Samarra, Iraq, called *Saglawiyah*, and less reliably, a rumor from Shammar tribesmen of a breed of naturally tailless Salukis.[16]

Violet had learned to speak Arabic in Kuwait and delighted in visiting with Bedouin women when Dickson made official and social visits. Having taken up botany as a hobby, she wrote *The Wild Flowers of Kuwait and Bahrain* as well as her personal reminiscences, *Forty Years in Kuwait*. She would be made a fellow of the Zoological Society and a Member of the British Empire in 1942. In 1973, at the age of 76, she had been a widow for fourteen years and continued to live in Kuwait. She continued her camping trips to visit Bedouin friends and lamented the dwindling game and camel herds, and the growing number of cars and trucks. Still fond of Salukis, she discussed them in a letter to the editor of the American Saluki Association's newsletter in 1973.[17] Violet died in 1991, a Dame Commander of the British Empire.

Another Connaught Ranger in Iraq who took a fancy to the breed was Colonel Pierce Charles Joyce. Prior to serving with Lawrence in the Arab Revolt, he had known Dickson in the Rangers, even though they served in two different battalions. Joyce also brought his bride to the desert and it was in Baghdad that she met his Salukis. On his retirement from the Iraqi Ministry of Defence, the Joyces would be the first serious breeders of Salukis in Ireland.

Pierce Charles Joyce was born in Galway, in the heart of the Gaelteacht — the Gaelic-speaking region in western Ireland. He was what the Irish called "a mighty man" — 6' 4" in height and with bulk to match. He was handsome, with a ready smile, twinkling eyes, dark brown hair, and a large mustache. His Norman ancestors (Joyeuse) had been given large tracts of Irish land in the 14th century and they prospered as bankers and merchants in Galway. Despite its location in the wilds of Connaught, Galway was a fairly cosmopolitan town, having been a major trade port with Spain and Portugal since the Middle Ages. The Joyces were

---

**The book was originally so massive that it had to be split into two more manageable volumes, the other being* Kuwait and Her Neighbors *which was published in 1956. Violet wrote the story of their life together in* Forty Years in Kuwait.

Lt. Col. Pierce Charles Joyce, C.B.E., D.S.O. wearing his Arab Revolt *kufiyah*, 1918. With the kind permission of Lowell Thomas Jr. Lowell Thomas Collection, James A. Cannavino Library, Archives & Special Collections, Marist College, Poughkeepsie, New York. © Lowell Thomas Jr. 1967.

one of the Fourteen Tribes of Galway — a group of founding families that were the business, political, and social leaders of the community.* By the mid–1800s, the Joyces were no longer involved in banking, but derived most of their income from land, both urban and rural. The Joyces were regarded by their tenants as fair and benevolent landlords in an era when subsistence farmers who could not meet their rent were evicted to starve.

They owned many properties, buildings, and houses in Galway, some of which still exist today. Pierce Charles's inheritance would even include fishing rights on the River Clare. Their principal home, Mervue†, was built on the high ground just outside Galway City. The three-story, Queen Anne–style mansion was constructed in the late 18th century and expanded on either side decades later. The grand view of Galway Bay inspired the name of the house. There were ornamental griffons on the roof and the fireplaces were beautifully carved out of green and black Connemara marble. In addition to the usual living quarters for family and servants, there was a ballroom, a chapel, and of course, kennels. The most notable feature was a marvelous semicircular greenhouse, which served as the main entrance to the mansion.

Pierce's grandfather (another Pierce Joyce) was an avid hunting and racing enthusiast and in 1839 was one of the founders of the County Galway Hunt which would later become the celebrated Galway Blazers.[18] A pack of foxhounds was kept by Grandfather Pierce at Mervue. He and his son, Pierce John, were known as two of the best horsemen in the locality and in 1869 the elder Pierce helped to establish the Galway Races.[19] To this day, it is a hugely popular sporting and social event in Ireland. The family was renowned for their hospitality and Mervue had been built with entertaining in mind. There were lively parties and the estate resounded with the music of waltzes, polkas, jigs, reels, and the popular tunes of the day. Their famous entertainments earned them the sobriquet of "the Merry Joyces." Such was the family and atmosphere that Deputy Lieutenant Pierce John's only surviving son was born into in 1878.§

*The Galway Joyces are from a distinctly different line than that of the author James Joyce, who also hailed from the west of Ireland.
†Sometimes spelled "Merview."
§Pierce Charles did have one sister.

Pierce Charles Joyce grew up with hounds and horses, guns and fishing tackle. He was educated at the local grammar school but then sent off to Beaumont College in Windsor. Upon graduating, he joined the 1st Battalion of the Connaught Rangers* in 1900, the British Army regiment that traditionally recruited in western Ireland. After some hasty training, he was sent to South Africa to join the rest of the battalion, who had been there since November 1899. The Rangers fought in several major and minor actions, including Reit Vlei, and the Relief of Ladysmith. Regimental historians reckoned that the Rangers marched nearly 4,774 miles during their two years and five months in South Africa.[20] After his arrival, Second Lieutenant Joyce did more training with a provisional battalion near Cape Town before joining his regiment in July 1900. His service in South Africa seems to have been pedestrian enough to avoid notice in the regimental history, with one near-fatal exception.

On May 31, 1902, at eight o'clock in the morning, Joyce and his sergeant were ambushed while reconnoitering a ridge above a supposedly friendly farmhouse, just six days before the cessation of hostilities. Trapped on a narrow trail, they were badly shot up by Boer snipers. When nine men from his patrol attempted a rescue, five of them were shot as well. The Boers captured the other four, looted their pockets, stole their weapons, and left them bleeding on the ridge. It was twenty-five hours before the mule-drawn ambulance wagons could be brought up to evacuate Joyce and the other wounded to the nearest hospital, a half-day's journey away. After the peace, the Rangers remained in South Africa until November, but most likely, Joyce was sent home on a transport ship in June or July.

Joyce recovered, was awarded both the Queen's and King's South Africa medals, and promoted to lieutenant, retroactive to April 1902. He soldiered on with the Rangers in Ireland until 1907, when he transferred to the Egyptian Army. There, Joyce held the regular Army rank of captain but was a *bimbashi* (major) in the Egyptian Army. He was stationed deep in the Sudan on the White Nile at Mongalla, a frontier post on the Sudanese-Ugandan border. It was surrounded by jungle and faced the Belgian post just across the river. There, amidst clouds of mosquitoes and daily rations of venomous snakes, *Bimbashi* Joyce commanded two companies of the 11th Sudanese, one of the finest regiments in the Egyptian Army.

In 1909 an elephant had attacked Joyce and thrown him to the ground with his trunk. Only the orderly's quick thinking saved Joyce's life. He fired a shot in the elephant's hindquarters and distracted the great beast from crushing the Irishman.[21] Joyce's relief turned out to be a man with whom he would later serve in the Arab Revolt — Capt. Walter Francis Stirling. Joyce was heartily glad to get out of the jungle to rest and heal in civilization.

Joyce returned to serve with the Egyptian Army and fought at the bloody first landing at Gallipoli. Promoted to major in 1915, he was formally transferred to the Egyptian Expeditionary Force and by 1917 he was acting as a lieutenant colonel and heading for Arabia. Sir Reginald Wingate, Governor General of the Sudan and Sirdar of the Egyptian Army referred to Joyce as "one of the best officers he had in the old 'Gippy Army.'"[22]

Joyce and T. E. Lawrence had actually met in Port Sudan in 1916 during a conference to discuss the proposed Arabian campaign and both were singularly unimpressed with each other. Joyce wanted desperately to tell him to get his hair cut and uniform pressed.[23] They met again two months later at Prince Ali's war council at Rabigh to plan strategy for defeating the Turks in the Arabian Peninsula and were still suspicious of each other. From Lawrence's point of

*Known until 1881 as the 88th Regiment of Foot, in the Peninsular Wars the regiment earned the nickname "The Devil's Own."

view, the tall Irishman was an unknown with respect to dealing with Arabs and his mixed Egyptian force was still untried. On the other hand, Joyce was "suspicious of a lieutenant with no executive command but with a definite political significance and therefore from my point of view entirely to be mistrusted."[24] Working together in the Hijaz the two men grew to respect and eventually to like each other. Joyce, as a brevet lieutenant colonel, was in overall command, so he took charge of the Arab Regulars — consisting of Egyptians, Arab townsmen, Iraqis who had formerly fought with the Turks, and later Ghurkas, small units of the British Army, and the Egyptian Camel Corps. He was content to leave wild raids and Bedouin to Lawrence.

Joyce also became O.C. (Officer Commanding) of the Al Aqabah base after its capture in 1917, relieving Raymond Goslett's temporary stint as O.C. and freeing the latter to concentrate on sorting out the Gordian knot of Al Aqabah supplies. Joyce had been depending on the reliable Goslett to keep his army on the march ever since their start at Al Wajh the year before. He was an active leader and while he focussed his energies on the Arab Army, he did go upcountry in the armored cars on the occasional railway bridge demolition raid. A convivial member of the officers' mess, he had hunting in common with the other hound fanciers of the Arab Revolt — Goslett, Stirling, Peake, Winterton, and Buxton.

Joyce's physical presence, good nature, unselfishness, and honesty made him a superb leader and well suited to organizing local troops. Lawrence considered him to be absolutely unflappable and possessed of an easy sense of humor equal to dealing with the frustrations in the cultural differences between East and West. He would write:

> He was rather Clayton-like, himself, a good cartilage to set between opposing joints, but with more laughter than Clayton, for he was broad and much over six feet in height. His nature was to be devoted to the nearest job without straining on his toes after longer horizon. ... Also he was more patient than any recorded archangel, and only smiled that jolly smile of his whenever I came in with revolutionary schemes, and threw new ribbons of fancy about the neck of the wild thing he was slowly rearing."[25]

Joyce had started the war with both South African medals (with five clasps) and the Egyptian medal and clasp for his Sudan service, and by the end of the war had been promoted to brevet lieutenant colonel and had earned the 1914–15 Star, British, and Victory medals, the 4th class orders of the Medjidieh and the Nile, D.S.O., four mentions in *Despatches*, the *Croix d'Officier*, the Legion of Honor, and the Arabian Order of the Nahda, 2nd class. He had been wounded badly enough to warrant recovery in a hospital and once had had a painful toothache that necessitated a trip to a Cairo dentist. After the armistice, Joyce remained on staff with the Egyptian government and for a time was governor of Luxor and eventually made C.B.E. In January 1921, he accepted a post at Baghdad as military advisor to the new Iraqi government and the future King Faisal.* The following year, with the creation of the Irish Free State, the British army disbanded a number of Irish regiments, including the Connaught Rangers.

In Iraq, Joyce had the local rank of colonel, with the official position of Advisor to the Minister of Defense, Jafar Pasha al Askari. The portly Jafar Pasha was an Iraqi military expert who served as a Turkish officer but secretly aided the fight for Arab independence. Switching sides late in 1917, he campaigned with Joyce and Lawrence and later became a member of Faisal's government in Syria. While Joyce was technically only an advisor, it was his job to

---

Faisal would be the first crowned king of Iraq in August 1921.

help Jafar recruit and forge an Iraqi army out of ex–Turkish soldiers and an assortment of townsmen and Bedouin.

Under the benign neglect of the Ottoman Empire, Iraq and its neighbors had functioned nominally without borders, and when tribal or religious feuds broke out or murder was done, Turkish troops set about retribution and restoring the local order. But with the defeat of the Ottoman Empire in 1918 and the creation of national borders, a new method of upholding the law needed to be devised. Besides setting up a constitutional monarchy for King Faisal, law enforcement was needed and that meant an army. The usual scheme was called into play — find former Turkish officers to lead, recruit locals and ex–Turkish soldiers, have British officers train the whole lot in military operations and then, it was hoped, leave them to run the show on their own when they were judged capable. That was Joyce's job and a difficult one it was.

Joyce joined the Baghdad social circle and became good friends with one of its leading lights, Gertrude Bell. They regularly played bridge, and attending Gertrude's dinner parties and P.S.A.s (Pleasant Sunday Afternoons) in her garden was de rigueur.[26] Bell, Joyce, Cheesman, and a few others were always taking motor excursions, visiting the nearby ruins of Ctesiphon,* riding, playing polo, picnicking, shooting, going to the cinema or the races, and attending all the social and government events. He renewed his acquaintance with Harold Dickson and met Violet for the first time (Gertrude's opinion of the latter had gone up by then). Joyce had become engaged in Cairo to Colin Florence Murray, the only daughter of Major General Robert Hunter Murray, C.B., C.M.G., of the Seaforth Highlanders.[27] She was a well-propertied prospect, bringing a sizeable estate and Red House in Yateley, Hampshire, to the marriage. Colin was slim, average in height, and had short dark hair. She followed the fashion of the other ladies and wore a topee with a large, sheer veil, and carried a parasol to fend off the tropical sun. Joyce brought his bride to Baghdad in late October 1921 and Gertrude thought they were delightful, genuine people — Colin had class and would be an example to the "second rate little minxes of which Baghdad society has mostly been composed."[28] Gifted with a lovely voice, Colin often sang at the officers' mess in Baghdad and Gertrude frequently invited the Joyces to her house for dinner and a game of bridge. While it is unknown whether or not Joyce had Salukis in Egypt or Arabia, he definitely kept them in Baghdad.

In 1923, the year the Joyces joined the Saluki or Gazelle Hound Club, they acquired a bitch from everyone's favorite local despot, the soon to be deposed Vali of Pusht-i-Kuh. They named her Risha of Luristan to mark the relationship to the Vali's hounds. Given this connection to Pusht-i-Kuh, Joyce was the most likely intermediary for both General Lance's negotiations to obtain one of the Vali's hounds, as well as one from the Daghestani prince, Daoud Bey.† There are few details recorded about the Joyce Salukis in Baghdad, but Kennel Club registrations and an article by Florence Amherst provide some tantalizing hints. The following year, Sheikh Ali Kerim gave the Joyces a smooth bitch named Shallah. From elsewhere they obtained a smooth male named Ghazal el Senak. Shallah was born near Samarra, some sixty miles north of Baghdad on the Tigris River, an area where a superior strain of Salukis was reputed to be found.

---

*Until Baghdad became the chief city of the Arab empire about 635 C.E., Ctesiphon had been a capital for the Parthians, Sassanians, Greeks, Romans, and Persians. Part of its mammoth vaulted hall still stands opposite the ancient capital of Seleucia ("Saluqiyyah" in Arabic).

†It is likely that Lance first met Joyce when the latter was governor of Luxor from April 1920 to January 1921. Lance had toured the tombs there looking for paintings of Salukis.

Samarra was a vast city that was for sixty years in the 9th century the capital of the Abbasid Empire and boasted many ruins from its glorious past, including a unique spiral ziggurat minaret. The once-walled modern town contains the shrine of Ali al–Hadi and Hasan al–Askeri, two of the twelve imams revered by the Shia, and the cave from which the 12th imam is expected to return.* When the Joyces eventually retired to England, they would choose Samarra as their kennel name.

Major Arthur Bentinck returned to Iraq in November 1925 as one of the "Forty Thieves", the Baghdad social circle's nickname for the officers working with the Iraqi Army.[29] He brought Feena and Rishan with him and bred at least one litter. When old enough, the puppies and their parents and a spaniel would accompany him on his rides and camping trips in the desert, even as far north as Al Mawsil, very near where Feena and Rishan were born. Bentinck always rode out with one or more soldier escorts and his servant, an Iraqi who wore military-style clothes, a fedora with upturned brim, and carring a holstered pistol. The soldiers and the servant doted on Bentinck's hounds and were happy to pose with them for snapshots. When old enough, one of Bentinck's young males, Waara of Kurdistan, was bred to the Joyces' bitch, Risha of Luristan, and the first Joyce litter was born in Baghdad in April 1927. One month later, their two smooths, Ghazal and Shallah, produced the litter that was to become the Samarra foundation stock.†

Joyce joined the Royal Exodus Hunt, whose members rode after jackal in the vicinity of the city and put on an annual ball at the Alwiyah Club. Formerly known as the Baghdad Hounds, it had been an all–Saluki pack in the years just after the war. D.C. Pim had been the master and inexplicably claimed "the distinction of being the only Hunt Master to have his entire 'field' taken prisoner by the Arabs."[30] The pack was the darling of the 110th com-

Major Bentinck, his servant, Iraqi Army soldiers, Feena, Rishan, and their puppies, Iraq, 1926–1927. The plane is a DH-9A — the same type that Flying Officer Sugden used to fly with his Saluki in Iraq. With the kind permission of the Earl of Portland.

*The magnificent golden dome over the shrine was destroyed in 2006 by anti–Shiite insurgents.
†The Joyces had a penchant for naming their puppies after Iraqi cities (Baiji, etc.).

Major Bentinck's servant and Iraqi soldiers with the pack (including a spaniel) taking a break on the day's trek. With the kind permission of the Earl of Portland.

pany of the Royal Indian Army Service Corps who changed its name to "Ex O Dus"—which sounded like Hindustani for the number 110.[31] In the early twenties, the hunt had imported foxhounds to gradually replace the long dogs, and moved the pack to the RAF cantonment at Hinaidi.[32] After the change of character of the Royal Exodus Hunt, the Saluki owners of Baghdad found their own opportunities to go coursing.

Mrs. Borrie, the wife of the director of hospitals at Basrah, was another devotee and sent reports to Gladys about the Basrah Hunt in southern Iraq, a small but eager club which used Salukis to course the local fox and jackal. Members would saddle up and meet early on Sundays and Thursdays, either on the Basrah side of the river Shatt al–Arab or at the police post on the opposite bank, and work the surrounding countryside, which consisted of both date orchards and "sporting country." Sometimes they would cross the river and hunt in the open country to the north of the city. Mrs. Borrie wrote, "The Saluki, although not a small dog, is extremely fast and once a jack is sighted, a very good run, although often all too short, ensues."[33]

Captain A. V. Cooper was a leading member of the Basrah Hunt. He had been a high-ranking officer of the Iraqi Police Force since 1919, having served in Baghdad, Najaf, and most recently Basrah. Cooper kept six hunting adults plus assorted puppies at Basrah — all of which were fawn colored except the best, which was a black-and-tan bitch presented to him by Sheikh Zobair.* When Captain Cooper visited the Lances in 1924, he was very interested to see how Salukis fared outside their native environment and remarked upon the heavier feathering and larger size of the Salukis in England — "fat and feathered" being his exact words. [34] Gladys accepted this with equanimity and, having considerable experience with Salukis in

---

*The breeder of Zobeida-el-Zobair, the dam of Florence Amherst's Ch. Zobeid.

the desert herself, she attributed these differences to the lack of wear and tear from brush and thorn, and a better diet. She had written to him requesting a speed test and he measured his hounds against a motor-car, finding that they could easily manage 25 miles per hour.

Interestingly enough, Bertram Thomas, the famous Arabian explorer, had also been curious about the speed of his Salukis and actually seems to be the first person to have left a record of measuring the speed against that of a car. In southeastern Iraq, at Ash Shatrah, in May 1921, he attempted to solve a debate about whether or not Salukis could bring down an adult gazelle. Thomas had heard of it being done, but his doubting Arab friends said that if it indeed had ever happened, it must have been a young gazelle or one that was heavy with foal. He tested his theory by driving his car after a fleeing gazelle with his pack of Salukis in pursuit. The hounds were fresh and in good condition, but could not match the 40 miles per hour needed to come up level with the gazelle.[35] That seemed to settle the question of catching gazelle as far as Bertram's group was concerned, although he does not say how long he kept up the chase.

Colin Joyce began corresponding with Florence Amherst about Iraqi Salukis, but oddly enough the latter seems to have been misled by her name for she frequently referred to her as *Mr.* Colin Joyce. At any rate, Colin passed along a considerable amount of Saluki lore to the ever-eager Florence. Colonel Joyce was used to living in harsh conditions, but his wife must have found this new life as initially trying as did Violet Dickson. Temperatures in Baghdad could range from below freezing to well into the triple digits. An old proverb goes, "When Allah made Hell, he did not find it bad enough, so he made Mesopotamia — and added flies."[36] Colin noted that winters in Iraq were cold enough to necessitate three or four coats for the hounds in the winter, and a thin coat in summer to protect them from the biting flies.[37] Ruth and Helen Hoffman, American twins who lived near the village of Ali al Gharbi* in eastern Iraq, observed Bedouin Salukis wearing blankets fastened with string or safety pins. They took pains to point out in their memoir, *We Married an Englishman*, "A child may go shivering in the winter on the desert, but a *saluki* always has a coat."[38]

Colin wrote affectionately about how devoted Salukis were to their masters and their horses, and when tired after a long day's trek, they would leap onto the horse's back and sit behind the saddle. At night, the hounds would curl up next to their favorite horses. They were fed native bread, meat, and milk, and relished dates and cheese. For meals on long journeys, she noted, they might only have dates and lumps of sugar from the saddlebags.[39]

One of Colin's anecdotes was repeated by Florence Amherst in a 1928 article in the *AKC Gazette*— yet another of many amazing accounts that stand as proof of the Saluki's homing instinct and incredible stamina. Colonel Joyce had known soldiers who, with their Saluki mascot, were taken 70 miles north of Baghdad by train (most likely to Samarra, where the railway line ended). There they remained for some time, but the Saluki, longing for his home, decamped a few days prior to the unit's return and was not to be found. Days later, back in Baghdad, his owner abandoned the last shred of hope of recovering his hound. Much to his surprise, several weeks later, the Saluki walked into the barracks, emaciated and exhausted, having crossed nearly a hundred miles of desert plains, mountains, and rivers swollen with flood.[40]

---

*On the Tigris River between Al Kut and Al Amarah.

19

The Lady and the Traveler

"I will have no lazy glutton for a lover of mine,
Who would cling to me always like a sluki."

Rwala Bedouin poem[1]

Perhaps the most famous Saluki owner in the British mandate of Iraq was Gertrude Margaret Lowthian Bell, C.B.E. Archaeologist, scholar, author, traveler, mountain climber, airplane enthusiast, anti-suffragist, diplomat, intelligence gatherer, and animal lover, she was known as Miss Bell, and both town and tent Arabs called her *al–Khatun* (the Lady). In Iraq, she was the Oriental Secretary to High Commisioner Sir Percy Cox, advisor and confident of King Faisal, and the Director of Archaeology. For a woman who lived amidst the gender constraints of the Victorian and Edwardian eras, Gertrude led a life that would have been extraordinary for any man.* In addition to being a Saluki owner, Gertrude would be directly responsible for another appearance of a Saluki in western literature.

She was born in 1868 to Hugh and Mary Bell. The Bells were a prominent and wealthy family that had made its considerable fortune as one of the major iron producers in England. Gertrude's mother died when she was very young and her father would later marry Florence Olliffe, with whom Gertrude would grow very close. Young Gertrude had reddish hair, blue eyes, a slender build, and would always be very particular about fashion. She took pains to be correctly dressed wherever she would travel in the world, whether city or desert. Her father and stepmother valued education, and in an enlightened move, unusual for the upper middle class in a time when education was thought to be too strenuous for the female constitution, they sent Gertrude away to boarding school in London.[2] When old enough, she was admitted to Lady Margaret Hall at Oxford and received honors in history.† After Oxford, she traveled extensively, taking a Cook's tour around the world, and making her own extended trips to Romania and Istanbul.

After living in Tehran for several months in 1892 she found herself gently and eagerly ensnared by Persian culture. It was the start of her lifelong love of the Middle East. She became fluent in Farsi, learned to translate classical Persian poetry, and mastered a number of Arabic

Opposite: **Gertrude Bell in her Baghdad garden, with a Saluki and another of her dogs. Taken by Vita Sackville-West, 1926. With the kind permission of the late Nigel Nicolson.**

*Much has been written about Gertrude Bell's life, notably biographies by Elizabeth Burgoyne, Janet Wallach, H. V. F. Winstone, Joesephine Kamm, and Susan Goodman. Of special interest is her own delightful correspondence, The Letters of Gertrude Bell, *edited by her stepmother, Lady Bell.*
†Women would finally be permitted to receive degrees in 1920.

Gertrude Bell.

dialects. In the early 1900s she trekked to Turkey, Jaffa, Jerusalem, Damascus, Palmyra, Petra, and the Moab Desert. Archaeology became another of her passions and she became fascinated by Byzantine churches and Seljuk castles. Gertrude was the first since Lady Blunt to travel openly in the desert as a Christian woman, but Gertrude did it with only her *rafiqs*. In 1911, when she was forty-two, she met the young T. E. Lawrence who was then excavating Hittite ruins at Carchemish. The two would become friends and the coming war in the Middle East would see them working together.

After the European War was declared, David Hogarth remembered Gertrude's talent for languages and vast knowledge of Arabian, Syrian, and Mesopotamian tribes (she had been the last European to visit Northern and Central Arabia).[3] In 1915, he whisked her away from Red Cross work in London to the Military Intelligence Department in Cairo. There she would help to complete the map of Northern Arabia and compile data and profiles on Bedouin personalities, temperaments, and loyalties. When Hogarth split his desert specialists off to form the Arab Bureau, Gertrude was sent to Basrah to help run the Mesopotamian branch in 1916. There she met Sir Percy Cox, the area's chief political officer. For Cox and the Arab Bureau she worked tirelessly to document tribal alliances, numbers, and movements. Gertrude wrote valuable intelligence papers and would become a respected Arabist of great influence.

To keep the information flowing, she maintained close friendships with the local Bedouin throughout the war, and one Sunday in 1919 a brace of grizzle Salukis showed up on her doorstep — the gift of Sheikh Fahad Beg ibn Hadhdhal. She had met the battle-scarred graybeard, who kept falcons and Salukis, on her travels in 1914. She impressed him no end and he became a staunch friend and ally. The same day that the gift arrived, Gertrude wrote to her stepmother:

> Another thing came in to-day, quite as important as the post — two most beautiful Arab greyhounds sent to me today by my old friend the paramount chief of the Anazeh, Fahad Beg. They had walked ten days down the Euphrates with two tribesmen to conduct them, and came in half starved. They are sitting beside me on my sofa as I write, after wandering about the room for half an hour whining. They are very gentle and friendly and I hope they will soon get accustomed to living in a garden instead of a tent. They are perfectly lovely and of course of the finest Arab breed. We've named them Rishan and Najmah — the feathered (that's because of his feathered tail) and the star....[4]

Three weeks after Najmah and Rishan arrived, they were behaving like angels and she had begun to persuade them that carpets were more appropriate for hounds and that sofas and chairs were for people. The pair settled in and grew accustomed to her other animals: a parrot, two spaniels, two guinea pigs, a tame gazelle, and a mongoose — although the Salukis never did quite regard her assorted birds as anything other than potential food.

Gertrude's very first desert dog was actually a Syrian pi-dog, "insatiably greedy" like all pariahs but friendly in disposition.[5] She wrote to her stepmother in 1905 that she had acquired "an extremely nice dog of the country" named Kurt — the Turkish word for wolf. He had yellow fur and was well mannered enough to sleep in her tent.[6] A month later, just outside Baalbek, on the road to Hims, Kurt was stolen. Her men recovered him, but eight days later on the track, Kurt went missing again — this time permanently. The unhappy Gertrude suspected that Kurt had been stolen after being tempted by food.[7] She had better luck with Fahad Beg's gift. Salukis were not new to Gertrude for she had seen "Slughy dogs" during her travels in central Turkey in 1907.[8] In 1914, she had even photographed Fahad Beg's recumbent white

Saluki in his tent on their first meeting.[9] She was devoted to her spaniels but the Salukis became her riding companions and a source of much pleasure. Armed with a riding crop for lashing biting mongrels, Gertrude and her hounds would go for walks and rides in the cool hours of the morning or evening.

> This morning I was out riding just after sunrise — it was difficult to decide whether the earth or the air was more solid. The dust bars hanging over the horizon were like slabs of desert in the sky, and in the uncertain light of sunrays, dust and damp, when I turned round to look for my dogs I couldn't see anything tangible, but I marked each one by the little golden dust cloud that it made as it ran. My dogs are very well. So's the parrot. But the mongoose has run away.[10]

Gertrude was not opposed to hunting — she had participated in many a shooting and hawking party — but left coursing to the other Saluki owners in Baghdad. She did have to be careful to keep Rishan and Najmah away from domestic birds. "I took my two dogs for a long walk in the desert where I could let them run loose owing to the fact that there are no hens in it. They jump on every hen they see and I never knew till I went out walking with them how many owners of hens there are in Baghdad."[11]

The mischievous Rishan seems to have been her favorite despite his own brand of havoc, for he appears more frequently in her letters than does Najmah. "Rishan is in terrible disgrace. First he jumped on the pantry table and broke all the crockery on it, including my dear little Persian jam-pot. He was looking for something to eat of course. Next he thought fit to roll in a beautiful bed of nasturtiums and destroyed half of them."[12]

In addition to his other bad habits, Rishan was notorious for his habit of stealing dates and killing chickens. Still, Gertrude's Armenian servant, Fattuh, said that "the Baghdadis are worse rogues than Rishan."[13] In late June 1920, he tore his chest open on a barbwire fence and was three weeks in healing. Three years later he was still misbehaving, for he went missing for nearly two weeks, finally appearing at his mistress's doorstep, thin and apologetic — "But doesn't say where he has been."[14] Nonetheless, Rishan was well-mannered enough to go along with Gertrude on picnics and shooting parties.

Winter was hard for animal and human alike. Gertrude noted that winter temperatures in Baghdad could drop to a freezing 18° F. Salukis, not having much flesh on their bodies to begin with, acutely felt the bite of the cold and would huddle close to the fireplace. Like the Joyce hounds, Gertrude's had cold-weather coats. Only when the fabric had become ragged and disgraceful would Marie, the maid, make new ones. At the opposite end of the thermometer, summer temperatures of 116° and above were not uncommon. All the windows were covered with mats to block out the sun and carpets were taken up to allow the stone floor to help cool the house. Hanging a wet sheet between the bed and the window allowed some sleep due to evaporative cooling from the night breeze, but there were regular interruptions when the sheet dried out and had to be resoaked during the night. At the peak of summer when the heat inside at night was unbearable, Gertrude and the Salukis retreated to the roof where the night breeze made it possible to sleep — she in her bed and they on their special mats. The only disadvantage to sleeping al fresco was being rudely awakened when Najmah and Rishan decided to bark defiance at the noisy pariahs of the vicinity, who in turn barked at other dogs and so forth, until the racket echoed back from the furthest districts — and set off Najmah and Rishan all over again.

By March 1921, Gertrude had been appointed Oriental Secretary to Sir Percy, High Commissioner in Iraq. Hers was a position of tremendous importance and a singular honor. When

it was decided to create a state out of Mesopotamia, Sir Percy and the three former archaeologists, David Hogarth, T. E. Lawrence, and Gertrude Bell, became the chief advocates for
Faisal (who was still smarting from his ejection from Damascus by the French) to be made
king of the new nation. Gertrude became an integral player in the new administration — one
that she considered the first Arab government in Mesopotamia since the Abbasids.[15] Faisal
trusted her and she became his adviser and confidant. There were a thousand details that
needed sorting out in order for the new state to have its own identity. Gertrude set up the
protocol for the new court and helped to design the flag and the medal for the national order.
Iraq would not have its own postage stamps until 1923. Evelyn Cheesman (Robert's sister)
was visiting her brother in Baghdad and codesigned the new pictorials — relegating the old
Turkish postage (over-stamped "Iraq in British Occupation") to trash bins or philatelic
albums.[16]

While Gertrude often protested that she did not care for society, she relished her status
and was generally the center of attention at any dinner, picnic, outing, or function. After
Faisal was crowned, he gradually took over the reins of office and Gertrude's roll in the government began to diminish. She had never ceased to be interested in preserving Iraq's antiquities and in recognition of this, Faisal appointed her Director of Archaeology in 1922. With
Sir Percy's retirement in 1923 there was still less for her to do outside her work in the new
museum of antiquities. By 1925 she was considerably disappointed with her lot in life and
had grown generally irritable. Her former good opinion of the Joyces had soured and she considered Joyce to be stupid and without initiative or ambition.[17]

Before 1925, Baghdad had been getting its mail via airplane for a couple of years (Gertrude
loved to fly) and an automobile route across the
desert had finally opened up, allowing regular
freight shipments and the arrival of something
that the city had not seen much of— tourists.
Baghdad was about to get its own office of
Thomas Cook & Sons and the new interest in
desert travel peeved Gertrude no end: "[U]pon
my soul I almost wish there weren't a desert
route — it brings silly females, all with intro-
ductions to me."[18] However, in February 1926
Gertrude warmly welcomed one particular
female visitor to her home.

The Honorable Victoria Sackville-West —
poet and dog lover — had traveled from London
through Trieste, Cairo, Aden, Bombay, Delhi,
Basrah, and Baghdad, via rail ship and motorcar, and would continue on through Persia,
Russia, Poland, and Germany before returning
home four months later to England. "Vita,"
as she was known, was on her way to see her
handsome husband, Harold Nicolson, who was
on the British Legation staff in Tehran — her
next major stop after Baghdad. In addition to
being a diplomat, he was a gifted historian and

The poet, author, traveler, and gardener Vita
Sackville-West. With the kind permission of the
late Nigel Nicolson.

journalist, and shared Vita's passion for literature, gardening and dogs. Gertrude had actually met Vita and Harold in Istanbul before the war and the three periodically renewed their friendship whenever their paths crossed. Like Gertrude, Vita was an enthusiastic traveler, and when she entered Gertrude's walled garden in Baghdad, she was greeted by Rishan and Najmah.

> A tall grey sloughi came out of the house, beating his tail against the posts of the verandah; "I want one like that," I said, "to take up to Persia." I did want one, but I had reckoned without Gertrude's promptness. She rushed to the telephone, and as I poured cream over my porridge I heard her explaining — a friend of hers had arrived — must have a sloughi at once — was leaving for Persia the next day — a selection of sloughis must be sent round that morning.[19]

Vita was so charmed by the pair that she had to have a Saluki of her own immediately. The two women exchanged news over breakfast and then the latter left to do some work in her office, promising to be back for luncheon with guests. Vita was left to her own devices in Gertrude's house.

> I had my bath — her house was extremely simple, and the bath just a tin saucer on the floor — and then the sloughis began to arrive. They slouched in, led on strings by Arabs in white woollen robes, sheepishly smiling. Left in command, I was somewhat taken aback, so I had them all tied up on the posts of the verandah till Gertrude should return, an army of desert dogs, yellow, white, grey, elegant, but black with fleas and lumpy with ticks. I dared not go near them, but they curled up contentedly and went to sleep in the shade, and the partridge prinked round them on her dainty pink legs, investigating. At one o'clock Gertrude returned, just as my spirits were beginning to flag again, laughing heartily at this collection of dogs which her telephone message (miraculously, as it seemed to me) had called into being, shouted to the servants, ordered a bath to be prepared for the dog I should choose, unpinned her hat, set down some pansies on her luncheon table, closed the shutters and gave me a rapid biography of her guests.[20]

Eventually, Gertrude selected a smooth Saluki as the most suitable and subjected her to a bath by the servants. She named the hound Zurcha — and Vita later said that it meant "yellow one."* Gertrude took Vita to tea with King Faisal and the two women passed a few pleasant days before Vita left for Tehran and Harold, with Zurcha curled up beside her.[†]

Gertrude's diminishing health and role in the government in Iraq had left her despondent and enervated. She only lived a few months after Vita's visit. Gertrude died in her sleep on July 12, 1926, having taken an overdose of sleeping medicine.[21] She was buried that day in a state funeral and a memorial plaque and bust were put up in the Baghdad Museum. The fate of her Rishan and Najmah is uncertain, but in 1938, Miss Helena I. H. Barr (Grevel Salukis & Irish Wolfhounds) met a hospital matron in Baghdad that claimed to have one of Gertrude's old Salukis.[22] Miss Barr reported that this was a small, pale cream bitch but as Gertrude only recorded having her two grizzle Salukis (and at least one of them a male) when she died, the matron's claim seems highly dubious.[§] With Gertrude's connections and friends, Rishan and

---

*In his article, "Three Remarkable Women and their Salukis" (The Saluki, Crufts Edition, 1996), Sir Terence Clark notes that "Zurcha" is not an Arabic word. Gertrude was fluent in Arabic and would not have made such a mistake. "Zurqa" sounds close but means blue — a term the Arabs use to describe a shade of fawn with blue tints.

†In the 1990 reprint of Passenger to Teheran, "sloughi" would be changed to "Saluki." I am grateful to Vita and Harold's son, the late Nigel Nicolson, O.B.E., for guidance in ferreting out Zurcha's story and allowing me to reproduce his mother's photographs.

§Gertrude never does note Najmah's sex but writes as if the Saluki was male.

Zurcha's first bath

Najmah doubtless found a home with one of the other Saluki fraternity in Baghdad — perhaps with the Joyces.

❖   ❖   ❖

Vita left Baghdad on the railway line to Persia which ran northeast across the plain, crossing the Tigris and then stopping in the foothills of the northern end of the snowy Zagros mountain range and the Pusht-i-Kuh. When the line ended she transferred her luggage to the overland Trans-Desert Mail motorcar. Vita and Zurcha settled into the front seat and headed off to Tehran

> with Zurcha, who although as leggy as a colt, folded up into a surprisingly small space and immediately went to sleep. I was glad to see this, as I had not looked forward to restraining a struggling dog over five hundred miles of country, and had not been at all easy in my mind as to what a slouhgi straight out of the desert would make of a motor. That yellow nomad, however, accepted whatever life sent her with a perfect and even slightly irritating philosophy. Warmth and food she insisted on; shared my luncheon and crawled under my sheepskin, but otherwise gave me no trouble. I was relieved, but felt it a little ungrateful of her not to notice that she was being taken into Persia.[23]

Knowing Vita was coming from Baghdad, Harold drove a considerable distance to meet her at Kermanshah. Late at night in the headlamps of the motorcar, he saw his beloved "Viti" with Zurcha curled on her knee.[24] Reunited, they motored on to Tehran, where Zurcha joined Harold's dogs (a spaniel and Afghan hound named Henry and Sally) at the Legation. The reunion was ecstatic — Vita thoroughly enjoyed the sights, sounds, and scents of Tehran and together they attended the coronation of Reza Shah Pahlavi — the man who had consolidated power in Persia and ousted the cruel Vali of Pusht-I-Kuh.

Harold and Vita were great dog lovers, but taking Zurcha on to Russia and then to England and quarantine would be difficult at best, so she was left with Harold. Vita only wrote about her once again, when she would call Zurcha "the dullest dog I ever owned ... she was faithful only to the best arm-chair."[25] Plucked out of the desert as an adult and given to a stranger, it is small wonder that Zurcha did not behave as did their spaniels, elkhounds, and German Shepherds. Still, Harold took good care of Zurcha and his other dogs at the Legation in the walled garden, a wonderful oasis of ponds, fountains, and shade trees. Vita returned to Tehran six months later in February 1927 and together with Harold they left for England in May.[26] Zurcha did not go with them.

Vita and Harold would have many other dogs, but never again a Saluki. At the age of seventy, Vita wrote that she gave Zurcha to a Persian prince who took her to Russia and lost her in Moscow.[27] Despite the fact that Vita considered Zurcha unsatisfactory as a dog, Harold liked her and he lovingly compared the sounds Vita made while drifting off to sleep to Zurcha's contented little grunts.[28] Years later, he would liken the Saluki's athletic grace to the physical manner of T. E. Lawrence. While Vita ultimately did not care for Zurcha, it was her own prose about the Saluki's elegance that was to make an impression on another author back in England. "I've bought a dog. The garden here was filled with dogs that were potentially mine, — all come in from the desert, led on leash by Arabs. This one is a marvel of elegance, — long tapering paws, and a neck no thicker than your wrist. So off we set together tonight, the sloughi puppy and I, to face the snows in the high passes."[29]

Opposite: **Vita's new Saluki gets a bath before the long drive to Tehran. With the kind permission of the late Nigel Nicolson.**

On February 28, the day she left Baghdad, Vita wrote that passage in a letter to Virginia Woolf.

Vita and Harold had a strong marriage that defied social conventions and pigeonholing. Each of them openly took lovers, and yet remained passionately in love and devoted to each other. Virginia and Vita were extremely close and the former was fascinated by Vita's adventures. Virginia wrote a highly unusual tribute on the heels of Vita's journey across Europe and the Middle East. She called it *Orlando*, said to be the "biography" of an immortal Elizabethan nobleman who, after a week-long sleep in Constantinople, wakes up to find his gender mysteriously (but not objectionably) changed to female. Orlando's adventures continue and she remains perpetually in her thirties throughout the centuries. In 1928, at the conclusion of the book, Orlando shows every indication of living for several more centuries. Vita posed as Orlando for several fanciful photographs to be included in the book. Vita and Harold's son, Nigel Nicolson, called *Orlando* "the longest and most charming love letter in literature."[30] Virginia Woolf had been inspired by Vita's description of her trim "sloughi" to include a faithful Saluki as Orlando's companion in Constantinople. After waking as a woman and imperturbably noting the change of gender, Orlando bathes, and then:

> First, she carefully examined the papers on the table; took such as seemed to be written in poetry, and secreted them in her bosom; next she called her Seleuchi hound, which had never left her bed all these days, though half famished with hunger, fed and combed him; stuck a pair of pistols in her belt; finally wound about her person several strings of emeralds and pearls of the finest orient which had formed part of her Ambassadorial wardrobe.[31]

Riding out on a donkey and accompanied by an old Gypsy and her "lean dog," Orlando then leaves Constantinople.* This was the fifth appearance of Salukis in western literature.†

---

*While the 1992 film of the book took some liberties with the sequence of events, it did have two Salukis keeping vigil over Orlando throughout several days of uninterrupted sleep.

†Vanity Fair, Kim, Seven Pillars of Wisdom, *and* Passenger to Teheran *being the others.*

PART VI: ECLIPSE

20

The Passing of the Caravan

"The dogs bark, but the caravan passes by."

Arab saying

In the decade before Britain went to war with Germany a second time, the world saw penicillin, nylon stockings, television service in both England and America, flashbulbs for photography, and both sound and color motion pictures for the first time. There was a great rush of both male and female aviators to cross oceans and continents — Amy Johnson flew solo from London to Australia in five days and Amelia Earhart went solo across the Atlantic and then disappeared over the Pacific. *Lady Chatterly's Lover*, *The Maltese Falcon*, *Brave New World*, and *Gone with the Wind* were published and *Carmina Burana* performed for the first time. The American stock market crashed, sending the country into the Great Depression, the Soviet Union continued to be ravaged by terrible famines, and Ibn Saud renamed his new kingdom. The Golden Gate Bridge and Empire State Building were finished and the *Hindenberg* exploded in New Jersey. Queen Elizabeth II was born and Thomas Edison, Rudyard Kipling, and King George V died. The king's heir, Edward VIII, shocked the British Empire by abdicating in order to marry Wallis Simpson, an American divorcée. Both Britain and America went off the gold standard, and England and France competed to build the biggest, fastest, and most opulent superliners with the SS *Ile de France*, SS *Normandie* and RMS *Queen Mary* vying for honors. The Olympics were celebrated in Amsterdam, Los Angeles, and — the last one for twelve years — Berlin. Vidkun Quisling organized the Norwegian Nazi Party and Konrad Henlein did the same in Czechoslavakia. Books were burned in Germany and civilians were slaughtered in the Spanish Civil War. President Roosevelt signed the U.S. Neutrality Act, and Neville Chamberlain became prime minister of Great Britain and pursued a policy of appeasement with the increasingly aggressive Germany. Japan invaded China, set up a puppet government, and resigned from the League of Nations. *Il Duce*, Benito Mussolini, annexed Abyssinia after years of bloody fighting and Adolf Hitler was appointed chancellor in Germany, later making himself war minister.

Breed popularity should have stuck in those ten years. Saluki registrations and show entries had been increasing. There were new imports from the Middle East, particularly Iraq. Club membership and participation was up, Salukis appeared on collectible cigarette cards, and there were frequent articles in the press. There were Saluki populations (some large, some small) in the United States, Australia, Bermuda, Belgium, British Malaya, Canada, Ceylon,

East Africa, Finland, France, Germany, the Netherlands, New Zealand, Western Samoa, South Africa, Spain, and Sweden (many of these descendants of Sarona Kelb). The word "Saluki" was formally added to the English lexicon with publication of the new *Oxford English Dictionary's Supplement and Re-Issue* in 1933:

> **Saluki** (sa̱lu̱·ki). Also salugi, selug(h)i. [Arab. *seluqi*, f. *Seluq*, a town in Greece famous for dogs.] A Persian Greyhound.

The necessary bricks and mortar were there for the sort of sustained popularity that Borzois had long enjoyed, but the house was not to be finished. Gradually, it all came apart.

✧   ✧   ✧

There were plenty of military importers of Salukis coming into England from Iraq in those years. Major General A. R. Hoskins, Flying Officer H. O. Fellowes, Captain Cooper of the Basrah Constabulary, and Captain Growden of Kirkuk, to name a few. Some of these Salukis disappeared after clearing quarantine, most likely to become pets, but others were seen in the show ring or in the coursing fields. Both Flying Officer Fellowes and Flight Lieutenant Rickards joined the SGHC in 1926. The latter set up the Fairford kennels and for the next seventeen months, Rickards made a great splash in the show scene with his three imports. In March 1928, he was posted back to Aden. He looked into shipping two Salukis to Canada, but there is no record in his papers, the club files, or doggy newspapers as to whether Abu Jedid and Beni' Saud went there or not. However, it is recorded that Rickards sold Um-el-Tayyib to Florence Amherst who had the good sense to buy the out-cross bitch for breeding stock and avoid Rickard's male — whose parentage was 50 percent uncertain. In September, 1928, she registered the bitch as an Amherstia but, curiously, does not seem to have bred her. That ended the Fairford Kennels. Rickards was eventually promoted to wing commander and awarded the O.B.E., but in 1937 was killed in a plane crash in Oman.[1]

In late 1927, Lt. Colonel Count Arthur Bentinck left Iraq for the second time and resumed his permanent rank of major on his return to England. Of his faithful Rishan and Feena or their Baghdad puppies, there is scant information. With the exception of one puppy, it is likely that they were all left with brother officers in their native country. In giving updates on the latest imports, Gladys in her *Dog World* column, October 1928, wrote that a black-and-white feathered Saluki from Iraq was due to clear quarantine the following month.[2] He was the son of Bentinck's Rishan of Kurdistan who had been mated to an RAF officer's bitch. She noted that the import was expected to be a show prospect, but does not say who his owner was. Presumably it was not Bentinck.*

Bentinck moved back to the family house at 53 Green Street in the fashionable Mayfair district, and settled in to life in London and his duties at the Coldstream Guards Headquarters, going on half-pay status in April 1928 due to continued health problems from his old war wounds. In 1929 he rejoined the SGHC and paid in arrears his membership subscription for 1928. Except for a short lapse, he had maintained a "Foreign Membership" for 1926 while he was in Iraq. He was welcomed back to the fold and began to regularly attend club meetings at Florence's flat at 6 William Street, Knightsbridge. Bentinck was appointed to the Saluki

---

*Many imported Salukis were brought in just as pets and were never registered or shown.

Racing Club committee and was elected as the SGHC delegate to the Kennel Club's Council of Representatives.*

That he registered his "Kurdistan" suffix in 1930 suggests that he intended to resume showing and breeding at some point but, Bentinck does not seem to have owned Salukis again. His membership lapsed (this time permanently) in 1931, and he faded out of Saluki activities.[†]

Also returning from Iraq in 1927, were the Merry Joyces with a pack of no less than eight Salukis.[§] With the Joyces well able to afford the shipping and quarantine costs, their pets became the largest single importation of Salukis into England.

Lt. Colonel Pierce Joyce, C.B.E., D.S.O., had had enough of trying to organize the Iraqi Army. In November 1925, with the arrival of a new inspector general and advisor to the Minister of Defense, Joyce was reduced to the lower rank of chief of general staff. At the time, Gertrude Bell thought he might well resign, for the latest scheme to get the Iraqi Army up to speed was dodgy at best.[3] Where Gertrude had initially been very fond of Joyce and Colin, by the end of 1925, seven months before her death, she had grown disenchanted with the couple—as she had with much else in her life. She wrote to her father that she believed Joyce to be "entirely without initiative"—just as she considered the rest of the top level British staff to be.[4]

Despite Gertrude's prediction that he would leave after the arrival of his new superior, Joyce stayed on in Baghdad. Although he never voiced any bitterness, his friends would later come to believe that like Colonel Lawrence, the Irishman was disappointed with the treatment of the Arabs by the European politicians and saw less and less opportunity to make a difference for the good of the country.** Joyce applied for half-pay status, and in June 1927, he and Colin left Baghdad with baggage, big-game trophies from the Sudan, leashed Salukis, and a gift horse from King Faisal. They took up temporary residence in Colin's dower house in Yately, Hampshire, before moving back to Mervue in the five-year-old Irish Free State. When their Salukis were released from quarantine, they eagerly took up dog shows as a hobby. In March 1928 they showed their six smooths at the Irish Kennel Club Annual Show, where Joyce put up the guarantee for the inaugural Saluki entry at an Irish dog show.[††] They were the only ones to be shown and their courser, Baiji of Samarra, took the prize that day.[§§] Colin became a life member of the IKC and registered their Samarra prefix.

Taking four of their smooths across the Irish Sea by ferry, they made a big splash in England by winning several prizes at the SGHC Member's Show in July of that year.*** The Joyces plunged headlong into club activities—meetings, showing, racing, and hare coursing. Colonel Joyce even competed in horse shows with his Arabian. They were wealthy enough to travel between the two countries as they pleased, occasionally boarding their Salukis at the

---

The Council discussed rules put forward by the Kennel Club Committee and could vote approval or disapproval, but had no real authority.

[†]*Curiously, Bentinck never spoke about Feena, Rishan, or their puppies to his family and it was not until long after his death that they became aware of this chapter in his life.*

[§]*One of these, Waara of Luristan, was a Baghdad-born grandson of Bentinck's Rishan.*

**Lord Killanin suggested this in Joyce's obituary in the* Irish Times.

[††]*To "guarantee" a class meant to put up the money for the prizes in case the entry fees should not be enough to cover the club's costs.*

[§§]*The IKC gives a Green Star as a championship award, as opposed to the English Challenge Certificate.*

***Dogs could move freely between England, the Irish Free State, Northern Ireland, the Isle of Man, and the Channel Islands, as long as they had gone through official quarantine or been born within the British Isles.*

Desborough boarding kennels. They purchased two feathered hounds with strong desert blood, one from Miss Francis Joan Mitchell and another from Mrs. Vereker-Cowley. At club meetings, Colonel Joyce talked up the St. Patrick's Day show in Dublin and seems to have been the organizer of a large Saluki entry at that show the following year.

With the Easter Rebellion of 1916, the factional violence of "the Troubles" and the bloody Civil War of 1921–22 now behind them, the Irish government was encouraging tourism and touting Ireland as a sportsman's haven — which it was, as C. S. Jarvis knew well. Fishing, shooting, and golf were the commodities, and the English sporting fraternity was buying. The Irish held sport of all kinds in high regard, for even during the worst of the Troubles, dog shows in Dublin were sacrosanct and free from violence — deadly enemies would compete in the ring with their dogs.* By the late 1920s, the Irish Kennel Club was keen to attract entries from England and special arrangements were made for exhibitors who took the ferry across the Irish Sea. A railroad siding brought trains full of owners and their dogs directly to the dog entrance at grounds southeast of the city — with a voucher from the show secretary, the dogs had traveled free. There were an indoor parking garage, large marquees to protect the benched dogs from wet weather, special kennels for dogs who were staying overnight, the usual cloak rooms, specialist club meeting rooms, press room, bar, vendor's stalls, and a public telephone.

At the 1929 St. Patrick's show in Dublin, Salukis were honored by being exhibited in the prestigious Ring No. 1, and were benched in Marquee No. 1 between the Bulldogs and Old English Sheepdogs, and across the aisle from the Alsatians and Borzois. There were seventeen entered and that year the IKC, in a nod to the English club and exhibitors, had changed the breed name from "Salukis" to "Salukis (or Gazelle Hounds)." Unfortunately, the six Samarras (entered separately in the "Smooth-Coated" variety) were absent on the day. Besides the Joyces, Mrs. Kay MacLean of Carrickmines was the only other Irish Saluki owner entered at that show. There were a few from England, including Joan Mitchell who brought over a Nablous bitch. The longest distance traveled was by the Misses E. M. and A. M. Doyle, who stepped off the ferry with three Salukis from Broxburn, near Edinburgh, Scotland.

The following year, 1930, sixteen Salukis made it to Dublin, seven of whom were registered to Colin Joyce. There were now a few more Saluki owners in Ireland, including Mrs. Rose Keegan, the wife of a well-to-do Dublin surgeon, who exhibited The Sirdar only once. He was bred in Ireland by Mrs. MacLean, and Mrs. Keegan obtained the full-grown hound through the Joyces. According to her son, Frank,† as glamorous as the Saluki was, their family only had him for a few months as The Sirdar could not be moved from his mother's bed, was aggressive toward other dogs in the park, and absolutely uncatchable when turned loose for a romp on the popular Dublin tidal flat known as Sandymount. The Sirdar was sent back to Colonel Joyce, but not before Mrs. Keegan took him and the seven-year-old Frank to pose for a studio portrait. She was so enchanted with The Sirdar's feathered tail, that she stood just off camera and held up its tip so that it would be fully displayed in the photograph.

And that was the peak of Saluki activity at Irish dog shows. There were no entries at the 1931 Dublin show, only one in 1932 (but absent on the day) and none in the years after. According to IKC records, there were never more than 26 Salukis registered in Ireland dur-

---

*Dog number 18 in the IKC registry, dated January 21, 1921, was Jess — Michael Collins's Irish Blue Terrier (now known as the Kerry Blue).

†Frank Keegan would marry a distant cousin of Colonel Joyce. I am grateful to him for sharing memories of his family and The Sirdar.

ing these years. Joyce took full retirement in 1932 and Mervue became their primary residence. Showing the Samarras in England stopped, although the Joyces did make occasional trips over for coursing and racing. Baiji, in particular, seems to have excelled at both and was coursed in competition at eight years old, an advanced age for hunting hares. Colin's life membership in the IKC was canceled for nonpayment of dues in 1935 and at the end of that year, the Joyces resigned from the SGHC.

They still kept Salukis at Mervue* and Colin made one last appearance in the show ring. In July 1936, the newly formed Galway Dog Show Society held its first and only show. The town went all out for the event and it was held in the town center on the grass of Eyre Square.† For the winners of certain classes, local merchants and dog fanciers offered special prizes, including cash, silver cups, a parcel of dog medicines, and a case of briar pipes.[5] It is somewhat surprising that the Joyces, as prominent members of the community, were not involved as members or sponsors, but Colin did enter the nine-year-old Beda in the "Any Variety (Not Classified)" category. Out of seven entries, it was a Pekingese that beat Beda. It was an ironic finish to contrast with the initial promise of the Samarras.

As a young teenager, John Lance was more keen on sports than dog shows, but nonetheless, when he and Geoffrey were home from boarding school, their parents would take them along as "kennel lads" for the boring job of holding dogs while their mother took them in the ring.[6] John was seventeen when he joined the SGHC under a "special" membership provision the year after the Sarona fire in 1929. He had at least one Saluki registered in his name and exhibited, but was not as devoted to the breed as were his parents. Four years later, John followed the family tradition by getting commissioned in the army and leaving home for India. He had joined his father's old regiment, now known as the 19th King George's Own Lancers. As befitting an officer and a gentleman, not to mention General Lance's heir, John took a brace of Saronas to India for companionship and coursing.§

The venerable Ch. Sarona Kelb had died in 1931 at the age of twelve. Fit to the last, the year before he had won his twelfth Championship Certificate at Crufts. Kelb had an outstanding record in the show ring and sired litters for many of the foundation kennels in England. Indeed, like Major Bayne-Jardine's Hama of Homs, there are few Saluki pedigrees today that do not include his name. Kelb would always be Lance's favorite and to the end of his days, the Brigadier would fondly remember the rough-and-tumble gazelle hunts with Seleughi, Kelb, Tor, Becky, and the rest of the pack in Palestine.

About the time that Kelb died, Gladys lost interest in keeping up their photo album. While she still had only minimal involvement with dog shows and club activities,** General Lance had been moving upward politically, serving on the Kennel Club Committee and their Shows Regulation Committee, and by 1935 he was prominent enough to be listed in *Who's*

---

*Joyce's niece, the late Maureen Smyth, recalls that he had some notion of crossing Salukis with greyhounds, but this does not seem to have happened. The Salukis were pampered and she remembers that one was named Risha and that a smooth stayed at her house at Oranmore for a time—characteristically taking up residence on the sofa.

†Renamed Kennedy Memorial Park in honor of President John F. Kennedy's visit there a few months before his assassination in 1963.

§Before going with his regiment to India in the early 1930s, Geoffrey Lance kept a Saluki while he was with the Somersetshire Light Infantry in Blackdown, Warwickshire.

**Gladys's recent weight loss had been gratifyingly noted in dog circles.

Who in Kent. That same year, he commissioned a portrait of himself in his brigadier's red-tabbed uniform, stroking an adoring Saluki*.

At the end of 1935, the Lance family was to suffer an even greater loss than that of Kelb or the kennel fire. Aside from brief home leaves, it had been a while since the Lances had seen their sons. Both were in India — Geoffrey with the Somerset Light Infantry and John with his father's old regiment. The Lances decided to visit them for the Christmas holidays. The trip to India was a happy reunion for the family and Gladys was back in the land that she knew as a young army bride. The Lances had a warm but enjoyable Christmas, but Gladys became ill soon after. The doctor was quickly summoned and soon diagnosed pneumonia. Despite the available medicines and attentive nursing, her tobacco-damaged lungs did not respond and Gladys's condition rapidly declined.[†] As the fever climbed, her breathing grew more and more shallow

Donald Wood 1935 portrait of Brigadier General Frederick Lance, M.C., with Kelb's son, Ch. Sarona Gulshere — Lance's ideal Saluki. With the kind permission of Trevor Lance.

and labored. With her husband and sons by her side, she died on New Year's Eve. Funerals have to happen swiftly in the tropical latitudes and Gladys was buried the next day.

Word was telegraphed to friends and family back in England and an obituary notice appeared in *The Times* on January 2. Will Hally was the Saluki correspondent for *Our Dogs* and his fond tribute to Gladys praised her as the real mover and founder of not only the Sarona Kennels but the Saluki or Gazelle Hound Club itself. She was remembered as a kind and guileless woman who brimmed with courtesy and enthusiasm. Even though her losses in the kennel fire had vanquished all desire to exhibit, Gladys had still remained active in the club and a staunch promoter of the breed. Hally expressed condolences on behalf of the club members and ended with a quote from a member's letter which summarized their feelings about Gladys, "one whom we all loved."[7]

Twenty days after Gladys's death, King George V died, and for the third time in 34 years, Britain mourned the passing of a monarch. Like his grandmother, Queen Victoria, and his parents, Edward VII and Alexandra, George V was a great dog enthusiast, and his favorite breeds were the Labrador Retriever and Clumber Spaniel.[§] Lance had had a special connec-

---

The Saluki in Donald Wood's portrait is almost certainly the five-year-old Ch. Sarona Gulshere, Kelb's son and successor. Lance considered Gulshere to be a superb courser with perfect conformation.

[†]*Antibiotics were not manufactured in quantity until the mid–1940s.*

[§]*As Prince of Wales, he used the kennel name "Wolferton" but on the death of his mother, who had done so much to popularize the Borzoi, he took over his parents' prefix — "Sandringham."*

tion with the King as his daughter, Princess Mary, the Princess royal, was the only member of the immediate Royal family to ever own a Saluki — and a Sarona at that.

A despondent widower, General Lance returned home to England and the now lonely Wentfield.* For 25 years, Gladys had been his only love and his best friend. The club members were sympathetic and at their meeting in March 1936 proposed a "Gladys Maud Lance Trophy" as a memorial. Florence, Joan Mitchell, Mrs. Crouch and the secretary were to work with a silversmith in designing a sterling salver as the trophy. For months after her death, comments would appear in the dog papers about Gladys's sportsmanship, gracious generosity, and cheerful personality. Despite Lance's grief, Gladys's cousin, who was active in the Shropshire Kennel Association, persuaded him to judge Salukis at their May show in Shrewsbury.[8] Lance would judge Salukis only infrequently after that.[†]

Lance had been a key player in the founding of the Curly Coated Retriever Club in 1933 and after Gladys's death, he showed his new breed under the Sarona prefix. He remained interested in Salukis, but without Gladys the enthusiasm was just not there any more. She had always been the dog-show half of the Lance team, whereas coursing was his primary interest. Since the fire, he and Gladys had exhibited occasionally — particularly at the local shows in Kent, but with her death there was no longer any motivation. The regular Sarona advertisements in the *Our Dogs* annuals stopped. Their last litter had been born in April 1934 and there would be no more Sarona puppies, although Lance did export a brace of young adults to Chicago in 1936.[9]

The Brigadier remained vice president of the club and returned to his duties as chair in October 1936 and was a member of the Kennel Club's field trials committee in 1937. That year he was again elected chair, but opted to become "co–vice president" with Miss Barr. He later resumed the office of vice president, a position which he kept through 1954. Lance remarried in 1938 and that event was to further change his life with dogs. Maud Sybil McHarg was a widow and former singer who married the Brigadier in a small ceremony in her hometown of Wokingham, Berkshire. She was forty-six and he was sixty-four. The new Mrs. Lance did not have Gladys's love of dogs and the Brigadier's remaining house Salukis were relegated to the kennels. Lance still limped from the bullet wound from the skirmish with Multan's bandits 29 years before, and fishing or a morning's shooting with his Curly Coated Retriever had replaced hunting with Salukis as his preferred pastime.

Whether by intent or accident, Francis Joan Mitchell escaped the publicity that always followed her good friends, Florence and Gladys. She lived a quiet life but was still active in the Saluki club. After her string of household relocations, in 1930 she moved finally to Beckenham, Kent, where she bought a house at 31 Beckenham Road.[§] The town had been the home of the Crystal Palace — that great Victorian glass and iron palace for the exhibition of science, industry, and art until it was destroyed by a fire in 1936. Grown from village to town, Beckenham's civic character seems to have been inspired by the Crystal Palace and it had remarkable cultural facilities for the time. In the early 1930s, there was a hospital, a new town

Gladys had left Wentfield to Bridadier Lance in her will.
†*At the Kennel Club Show in October 1929 he judged Afghan hounds.*
§*In 1966, the county line was redrawn and Beckenham became part of the Bromley Borough of Greater London. Joan Mitchell's house is still there on the corner of Elm Road but the number has been changed from 31 to 29.*

hall, public baths, a technical institute, schools of music and art, two cinemas, a Woolworth's, and a new block of shops. By the end of the decade, there would be a new central library, a third cinema, and the public baths would be enlarged.[10] In a time when motorcars were beyond the means of the average person, the population of Beckenham had more than the average community and boasted a first-rate garage, incongruously built to resemble a Japanese pagoda and called by everyone "the Chinese Garage."[11]

Across from Joan's corner house were the public baths and technical school, on the other side of the broad Beckenham Road, the art school. Just across Elm Road was the Baptist church. The train station and town center were just short walks away. Her house had three stories and was constructed of red brick, decorated with white-painted, wooden gingerbread. A generously sized corner lot, it had a very large garden enclosed by a brick wall and was perfect for the few Salukis she was keeping. Joan was 56 and this was the last time that she would name a house "Nablous."

Joan continued to participate only in Saluki activities that were of interest to her. She rarely entered her Salukis at the all-breed dog shows but did serve on the SGHC Committee and nearly always attended club shows and meetings. She was well-liked and highly regarded by the other members, many of whom recalled her sweet disposition and devotion to the breed.[12] Her great niece, Mrs. J. A. Berrisford, remembers her as being utterly uninterested in conventional things, refusing to talk about popular topics just because they were the whim of the moment. But Saluki lore and history were always of interest and while dog shows were not the most scintillating of topics for Joan, she was very enthusiastic indeed about performance events. She used to journey frequently to the Saluki races at Dartford Stadium and to the fields of Kent for hare coursing — where her hounds did respectably well.*

In the show ring, the Syrian types usually were put up over Joan's Nablous Salukis and she would never make up her own champion. She and Florence had been working hard for over a decade to preserve and promote what they believed to be the correct Saluki conformation — the lighter Mesopotamian type — and in 1935 it was still an issue for them. That year, Joan made a statement by donating a large brass *dallah* (coffeepot) and matching *tazza* (basin) to be a special prize at the Kennel Club, Crufts and Saluki Club shows only. Unlike Florence and Gladys, Joan left little in writing about Salukis, but her philosophy about breed type is glimpsed in the award conditions for her trophy. The Ebni & Binte El Nablous Perpetual Trophy was awarded to "the best dog or bitch of the Gazelle type especially as to color, expression of eyes, and elegance in moving, size as to the standard of the Saluki Club."[13] In 1951, Joan wrote her last words on the breed in a letter to the club. "There seems to be a little misunderstanding about the trophy I offered. The color question seems to be a bit difficult, I think possibly through the use of the term 'deer-color,' which is a shaded fawn. This embraces plain fawn, red-fawn, golden-fawn, biscuit-fawn etc. Deer-color, which has so many lovely shades, was taken I believe, from the young of the deer, gazelle, and other animals of this type."[14]

During the 1930s, she still bred from time to time and in January 1939 had to fight her own illness and nurse an entire litter sick with distemper. There was no vaccine for the extremely contagious disease and periodically epidemics would sweep through the doggy community, taking a heavy toll. Treatment was mostly confined to fighting fluid loss and inflamma-

---

*While litter registrations and show entries were dropping off, coursing enjoyed a sustained popularity among many of the Saluki fancy.

tion, and hoping that the stricken dog (young or old) would be strong enough to survive — and survive without lasting effects. While today nothing is thought about making a quick call to the doctor or veterinarian, at that time telephones were still far from being a common utility. Many older people just didn't like the idea of speaking to a disembodied voice and refused to use the telephone.* Whether by budgetary constraints, indifference, or personal dislike, there was no telephone at Nablous. Housebound by her own illness and that of the puppies, Joan could only communicate with the outside world through letters or the use of a neighbor's telephone. Joan seems to be one of the few Saluki breeders who would write openly about having distemper in her kennel, and she would fight to save her hounds from the disease several times over the years. It is ironic that the famous Wellcome Research Laboratories, located just over a mile from Joan's house, first produced the prototype canine distemper vaccine in 1928–29.[15]

After the death of her kennel manager, Capt. Widden, in 1927, Florence Amherst's London kennel arrangements changed radically. She seems to have divided her Salukis between Foulden Hall and Miss Desborough's kennels (now at High Beech, Essex). She still lived in her flat at No. 6 William Street (just off Knightsbridge Road near Belgrave Square) and may have kept one or two favorite Salukis there. Knightsbridge was a familiar neighborhood for her as it was a half-mile from the old Amherst residence in Grosvenor Square. In the oppo-

Florence Amherst (in her seventies) walking her Salukis with Guy Desborough, about 1931. Unknown but republished in *Saluki Heritage* (1984).

Wilfred Jennings-Bramly also considered himself a poor "telephonist" and refused to use them while serving in Egypt unless there was a military necessity.

site direction and about the same distance, were both the institution that her father had admired and patronized — the Royal Geographical Society — and the house where he had died. Also, near the RGS was the Natural History Museum where her first Saluki, Luman, was mounted in a glass case.

Out of the goodness of her heart, Florence made periodic donations of a few shillings to help the club along. She continued entering shows, both to promote the Amherstia type and to support the club with the entry monies. Her entry of eleven Salukis at the Member's Show in 1929 was the peak and after that, her participation was considerably less, usually one or two per show. Another turn for the worse in her finances necessitated Florence's move to even smaller quarters in 1930.

Just a block from her William Street place, she took up residence in a courtyard off a quiet side street at No. 1 & 2 Kinnerton Studios and filled the place up with her belongings — including a piano, Egyptian souvenirs, antiques, and her massive collection of paintings, letters, articles, notes, and photographs pertaining to Salukis.* The cramped, two-story house was full of boxes and bric-a-brac, and when "Great Aunt Fluff" entertained her nieces and nephews and their young children, she had to sit on her bed so that her guests could have the chairs.[16] It was the last house that would see her as an independent woman and her few remaining Salukis lived at the Desborough boarding kennels. Of her immediate family, only Alicia in Dorset and Geraldine in Scotland were still alive. Florence was 70 that year and having

Far from the magnificent Didlington Hall, the white building on right with two doors under the long lintel was Florence Amherst's last house, as it looked in 1996.

Most likely renumbered to what is now 1 Studio Place.

health problems. In November, she drew up her will and named her sister Alicia trustee and executrix.

Florence would frequently write to American Saluki fancier Edward K. Aldrich Jr. of Providence, Rhode Island, with news of English shows, breed history, and pedigree information. Ultimately she would become his mentor and much of what she wrote he would repeat in his Saluki columns for the American Kennel Club Gazette. To start his Diamond Hill kennels, Aldrich would purchase one of her bitches that had been shipped to another fancier in the States. In 1930, Aldrich saw that Florence was made an honorary member of the fledgling Saluki Club of America, an honor that was never accorded to General Lance even though several Saronas had been imported to the United States.

The American fanciers were keen to increase breed popularity and, fueled by the continuing interest in Tutankhamun, one of them came up with the notion of describing Salukis as "the Royal Dog of Egypt" in the late 1920s or early 1930s. This catchy but incorrect appellation firmly stuck in the public's mind and even today is hard to dislodge.* They hoped for large entry at one of their shows and were sure that a famous breeder from England would do the trick. In 1935, Florence Amherst was invited to judge in America, but after several months of letters passing back and forth across the Atlantic, ultimately she had to decline. Florence had never become a Saluki judge in England and the AKC would not permit a non-judge to officiate at a show — not even the founder of the breed.[17]

In early 1936, Florence became seriously ill and missed the Annual General Meeting at Crufts, a rare occurrence up until that point. She wrote a letter of apologizing for being unable to attend and missed several committee meetings that year. During her year long convalescence, she conceived the idea of pulling her store of hundreds of articles, letters, notes, and photos together into the first book about Salukis.[18] Apparently she had had the idea before but felt that articles about the breed could be disseminated more widely and easily than a bound volume. She certainly did not want this to be a massive tome, but something for easy reference — "a sort of patchwork from all points of view of an inexhaustible subject."[19] Even though housebound, she corresponded with some regularity to Aldrich and was always happy to answer queries about anything to do with Salukis. The book did not happen that year, but she was finally well enough to participate as acting chair again in September, one month before General Lance returned to chair meetings. Florence's recovery seems to have been incomplete for in December she was again ill, and missed the Annual General Meeting for the consecutive second year. The only hint about the nature of her illness comes from Aldrich's January 1937 column where he says that Florence "is now able, after a year's illness, to be up and about and resume her interest in Saluki affairs."[20]

Florence was ever the generous host, but not having room for many guests at No. 1 & 2 Kinnerton Studios, she would host a luncheon for the Members' Show committee at a nearby hotel. When SGHC committee meetings were held in her cramped quarters, their "popular president" would always provide tea, sandwiches, and cigarettes. At 77, her eyesight was getting poor and she needed a magnifying glass to examine photographs. She was still determined to write her book and contribute material to Aldrich's column, but she was not as productive as she hoped — "owing to the fact of not being very well," according to Aldrich,

*Salukis truly were favored by royalty, but any Egyptian who hunted would have owned them. Likewise, a lack of knowledge about Islam on the part of an American fancier led to the mistaken assertion that Salukis were "sacred" to Muslims. This sacrilegious publicity nugget also stuck as part of the breed folklore but in recent years, thankfully, seems to be fading away as understanding of Islam becomes more widespread.

"and having many irons in the fire besides Salukis."[21] Throughout the 1930s, Florence still had an official role as delegate to international poultry conferences, and she served on the committee of the Ladies Kennel Association — "The Ladies Branch of the Kennel Club" — and was listed as an SGHC-approved judge in a club publication that year. While still not an official Kennel Club judge, Florence, as a breed expert, was listed on the panel of judges approved by the SGHC, along with several other fanciers such as A. Croxton Smith, Miss Barr, Mrs. Crouch, Will Hally, Miss Kerrison, and Brigadier General Lance.

Florence was living alone now in her small house and even if she had room for one of her quiet, older hounds, she was physically unequal to the task. As Foulden Hall had been sold sometime after 1935, her last Salukis were kept at the Desborough boarding kennels. In April 1937, two signal events happened to Florence. One was the birth of the last litter of Amherstia puppies. In the four decades that she had been breeding, she had registered 199 puppies from 50 litters, far more than any other breeder.[22] The other was the death of the magnificent Zobeid at the advanced age of fifteen years. Florence was sufficiently moved at the loss of her first and only champion to mention his passing to Aldrich in her letters. In July one of her bitches died and, as with Luman, Florence donated the body to the Natural History Museum, but this time the skin and skeleton were preserved separately and put in storage.*

By November 1938, she had told Aldrich again that she still intended to have a "plunge" at the book. Since publishing his seminal work *Dogs, Their History and Development*, Edward Ash had been a great supporter of Salukis and frequently turned to Florence and Miss Barr for information and photos. He had revised Robert Leighton's 1907 *The New Book of the Dog* and it had been out for less than a year when Ash died in early 1939. In the summer of that year, Florence took a nasty fall and was again several months in recovering from the injury, presumably a fracture. Her book was never written and her extensive research notes and drafts would be lost[†] but some hint of what it might have been may be seen in *Hutchinson's Popular & Illustrated Dog Encyclopædia*.

This mammoth undertaking was released in 1935 in regular installments (a total of fifty were projected) at seven pence per number. In 1923, Walter Hutchinson had used this format with *Hutchinson's Animals of All Countries: The Living Animals of the World in Pictures and Story*, and boasted that it contained "Every known thing in the world of Natural History."[23] When he published his dog encyclopedia, Hutchinson figured out a way to make money a second time on the same work, by also offering a service where people could send in their collected installments to be bound into three volumes. Cleverly, each installment ended in a "cliff hanger," an entry that covered only part of a breed, so that people would have to buy the next installment to have it completed.

Hutchinson's Number 43 featured a painting of Rihan, one of Florence's Salukis, on the cover with a full-page version of the portrait inside. It included the end of the St. Bernard section, Saint Vitus' Dance, Sal Volatile (smelling salts), Salicylic Acid, Saline Purgatives, Saline Solution, Saliva, Salivary Glands, Salmon Poisoning, Salol, Saltpetre, the Saluki or Gazelle Hound, & the beginning of Samoyeds. The Saluki history and lore were written by

---

*Curiously, Florence's Farhan (Zobeid's brother) is mounted in the National Museum of Scotland in Edinburgh. One of Zobeid's daughters, Amherstia Battil was sold to Canada and after her death, was mounted in the Royal Ontario Museum in 1937 (Ingrid Romanowski, letter to the editor, The Saluki, Winter/Spring 1995, 6).

[†] The first book exclusively about Salukis would not be published until 1962. The Saluki in History, Art, and Sport, by Hope and David Waters, remains a standard reference to this day.

Florence (who Hutchinson acknowledged on the cover as a leading contributor), and Gertrude Desborough contributed the practical information on Saluki husbandry. As this work would be more widely distributed and easier to find than Amherst's chapters in Leighton and Ash, and her sundry articles, it would become the chief reference for future Saluki historians and perpetuate two errors in breed histories — that she had acquired Luman and Ayesha in 1897 from Prince Abdullah in the Transjordan.

By the early 1930s, the personality of the SGHC was changing slowly. The first members of the club who had actually been to the Middle East were getting on in years and less active in the club. Some were even losing the physical capacity to keep dogs. Miss Kerrison resigned as secretary of the Coursing Section in 1934. Other "flash in the pan" members just lost interest and dropped out. There were two member deaths in 1937 — Mr. L. Crouch Esq., who had been treasurer, and Miss Beryl Thynne (who had changed the name of her Sarona puppy to Tut-ankh-amen in the fervor of Tutmania). New names and prefixes begin to appear in the show reports and club minutes — Commander L. S. N. Adam (Haredam), who named his Salukis after warships; Major Dispenser-Robertson (Wilbury), a great coursing enthusiast; Capt. L. Ames (Ayot); Capt. F. C. & Mrs. Cowper (Garrymhor); Mrs. Cecil Franklin (Zahara); Mrs. Coston (El Hor); Mrs. B. H. Goom; Mrs. R. G. Michelmore (Nal); Miss June Applebee (Lineage); Mrs. H. M. Parkhouse (Shammar); Miss Gwen Angel (Mazuri)— who would become a famous breeder, columnist for *Dog World*, and dedicated collector of Saluki information; and Irish Wolfhound breeder Lady Inglis Gardner (Knightellington), the founder of the only three-generation dynasty in England based on her first Saluki bought from Joan Mitchell, and who became president of the SGHC after Florence's death.*

The year 1930 saw 131 Salukis registered in England. It was the second highest number since the breed was recognized in 1923, the apex being 1927 with 146 registrations. Inexplicably, there were only 55 registrations in 1931. That year saw the start of regular pleas in the SGHC Annual Report to register litters and keep the numbers up, but there would not be more than 71 Salukis registered annually in the years between 1931 and 1939. In fact, of the seven recognized sighthound breeds (Afghans, Borzois, Scottish Deerhounds, Greyhounds, Irish Wolfhounds, Salukis, and Whippets), Salukis would have the second-lowest number of registrations in 1938 (71) with Scottish Deerhounds at the low of 53. In 1939, with only 39 registrations, Salukis traded places with the Deerhounds (48) for the low point.[†]

Saluki show entries dropped and the usual number of separate dog and bitch classes could no longer be guaranteed by club funds, and the sexes now had to be shown together. Before, the club had had enough on the ledgers to make generous donations to dog charities but show income was now needed to cover basic operating expenses. Ribbons were awarded at the Member's Show instead of prize money and members were asked to donate 10 percent of their cash winnings from other shows to help guarantee classes.[24] With more lapses and resignations than new subscriptions, membership was tapering off— and with it, revenue for operating expenses, putting on the Member's Show, guarantees, prize money, and the club's annual report. In 1937, the club's income amounted to only £25 4s.[25] Foot-and-Mouth dis-

---

*Lady Gardner's daughter, Helen Baker, took over the line, and Helen's daughter, Mrs. Rosemary Lewis, continues it to this day.

[†]1939 was admittedly an unusual year, as dog activities were curtailed with the outbreak of war in September.

ease broke out in England again that year and the resulting ban on movement of animals made the Saluki slump even worse.

In the show ring, the embers of the old Syrian/Mesopotamian type controversy had all but died out, but in early 1936 they were fanned into flames by the letters of Mrs. M. Towgood, a self-proclaimed breed expert. For over four months, an unceasing barrage of letters was sent to the Saluki columnist for *Our Dogs*, Will Hally. Despite Hally's initial praise for her background in the breed, because his opinions differed from hers, he found himself the focal point of Mrs. Towgood's vitriolic attacks.

Her husband had lived in Lower Egypt where he did survey work as a civil engineer. In the course of his travels, he would see Salukis belonging to the desert tribesmen and villagers, and acquired one in 1910. His fiancée was so taken by them that the hounds played a part of their wedding ceremony.[26] The Towgoods acquired several pale-colored Salukis in addition to a pair of Pekingese. After nearly two decades of living in Egypt and Palestine, they returned to England and settled in Gainsborough, Lincolnshire, leaving their Salukis behind. They bought three of Florence Amherst's sand-colored puppies — which Mrs. Towgood considered to be the correct type and color — "cream in its various shades to gold: though my brother further south had a brace which might almost be called a light red."[27] In Palestine, she had seen some of the Syrian grizzles, which she described as "rather larger dogs with dark backs and heads shaded to cream legs and feet."[28]

She was appalled at both the prevalence and popularity of parti-colored Salukis with what she referred to as "odd markings or patches," "white stockings," and "spots over the head and muzzle."[29] It was her opinion that the black-and-tan Ch. Sarona Kelb and the black-and-white parti-color Ch. Orchard Shahin were "two dogs of odd color."[30] Because she herself had never seen them in Egypt or Palestine, they were clearly incorrect and she suggested that they were the result of crossbreeding with setters and Borzoi.[31] She further intimated that size and bone of the Sarona stock were perhaps derived from Great Danes.

Besides campaigning for the colors Mrs. Towgood considered to be true and correct — "both desert shades and Syrian darkbacks"* — in both the weekly dog newspapers, she adamantly objected to nearly everything about Salukis in England — height, feathering (too much), size versus ability to bring down gazelle, lack of chest, too much chest, and the unacceptable imports that were coming in from Iraq. She would contradict herself by urging strict enforcement of the breed standard while discounting any Saluki that did not fit her own personal standard.

Mrs. Towgood belonged to her own exclusive society of Saluki experts — one that by definition rejected anyone else from admission. She considered that the only true Saluki experts were those who had been breeders of the Mesopotamian type for many years in the Middle East (she also proclaimed herself to be a breeder of Japanese rats, horses, and camels). By her standards, no one else in England was an expert — including Florence, the Lances, and Joan Mitchell. Seemingly, the only reason that Florence Amherst's puppies were good enough for Mrs. Towgood was that they were the "correct" color and size. Perhaps also working in Florence's favor was that Prince Abdullah of Transjordan had, at different times, given Salukis to both women — and Florence had been breeding from hers in England.† Like a broken gramophone record, the fancy quickly grew sick of hearing Mrs. Towgood and she eventually faded away.

---

*An interesting term for the grizzle coat pattern, which had also been called "wolf or deer colored" by various Saluki fanciers.
†Amherstia Sabirah and Sharifa were imported in 1926.

Salukis still appeared as glamor dogs in the popular press. The budding actress Miss Norah Baring posed with one for a full-page portrait in a 1930 edition of *The Sketch*.[32] Obviously the combination was a hit, for a year later *The Sketch* featured a study of socialite Miss Rosemary Nicholl and a cream Saluki wearing matching jeweled chokers. A charming drawing of Saluki exhibitors at Crufts that featured Mrs. Lance, Mrs. Parkhouse, and an unidentified tweedy gentleman, appeared under the caption "Looking at Life" in *The Daily Mail* in 1934.[33] But the sustained popularity of the Borzoi and other breeds did not come to the Saluki, despite the best efforts of the members. Curious and exotic as they were, Afghans were considered more so and therefore trendier. Dog author Mitford Brice wrote in 1934, "It is my belief that when the romance of his history and the charm of his character are more clearly understood, the Saluki will obtain a magic hold on the affections of the so-called unromantic Englishman."[34] Of course, the fanciers of the SGHC were convinced of this, as well. Puppies had been given to royals and peers, sympathetic journalists wrote about them at seemingly every opportunity, and even when the royalty of Hollywood, California, acquired the elegant Saluki, the spark missed the tinder.

In October 1927, Miss Barr (Grevel Salukis) sold three puppies to a film star and was relieved to hear that they were fine after the "long and awful journey" from England to Hollywood.[35] Edward Aldrich turned down a confidential offer through a Hollywood film star's agent to buy an entire litter of eleven puppies for coursing and showing. A year later, with eight in the litter still remaining, the offer was increased and once again declined. Aldrich wanted to establish a record by seeing that the entire litter became champions and he intended to keep close tabs on them. He gave the agent a list of breeders in the States and presumably the unnamed actor acquired them from elsewhere.[36]

In May 1936, one of the breed's American fanciers, Mrs. Sylvia Watt of Oakland, California, expressed high hopes that Salukis would be used in the proposed film about T. E. Lawrence, *Revolt in the Desert*.[37] Colonel Walter Stirling had been hired by the film's director, Alexander Korda, as technical and military advisor, but for a variety of reasons, that version of Lawrence's experiences in the desert would never be made.* That same year, director Michael Curtiz was said to have included Salukis in *The Charge of the Light Brigade*.[38] Starring Errol Flynn, David Niven, and Olivia de Havilland, it was a typical Hollywood mishmash of history. The Saluki footage did not survive the editing, but Surat Khan's palace in "Suristan" or the leopard hunt would be the most likely scenes for the hounds. In fact, the first Saluki to appear on the silver screen was the animated one in Disney's *Society Dog Show*, (1939).[39] Real Salukis would finally make fleeting appearances in *Blondie in Society* (1941) and *An Ideal Husband* (1947).[40] Perhaps too exotic, too hard to train, or just too scarce, Salukis just did not catch the fancy of Hollywood.

For years, Salukis, along with the other breeds, were featured on collectible cigarette cards, and the 1939 edition of *Collins' Dog Lovers Diary* had a Saluki portrait in a prominent

---

Mrs. Watt called the film Lawrence of Arabia *when its actual title was* Revolt in the Desert *(see L. Robert Morris and Lawrence Raskin,* Lawrence of Arabia: The 30th Anniversary Pictorial History, *New York: Doubleday, 1992).* Lawrence of Arabia *was finally made in 1962—without Salukis.*

position with a glowing description of the breed.* But despite these print appearances and the persistent efforts of the Saluki or Gazelle Hound Club, Saluki popularity declined. Even the venerable A. Croxton Smith was perplexed by the situation: "For some reason or other that no one can explain, there was a falling away as 1939 approached and for the first year or two, too, after peace was declared there was not a great deal doing in the breed."[41] The decline continued until September 3, 1939, when Prime Minister Neville Chamberlain declared war on Germany after its invasion of Poland two days before.

The outbreak of the second European war put a halt to most English doggy activities of all kinds. Showing stopped at first, but then resumed on a greatly reduced scale. German submarines took a heavy toll on the ships that carried food and supplies to England. As had happened during the Great War, rationing was enforced and feeding good red meat to dogs became difficult and expensive, if not illegal. The government encouraged the owners of kennels and hound packs to euthanize them in order to save food resources, and breeding virtually ceased, except where it was deemed necessary to preserve specimens. Hundreds of purebred dogs were "ploughed under" as a more humane solution than subjecting them to starvation and bombing.[42] Mrs. Crouch, the owner of the first Saluki champion, would have all her Orchards put down when she could no longer find sufficient food for them.[43]

Horace Parkhouse took over the club's frozen funds and out of his own pocket paid out the fees needed to keep the club alive. The SGHC voluntarily suspended its activities "until they could be started again in happier times."[44] Dog shows were now few and far between and no championship shows were held during the war. Gasoline was rationed, making travel to shows (for the few who had automobiles) a disproportionate luxury — and driving more than twenty-five miles to a show was banned. The railroad was something of an alternative, but trying to take two or three Salukis on a crowded train was "rather a nightmare."[45] Bombs dropped by the Luftwaffe took a terrible toll on London and other cities. By the midpoint of the war, the outlook was somewhat brighter. Miss Barr (Grevel), Mrs. Coston (El Hor), Mrs. Parkhouse (Shammar), Gwen Angel (Mazuri), and Lady Gardner (Knightellington) were chiefly responsible for ensuring continuity of the breed by having a few litters. Gwen Angel is said to have attempted rescuing Salukis from Holland and France during the German occupation. In the closing months of the war, she wrote to prospective Saluki buyer June Applebee, "Yes, I am still breeding Salukis, they are far too fascinating to give up just because of Hitler!"[46] By 1944, breeders hoping to cash in on the shortage of purebred dogs were having litters in anticipation of the war's end. Postwar imports of Salukis would eventually reinvigorate the breed. But it would not be until the years after the war when rationing finally ended, the British economy was recovering, autos became more affordable and available, and the second wave of officers returned with hounds from the Middle East, that Salukis would begin to rise in popularity once more.

---

*In addition to being a personal diary, this pocket edition had a wealth of information on laws, quarantine, Kennel Club regulations, breeding, disease, treatment, travel guidelines, etc. I am indebted to my late uncle Patrick "Mogan" Duggan for giving me his copy.

21

Epitaphs

"To speak the name of the dead is to make them live again."
                                      Ancient Egyptian inscription

With the end of the Second World War, the face of the earth had changed. The Victorians and Edwardians linked by their adventures in the Middle East and their Salukis began to pass from the scene. The need for mapping, documentation of native customs, and the obsessive collection of biological specimens was fading, although the soldiering continues inevitably. Soldiers are always being shipped off to defend or capture something "strategic" in the desert and if the reader doubts this, just review the history of the hard-marching legions of Rome, the white kepi'd foreign volunteers of the Légion étrangère, Alexander the Great's hoplites, the war chariots of Rameses, Mussolini's *Fascisti*, and Napoleon's army of soldiers, scholars, and artists. Consider the British Redcoats, Rommel's diesel-tracked Afrika Korps, Turkish Mameluks and mail-fisted Crusaders, and the camouflaged armies of Operations Desert Storm and Iraqi Freedom. They and more have all been there fighting for sandy real estate in the cradle of civilization. It was always so and likely always will be.

The hardships, privation, and at times outright slaughter of the Second World War nearly wiped out the Saluki population in Europe.* Besides England, only small numbers remained in Germany and the Netherlands. The same was the case on the other side of the world, the United States, Canada, and Australia. Another generation of Saluki fanciers would take over the work to reestablish the breed in the West. Once again, soldiers returning from the Middle East brought Salukis home with them and for the first time, oil workers did so too. Not only were hounds periodically imported to the West, but, from time to time, good specimens were exported back to the Middle East. With the booming oil industry, urban growth, newly affordable travel, asphalt roads and automobiles, and passenger and cargo airplanes, the Middle East was no longer the isolated domain of Bedouin and hardy adventurers. Air-conditioned trucks and houses replaced camels and black tents, and only in the most remote areas is there a need for falcons and Salukis to catch meat for the pot.

In 1971, two Americans, William R. Polk and William J. Mares, recreated a caravan journey from Riyadh to Amman, and were hard-pressed to find sufficient serviceable camel saddles or indeed anyone who knew the area well enough to serve as a *rafiq* or guide. Ultimately, it took several weeks of scouring central Arabia to come up with six camels and six saddles. Prince Salman, Amir of Riyadh, tried to talk them out of the hazardous journey, as the desert

---

After surviving disease, rationing, and hunger, entire kennels of German Salukis were shot by Russian soldiers at the end of the war.

tracks and wells were no longer maintained. Such treks were not done any more and wouldn't they like to take a truck as everyone else did? The Amir only consented to the journey after many days of negotiation (and he loaned them a Saluki) but they had to agree to be met by the Amir's men in trucks each night who brought camel fodder for the first week.[1] The Amir's fears about the state of the tracks and wells were well-founded — the two men and their guide nearly died of thirst in the terrible furnace of the Great Nafud desert. The old Bedouin way of life was truly passing and Salukis no longer had the integral role that they once did.

Wilfred Edgar Jennings-Bramly, M.C., M.B.E., Keeper of the Giza Zoo, explorer, and Saluki importer to Florence Amherst, lived an extraordinary life that easily surpasses fiction. After The Great War, the "Walking Englishman" designed and constructed Burj al Arab, a town near Alexandria, that was to have been a center for the carpet industry. He built a Moorish-style home there and was quite happy in the desert. The local Bedouin were utterly devoted to him. During World War II, when he was in his late sixties, he organized the local Bedouin to help with the defense of Alexandria against the threat of the Afrika Korps. "Wiffy" and Phyllis refused to move from their home and when Rommel's troops were approaching the horizon, the tribesmen asked if it was time to evacuate. Jennings-Bramly pointed to Phyllis and said that when she left it might be time for them to go.[2] Rommel never forced them to move but the Egyptian government did when they purged the country of colonial remnants and the British. In 1951, Jennings-Bramly was compelled to leave the land he so loved. He returned to the home of his grandparents in Florence, Italy. There, at 88 years old, the man who gave Florence Amherst the brace of Salukis that founded the breed in the West died on March 2, 1960.

Captain Raymond Goslett, M.C., the Saluki fancier and supply wizard of Al Aqabah, despite being essentially a very private man, was well known by friends and family for his sense of humor and fund of stories. After the Arab Revolt, he returned to England where he became a keen enthusiast for fine British automobiles and shooting with his Labrador. He continued working in the family business Alfred Goslett Furniture Co. (which still does business in London, although the family interest was sold long ago). Goslett also kept up a warm correspondence with Lawrence and the family firm supplied the bathtub, boiler, and plumbing for Lawrence's austere house, Cloud's Hill in Dorset. Goslett died at his home, Sunnyside Cottage, Denham, Buckinghamshire, January 3, 1961, at the age of 75.

Like many soldiers, Goslett never talked about the war or his Salukis, Snorter and Musa, but his son, Mr. John H. Goslett, remembers a souvenir *kaffiyeh* brought home from Al Aqabah and treasures his father's medals. One of his father's snapshots of T. E. Lawrence in white robes at Al Aqabah might well have been the model for the most well-known costume in the film *Lawrence of Arabia*. It was a vision that catapulted Lawrence into the limelight again and young Peter O'Toole to stardom.* John Goslett made a permanent loan of his father's marvelous photographs of the Arab Revolt to the Imperial War Museum.

Lt. Colonel Pierce Charles Joyce, C.B.E., D.S.O., also maintained his friendship with T. E. Lawrence after the war and they frequently exchanged letters until the latter's death in

---

Mr. John H. Goslett was kind enough to give me a copy of the famous photograph. Goslett's photo and a corresponding still of the film's Lawrence are reproduced on page 101 of Lawrence of Arabia *by L. Robert Morris and Lawrence Raskin (1992).*

the 1935 motorcycle accident. The Samarra Salukis disappeared in Galway during the 1930s and the line was lost to the gene pool. Joyce and Colin seem to have found it hard to live in Ireland and keeping up the palatial Mervue was expensive. They sold it to the City of Galway Corporation in the late 1950s. Colin's brother had died and left her his house so they moved into Firtrees, in Crowthorne. Joyce gave his hunting trophies to the Irish Army headquarters at Renmore barracks. Mervue became a city hospital and Joyce was brokenhearted when he learned that his former home had become so dilapidated that the city could no longer afford the maintenance and sold it in 1953 to the Royal Tara Ltd., a firm that manufactured fine china. Renovated after a fire in the late 1950s, the building is still owned by Royal Tara and visitors can still see the ballroom (now a cafeteria) and the fine Connemara marble fireplaces in the showrooms.

Joyce had a quiet retirement and periodically gave interviews about T. E. Lawrence. In his last years, he seems to have been chronically ill and was often comforted by the local minister. At the age of 87, Joyce died at Firtrees, on February 1, 1965, and Colin died on June 26, 1968. His estate was considerable as it included two Galway houses, Glenina Mervue and Herd's Cottage, and land, a shop in the town center, and hereditary fishing rights on the River Clare. Many of the Joyce family buildings still stand in Galway but the memory of the Joyce's Salukis has faded. To this day, the older residents of Galway City still remember Colonel Joyce as a great man.

Six years after Major C. W. Bayne-Jardine, C.B.E., M.C., and Hama were unhappily parted, he was posted back to India in 1928. After some years, he returned to England and married in 1930. Living in Kent very near Brigadier Lance's home, the two men renewed their friendship. During World War II Bayne-Jardine commanded an anti-aircraft brigade — accounting for some 200 downed German planes. He was awarded the C.B.E. and retired in 1945 as an honorary brigadier general and moved his wife, son, and two daughters to their small estate in East Lothian in Scotland. Happy with the quiet life of the country, he was an elder of the kirk and a county councilor. Still quiet and undemonstrative, he told good stories but never talked about the Great War — or Hama. He died on March 22, 1959.

Major Count Arthur Bentinck, D.S.O., the man who imported Salukis back to Iraq, at the age of 46 was still plagued by his old wounds. He retired from the army in 1933 and had already left the Saluki chapter of his life behind. In 1934 he joined an international police force which oversaw the territorial plebiscite in which the people of the Saar region (with its valuable coalfields) voted for annexation by the new Nazi government in Germany. In 1936, he volunteered for the British Ambulance Service in Abyssinia where he learned to speak Amharic, the national language. In 1942 he rejoined the Coldstream Guards and served with distinction as a staff officer in India, Burma, China, Egypt, and, after the war, Somalia. Bentinck was mentioned in *Despatches* and despite being in his late fifties, saw some action, for he was awarded the Distinguished Service Order, given for gallantry or distinguished service in the face of the enemy. Arthur Bentinck never married, but was a favorite uncle in the family. He died at age 75 on November 26, 1962.

Brigadier General Frederick Fitzhugh Lance, M.C., continued to serve on various Kennel Club committees and in 1946 became vice president of the Saluki Club and served through 1949, although he rarely attended meetings toward the end. Lance's passion for Salukis had waned since Gladys's death. In November 1945, Lance sold Wentfield but continued to live there for some time until he and his second wife, Maude Sybil, moved to Wentshaw, a lesser house on his estate. He donated a quantity of Sarona memorabilia as trophies, and in 1950 he donated his photo album, book of press cuttings, and printing blocks* to the Saluki Club. The Sarona photo album is a stunning collection of images from the early history of the breed — Lance and Kelb in the Middle East, Bentinck's hounds in Iraq, Bayne-Jardine's Hama, the early litters at Sarona Kennels, exercise in the garden, dog shows, and coursing meets, all carefully mounted on black paper in an album purchased at Harrod's, with detailed captions in white script by Gladys. The SGHC's committee, wishing to share the wonderful histori-cal resources, agreed to let members borrow the album and book of press cuttings each for a fee of two shillings and sixpence. On July 28, 1954, Vice President Brigadier General Lance was invited back for what was probably his last Saluki judging assignment. He was 81 and as smartly dressed as ever.

Of his sons, Geoffrey and John, the former was killed in Normandy in 1944. John mar-ried Daphne, his brother's widow, and adopted Geoffrey's only child, Trevor.† After retiring from the 19th Lancers and India, John Lance and family emigrated first to Kenya and, after the Mau Mau uprisings, to New Zealand. One or two Salukis were exported to New Zealand but the Sarona line never flourished there.

No longer physically able to keep up his home and property at Wentfield, by 1959 or 1960 Brigadier Lance had moved to the city at number 7 Ephraim Court, Molyneux Park Road, Tunbridge Wells —fifteen miles away from his former home. He died at the Homeo-pathic Hospital in Tunbridge Wells at the age of 89 on December 11, 1962, and was cremated. His estate of £32,000 was divided between his second wife Maud Sybil and his son John.§

Wentfield is still there on top of that marvelous hill in Kent, although the property has been reduced since Lance's day. Sadly, much of the Saluki artwork the Lances collected has been dispersed, although Trevor Lance still has his grandfather's portait. A pair of small sil-ver cups donated by the Lances is still awarded to the best dog and bitch at Crufts. The two Sarona albums went missing for several years and in the early 1970s the SGHC magazine, *The Saluki,* ran notices asking for their return. Fortunately the most important of the two, the Sarona photo album, mysteriously popped up in the secretary's mail delivery one day and now resides permanently in the care of the Kennel Club Library in London. The Lances' Sarona album is a fitting personal memorial to the couple whose love of Salukis and talents for networking and publicity combined to win Kennel Club recognition for the breed.

Francis Joan Mitchell grew old at Nablous house in Beckenham where she kept cats and a few Salukis as long as she was able. Her grandniece, Mrs. J. A. Berrisford, remembers vis-iting her easy-going aunt during the 1940s. Joan's hair had gone white by then and she was getting a little vague in her old age. When family members would come to visit, it would take an awfully long time for Joan to think about offering her guests tea or a meal. Still, she was kind and in 1944 at the age of 70, despite a bad leg injury, cared for her invalid sister as well as her cats and Salukis.

Joan came close to being a wartime casualty in 1944 when a German V-1 rocket bomb (known as variously as Doodlebug, Buzz Bomb, or The Squirt) destroyed several buildings and killed 44 people in a crowded café on Beckenham Road just four blocks west of her house.[3]

Acid-etched metal plates used to reproduce photographs in print.
†*With so many casualties from the war, at that time it was fairly common practice for a man to marry his brother's widow in order to provide for her and any children.*
§*Lance had strongly disapproved of John's first wife, Shelagh Gildea, and specifically disinherited any children from that marriage (there were none).*

After the war, at the July 24, 1946, club meeting with Brigadier Lance as the chair, Joan Mitchell and a charter member, Mrs. Crouch, were made honorary members in recognition of their services. In 1950 Joan asked the club if she might present the trophy she had donated at the Richmond show as well as the club show (which at that time was held at Crufts). That seems to be her last official club activity.

At age 79 on May 23, 1954, the mistress of Nablous died at Westminster Hospital, where she had been trained as a nurse fifty years before. Joan's trophy is still awarded at the club show and her house still sits at the corner of Beckenham Road and Elm Road (although the houses have been renumbered), just across from the Elm Road Baptist church. The large garden and wall are still there, as is the lovely stained and jeweled glass windows alongside the front door. The exterior of the house has not changed much except for a small addition. It is an appropriate coincidence that the home of a woman who spent so much of her life dedicated to the care of the sick is now a private medical clinic.

Howard Carter lapsed into inactivity after the final clearance of Tutankhamun's tomb in 1931. He did occasional lectures but never excavated again. There is no evidence that he had much — if any — contact with Florence Amherst in the years during and after his work on the tomb. He died on March 2, 1939, and his obituary recalled his spectacular find in the Valley of the Kings: "The discovery stirred the whole civilized world more perhaps than any other archaeological success had ever done."[4] Tutankhamun's treasures are well-known and documented, and one can easily find depictions of the pharaoh's Salukis on many of the funeral objects.

The Amhersts' town house at Number 8 Grosvenor Square no longer exists and was most likely destroyed during the bombing raids of the Blitz. The old Didlington Hall was torn down in 1950 but in the last few years, a modern Didlington Manor has risen like a phoenix under the care of new owners.* Several of the old outbuildings and estate houses remain, and the grounds, while much reduced in acreage, are as stunning and lush as they were in Didlington's heyday. Pheasant and brown hare pop out of the hedgerows, the lake and Castle Cave are still there, as is the large swimming pool with its colonnade, and the ruins of the hydraulic ram that supplied the house with water from the lake. Nearby St. Michael's still houses the Amherst crypt and continues to serve the people of the Didlington community — but the carved dogs on the church pews have been sawn off and stolen. The old pet cemetery's tombstones and statue of the hunter and his dog were vandalized during a tank regiment's occupation during the war. Five of the seven statues of Sekhmet that used to guard the Amherst home now sit watchfully in the Egyptian galleries of the Metropolitan Museum of Art in New York.†

The last years of Florence's life were spent in a tiny house at number 1 & 2 Kinnerton Studios, Wilton Place, in a mews just off Knightsbridge Road in London. The house is still there, although the courtyard's name has been changed to Studio Place. The cramped house had two floors and no garden. As Florence's great niece, Lady Lanyon, described it:

Didlington Hall was honored in a curious way that recalls the 1856 honeymoon of Lord and Lady Amherst of Hackney. A class of steam locomotive engines was named after great halls and manors — Didlington being one of them. Built in Gloucester in 1942 but not named until after the war in 1946, Didlington Hall gave twenty-two years of service before being scrapped in 1964. Great Western Archive http://www.greatwestern.org.uk/m_ in_hal_hall69a.htm (accessed June 18, 2008).

†*Collection numbers MMA15.8.1–4, & 7. Two of the Amherst statues were sold to the Royal Ontario and San Antonio Art Museums, but the one from the Nafissah photograph of 1909 can still be seen at the Met.*

Her flat was crammed with possessions, including an upright piano. There was hardly any floor space left. As a child, my memories are of my Great Aunt sitting on her bed in a hat surrounded by boxes — a fur coat and a pair of galoshes handy — in case she went out! Some of these possessions must have been priceless. In fact after her death two of the packing cases marked 'Very Valuable' were, on being opened, found to contain quantities of Nile mud! Possibly it was thought to have healing properties![5]

Her papers seem to have been scattered after her death. Neither the present Lord Amherst of Hackney nor any of her relatives were aware that Florence had corresponded with T. E. Lawrence. It is intriguing to speculate that they may yet exist, tucked away in a sheaf of papers or a cigar box somewhere.

Florence's last two residences, being in the heart of Knightsbridge area, were not suitable for dogs, and her increasing health problems had necessitated the Amherstia hounds being boarded with her friend Gertrude Desborough at High Beech, Essex. Florence's last litter was born there in 1937, and when Gertrude died two years later, there was no one to take on the stewardship of the Amherstia line. Florence, however incapacitated by age and poor health, still hosted club meetings and read the weekly dog publications. Periodically she was moved to write to the columnists, commenting on the articles and letters concerning Salukis, and her last Christmas greeting to the club members was sent via Gwen Angel's *Dog World* column in 1944. With unofficial "honorary" status but limited participation, Florence remained a committee member of the Ladies Kennel Association and president of the Saluki or Gazelle Hound Club. During the Blitz and early years of the war, she would periodically leave London and stay with her sister Alicia in Dorset. In 1944, two years before she died, she had an American bomber crewman to a most amazing tea — and what would almost certainly be her final Saluki curtain call.

In 1942, a Saluki fancier, Master Sergeant Carl Oakley of Boston, Massachusetts, went to England with the 381st Bomb Group. He was a flight engineer on a B-17 and only flew three missions before being severely wounded in the back and legs by flak. Recuperating in the Old Churchill Hospital in Oxford, he spent three months in traction and a further three months learning to walk again and convalescing. Lady Elsie Mendel (wife of Sir Charles Mendel), whom he had met in Hollywood prior to the war, took a particular shine to Oakley and sent all her friends to visit him at the hospital. When Oakley was discharged from the hospital, he was to be shipped home to the States as unfit for active service but his commanding officer interceded, with the promise that Oakley would receive complete medical care and therapy at their air base in Ridgewell, Essex. Oakley, as a noncombatant, was placed in charge of organizing the repair and refurbishment of damaged bombers. It took large amounts of phenobarbital to dull his pain and keep him going.

Oakley was a good friend of Edward Aldrich and had two Salukis from his Diamond Hill kennels, one of which was out of Aldrich's Amherstia bitch (one of the few Salukis that Florence had exported). When Oakley shipped out to England, Anne Marie Paterno (El Retiro Kennels) volunteered to keep his hounds. Aldrich wrote to Oakley regularly during the war, and at one point mentioned that he was worried about Florence after not having any word from her for some time. In 1944 he sent Oakley a letter of introduction, with Florence's address and telephone number, and asked if he would try to find out if she was well. While convalescing, Oakley telephoned Amherst and a visit was agreed upon and leave from the hospital arranged — provided a nurse accompanied him, as he was still shaky on his feet. They took the train from Oxford to London and, by private agreement, the nurse dropped him off at a friend's house in St. John's Wood — leaving each of them unencumbered. Automobile transportation was difficult to arrange in England during the war, as petrol was strictly rationed. Oakley was given a lift to his meeting with Florence by a friend who was a high-ranking official with the De Havilland Aircraft Company, who had connections to get extra petrol, despite its short supply.

At age 84, the venerable Florence Amherst was very tired and not well, but despite her poor health graciously received Oakley and had tea served by her male caretaker who lived upstairs.* Florence was bedridden on the ground floor and the only furniture in the cluttered room was a chair, dresser, and her bed. What astonished Oakley was that every square inch of wall and ceiling were covered with photographs of Salukis. They had been pasted and tacked there by Florence's devoted attendant so that she could enjoy them without having to leave her bed. Though frail, she was bright and lucid during their conversation and her memories of the dogs were as clear as ever. She told Oakley of her first Saluki, Luman, and how he was preserved at the British Museum. With great animation, Florence pointed out particular photos on the walls and ceiling and discussed pedigrees, and even showed Oakley a photo of his dog's dam, which Aldrich now owned. She was full of interest in Aldrich's doings, Oakley's own Saluki, the breed in America, and, as was inevitable in those days, they talked about the war. Oakley remembers her as being clearly unhappy about her situation, as she was far from relatives, friends, and her beloved hounds, and she seldom had visitors.[†] Oakley said goodbye that day with a promise to call again, but that would be the first and only time he would see her.

Germany's surrender was official on May 8, 1945, and two months later Oakley was due to return to the States with the 381st Bomb Group before joining the final assault on Japan. He called Florence for a farewell visit, but the caretaker informed him that she was too ill to receive company or even speak on the telephone. When her condition became too serious for her attendant to cope with, she was transferred to Tugvor House Nursing Home, Richmond, Surrey. As happens with so many frail, elderly women, one day Florence fell and broke her hip. The shock of the injury produced complications and eventually, heart failure. She died on August 9, 1946, at the age of 86. She is believed to be buried near her mother at All Saints churchyard at Foulden, two miles down the road from their beloved Didlington.[§]

Florence died with total assets amounting to £12,247** — a decent sum despite her living circumstance. Her will stipulated that her estate be divided into equal shares with any of her living sisters and certain nephews. No specific mention was made of any of her Saluki art or memorabilia. Her possessions were divided among her relatives. Heaven knows what happened to the two cases of dried mud from the Nile, but doubtless they enriched a garden or building site in London.

From the estate, her nephew executors, William Alexander Evering Cecil, C.B.E., 3rd Baron Amherst of Hackney, and the Right Honorable Robert William Evelyn, Lord Rockley, donated two paintings to the Saluki or Gazelle Hound Club in 1947, and two years later the club decided to award them as trophies. One of the portraits was a hound that more closely

---

Oakley remembers that the caretaker spoke with an accent and suggests that he might have been Italian.

[†]*Nephew Jack Cecil was in England during the war and did visit Florence when he was on leave in London. Alicia died in 1941 leaving only Florence and Geraldine. In 1956, the latter would be the last Amherst daughter to die.*

[§]*The records are obscure on that point and I was not able to find her headstone in the churchyard.*

**£349,130.71 in 2006 (MeasuringWorth.com).*

resembled an Afghan than a Saluki, so in 1950 the club voted to offer it to the Southern Afghan Club. Apparently three different Afghan clubs had the same opinion of the alleged resemblance, for all declined the painting. The Saluki Club finally offered the painting to Crufts as a trophy for the best Afghan, but its current whereabouts is unknown.

The other painting was a head study of Sultan,* Florence's first successful show dog and said to be her favorite.[†] Originally painted in 1913, this became known as the "Amherstia Picture," and was awarded by the club committee for "the best Saluki whose sire or dam shall have been imported." The picture was listed on the club trophy manifest through 1964, but by 1972 it too had disappeared. A silver Sheffield candlestick was also presented by her executors and known as "the Florence Amherst Trophy." It was awarded for the best dog or bitch at the club show, but by 1963 it was in bad condition and now, like the paintings, has gone missing.

Florence's massive accumulation of Saluki photos and papers did not particularly interest her family and seems to have been thrown away when her house was cleared — including the letters from T. E. Lawrence and Howard Carter's painting. Also lost was the draft of her manuscript on Salukis. While the great majority of her Saluki memorabilia and art have vanished, one significant piece is treasured to this day. Florence's copy of the bronze Cellini Saluki plaque still is still proudly awarded at the Saluki or Gazelle Hound Club show for best imported Saluki. Combining Florence's three strongest passions — history, art, and Salukis — there is no more appropriate memorial than the Cellini plaque for the scholar who researched and championed the breed for so many years by herself.

Near Aylesbury in Hertfordshire, in the small town of Tring, just off the narrow High Street, is a magnificent half-timber building built by Lord Rothschild. It is an annex of the British Museum, Natural History Division, and holds Lord Rothschild's extensive collection of mounted birds as well as an amazing accumulation representing Victorian collecting mania. There are drawers filled with delicate butterflies and bird's eggs, sharks suspended from the ceiling, an elephant, incredibly long pythons stretched to full length, enormous sea lions perched on top of other cases crammed with specimens, whole orders of the primate and giant feline families, tiny titmice, costumed fleas, and the titanic skeleton of a prehistoric sloth. Amidst this visual cacophony of specimens is an exhibit unique in the world. Filling one of the long aisles is a collection of various breeds of domestic dogs that were donated in the interest of science. The exhibit includes celebrities like Farthest North, the leader of Lt. Peary's team of Eskimo Dogs, Mick the Miller and Fullerton — top-winning racing Greyhounds, and the Pekingese Verity Minni-Atua, whose owner twice refused offers of a 1,000 guineas for the dog.[6]

Luman, Florence Amherst's beloved first Saluki, stands in the long glass case flanked by a pariah dog, a dingo, another Saluki, two Afghans and a Borzoi. An old dog when he died, his face is now white, his ears and tail have lost much of their feathering. His once deep-golden coat has faded to a cream color as a result of the Edwardian taxidermist's harsh chemicals and decades of exposure to unfiltered sunlight. Perhaps puzzled by having to mount the

---

Private correspondence with Hope Waters, October 2, 1996.
[†]*Many modern Salukis can be traced back to Sultan through his great grand daughter, Amherstia Omara, who occurs in most Amherstia pedigrees.*

His coat faded by taxidermist chemicals and sunlight and his face white with age, Luman (surrounded by a dingo, second Saluki, and a Borzoi) stands in the Natural History Museum Annex at Tring. © The Natural History Museum, London.

very first "Arabian greyhound" with scant reference material, the taxidermist may have relied on greyhound anatomy as a model for building Luman's back, as it now has a greyhound-like arch, which was not there when he was alive.

Originally, Luman and the other dogs stood in the British Museum in London with small wooden placards hung from their necks to identify them to museum visitors. After the collection was partially damaged in the bomb raids of the Blitz and other displays began to crowd it, in the 1950s the domestic dog display was put into storage. In 1967, the Saluki or Gazelle Hound Club persuaded the curator to take Luman out of storage and loan him for a special display at the Hound Show in Alexandra Palace where English Saluki fanciers were able to come face to face with the great grandfather of the breed.[7] The following year, Luman and the rest of the collection were returned to display cases — this time in Tring to join Lord Rothschild's collected mélange.

Luman, "the Flash of Light," now with dull glass eyes, stands today as mute witness to the history of the breed in the West. If he could talk, what stories could he tell of the Bedouin in Lower Egypt, his adventures with the Walking Englishman, the voyages across the Mediterranean and the English Channel, the train journey to Norfolk and final carriage ride to Didlington Hall. He could tell of life with the Amhersts, visits from archaeologists, politicians, and royalty; the local Jubilee Celebration, exhibitions at the early dog shows and the first public interest in the breed; the devastation caused by the family bankruptcy, and, of course, of his devoted mistress, the doyenne of Salukis, the Honorable Florence Amherst.

Luman's fate is fittingly ironic. In a strange mimicry of Egyptian funerary rituals, his body parts have also been separated and preserved for eternity. Some thirty miles away in London, deep within the catacombs of the British Museum, locked in a cupboard, is the canopic cardboard box that contains most of Luman's disarticulated skeleton — the delicate feet bones having been left in the mount to give proper shape to his paws. The box also contains his last collar — the piece of string and small wooden cartouche that once hung about his neck. Like the effigies in the pharaoh's tombs, Luman's corporeal likeness stands preserved in Tring and stares wide-eyed at us from the depths of history.

APPENDIX 1

History Repeats Itself—Major Moss

After World War II, British soldiers again returned to England with their pet Salukis, and the circumstances that had led to breed recognition after the Great War were largely repeated — except that this time the breed was being reestablished. As they had done in Frederick Lance's time, the British Army deployed cavalry in the Middle East but with even less effect. The Cheshire Yeomanry earned the distinction of becoming the last British cavalry regiment to serve in action and the man entrusted with the health of their mounts was Major William Philipson Moss, M.C., R.A.V.C — owner of the first postwar, desert-bred Salukis in England.*

Born in 1896 in Gateshead, Northumberland, Billy Moss studied at the King Edward VII School of Art at Armstrong College, University of Durham, in Newcastle-Upon-Tyne, and displayed a talent for capturing the essence of animals.† In 1914 at the age of eighteen, he enlisted in the 2nd Battalion of the Royal Irish Rifles. While the first battles were raging in France, Moss went through officer training and his regiment was taught soldiering more suited to the Crimean War than a conflict fought with airplanes, poison gas, and high-powered explosives.

In the quagmire of No-Man's-Land, Lieutenant Moss saw his share of bloody and futile battles. He led grenade attacks, cleared trenches of dead bodies, and was one of seven survivors when his group of thirty men held a German trench for a week against withering fire. Wounded three times, the worst was at the massacre of the Somme, where a bullet smashed into Moss's knee, knocking him into a mud crater. Wracked with pain and unable to walk, he was stuck a hundred yards away from the British trenches. With small-arms fire and mortar explosions all around, he huddled there for hours until his batman, Rifleman Hood, was able to race out under the murderous spray of German machine guns and drag him to safety.

The twenty-year-old Moss was invalided home and married Mary Frances Watson in Bexhill-on-Sea in December, 1916. His shattered leg took years to heal properly and he would see no more active service in France. After the armistice in 1918, Moss was at loose ends for employment, and, with a wife and his young son, John, to support, he enrolled in veterinary school. After graduation, he worked as a government inspector during the epidemics of foot-and-mouth disease in the mid–1920s. Looking for new challenges, he set up a private veterinary practice in Woking, Surrey. There, he demonstrated an unexpected knack for improvising

*Condensed from "The Sketchbook of Major Moss," by Brian Duggan and Ken Allan, Saluki International 5, no. 10 (Spring/Summer 1997).
†The author wishes to thank John and Margaret Moss for their kindness in allowing this story to be told. Particular thanks go to Claire Jowett, who made Ken Allan of Saluki International aware of this hidden treasure.

253

Major William Philipson Moss, R.S.V.A. (center), with Selwa and Selma. With the kind permission of John Moss.

treatments for exotic circus and zoo animals (which had not been part of the veterinary college curriculum)—a skill which would later serve him well.

When the Second World War broke out in 1939, Moss reenlisted, and in March 1940 he was posted to the Cheshire Yeomanry as Veterinary Officer. Along with the North Somerset Yeomanry and Yorkshire Dragoons, the Cheshires formed the 5th Cavalry Brigade, the last unmechanized unit of British cavalry. They were shipped to the Middle East to fight the Syrians allied with the French Vichy Government.*

Unlike the tanks and trucks of the rest of the army, horses require care and feeding around the clock, seven days a week. Moss had his work cut out for him, for the regimental mounts were mostly commandeered hunters, and while accustomed to work on rough terrain, the horses had to learn military drill and be trained to tolerate the noise of military band music, gunfire, and explosions. Each horse had to be in top condition in order to carry rider, saddle, weapons, ammunition, and assorted equipment—a load of over 200 pounds.

Each day the horses were fed, watered, groomed, and exercised, their hooves cleaned and their manure shoveled. They were inspected for disease, worms, injuries, and poor health, and had their teeth filed and hooves regularly trimmed and shod. Moss, the farrier sergeant, and troop farriers oversaw all care of the horses. Moss had unconventional ideas about health care for the horses and was not afraid to flout army regulation in the interest of the health of his charges. Convinced that steel shoes and nails were actually unhealthy, he ordered that the

---

*Ironically in World War II, the British Army had to reconquer Syrian territory which they had already fought for and won at the end of First World War.

horses were to be left unshod whenever possible. Meticulous attention by Moss and his farriers to the cleaning and trimming of hooves clearly paid off, as witnessed by the successful
health and service of their horses in a hostile land and climate.

Busy as he was with a few hundred horses, the dapper "Mossy" did not neglect his passion for art. With charcoal pencils and pastels he drew camp life, landscapes, men and horses.
He did portraits of his fellow officers on horseback accompanied by their foxhounds and terriers, he sketched the regiment crossing rivers, and the troopers tending to their mounts. The
Cheshires thought themselves very fortunate indeed to have a man who was equally skilled
with lancet and charcoal pencil.

On June 8, 1941, the Cheshire Yeomanry advanced into Syria as part of the 25th Australian Brigade. They covered forty-five miles in one long day. At dawn the next morning,
machine-gun fire from a village on the far side of the Litani River threatened the regiment.
The Cheshires advanced to capture the village, but the Syrians quickly retreated when faced
with the threat of a massed cavalry attack. Meanwhile, the Australians near the coast were
suffering heavy casualties and the Cheshires were next ordered to attack the Vichy left flank.
On June 10, a squadron was sent forward to reconnoiter, and the French officers, mistakenly
believing an attack by a large force was on the heels of the patrol, retreated. There would be
no more opportunities for a cavalry charge, and they finished the campaign with patrols and
reconnaissance work. At the end of the Syrian Campaign in early 1942, the Cheshire Yeomanry were reorganized as a mechanized unit within the Royal Signals and they gave up their
horses. Major Moss had unknowingly gained the singular distinction of being the last artist
to draw British cavalry in action.

Along with their departing horses went the Chesire's need for a veterinary officer. Moss
soon transferred to a British Druze Regiment to care for not only their horses but their camels
as well. His experiences in treating exotic animals back in England provided a good foundation for this new challenge. Moss moved easily among the desert tribesmen and sketched soldiers and camp scenes — and with their consent, made portraits of their women. Salukis in
the regiment were a common sight and from his friend Captain Ness he acquired two cream-
colored, feathered bitches. Selwa and Selma became his constant companions throughout
Palestine, Syria, the Jordan Valley, and ultimately, Cyrenaica. In a letter to *The Field*, he wrote
about their hardiness and homing ability:

> Although not demonstrative, these Salukis are faithful companions and I too have known
> several instances where dogs have traveled surprising distances to reach their master if they
> have been separated. When I was in the Middle East, my two bitches trekked many hun-
> dreds of miles with me. They always kept pretty close while we were on the move, but as
> soon as they had seen my kit unpacked they did not mind "exploring" a little on their own,
> and never had any difficulty in finding their way back to camp in the many strange places
> we visited.[1]

The vet sketched the hounds in repose and in their business about the camp among the
soldiers, camels, and horses. His surviving works show that several Salukis were a normal feature of camp life (one British regiment was known to have had at least 80 of the hounds bred
from Arab stock). Moss's hounds were treated indulgently, even after young Selwa and Selma
once stealthily entered the sanctity of the mess tent and gobbled the entire first course while
the stewards were setting out the meal.

Wherever he traveled, Moss found camaraderie between Saluki owners, whether army
or tribesmen. He developed close friendships with other officers and soldiers that owned

Salukis, and together they hunted in their off-duty hours. Selwa and Selma became excellent hunters and could handily take down fox, jackal, hare, and gazelle. He rode with tribesmen and his brother officers on hell-for-leather Saluki hunts after jackal and hare, and later drew the scenes from memory.

In 1943, Moss was transferred to Cyrenaica, over 500 miles west of Alexandria in what is now Libya, where he served with the British Military Administration, Veterinary and Remount Head Quarters, until late 1944. As Chief Veterinary Officer he ran the military veterinary hospital in D'Annunzio (Al-Baidhah), hunted with his hounds, and painted the local Senussi tribesmen in his spare time. When he was authorized for demobilization, Moss determined to take his Salukis back to England. While Mary waited impatiently, he postponed returning home because one of the Salukis was in whelp. When he finally did leave, on the first leg of his journey home, he let Selwa and Selma stretch their legs alongside the truck in their accustomed fashion.

> [W]e continued with a speedometer showing 30 m.p.h. They stopped to empty themselves and then laid themselves flat at full speed a few hundred yards away from the road on going until level with the car. After this they continue in, a loping canter at 30 m.p.h. for about 8 miles. When they were brought in their easy breathing showed that they had scarcely exerted themselves at this average speed. I need hardly say that the other travelers were very greatly impressed at this grand display.[2]

Moss landed at Liverpool on January 3, 1945, and Selwa and Selma entered quarantine. The scarcity of desert bloodlines and reduced breeding stock in wartime England generated quite a bit of interest the pair. Selwa and Selma had the honor of being the first desert-bred Salukis to be registered in England after the end of the war.[3]

Buying a hillside farm near Bexhill-on-Sea with plenty of room for his hounds to run, Moss tried breeding Guernsey cows to sell to dairy farms. Moss joined the Saluki or Gazelle Hound Club in 1946 and judged breed classes on a few occasions. His Salukis were registered with the Kennel Club under the prefix Rashilal (a cape on the coastline of Cyrenaica). Selma was bred to Bully — a Saluki imported from Egypt by Naval Commander A.E. Lockington — and a litter of puppies was born later in 1946. Selwa and Selma loved the farm but were prone to killing chickens on a neighbor's farm. Ironically, and most likely in retaliation for the chicken carnage, the former chief veterinary officer in Cyrenaica was reported to the RSPCA by the neighbors who claimed that his trim Salukis were being starved.

Moss's activity in the Saluki Club declined but he bred at least one more litter. After Selwa and Selma died, Moss traded a watercolor of Bedouins, Salukis, camels, and horses to Hope Waters (Burydown Salukis) for another Saluki. In the years after the war, he wrote and illustrated a few articles on hunting in the East with Salukis and eventually would be commissioned by the Ministry of Information to execute a series of illustrations of the Syrian and Senussi Campaigns as part of a program to document various aspects of the war.

Referring to his well-traveled sketchbooks, he did several paintings of the men, horses, and Salukis who had been his comrades in arms. The Imperial War Museum purchased some of his work, as did a Bond Street gallery, private collectors and the Emir el Attrash of Druze. In December 1959, Moss and his work were honored with a show entitled "Drawings and Paintings of the Bedouin Arab" in Fletching, East Sussex. Moss's work ranged from cartoon-style caricatures and thumbnail studies for later works, to charcoal portraits of great character and strength, and studies in pastel, watercolor, and oil, showing not only a detailed knowledge of canine form and anatomy, but mannerisms characteristic and distinctive of the Saluki.

Charcoal study (ca. 1943) of Druze trooper and Salukis by Major William Philipson Moss, R.S.V.A. With the kind permission of John Moss.

William Moss died in 1979. To this day, his family and a few fortunate Saluki fanciers treasure his paintings and drawings. Preserved at the family farm near Hastings is a box containing photographs, sketches, letters, and magazine clippings about Moss's army career, his art, and his Salukis. His attachment to Selwa and Selma was as strong as that of any of the Great War veterans to their hounds. In that box lies a token of that bond — a wide leather collar, now brittle with the passage of years, with a dull brass plate, hand-stamped to read:

Maj. W.P. Moss. M.C.
R.A.V.C.
"Selwa"

APPENDIX 2

Wilfred Jennings-Bramly, the Walking Englishman

"I heard that the Beduins gave me the name of the 'Walking Englishman,' and once or twice were kind enough to say that I was one of themselves."[1]

Wilfred Jennings-Bramly, M.C., M.B.E., was the Saluki nexus for the breed's history in England. His intriguing dealings with the Honorable Florence Amherst and her father, Lord Amherst of Hackney, are a quick glimpse into a remarkable life and career. Largely unknown outside of his family and a few scholars, it is worth a few pages to sketch out something of Wilfred's life.

Born in 1871 to John and Bertha Jennings-Bramly, he was the second child and oldest son of six siblings. John was a career major in the Chestnut Troop of Royal Horse Artillery. Bertha had progressive ideas on education and at the tender age of five he was sent with a governess to live in Germany. Probably dyslexic, Jennings-Bramly would later attribute his Elizabethan spelling quirks to having to learn German at the same time that he was getting a grip on English. One day while walking in his schoolboy's sailor suit he met two large men who turned out to be Kaiser Wilhelm and Chancellor von Bismarck. Years later, Wilfred would suggest at dinner conversations that his meeting with the German kaiser and chancellor was on a much loftier and political level.

When he returned to England, he was educated at Malvern and Winchester, and displayed a passion for collecting animals, filling the cupboards of his room with birds, small mammals, and snakes. During his time at Malvern, Wilfred began to enjoy taking dares and making wagers with his fellow schoolboys. By 1890, he had grown into a handsome young man. Of slender build, five foot eight, Wilfred was strikingly good-looking with reddish-brown hair and piercing blue eyes. Humorous by nature, he had an engaging personality and was gifted with talents for horsemanship, storytelling, and mimicry. "Wiffy" decided to enter officer training, but flunked the Sandhurst entrance exam six times with his bad spelling, until on the seventh attempt, another student's nosebleed distracted him from making deliberate attempts to spell correctly.

Wilfred's mother, Bertha, had strong family connections to the Khedive's government in Egypt. Her father, John Wingfield Larking, had been British consul in Alexandria and agent in England for the Khedive Mohammed Tewfik (Tawfiq) Pasha, and her brother, Col. Cuthbert Larking, was Tewfik's aide-de-camp. Bertha had been born in Egypt and her mother,

Rosina, was the daughter of Pellegrino Tibaldi, Mohammed Ali Pasha's ill-fated advisor.* After Tibaldi's murder in 1811, Rosina's mother married Thurburn of Mertyl (H.M. Consul in Alexandria prior to Larking's tenure), and after his death, married Larking himself.

In the summer of 1890, Bertha suggested that before Wilfred joined the army that he visit Egypt and stay with family friend Boghos Nubar Pasha — the Khedive's prime minister. After three months, he was homesick but decided to stay in Egypt. Family tradition has it that the Khedive wanted him for a minister but, lacking any experience in government processes, the nineteen-year-old Wilfred was sent to Alexandria to work as a clerk for Monsieur Alfred Caillard, Director General of Customs.

Quickly bored with office work, he persuaded Caillard to let him do field work and soon he was speaking passable Arabic and displayed a distinct talent for disguises and skulking in bazaars

Captain Wilfred Jennings-Bramly, M.C., 1918. With the kind permission of Jasper Scovil.

in order to catch hashish and salt smugglers. When the Khedive died unexpectedly in 1892, any nepotistic hope of a high-ranking government position disappeared. When Wilfred was about to return to England in 1893, Nubar Pasha found him a post as the keeper of the new Zoological Gardens at an abandoned palace in Giza. Collecting animals for the zoo was a perfect excuse to go on desert expeditions to catch animals or explore. He continued to work on his Arabic and disguises, and when confronted by inquisitive Bedouin, developed the clever ruse of explaining his odd appearance and accent by claiming to be from a place so far away that they could not possibly know anything about it. Also, Wilfred was not above masquerading as a British colonel when the need arose, to impress the local tribesmen. The Bedouin called him "the Walking Englishman" because of his preference for walking rather than riding a camel, as well as his unusual tolerance of desert heat. As described in chapter 2, under his creative supervision the Giza Zoo became a popular attraction for the citizens of Cairo.

Weary of record keeping (which would never be his strong suit) and the zoo, he left in 1898, and until 1904 did mapping surveys of springs, wells, and tribes in Egypt and Sinai for the Palestine Exploration Fund and the Royal Geographical Society — and in the Sudan for the army (where he took up camel racing over fifty-mile courses).† Always disenchanted with paperwork, his survey work (when completed) was interesting but never up to the standards of those organizations. Wilfred made two singular wagers during this period — one in which he went from Alexandria to Florence in Bedouin costume and speaking nothing but Arabic, and the other where he said he could go for thirty days in the desert existing on nothing but

---

Tibaldi advised against the Pasha's plan to exterminate Mamluk rule and was poisoned for his counsel. As a young girl of five, Rosina remembered vividly her father's painful death and seeing the heads of the slaughtered Mamluks paraded through the streets of Cairo on cavalry lances.

†*For an account of his calamitous expedition to Siwa in 1896, see my article "Ordeal," Saluki International, Annual #2, 2007.*

Nestlé's condensed milk (much to the disgruntlement of his servant). He won the first bet but the results of the second are not recorded.

In 1901, he proposed marriage to Phyllis Noel Justina Isabel Mary de Cosson (daughter of the famous arms and armor expert, Baron de Cosson) but got cold feet and postponed the marriage by a year. They were married in Florence, Italy, the home of her parents, and lived there for a time. After moving to Egypt, they had Lady Anne Blunt and her husband, Wilfrid Scawen, as neighbors in Ain al Shams, north of Cairo. While Wilfred and Phyllis got on well with Lady Anne, the two men disliked each other intensely — the staunch anti-imperialist Blunt considering Jennings-Bramly to be the embodiment of everything he considered wrong with the Anglo-Egyptian government. A wall was eventually built between their gardens so that the two would not have to see each other.

Wilfred and Phyllis had two daughters, Vivien Dorothy and Judith Antoinette, who shared their father's love of costume and used to dress up in Arab robes and pose for photographs. The girls stayed in Florence with their maternal grandparents when Phyllis was able to be with Wilfred in Egypt, and would eventually come to live with their parents in 1912. In 1904, Wilfred was made Commander and Inspector of Sinai, which meant he was the only Englishman with a handful of *bashi-bazouks** to map the landscape, and keep an eye on the small police posts that guarded the pilgrim's road to Makkah all the while preventing rampant smuggling and mayhem. Wilfred once went with a party of Bedouin clandestinely into Palestine, got arrested by Turkish troops and escaped out of a second-story window, stealing away into the night.

As Sinai adjoined the Ottoman Empire's territory, some diplomatic niceties had to be maintained, but the Turkish Army largely relied upon paid Bedouin to alert them to intruders. Upon hearing in 1906 that some sort of Turkish force had established a camp at Al Aqaba (instigated by the Sultan's German advisors in Constantinople), Lord Cromer sent Wilfred to investigate and reinforce Egypt's border claim there. Strategically located at the head of the Gulf of Aqaba, the small port was a key entrance point for both land and sea entrance to Eastern Sinai, Northern Arabia, the Transjordan, and Palestine. Even though Cairo rejected his radical thinking, eight years before World War I Jennings-Bramly was making the case for the strategic importance of Sinai and the Bedouin tribesmen.

Upon finding a sizeable Turkish force at Al Aqaba, Wilfred used one of his old ruses by pretending to have army authority and giving ultimatums to the Turkish colonel. Over five months, the situation escalated, with the arrival of up to three divisions of Turkish soldiers reinforcing their position while Wilfred and some two hundred men camped in a small fort on an island offshore from Al Aqaba — debating the Turkish colonel, issuing withdrawal demands, and sending telegrams to Cairo pleading for a warship so that he could settle everything. His high-handed approach escalated the situation into a border incident that nearly sent Egypt and England to war with the Ottoman Empire.[†] Now known as the Aqaba Incident or Tabah Crisis (Tabah being a small village on the gulf opposite Aqaba), it was only settled when diplomats were sent to renegotiate the mutual border and Wilfred was removed from his post. The Turkish plenipotentiary unwittingly paid the former inspector a great compliment by saying, "My dear sir, put the boundary where you like, but, please, remove Bramly a thousand miles from Sinai."[2]

Irregular Turkish soldiers noted for indiscipline and wild behavior.
†*Jennings-Bramly's former neighbor, Wilfrid Scawen Blunt, blamed him for the whole situation.*

Somewhat disgraced, Wilfred was sent back to Egypt. In Cairo a couple of years later, Lord Cromer employed him in the Recruiting Department to sort out which Egyptians were eligible for military conscription. In return for their military support, in the early 1800s Muhammad Ali Pasha had guaranteed the Bedouin descendants of the seventh-century Muslim conquerors exemption from conscription. Since then, many had settled to become farmers or merchants, and naturally, every fellah claimed Bedouin lineage to avoid army service. With perhaps 20,000 Bedouin in Egypt, Wilfred had the massive job of trying to sort out 600,000 claimed exemptions.[3] A detailed interview about their ancestry with cross-comparisons and simple quizzes about things only a real Bedouin would know about (such as the name of a particular tent pole) helped Wilfred distinguish imposters from the genuine article. After finishing the Cairo part of the survey, he and Phyllis lived on a *dehabiyeh* (native boat) and would ride inland to visit the Bedouin encampments. Together, they accumulated massive amounts of tribal data that friend and author G.W. Murray would later incorporate into his book *The Sons of Ishmael*. Although Wilfred had authored a number of articles for the *Palestine Exploration Fund Quarterly Statement*, the London Zoological Society, and *Sudan Notes and Records*, he modestly refused Murray's offer of coauthor credit.

With the outbreak of World War I, Phyllis became very ill and she and their daughters went back to her parents' home in Florence. Wilfred was commissioned as an intelligence staff officer with the rank of temporary captain and worked first in the Western Desert and later with T.E. Lawrence in Sinai (Lawrence thought highly of him). The precise nature of Wilfred's war work is somewhat murky, but it must have been meritorious, as he was awarded the Military Cross for his service.

After the war, Wilfred, Phyllis, and their daughters moved to back to the desert where for a time, he was commandant of the Wadi Natrun district and later the Western Desert. Over the next two decades, with scant funding from the government, he used his own wits and resources to build a town forty miles west of Alexandria. Called Burg-al-Arab (Town of the Arab), he was convinced it would become an important stop on the caravan route to Alexandria and Cairo, and in 1919 established a carpet-weaving factory there to employ the local women. There was a factory tower, windmill, railway station and — being only two miles from the Mediterranean — a lighthouse. T.E. Lawrence thought well of Wilfred's civic architecture and commended it to E.M. Forster, who in turn noted it in his 1922 book *Alexandria: A History and Guide*.

Wilfred built a stone home on a ridge overlooking the town and ocean with an oasis of tamarisk trees and olive groves — an imitation of a Moorish manor with an Elizabethan-style great hall, and called it *Dar-al-Badia* (House of the Desert). Phyllis had always been more of a dog person than Wilfred (already owning a poodle when they married, he gave her a Borzoi as a wedding present). Wilfred did not care for her terriers, which had the run of Dar-al-Badia, and he used to gently annoy them with his walking stick. Known as "Ramley Bey" to the locals, he enjoyed spending time with them and spinning stories to entertain. He was well respected by the Bedouin and was actively sought out to settle legal disputes and feuds. Wilfred remained on a captain's half-pay until 1924 when he retired from government service and devoted his energies to his town and home. He and Phyllis hosted Lord Lloyd, High Commisioner in Egypt, Harold Nicolson, Lord Allenby, officers of General Montgomery's 8th Army, Major Bagnol of the Long Range Desert Group, Jane Jarvis (apparently traveling without her husband, C.S.), desert explorer and author Freya Stark, and Count László Almásy, the Hungarian pilot, motorist, and explorer who was the model for Michael Ondaatje's protagonist in his novel *The English Patient.*

When war was declared against Germany in 1939, Jennings-Bramly was 68, yet he volunteered for the Reserve Army. He was given the local rank of major and once again applied his unique talents to intelligence gathering. In what was called "the Arab Force Scheme," he recruited Bedouin of the area to the British side and through them kept an eye on Rommel's advance toward Alexandria. With German tanks advancing in their direction, Wilfred and Phyllis stood fast and never did evacuate. General Montgomery defeated Rommel at El Alamein in 1942 — just over the horizon from Dar-al-Badia. It was the turning point in the North African campaign for the British, and for his services Wilfred was awarded M.B.E.

After victory in Europe, life for the Jennings-Bramlys returned to their routine of producing olive oil, entertaining guests, and visiting Bedouin friends. Their last years at Dar-al-Badia were comparatively calm until rising Egyptian nationalism began to cause unrest. In 1956, in a rebellion against the last vestiges of British colonialism, all English residents were deported. After sixty-five years in Egypt, Wilfred and Phyllis left their beloved home and took up residence in Florence, Italy, at the old home of his maternal grandparents.

In his last years, Wilfred began compiling autobiographical notes and even wrote a line or two of poetry. His brief and somewhat truncated biography was privately published for the family. He died in Florence on March 2 1960.

Perhaps Wilfred Jennings-Bramly's best epitaph is his own summation of his life in the desert and affection for its tribesmen — "I came to Egypt for three months, but stayed for sixty-five years."

Glossary of Foreign Words and Anglo-Indian Slang

'aba' (*Arabic*): a man's cloak-like overgarment.

'iqal (*Arabic*): the head cord used to bind a man's *kaffiyeh*) in place. May be used as a camel hobble if necessary.

baksheesh: monetary gratuity, alms, bribe, or gift depending on the outlook of the giver.

barraked: English corruption of the Arabic "*barraka*" — to make a camel kneel for loading or mounting.

bastinado: beating — particularly on the soles of the feet.

bazaar-wallah (Anglo-Indian slang): shopkeeper.

Bedu or *Badu:* nomadic tribesmen (singular: *Badawi*).

bait sha'r (*Arabic*): a tent made of woven goat hair — literally "house of hair"

bey (Turkish & Egyptian): also *beg*. Lord — also the rank below that of pasha.

bimbashi: the rank of major in the Egyptian army.

bismillah: Muslim ritual invocation when slaughtering an animal for food (this formula is also known as "*basmala*").

bobbery (Anglo-Indian slang): wild, tumultuous, or uproarious — often aptly used to describe a hunting pack with several breeds of dogs.

dallah (*Arabic*): long-spouted teapot or coffeepot.

dehabiyeh (or *dhahabiya*h): an Egyptian boat with living quarters.

dhabh (*Arabic*): sacrifice — specifically the prescribed throat-cutting to make the meat lawful (*halal*).

effendi (Turkish): honorific term for a gentleman or professional man, common to many Middle Eastern countries.

efrit (or *'ifrit*): (*Arabic*): a ghost.

fantasse (or *fintas*): twelve-gallon water tank carried in pairs by camels (plural: *fanatis*).

fellaheen (or *fallahin*): Egyptian peasants. Singular: *fellah*.

gebel (or *jabal*): (*Arabic*): mountain.

grizzle: originally meaning the color gray, by the mid 1930's in England, used to describe the color pattern of one darker color on the head, back, and sides with a lighter shade on the face, legs, and belly.

halal (*Arabic*): lawful — in accordance with Muslim practice.

hamla (*Arabic*): a baggage caravan.

haqq al-bait (*Arabic*): literally, the law of the tent. Obligatory shelter, food, and drink for any who may ask.

howdah (Persian; in Arabic: *haudaj*): camel litter.

jambiyah (*Arabic*): a specific type of curved dagger.

jerba or *qirba* (*Arabic*): waterskin made from goatskin.

jinni (or *djinn*) (*Arabic*): an evil spirit.

kaffiyeh (*Arabic*): a lightweight headcloth. Similar to a *shemagh* (colloquial Arabic), a heavier, often patterned head cloth, usually worn in winter.

kaimakam (or *qaimaqam*) (Turkish-Egyptian): district administrative officer, sometimes the rank of colonel.

kasr (or *qasr*): (*Arabic*): a castle or fort.

kopje (Boer): a stone outcrop or hill.

kurta (Urdu and Hindi): collarless tunic worn by Indian cavalry regiments.

lungi (Urdu): traditionally a garment knotted around the waist, it came to mean the turban or *pagri* worn by Indian cavalry, with distinctive regional wrapping styles.

maher (Arabic): front arch of the camel saddle.

memsahib (Anglo-Indian): lady, originally "madam *sahib*," the wife of the *sahib* or gentleman of the house.

omdah (Turkish): a village headman or leader.

nasrani (Arabic): a Christian (from Nazarene).

pagri (or *puggaree*): (Hindi): a turban. In military use, it can also be pleated cloth and wound around a pith helmet.

parti-color: said to have originated from the elaborately marked hose that men wore during the Italian Renaissance, in this book it refers to a predominantly white dog with overlaid markings or spots of black, red, brown, etc.

pasha (Turkish/Egyptian): honorific term for a person of rank and station.

pukka (Hindi): slang for proper, good, true, first-class, or genuine.

punkah-wallah (Hindi): the person, usually a young boy or old man, who rhythmically pulls the ceiling fan cord in order to cool a room.

rafiq (Arabic): a local escort and guide.

Raj (Hindi): literally "kingdom"—the term for the British colonial rule in India 1858–1947.

sahib (Hindi/Bengali): respectful term for a gentleman. Originally derived from the Arabic "*sahib*" (friend).

El-Sham (or *ash-Sham*): (Arabic): Damascus and the area surrounding it.

shawabty: ancient Egyptian burial figurine which would come to life in the next world and perform work for the deceased.

sheikh (or *shaikh*): (Arabic): a leader of a tribe or clan. Also applied to elders.

shikari (Hindi): literally "hunter," but used by the British to refer to a guide, gun bearer, or tracker.

sirdar (Persian): leader. The title of the commander in chief of the Anglo-Egyptian Army.

souk (or *suq*) (Arabic): an open market or shop area.

tarbush (Turkish-Egyptian): head covering in the form of a truncated cone and often confused with a fez. The lack of a brim allows Muslims to pray without removing their headgear.

tawa (Arabic): an iron plate, used for baking.

tazza (or *tasa*): (Arabic): shallow cup or basin.

thaub (Arabic): men's white smock with long, wide sleeves.

topee (Hindi: *topi*): a lower-crowned, civilian version of the pith helmet worn in the tropics. Made of lightweight cork or pith to provide shade for the head.

wadi (Arabic): a water course (generally dry), which can range in size from a ravine to a valley.

wallah (or *walla*) (Hindi): fellow or person.

wazir (Arabic): minister; also "*vizier*."

British Titles, Orders, Awards, and Honors

C.B.E.: Commander of the Order of the British Empire

C.G.I.E: Knight Grand Commander of the Order of the Indian Empire

C.I.E.: Companion of the (Order of the) Indian Empire

C.M.G.: Companion of the Order of St. Michael and St. George

C.S.I. Companion of the Star of India

C.V.O.: Commander of the (Royal) Victorian Order

D.S.O.: Distinguished Service Order

F.R.C.V.S.: Fellow of the Royal College of Veterinary Surgeons

F.R.G.S.: Fellow of the Royal Geographical Society

F.S.A.: Fellow of the Society of Antiquities

F.Z.S.: Fellow of the Zoological Society

K.C.B.: Knight Commander of the Bath

K.C.I.E. Knight Commander of the Indian Empire

LL.D: Doctor of Laws

M.C.: Military Cross

M.B.E.: Member of the Order of the British Empire

O.B.E.: Officer of the Order of the British Empire

R.A.: Royal Academy *or* Royal Artillery, depending on the context

R.A.V.C.: Royal Army Veterinary Corps

Notes

Prologue

1. T. E. Lawrence to D. Hogarth, Bodleian Library, MS. Eng. D. 3355, fols. 161.
2. David Garnett, ed., *The Letters of T. E. Lawrence*, 2nd ed. (New York: Doubleday, 1939), 150.
3. Jeremy Wilson, *Lawrence of Arabia* (New York: Atheneum/Macmillan, 1990), 626.

Chapter 1

1. Alfred W. Pollard, "The Amherst Library," *Country Life Magazine*, October 27, 1906, 581.
2. Baroness Strange, letter to the author, January 7, 1994.
3. *Sunday Times* clipping, Hackney Archives, London, Acc. No. D/F/AMH 331.b.
4. Laureen Baillie and Paul Sievking, eds., *British Biographical Archive* (New York: Saur, 1984), microfiche #288–298.
5. Ibid.
6. James W. Trimbee and Jean Trimbee McKenzie, *A Trail of Trials* (Edinburgh: Pentland Press, 1995), 52–62.
7. David Butters, Swaffham Museum, letter to the author, December 17, 1996.

Chapter 2

1. Alicia M. J. Amherst, "The Journal," December 1894–June 1895, Vol. I, 1.
2. Ibid., 1–16.
3. Ibid.
4. M. Naville, Percy E. Newberry, and George Willoughby Fraser, *The Season's Work at Ahnas and Beni Hasan* (London: Gilbert & Rivington Ltd. for the Egyptian Exploration Fund, 1891), 12.
5. Thomas Cook & Sons, *Dahabeahs on the Nile: Under the Arrangements of Thomas Cook and Sons*, London, 1891.
6. Alicia M. J. Amherst, Vol. II, 22.
7. Lady Margaret Amherst of Hackney, *A Sketch of Egyptian History* (London: Methuen, 1904), 140.
8. Lady William Cecil, *Bird Notes from the Nile* (London: Archibald Constable and Co., 1904), 31.
9. Albert M. Lythgoe, "Statues of the Goddess Sekhmet," *Bulletin of the Metropolitan Museum of Art*, Part II (October 1919): 3, 6.
10. T. G. H. James, *Howard Carter: The Path to Tutankhamun* (London: Keegan Paul International, 1992), 2.
11. Alicia M. J. Amherst, Vol. II, 32.

Chapter 3

1. Edward C. Ash, *Dogs: Their History and Development*, vol. 1 (London: Ernest Benn Limited, 1927), 197.
2. Margaret S. Tyssen Amherst, *In a Good Cause* (London: Wells, Gardner, Darton, 1885), 267.
3. Austen H. Layard, *Discoveries at Nineveh and Babylon* (New York: G. P. Putnam, 1853), 48.
4. "The Hon. Florence Amherst and her Salukis at Amherstia Kennels," *Dog World*, May 20, 1926, 612.
5. Lady Anne Blunt, *Bedouin Tribes of the Euphrates* (New York: Harper & Brothers, 1879), 181.
6. Ibid., 307.
7. Lady Anne Blunt, *A Pilgrimage to Nejd*, vol. 1 (London: J. Murray, 1881), 37.
8. Rosemary Archer and James Fleming, eds., *Lady Blunt: Journals and Correspondence 1878–1917* (Cheltenham, Gloucestershire: Alexander Heriot, 1986) 59.
9. Blunt, *A Pilgrimage to Nejd*, vol. 1, 73–74.
10. Ibid., vol. 2, 168.
11. Ibid., vol. 1, 74.
12. Charles M. Doughty, *Travels in Arabia Deserta* (London: J. Cape & The Medici Society Ltd., July 1926), 517.
13. Ibid., 131.
14. John Hayman, ed., *Sir Richard Burton's Travels in Arabia and Africa: Four Lectures from the Huntington Library Manuscripts* (San Marino: Huntington Library, 1990), 5, 21.
15. Richard Burton, *Personal Narrative of a Pilgrimage to Al-Medinah & Meccah*, vol. 2 (New York: Dover Publications, 1964), 104–105.
16. Edward K. Aldrich, "Salukis," *American Kennel Club Gazette*, May 1946, 54–55.
17. Advertisement, *Dog World Annual*, 1960, 119.
18. Hope Waters and David Waters, *The Saluki in History, Art, and Sport* (Newton Abbot, England: David & Charles, 1969), 54.
19. James Watson, *The Dog Book* (New York: Doubleday, Page, 1906), 630.
20. Walter Hutchinson, *Hutchinson's Dog Encyclopædia*, part 43 (London: Hutchinson, 1935), 1549.

Chapter 4

1. *Thetford and Watton Times*, September 4, 1897, 6.
2. Ibid.
3. Florence Amherst, "Oriental Greyhounds," *The New Book of the Dog*, ed. Robert Leighton (London: Cassell, 1907), 478.
4. Florence Amherst, "The Gazelle-Hound," *Every*

Woman's Encyclopedia, 1910–1912, reprinted in *Saluki International*, #20 (Spring/Summer 2002), 52.

5. "The Hon. Florence Amherst and Her Salukis at Amherstia Kennels," *Dog World*, May 20, 1926, 612.

6. Fernand Mery, *The Life, History, and Magic of the Dog* (New York: Grosset & Dunlap, 1968), 107.

7. Brian Duggan, "Ordeal," *Saluki International*, Annual #2, 2007, 51.

8. Lord Amherst to George Armstrong, October 26, 1898, Papers of W. E. Jennings-Bramly: PEF/DA/BRA/6 (London: Palestine Exploration Fund).

9. Basil Thomson to Sir Charles Wilson, November 9, 1898, Papers of W. E. Jennings-Bramly: PEF/DA/BRA/9 (London: Palestine Exploration Fund).

10. Basil Thomson to George Armstrong, August 23, 1899, Papers of W. E. Jennings-Bramly: PEF/DA/BRA/1/28/1–2 (London: Palestine Exploration Fund).

11. Jennings-Bramly to George Armstrong, no date, Papers of W. E. Jennings-Bramly: PEF/DA/BRA/27 (London: Palestine Exploration Fund).

12. Vivien Betti, conversation with author, March 16, 1997.

13. Basil Thomson to Sir Charles Wilson, December 24, 1899, Papers of W. E. Jennings-Bramly: PEF/DA/BRA/35 (London: Palestine Exploration Fund).

14. Sir Charles Wilson to George Armstrong, July 20, 1901, Papers of W. E. Jennings-Bramly: PEF/DA/BRA/44 (London: Palestine Exploration Fund).

15. Jennings-Bramly to George Armstrong, August 1902, Papers of W. E. Jennings-Bramly: PEF/DA/BRA/49 (London: Palestine Exploration Fund).

16. E. A. Reeves (Royal Geographical Society) to George Armstrong (Palestine Exploration Fund), November 4, 1904, Papers of W.E. Jennings-Bramly: PEF/DA/BRA/52 (London: Palestine Exploration Fund).

17. Florence Amherst, "Oriental Greyhounds," 476.

18. W. E. Jennings-Bramly, "Bedouin of the Sinaitic Peninsula," *Palestine Exploration Fund Quarterly Statement* (October 1909): 254.

19. Cherry Drummond, *The Remarkable Life of Victoria Drummond, Marine Engineer* (London: Institute of Marine Engineers, 1994), 25–26.

Chapter 5

1. Lady Margaret Amherst of Hackney, *A Sketch of Egyptian History* (London: Methuen, 1904), 37.

2. Ibid., 57.

3. Ibid., 111, 113.

4. Florence Amherst, "Saluki, or Gazelle Hound," in *Hutchinson's Dog Encyclopaedia*, ed. Walter Hutchinson (London: 1935), part 43, 1545.

5. Griffith, Francis L., *Beni Hasan, Pt. IV* (London: Egypt Exploration Fund, 1900), 1.

6. M. Naville, Percy Newberry, George Willoughby Fraser, *The Season's Work at Beni Hasan 1890–1891* (London: Egypt Exploration Fund, 1891), 11.

7. Griffith, 1–2.

8. T. G. H. James, *Howard Carter: The Path to Tutankhamun* (New York: Keegan Paul, 1992), 129.

9. Edouard Naville, *The Temple of Deir el Bahari*, vol. 3 (London: Egyptian Exploration Fund, 1894–1908), 13.

10. Hope Waters and David Waters, *The Saluki in History, Art, and Sport* (Newton Abbot, England: David & Charles, 1969), 20.

11. Norman De Garis Davies, *The Tomb of Rekhmire at Thebes* (New York: Arno Press, 1973), 26–27.

Chapter 6

1. "The Hound Show at Ranelagh," *Country Life Illustrated*, June 16, 1900, 783.

2. Hugh Dalziel, *British Dogs*, vol. 1, 2nd ed. (London: L. Upcott Gill, 1887). The first edition was published serially between 1879–80.

3. "Kennel Notes," *Country Life Illustrated*, July 16, 1898, 60.

4. Herbert Compton, *The Twentieth Century Dog (Sporting)* (London: Grant Richards, 1904), 445.

5. H. W. Bush, "Greyhounds (Eastern)," in *Kennel Encyclopædia*, vol. 2, ed. J. Sidney Turner (London: Sir W. C. Leng, 1908), 747.

6. William Youatt, *The Dog* (London: Longmans, Green, 1886) 42.

7. *The Kennel*, April 1911, 24.

8. A. Croxton Smith, "Major Bell-Murray's Afghan Hounds," *Country Life*, December 2, 1922, 717.

9. Wilfrid Scawen Blunt, *My Diaries: Being a Personal Narrative of Events, 1888–1914*, vol. 2 (New York: Alfred A. Knopf, 1921), 38.

10. Rosemary Archer and James Fleming, eds., *Lady Anne Blunt: Journals and Correspondence 1878–1917* (Cheltenham, Gloucestershire: Alexander Heriot, 1986), 290.

11. Philip Graves, *The Life of Sir Percy Cox* (London: Hutchinson, 1941), 323.

12. *Saluki or Gazelle Hound Club Annual Report*, 1930, 2.

13. Charles Lock Mowat, *Britain Between the Wars 1918–1940* (Chicago: University of Illinois Press, 1958), 231.

14. *Crufts Show Catalog*, 1898, 30.

15. James W. Trimbee and Jean Trimbee McKenzie, *A Trail of Trials* (Edinburgh: Pentland Press, 1995), 56–57.

16. Theo Aronson, *Royal Vendetta: The Crown of Spain 1829–1965* (Indianapolis: Bobbs-Merrill, 1965), 180.

Chapter 7

1. T. G. H. James, *Howard Carter: The Path to Tutankhamun* (London: Keegan Paul International, 1992) 136.

2. "Introduction to the Amherst Family Papers," The Hackney Archives, Rose Lipman Library, London, Acc. No. 1982/1.

3. Laureen Baillie and Paul Sievking, eds., *British Biographical Archive* (New York: Saur, 1984), microfiche #288–298.

4. Cherry Drummond, *The Remarkable Life of Victoria Drummond, Marine Engineer* (London: Institute of Marine Engineers, 1994), 39.

5. "The Slughi or Gazelle-Hound," *Country Life*, 1906, 47–49.

6. Kim Dennis-Bryan and Juliet Clutton-Brock, *Dogs of the Last Hundred Years at the British Museum (Natural History)* (London: British Museum, 1988), 15–16.

7. Brian Patrick Duggan, "Origins of the First Breed Standard," *Saluki International* no. 18 (Spring/Summer 2001), 30.

8. Florence Amherst, "Oriental Greyhounds," *The New Book of the Dog*, ed. Robert Leighton (London: Cassell, 1907), 474.

9. J. Sidney Turner, *The Kennel Encyclopædia* (London: Sir W. C. Leng, 1908), 746.

10. Amherst, 475.

11. James, 136.

12. Jean Strouse, *Morgan: American Financier* (New York: Random House, 1999), 606.

13. Ibid.

14. A. Croxton Smith, *Everyman's Book of the Dog* (London: Hodder and Stoughton, 1909), 253.

15. A. Croxton Smith, "Kennel Notes," *Country Life*, August 27, 1910, 305.

16. Warren R. Dawson and Eric P. Uphill, *Who Was Who in Egyptology* (London: Egypt Exploration Society, 1995), 14.

17. David Butters (Swaffham Museum), letter to the author, December 17, 1996.

18. *Didlington Estate Sale Catalog 1910*, Norfolk Record Office, MC 68/1[518x8].

Chapter 8

1. T. E. Lawrence to Florence Amherst, Bodleian Library, MS. Eng. D. 3327, fols. 6a–b.

2. Edward K. Aldrich, "Salukis," *American Kennel Club Gazette*, March 1, 1940, 41.

3. *A Guide to the Domesticated Animals (Other Than Horses) Exhibited in the Central and North Halls of the British Museum*, The British Museum (London: British Museum, 1912), 32.

4. Ibid.

5. Jean James, "'Salukis' by The Honourable Florence Amherst," *The Saluki* 7, no. 2 (Autumn/Winter 1975), 4.

6. Florence Amherst, "The Gazelle Hound or Saluki Shami," *Saluki International* 5 no. 9 (Autumn/Winter 1996), 37–39.

7. Edward K. Aldrich, "Salukis," *American Kennel Club Gazette*, March 1, 1937.

8. Freeman Lloyd, "Dogs and Their Owners," *Dress and Vanity Fair*, October 1913, 110.

9. Jeremy Wilson, *Lawrence of Arabia: The Authorized Biography of T. E. Lawrence* (New York: Atheneum, 1990), 99.

10. T. E. Lawrence to Florence Amherst, Bodleian Library, MS Eng. D. 3327, fols. 4–5.

11. Robert Graves and Liddell Hart, *T. E. Lawrence to His Biographers* (Garden City: Doubleday, 1963), 74.

12. T. E. Lawrence, *The Letters of T. E. Lawrence*, edited by David Garnett, 2nd ed. (New York: Doubleday, 1939), 150.

13. Edward K. Aldrich, "Salukis," *American Kennel Club Gazette*, June 1, 1940, 31.

14. Lawrence to Amherst, Bodleian Library, MS Eng. D. 3327, fols. 6a–b.

15. T. E. Lawrence to David Hogarth, Bodleian Library, MS. Eng. D. 3335, fols. 141b–42.

16. T. E. Lawrence to Florence Amherst, Bodleian Library, MS. Eng. D. 3327, fols. 7–8.

17. T. E. Lawrence to Fareedah el Akle, Bodleian Library, MS. Eng. C. 6737, fols. 88a–b.

18. T. E. Lawrence, *T. E. Lawrence: The Selected Letters*, edited by Malcolm Brown (New York: W.W. Norton, 1989), 40.

19. T. E. Lawrence to Fareedah el Akle, Bodleian Library, MS. Eng. C. 6737, fols. 89a–b.

20. Jeremy Wilson, *T. E. Lawrence* (London: National Portrait Gallery Publications, 1988) 43.

21. T. E. Lawrence to Fareedah el Akle, Bodleian Library, MS. Eng. C. 3327, fol. 133.

Chapter 9

1. Albert M. Lythgoe, "Statues of the Goddess Sekhmet," *Bulletin of the Metropolitan Museum of Art*, Part II, October 1919, 3.

2. *Crufts Catalog*, February 1915, 115.

3. A. Croxton Smith, "Ladies Kennel Association Show," *Country Life*, June 19, 1915, 883.

4. "The Amherstias: Recollections and Reflections," *Saluki Heritage* no. 6 (1984), 38.

5. Cherry Drummond, *The Remarkable Life of Victoria Drummond, Marine Engineer* (London: Institute of Marine Engineers, 1994), 58.

6. Ibid., 53.

7. George Cecil, letter to author, February 17, 2003.

Chapter 10

1. Jeremy Wilson, *Lawrence of Arabia: The Authorized Biography of T .E. Lawrence* (New York: Atheneum, 1990), 152–3.

2. T. G. H. James, *Howard Carter: The Path to Tutankhamun*, 176.

3. Ibid.

4. Ibid., 175–6.

5. Ibid., 177.

6. Wilson, 257.

7. Ibid., 287.

8. R.C.R. Owen to Wilfred Jennings-Bramly, March 8, 1906 Royal Geographical Society, RGS/LMS/B 40.

9. Robert Graves and Liddell Hart, *T.E. Lawrence to His Biographers*, vol. 2 (Garden City, NY: Doubleday, 1963), 89.

10. Conversation with Vivien Betti, April 29, 1997.

11. Jeremy Wilson, *T. E. Lawrence* (London: National Portrait Gallery Publications, 1988), 50.

12. T. E. Lawrence to P.C. Joyce, November 13, 1917, Bodleian Library, MS. Eng. D. 3327, fol. 238 [with fols. 239–40 (short enclosures)].

13. S. C. Rolls, *Steel Chariots in the Desert* (London: J. Cape, London, 1937), 78–79, 143.

14. Ibid., 144.

15. Eric Barrass, letter to author, November 11, 1993.

16. Lowell Thomas, *With Lawrence in Arabia* (New York: Garden City, 1924), 314.

17. Bodleian Library, MS. Photograph C. 123/1, fol. 96.

18. Joel C. Hodson, *Lawrence of Arabia and American Culture* (Westport, CT: Greenwood Press, 1995), 18.

19. Bodleian Library, MS. Photograph C. 123/1, fol.84.

20. "Akaba Staff 1918, Lowell Thomas," Lawrence, T. E., LR P420, Harry Ransom Center, University of Texas at Austin.

21. Bravida, "100 Per Cent Dog," *Blackwood's Magazine*, February 1924, 254.

22. Horace W. H. White, "Reminiscence," *The Saluki*, Summer/Autumn 1987, 32–33.

23. T. E. Lawrence, *Seven Pillars of Wisdom*, Complete 1922 Oxford Text (Fordingbridge, Hampshire: J. and N. Wilson, 2004), 284.

24. Ibid., 288.

25. Alois Musil, *Arabia Petraea*, vol. 1 (Vienna: Kaiserliche Akademie der Wissenshcaften, 1907), 280.

26. Lawrence, *The Seven Pillars of Wisdom*, 694.

27. Lord Winterton, "Arabian Nights and Days," Part I, *Blackwood's Magazine* 207 (May 1920), 586.

28. Rex Hall, *The Desert Hath Pearls* (Melbourne: Hawthorne Press, 1975), 87.

29. Lawrence, *Seven Pillars of Wisdom*, 491.

30. Winterton, 594.

31. Winterton, "Arabian Nights and Days," Part II, *Blackwood's Magazine* 208 (June 1920), 756.

32. Maurice Andrew Brackenreed Johnston and K.D. Yearsley, *Four-Fifty Miles to Freedom* (Edinburgh: Blackwood & Sons, 1919), 59.

33. C. H. Stockley, "Hunting with Salukis in Northern Anatolia," *Dog World*, December 30, 1927, 1795.

34. Johnston and Yearsley, 59.

35. Alan Bott, *Eastern Nights and Flights* (Garden City, NY: Doubleday, Page, 1919), 77.

36. T. E. Lawrence, *Seven Pillars of Wisdom*, 798–800.

37. Walter Stirling, *Safety Last* (London: Hollis and Carter, 1953), 136.

Chapter 11

1. T. A. Heathcoate, *The Indian Army* (Newton Abbot: David & Charles, 1974), 84.

2. Byron Farwell, *Mr. Kipling's Army* (New York: W. W. Norton, 1981), 208.

3. Lionel Dawson, *Sport in War* (New York: Charles Scribner's Sons, 1937), 75.

4. Ibid., 76–77.

5. Charles Allen, ed., *Plain Tales from the Raj* (London: Futura Publications, 1983), 132.

6. Dawson, 79.

7. Rudyard Kipling, *Kim* (Oxford: Oxford University Press, 1998), 141.

8. E. G. Walsh, *Lurchers and Longdogs* (Gloucestershire: Standfast Press, 1977), 102.

9. Edward C. Ash, *Dogs: Their History and Development*, vol. 1 (London: Ernest Benn Limited, 1927), 196.

10. Edward K. Aldridge, "Salukis," *American Kennel Club Gazette*, March 1947, 64.

11. F. F. Lance, "The Saluki," in *Hounds and Dogs: Their Care, Training, and Working, The Lonsdale Library, Vol. XIII*, A. Croxton Smith, ed. (London: Seeley, Service, 1932), 260.

12. Lord Saltoun, *Scraps*, vol. II (London: Longmans, 1883), 257 et seq.

13. Edward K. Aldridge, *American Kennel Club Gazette*, July 1947, 78.

14. Kipling, *Kim*, 129.

15. H. Hudson, *History of the 19th King George's Own Lancers 1858–1921* (Aldershot: Gale & Polden, 1937), 115.

16. W. F. Stirling, *Safety Last* (London: Hollis and Carter, 1953), 94.

17. Saskia Jungeling and Han Jungeling, "The History of the Saluki in the Netherlands, Part 1," *Saluki World*, Fall 1971, 28.

18. Hudson, 249.

Chapter 12

1. "Salukis," *American Kennel Club Gazette*, September 1936, 32.

2. Bravida, "100 Per Cent Dog," *Blackwood's Magazine*, February 1924, 248.

3. Correspondence, *The Illustrated Kennel News*, October 6, 1919.

4. W. T. Massey, *The Desert Campaigns* (London: Constable, 1918), 126.

5. E. V. Knox, "Proof Positive," *Dog Stories from Punch*, 5th ed. (London: Clement Ingleby, 1926), 55.

6. Bravida, "The Armageddon Hunt," *Blackwood's Magazine*, Jan. 1924, 19.

7. G. M. Angel, "Salukis," *Dog World*, October 10, 1941.

8. D. C. Pimm, "Hunting with the Exodus at Habbaniya," *The Field*, June 14, 1941, 738.

9. Lionel Dawson, *Sport in War* (New York: Charles Scribner's Sons, 1937), 87.

10. R. M. P. Preston, *The Desert Mounted Corps: An Account of Cavalry Operations in Palestine and Syria, 1917–1918* (London: Constable, 1921), 301.

11. G. E. Badcock, *A History of the Transport Services of the Egyptian Expeditionary Force 1916–1917–1918* (London: Hugh Rees, 1925), 320.

12. Ibid., 319.

13. Quoted in H. Hudson, *History of the 19th King George's Own Lancers, 1858–1921* (Aldershot: Gale & Polden, 1937) 211.

14. Letter to the editor, *Country Life*, May 128, 921, 656.

15. Letter to the editor, *Country Life*, July 12, 1919, 64.

16. Naftali Thalman, "Introducing Modern Agriculture into Nineteenth-Century Palestine: The German Templars," in *The Land that Became Israel*, edited by Ruth Kark (New Haven, CT: Yale University Press, 1990), 90–91.

17. Bravida, "The Armageddon Hunt," 30.

18. Ibid.

19. G. G., "Astride v. Side-Saddle," *Country Life*, December 12, 1925, 921–2.

20. *Palestine and Transjordan* (England: Geographical Handbook Series, Naval Intelligence Division, 1943), 322.

21. F. Fitzhugh Lance, "Gazelle Hunting in Palestine," *Cavalry Journal* no. 51, reprinted in *Saluki International*, Spring/Summer 2004, 17–18.

22. H. Hudson, *History of the 19th King George's Own Lancers, 1858–1921*, 370.

23. Florence Amherst, "The 'Saluki Shami' or Gazelle Hound," *Dog World: Dogs of the Year 1924–25*, 16.

24. "Salukis," *American Kennel Gazette*, June 1, 1940, 32.

25. Esther Bliss Knapp, "Salukis," *American Kennel Club Gazette*, July 1955, 53–54.

26. "Salukis," *American Kennel Gazette*, September 1, 1936, 32.

27. Salukis," *American Kennel Gazette*, November 1, 1936, 37.

28. S. S. Flower, *Report on the Zoological Service for the Year 1920* (Cairo: Government Press, 1921), 10–11.

29. Byron Farwell, *Mr. Kipling's Army* (New York: W. W. Norton, 1981), 42.

30. *Kennel Gazette*, June 1919, 109.

31. Ibid., January 1919, 2.

32. Ibid., February 1919, 23.

Chapter 13

1. *The Field*, December 2, 1922, 813.

2. A. Croxton Smith, "A Great Show of Sporting Dogs," *Country Life*, February 18, 1922, 199.

3. T. G. H. James, *Howard Carter: The Path to Tu-*

tankhamun (London: Keegan Paul International, 1992), 208–209.

4. Warren R. Dawson and Eric P. Uphill, *Who Was Who in Egyptology* (London: Egypt Exploration Society, 1995) 14.

5. *Kelly's Directory of Kent*, 1930.

6. *The Field*, June 28, 1923, 989.

7. Colin Bayne-Jardine, letter to the author, April 30, 2002.

8. Colin Bayne-Jardine, *The Retreat from Syria*, unpublished manuscript, 4.

9. Ibid.

10. Ibid., 7.

11. Bravida, "The Armageddon Hunt," *Blackwood's Magazine*, January 1924, 24.

12. Ibid., 11.

13. Ibid., 16.

14. Colin Bayne-Jardine letter to the author, April 30, 2002.

15. Ibid.

16. June Applebee-Burt, "The Influence of the Desert-Bred Saluki in Britain," in *Saluqi: Coursing Hound of the Middle East*, edited by Gail Goodman (Apache Junction, AZ: Midbar, 1995), 357.

17. Noel Botham and Peter Donnelly, *Valentino: The Love God* (New York: Ace Books, 1976), 100.

18. Ibid., 104.

19. Charles Loch Mowat, *Britain Between the Wars 1918–1940* (Chicago: University of Chicago Press, 1955), 250.

20. Ibid.

21. "Cinema Supplement," *London Times*, February 21, 1922, xvii.

22. Joel C. Hodson, *Lawrence of Arabia and American Culture* (Westport, CT: Greenwood Press, 1995), 66.

23. "The Voice from the Minaret," Internet Movie Database, http://www.imdb.com/title/tt0014583 (accessed June 15, 2008).

Chapter 14

1. Howard Carter and A. C. Mace, *The Tomb of Tut-Ankh-Amen*, vol. 2 (New York: Cooper Square Publishers, 1963), 17.

2. Katherine Stoddart Gilbert, Joan K. Holt, and Sara Hudson, eds. *Treasures of Tutankhamun* (New York: Metropolitan Museum of Art, 1976), 12.

3. T.G.H. James, *Howard Carter: The Path to Tutankhamun* (London: Keegan Paul International, 1992), 217.

4. Ibid., 215.

5. Zaki El Habashi, *Tutankhamun and the Sporting Traditions* (New York: Peter Lang Publishing, 1992), 139.

6. James, 218.

7. Ibid., 230.

8. Carter and Mace, vol. 1, 111.

9. El Habashi, 153.

10. James, 151.

11. Carter and Mace, vol. 2, 16.

12. "An Egyptian Treasure: Great Find at Thebes: Lord Carnarvon's Long Quest," *London Times*, November 30, 1922, 13.

13. *Tatler* (London), January 10, 1923.

14. "Kennel Notes, Miscellaneous," *The Field* (London), February 1, 1923, 170.

15. *Cruft's Catalog*, 1923, 173.

16. Robert Leighton, "Cruft's Show: Persian Greyhounds," *The Kennel Gazette*, February 1923, 95.

17. "Minutes of the Inaugural Meeting of the Saluki or Gazelle Hound Club," *The Saluki*, 1998 Champion Show Edition, 10–13.

18. J. McLeish and J. Applebee, "History of the Saluki or Gazelle Hound Club," in *The Saluki Book of British Champions 1923–1973*, Ann Birrell and Hope Waters, eds. (New Malden & Haselmere, Surrey: Trendell's, 1981) n.p.

19. "Salukis," *American Kennel Club Gazette*, February 1, 1936, 33.

20. A. Croxton Smith, *Dogs Since 1900* (London: Andrew Dakers Limited, 1950), 75.

21. "Ladies Kennel Association Notes," *Tatler* (London), February 28, 1923.

22. "Minutes of the Inaugural Meeting of the Saluki or Gazelle Hound Club," 10–13.

23. Ibid.

24. McLeish and Applebee, n.p.

25. Brian Patrick Duggan, "Origins of the First Breed Standard," *Saluki International* no. 18 (Spring/Summer 2001), 30.

26. A. Croxton Smith, "The Father of the Greyhounds," *The Field*, May 1923, 28.

27. June Applebee-Burt,"The Influence of the Desert Bred Saluki in Britain," in *The Saluqi: Coursing Hound of the East*, edited by Gail Goodman, 357.

28. G.M. Lance, "Salukis," *Dog World*, March 5, 1925.

29. "Kennel Notes, Miscellaneous," *The Field*, June 28, 1923, 989.

30. *Kennel Club Calendar and Stud Book*, 1923, 15.

31. Ibid.

Chapter 15

1. Robert Leighton, "Foreign Dogs: Salukis," *The Kennel Gazette*, October 1923, 710.

2. *The Field*, March 8, 1923, 358.

3. Leighton, "Foreign Dogs: Salukis," 710.

4. F.F. Lance, "Salukis," *The Kennel Gazette*, October 1924, 757.

5. G. M. Lance, "Salukis," *Dog World*, May 28, 1925.

6. Cherry Drummond, *The Remarkable Life of Victoria Drummond, Marine Engineer* (London: Institute of Marine Engineers, 1994), 104.

7. Gerald De Gaury, *Three Kings in Baghdad: 1921–1958* (London: Hutchinson, 1961), 77.

8. Ibid.

9. A. J. Barker, *The Bastard War: The Mesopotamian Campaign of 1914–1918* (New York: Dial Press, 1967), 80.

10. Gertrude Bell to her father, February 7, 1921, Gertrude Bell Archives, Newcastle University, http://www.gerty.ncl.ac.uk.

11. De Gaury, *Three Kings in Baghdad*, 77.

12. George N. Curzon, *Persia and the Persian Question* (New York: Barnes & Noble, 1966), 280.

13. Freya Stark, *The Valley of the Assassins* (London: John Murray, 1947), 148.

14. Curzon, *Persia and the Persian Question*, 280.

15. Gertrude Bell to her father, March 12, 1921, Gertrude Bell Archives, Newcastle University, http://www.gerty.ncl.ac.uk.

16. Freya Stark, *The Valley of the Assassins* (London, John Murray, 1947), 48–49.

17. Amin Banani, The *Modernization of Iran 1921–1941* (Stanford, Calif.: Stanford University Press, 1961), 41.

18. Gertrude Bell to her father, January 15, 1925,

Gertrude Bell Archives, Newcastle University, http://www.gerty.ncl.ac.uk.

19. Arnold T., Wilson, *Loyalties: Mesopotamia 1914–1917*, vol. 1, 3rd ed. (London: Oxford University Press, 1936), viii–ix.

20. Gertrude Lowthian Bell, *Amurath to Amurath*, 2nd ed. (London: Macmillan, 1924), 247–248.

21. A. W. D Bentinck, "Imported Salukis," *Country Life*, November 15, 1924, 769.

22. A. Croxton Smith, "The Significance of Crufts," *Country Life*, February 23, 1924, 271.

23. Ibid., 272–273.

24. G. M. Lance, "Salukis," *Dog World*, December 10, 1926.

25. Register of Nurses, Westminster Training School, 1899–1949 (H02/WH/C02/01014), London Metropolitan Archives.

26. *Palestine and Transjordan.* Geographical Handbook Series (Great Britain, Naval Intelligence Division, 1943), 190.

27. Ibid., 332.

28. Member's Roll, Royal College of Nursing, 1923, 414.

29. "Obituary for Joan Mitchell, 1954," *The Saluki* 19, no. 1 (1977).

30. G. M. Lance, "Salukis," *Dog World*, September 26, 1924, 1227.

31. Ibid., 757.

32. Jeremy Wilson, *T. E. Lawrence* (London: National Portrait Gallery Publications, 1988), 135.

33. Jeremy Wilson, *Lawrence of Arabia* (New York: Atheneum, 1990), 625.

34. Ibid., 626.

35. Joel C. Hodson, *Lawrence of Arabia and American Culture* (Westport, CT: Greenwood Press, 1995), 51.

36. T. E. Lawrence to David Hogarth, Bodleian Library, MS. Eng. D. 3335, fols. 141b-142.

37. Nigel Nicolson, ed., *Harold Nicolson, Diaries and Letters 1930–1939* (New York: Atheneum, 1966), 154.

Chapter 16

1. *Saluki or Gazelle Hound Club Annual Report 1928*, 2.

2. G. M. Lance, "Salukis," *Dog World*, December 5, 1924, 1707.

3. Ibid.

4. "Sarona Salukis Classified Advertisement," *Dog World*, Sept. 3, 1925.

5. "Sarona Salukis Classified Advertisement," *Dog World*, Aug. 6, 1926.

6. *The Kennel Gazette* (London), March 1925, 165.

7. G. M. Lance, "Salukis," *Dog World*, April 29, 1926.

8. Ibid., April 15, 1927.

9. Francis Joan Mitchell to Natural History Museum, April 24, 1926.

10. Ken Allan, "The Sarona Album," *Saluki International* 3, no. 6 (Spring/Summer 1995), 42.

11. Arthur Craven, *Dogs of the World* (Manchester: A. Craven, 1930), 169.

12. Charles Loch Mowat, *Britain Between the Wars 1918–1940* (Chicago: University of Chicago Press, 1955), 249.

13. Ibid.

14. G. M. Lance, "Salukis," *Dog World*, November 11, 1927.

15. *Saluki or Gazelle Hound Club Annual Report 1927*, 3.

16. "The Saronas: Recollections and Reflections," *Saluki Heritage* #5 (Autumn 1983), 49.

17. R. E. Cheesman, *In Unknown Arabia* (London: Macmillan, 1926) 125.

18. C. S. Jarvis, *Arab Command* (London: Hutchinson & Co., 1942), 53.

19. C. S. Jarvis, *Yesterday and To-Day in Sinai* (Edinburgh: William Blackwood & Sons, 1931), 211–12.

20. Hope Waters and David Waters, *The Saluki in History, Art and Sport* (Newton Abbot, Devon: David & Charles, 1969), 34.

21. "Saluki Column," *Dog World*, August 27, 1925, 1324.

22. T. G. H. James, *Howard Carter: The Path to Tutankhamun* (London: Keegan Paul International, 1992), 249.

23. Catherine Kuhl and Carlene Kuhl, "Eastern Influences on the American Saluki," in *Saluqi: Coursing Hound of the Middle East*, edited by Gail Goodman (Apache Junction, Arizona: Midbar, 1995), 436.

24. Charles Belgrave, *Personal Column* (London: Hutchinson, 1960), 20.

25. Ibid., 79.

26. "The Soldier's Dog: A Perilous Privilege," *Dog World*, October 22, 1925.

27. Ulrich Thieme and Felix Becker, *Allgemeines Lexicon der Bildenden Künstler*, vol.I (Leipzig: E. A. Seeman, 1907), 274.

28. John Pope-Hennessy, *Cellini* (New York: Abbeville Press, 1985), 225.

29. Ibid., 226.

30. "Salukis," *American Kennel Club Gazette*, August 1, 1941, 22.

31. G. M. Lance, "Salukis," *Dog World*, November 4, 1927.

32. "Dogs of the Bible: The Newest Fad," *Literary Digest*, February 26, 1927, 46.

33. Jeremy Wilson, *T. E. Lawrence* (London: National Portrait Gallery Publications, 1988), 148.

34. Percival Christopher Wren, *Beau Sabreur* (New York: Permabooks, 1953), 87–88.

35. "Our Leading Light," *Dog World*, August 27, 1925, 1317.

36. G. M. Lance, "Salukis," *Dog World*, July 15, 1926.

37. The Hackney Archives, Rose Lipman Library, London, Acc. No # D/F/AMH #333.

38. *London Times*, February 7, 1926, 17.

39. G. Cooper (press officer, Kent County Fire Brigade), letter to the author, February 5, 1997.

Chapter 17

1. C. S. Jarvis, *The Back Garden of Allah*, 9th ed. (London: John Murray, 1949), 163.

2. E. T. Williams and C. S. Nicholls, eds., *Dictionary of National Biography*, 1961–1970 (Oxford: Oxford University Press, 1981), 189.

3. R. E. Cheesman, "The Fifth Battalion 'The Buffs' (East Kent Regt.) and the Wye College Contingent," *Journal of the Agricola Club* 9, no. 49 (1939), 317.

4. Ibid., 321.

5. Williams and Nicholls, 189.

6. Ibid., 190.

7. R. E. Cheesman, *In Unknown Arabia* (London: Macmillan, 1926), 253–254.

8. Ibid., 301.

9. Ibid., 269.

10. Ibid.

11. Ibid., 276.

12. Ibid., 279.

13. Ibid., 281–5.

14. G. Rex Smith, "The Saluqi in Islam," in *Saluqi: Coursing Hound of the East*, edited by Gail Goodman (Bramble Junction, Arizona: Midbar, 1995), 91.

15. Cheesman, *In Unknown Arabia*, 302.

16. Ibid., 304

17. Ibid.

18. Ibid.

19. Ibid., 333–334.

20. R. E. Cheesman, *Lake Tana and the Blue Nile* (London: Frank Cass, 1968), 1.

21. C. S. Jarvis, *Half a Life*, 2nd ed. (London: John Murray, 1943), 77–78.

22. Ibid., 161.

23. Ibid., 197–198.

24. C. S. Jarvis, *Happy Yesterdays*, 2nd ed. (London: John Murray, 1951), 114.

25. C. S. Jarvis, *Desert and Delta*, 4th ed. (London: John Murray, 1947), 74–75.

26. C. S. Jarvis, *The Back Garden of Allah*, 9th ed. (London: John Murray, 1949), 87.

27. C. S. Jarvis, *Innocent Pursuits* (London: John Murray, 1953), 88.

28. C. S. Jarvis, *Three Deserts*, 10th ed. (London: John Murray, 1947), 40.

29. Ibid., 61–62.

30. Walter F Stirling, *Safety Last*, 2nd ed. (London: Hollis & Carter, 1953), 110.

31. C. S. Jarvis, *The Back Garden of Allah*, 62.

32. C. S. Jarvis, *Heresies and Humours*, 2nd ed. (London: Country Life, 1945), 126.

33. Jarvis, *Three Deserts*, 243–244.

34. Ibid., 238–239.

35. Ibid., 230.

36. Jarvis, *Heresies and Humours*, 78.

37. J. H. C. Lawlor, Letter to the editor, *The Field*, March 11, 1944.

38. Jarvis, *Three Deserts*, 270.

39. Ibid., 258.

40. Ibid., 256.

41. Scudamore Jarvis, "A Sinai Wandering," *Blackwood's Magazine*, July 1930, 42.

42. Jarvis, *Three Deserts*, 255–256.

43. Ibid., 257.

44. Ibid., 267–269.

45. Ibid., 269.

46. C. S. Jarvis, *Yesterday and Today in Sinai*, 2nd ed. (Edinburgh: William Blackwood & Sons, 1931), 62.

47. Ibid., 301.

48. Jarvis, *Desert & Delta*, 288.

49. Jarvis, *The Back Garden of Allah*, 62–63.

50. Jarvis, *Three Deserts*, 260.

51. Ibid., 264–5.

52. Jarvis, *Desert and Delta*, 46.

53. Jarvis *Three Deserts*, 265–66.

54. Ibid., 271.

55. Ibid., 275.

Chapter 18

1. Florence Amherst, "The Dog of the Burning Sands," *American Kennel Club Gazette*, August 1, 1928, 96.

2. Michael Armitage, *The Royal Air Force: An Illustrated History* (London: Arms & Armour Press, 1993), 38.

3. Florence Amherst, "Saluki, or Gazelle Hound," in *Hutchinson's Dog Encyclopaedia*, ed. Walter Hutchinson (London: 1935), part 43, 1552.

4. J. A. McDonald, *The Royal Air Force Quarterly*, January 1939, 26–27.

5. James Offer, letter to the author, February 16, 1999.

6. Terence Clark, "Salukis of the Fairford Kennels," *The Saluki*, Crufts Edition, 2000, 44–48.

7. J. A. McDonald, *The Royal Air Force Quarterly*, January 1939, 30.

8. Ibid., 31.

9. H. R. P. Dickson, *The Arab of the Desert* (London: George Allen & Unwin, 1949), 7.

10. H. R. P. Dickson, *Kuwait and Her Neighbours* (London: George Allen & Unwin, 1956), 199.

11. Violet Dickson, *Forty Years in Kuwait* (London: George Allen & Unwin, 1971), 23.

12. Ibid., 24.

13. Ibid., 29.

14. H. R. P. Dickson, *The Arab of the Desert*, 377.

15. Ibid., 378.

16. Ibid.

17. Violet Dickson, "Arabian Remembrances," *American Saluki Association Newsletter*, July 1973, 28–29.

18. Gordon St. George Mark, "The Joyces of Merview Part II," *The Irish Genealogist* 9 no. 1 (1994), 91.

19. Ibid.

20. H. F. N. Jourdain, *The Connaught Rangers*, vol. 1 (London: United Service Institution, 1924), 598.

21. W. F. Stirling, *Safety Last* (London: Hollis & Carter, 1953), 32–32.

22. Obituary of Col. Joyce, *The Ranger Magazine*, #73, July 1965, 6–7.

23. Transcript of BBC Interview with Col. P. C. Joyce, July 14, 1941, University of London, King's College, Centre for Military Archives.

24. Ibid.

25. T. E. Lawrence, *Seven Pillars of Wisdom*, Complete 1922 Oxford Text (Fordingbridge, Hampshire: J. and N. Wilson, 2004), 349.

26. Bertram Thomas, *Alarms and Excursions in Arabia* (London: George Allen & Unwin, 1931), 71.

27. Robert O. Collins, ed., *An Arabian Diary: Sir Gilbert Falkingham Clayton* (Berkeley and Los Angeles: University of California Press, 1969), 159.

28. Gertrude Bell to her parents, January 5, 1922, Gertrude Bell Archives, Newcastle University, http://www.gerty.ncl.ac.uk.

29. Gertrude Bell to her father, November 17, 1925, Gertrude Bell Archives, Newcastle University, http://www.gerty.ncl.ac.uk.

30. G. M. Angel, "Salukis," *Dog World*, October 10, 1941.

31. D. C. Pim, "Hunting with the Exodus at Habbaniya," *The Field*, June 14, 1941, 738.

32. Ibid.

33. G.M. Lance, "Salukis," *Dog World*, March 26, 1925, 508.

34. Ibid., December 12, 1924, 1743.

35. Bertram Thomas, *Alarms and Excursions in Arabia*, 285–286.

36. A. J. Barker, *The Bastard War: The Mesopotamian Campaign of 1914–1918* (New York: Dial Press, 1967), 4.

37. Amherst, "The Dog of the Burning Sands," 32.

38. Ruth and Helen Hoffman, *We Married an Englishman* (London: Carrick & Evans, 1938), 121.

39. Amherst, "The Dog of the Burning Sands," 96.
40. Ibid.

Chapter 19

1. Alois Musil, *The Manners and Customs of the Rwala Bedouins* (New York: American Geographical Society, 1928), 208.
2. Susan Goodman, *Gertrude Bell* (Leamington Spa: Berg Publishers, 1985), 11.
3. Janet Wallach, *Desert Queen* (New York: Doubleday, 1996), 149.
4. Lady Bell, *The Letters of Gertrude Bell*, vol. 2 (New York: Horace Liveright, 1927), 471.
5. Gertrude Lowthian Bell, *The Desert and the Sown* (London: William Heineman, 1907), 168.
6. Lady Bell, vol. 1, 178.
7. Ibid., 200, 204.
8. Gertrude Bell Diaries, May 8 and 14, 1907, Gertrude Bell Archives, Newcastle University, http://www.gerty.ncl.ac.uk.
9. Gertrude Bell, Photograph Album, "Syria, Jordan, Saudi Arabia, Iraq 1913–1914," X-86, Gertrude Bell Archives, Newcastle University, http://www.gerty.ncl.ac.uk.
10. Lady Bell, vol. 2, 498.
11. Gertrude Bell to her stepmother, January 18, 1920, Gertrude Bell Archives, Newcastle University, http://www.gerty.ncl.ac.uk.
12. Lady Bell, vol. 2, 487.
13. Gertrude Bell to her father, June 1, 1920, Gertrude Bell Archives, Newcastle University, http://www.gerty.ncl.ac.uk.
14. Lady Bell, vol. 2, 674.
15. Gertrude Bell to her father, November 1, 1920, Gertrude Bell Archives, Newcastle University, http://www.gerty.ncl.ac.uk.
16. Arnold T. Wilson, *Loyalties: Mesopotamia 1914–1917*, vol. 1, 3rd ed. (London: Oxford University Press, 1936), 322.
17. Gertrude Bell to her father, June 17, 1925, Gertrude Bell Archives, Newcastle University, http://www.gerty.ncl.ac.uk.
18. Lady Bell, vol. 2, 725.
19. Vita Sackville-West, *Passenger to Teheran* (London: Leonard & Virginia Woolf at the Hogarth Press, 1926), 59.
20. Ibid., 59–60.
21. Janet Wallach, *Desert Queen*, 373.
22. Edward K. Aldrich, "Salukis," *American Kennel Club Gazette*, January 1, 1939, 32.
23. Sackville-West, *Passenger to Teheran*, 65–66.
24. James Lees-Milne, *Harold Nicolson: A Biography 1886–1929* (London: Chatto & Windus, 1981), 267.
25. Vita Sackville-West, *Faces: Profiles of Dogs* (Garden City: Doubleday, 1962), Ch. 3, "The Saluki or Gazelle Hound."
26. Nigel Nicolson, *Portrait of a Marriage* (New York: Atheneum, 1974), 213–214.
27. Sackville-West, *Faces*, Ibid.
28. *The Vita Sackville-West and Harold Nicholson Manuscripts, Letters and Diaries, from Sissinghurst Castle, Kent, the Huntington Library, California, and Other Libraries*, reel 9 (Brighton, Sussex: Harvester Microform, 1988), March 19, 1926.
29. Louise DeSalvo and Mitchell A. Leaska, ed., *The*

Letters of Vita Sackville-West to Virginia Woolf (New York: William Morrow, 1985), 109–110.
30. Nicolson, 202.
31. Virginia Woolf, *Orlando: A Biography* (New York: Harcourt, Brace & Jovanovich, 1956), 140.

Chapter 20

1. Sir Terence Clark, "Salukis of the Fairford Kennels," *The Saluki*, Cruft's Edtion 2000, 44–48.
2. G.M. Lance, "Salukis," *Dog World*, October 19, 1928, 157.
3. Gertrude Bell to her father, June 17, 1925, Gertrude Bell Archives, Newcastle University, http://www.gerty.ncl.ac.uk
4. Ibid., June 17, 1925, and December 2, 1925.
5. *Catalogue of the Galway Dog Show Society's First Annual Show*, Irish Kennel Club Archives, July 9, 1936, 10.
6. John Waterlow Lance, letter to the author, October 8, 1993.
7. Ibid.
8. W. Hally, "Saluki Subjects," *Our Dogs*, March 13, 1936.
9. "Salukis," *American Kennel Club Gazette*, February 2, 1938, 50.
10. H. Rob Copeland, *The Village of Old Beckenham* (Bromley: H. Rob Copeland, 1970), 59.
11. John Wagstaff and Doris Pullen, ed., *Beckenham: An Anthology of Local History* (London: Historical Association, 1984), 55.
12. Joan McLeish, "The Ebni & Binte El Nablous Trophy," *The Saluki*, Winter/Spring 1985, 5.
13. Ibid.
14. June Applebee, *The Saluki* 6, no.1 (Spring/Summer 1974), 26.
15. John Wagstaff and Doris Pullen, *Beckenham*, 37.
16. "The Amherstias: Records and Reflections," *Saluki Heritage* 6, 38–39.
17. "Salukis," *American Kennel Club Gazette*, September 1, 1935, 37.
18. Ibid., June 1, 1936, 28.
19. Ibid., November 1, 1938, 31.
20. Ibid., January 1, 1937, 34.
21. Ibid., March 1, 1937, 37.
22. Lesley Wiggins, "Amherstia Records," *Saluki Heritage* no. 6, 45.
23. Advertisement for Hutchinson's Animals of All Countries, *The Times*, January 19, 1923, 15.
24. J. McLeish and J. Applebee, "History of the Saluki or Gazelle Hound Club," in *The Saluki Book of British Champions 1923–1973*, edited by Ann Birrell and Hope Waters (New Malden & Haselmere, Surrey: Trendell's, 1981), n.p.
25. Ibid.
26. M. Towgood, "Saluki Affairs," *Our Dogs*, May 29, 1936, 685.
27. Ibid., February 14, 1936, 478.
28. Ibid.
29. Ibid.
30. Ibid., April 17, 1936, 205.
31. Ibid., April 10, 1936, 127.
32. *The Sketch*, September 24, 1930.
33. "Looking at Life: Parade at Cruft's Dog Show Yesterday," *The Daily Mail*, February 8, 1934.
34. Mitford Brice, *The Tale of Your Dog* (London: William Heinemann, 1934), "The Saluki" chapter, n.p.

35. "Saluki Subjects," *Our Dogs*, October 28, 1927.

36. "Salukis," *American Kennel Club Gazette*, December 1, 1934, 79; "Salukis," *American Kennel Club Gazette*, September 1, 1935, 37.

37. "Salukis," *American Kennel Club Gazette*, May 1, 1936, 29.

38. Ibid.

39. Brian Duggan, "The Saluki Filmography," *Saluki International* 5, no. 9 (Autumn/Winter 1996), 21.

40. Ibid.

41. A. Croxton Smith, *Dogs Since 1900* (London: Andrew Dakers, 1959), 74.

42. Lee M. Schoen, "Civilian Dogs in England," *American Kennel Club Gazette*, November 1944, 11.

43. Tom Rook, "Back to Our Roots," *The Saluki*, Winter/Spring 1987, 6.

44. J. McLeish and J. Applebee, "History of the Saluki or Gazelle Hound Club," n.p.

45. G. M. Angel, "Salukis," *Dog World*, December 1, 1939.

46. June Applebee, "Mazuri Is Swahili for Good or Beautiful," *The Saluki*, Summer/Autumn 1985, 18.

Chapter 21

1. William R. Polk and William J. Mares, *Passing Brave* (New York: Alfred Knopf, 1973), 39.

2. Freya Stark, *East Is West*, 4th ed. (London: John Murray, 1947), 79.

3. Eric Inman and Nancy Tonkin, *Beckenham* (Chichester, West Sussex: Phillimore, 2002), 127.

4. Obituary for Howard Carter, *The Times*, March 3, 1939.

5. "The Amherstias: Recollections & Reflections," *Saluki Heritage* no. 6 (1984), 38–9.

6. Kim Dennis-Bryan and Juliet Clutton-Brock, *Dogs of the Last Hundred Years at the British Museum (Natural History)* (London: British Museum, 1988), 26, 71, 100.

7. June Applebee, "Luman and Another," *The Saluki*, Winter/Spring 1985, 31.

Appendix 1

1. "Salukis," *American Kennel Club Gazette*, October 1946.

2. W. P. Moss, "Hunting Salugis," *Sport and Country*, January 4, 1946.

3. June Applebee-Burt, "The Influence of the Desert-Bred Saluki in Britain" in *The Saluqi: Coursing Hound of the Middle East*, edited by Gail Goodman (Apache Junction, Arizona, Midbar, 1995), 365.

Appendix 2

1. Wilfred Edgar Jennings-Bramly, "A Journey to Siwa in September and October, 1896," *The Geographical Journal* 10 (1897), 599.

2. G. W. Murray to *The Times*, March 23, 1960.

3. Ibid.

Bibliography

Books and Book Excerpts

Agate, James Evershed. *Lines of Communication: Being the Letters of a Temporary Officer in the Army Service Corps*. London: Constable, 1917.

Al-Sayyid, Afaf Lufti. *Egypt and Cromer: A Study in Anglo-Egyptian Relations*. London: John Murray, 1968.

Allan, Diana, and Ken Allan. *The Complete Saluki*. New York: Howell Book House, 1991.

Allen, Charles, ed. *Plain Tales from the Raj*. London: Futura Publications, 1983.

Amherst, Alicia. *A History of Gardening in England*. 3rd ed. New York: E. P. Dutton, 1910.

Amherst, Florence. "Oriental Greyhounds." In *The New Book of the Dog*, edited by Robert Leighton. London: Cassell, 1907.

_____. "Saluki, or Gazelle Hound." In *Hutchinson's Dog Encyclopædia*, edited by Walter Hutchinson. London: Hutchinson, 1935.

Amherst, Margaret Susan Mitford-Tyssen. *In a Good Cause*. London: Wells, Gardner, Darton, 1885.

Amherst of Hackney, Lord, and Basil Thomson. *The Discovery of the Solomon Islands by Alvaro De Medaña in 1568*. Vol. I. London: The Hakluyt Society, 1901.

Amherst of Hackney, Lady Margaret. *A Sketch of Egyptian History*. London: Methuen, 1904.

Applebee-Burt, June. "The Influence of the Desert-Bred Saluki in Britain." In *Saluqi: Coursing Hound of the Middle East*, edited by Gail Goodman. Apache Junction, Arizona: Midbar, 199).

Archer, Rosemary, and James Fleming, eds. *Lady Blunt: Journals and Correspondence 1878–1917*. Cheltenham, Gloucestershire: Alexander Heriot, 1986.

Armitage, Flora. *The Desert and the Stars: A Biography of Lawrence of Arabia*. New York: Henry Holt, 1955.

Armitage, Michael. *The Royal Air Force: An Illustrated History*. London: Arms & Armour Press, 1993.

The Army in India, 1850–1914: A Photographic Record. London: Hutchinson, in association with the National Army Museum, 1968.

Aronson, Theo. *Royal Vendetta: The Crown of Spain 1829–1965*. Indianapolis: Bobbs-Merrill, 1965.

Ash, Edward C. [Cecil] *The Book of the Greyhound*. London: Hutchinson, 1933.

_____. *Dogs and How to Know Them*. London: Epworth Press, 1925.

_____. *Dogs: Their History and Development*. 2 vols. London: Ernest Benn Limited, 1927.

_____. *The New Book of the Dog*. New York: MacMillan, 1939.

_____. *The Practical Dog Book*. New York: Derrydale Press, 1931.

_____. *Puppies: Their Choice, Care, and Training*. New York: MacMillan, 1934.

Badcock, G. E. *A History of the Transport Services of the Egyptian Expeditionary Force 1916–1917–1918*. London: Hugh Rees, 1925.

Baedeker, K. *Egypt and the Sudan: Handbook for Travelers*. 8th ed. London: Baedeker, 1929.

Baillie, Laureen, and Paul Sievking, eds. *British Biographical Archive*. New York: Saur, 1984.

Baily's Hunting Directory 1927–1928. London: Vinton, 1927.

Banani, Amin. The *Modernization of Iran 1921–1941*. Stanford, CA: Stanford University Press, 1961.

Barker, A. J. *The Bastard War: The Mesopotamian Campaign of 1914–1918*. New York: Dial Press, 1967.

Beaumont, Roger. *Sword of the Raj: The British Army in India, 1747–1947*. Indianapolis: Bobbs-Merrill, 1977.

Belgrave, Charles. *Personal Column*. London: Hutchinson, 1960.

Bell, Gertrude Lowthian. *Amurath to Amurath*. 2nd ed. London: Macmillan, 1924.

_____. *The Desert and the Sown*. London: William Heinemann, 1907.

Bell, Lady. *The Letters of Gertrude Bell*. 2 vols. New York: Horace Liveright, 1927.

Bentinck, Henry. *The Letters of Major Henry Bentinck*. London: Robert Scott, Roxburghe House, 1919.

Blunt, Anne. *Bedouin Tribes of the Euphrates*. New York: Harper & Brothers, 1879.

_____. *A Pilgrimage to Nejd*. 2 vols. London: J. Murray, 1881.

Blunt, Wilfrid Scawen. *My Diaries: Being a Personal Narrative of Events, 1888–1914*. 2 vols. New York: Alfred A. Knopf, 1921.

Botham, Noel, and Peter Donnelly. *Valentino The Love God*. New York: Ace Books, 1976.

Bott, Alan. *Eastern Nights and Flights*. Garden City & New York: Doubleday, Page, 1919.

Brewer, Douglas, Terence Clark, and Adrian Phillips. *Dogs in Antiquity—Anubis to Cerberus: The Origins of the Domestic Dog*. Warminster, England: Aris & Phillips, 2001.

Brice, Mitford. *The Tale of Your Dog*. London: William Heinemann, 1934.

Brown, William Robinson. *The Horse of the Desert*. New York: Derrydale Press, 1929.

Burton, Richard. *Personal Narrative of a Pilgrimage to Al-Medinah & Meccah*. Vol. 2. New York: Dover Publications, 1964.

Bush, H. W. "Greyhounds (Eastern)." In *Kennel Encyclopædia*, vol II., edited by J. Sidney Turner. London: Sir W. C. Leng, 1908.

Carman, W. Y. *A Dictionary of Military Uniform*. New York: Charles Scribner's Sons, 1977.

Carter, Howard, and A. C. Mace. *The Tomb of Tut-Ankh-Amen*. 3 vols. New York: Cooper Square Publishers, 1963.

Cecil, Lady William. *Bird Notes from the Nile*. London: Archibald Constable, 1904.

Chappell, Mike. *British Cavalry Equipments 1800–1941*. London: Osprey Publishing, 1983.

Cheesman, Evelyn. *Things Worthwhile*. London: Hutchinson, 1957.

Cheesman, R. E. *In Unknown Arabia*. London: Macmillan, 1926.

_____. *Lake Tana and The Blue Nile*. London: Frank Cass, 1968.

Christiansen, Keith, ed. *Giambattista Tiepolo 1696–1770*. New York: Metropolitan Museum of Art, 1996.

Cohen, Morton, ed. *Rudyard Kipling to Rider Haggard: The Record of a Friendship*. Florham, NJ: Fairleigh Dickinson University Press, 1965.

Collins, Robert O., ed. *An Arabian Diary: Sir Gilbert Falkingham Clayton*. Berkeley: University of California Press, 1969.

Compton, Herbert. *The Twentieth Century Dog. Vol. II, Sporting*. London: Grant Richards, 1904.

Cooper, Jilly. *Animals in War: Valiant Horses, Courageous Dogs, and Other Unsung Animal Heroes*. Guilford, CT: Lyons Press, 2002.

Copeland, H. Rob. *The Village of Old Beckenham*. Bromley: H. Rob Copeland, 1970.

Craster, J. M. *Fifteen Rounds a Minute: The Grenadiers at War, August to December 1914*. London: Macmillan, 1976.

Craven, Arthur. *Dogs of the World*. Manchester: A. Craven, 1930.

Cunliffe, Juliet. *Popular Sighthounds*. London: Popular Dogs, 1992.

Curzon, George N. *Persia and the Persian Question*. 2nd ed. New York: Barnes & Noble, 1966.

Dalziel, Hugh. *British Dogs*. Vol. I. 2nd ed. London: L. Upcott Gill, 1887.

Davies, Kristian. *The Orientalists: Western Artists in Arabia, The Sahara, Persia, & India*. New York: Laynfaroh, 2005.

Davies, Norman De Garis. *The Tomb of Rekhmire at Thebes*. New York: Arno Press, 1973.

Dawson, Lionel. *Sport in War*. New York: Charles Scribner's Sons, 1937.

Dawson, Warren R., and Eric P. Uphill. *Who Was Who in Egyptology*. London: Egypt Exploration Society, 1995.

Day, J. Wentworth. *The Dog in Sport*. London: George G. Harrap, 1938.

De Gaury, Gerald. *Three Kings in Baghdad: 1921–1958*. London: Hutchinson, 1961.

_____, and H. V. F. Winstone. *The Spirit of the East: An Anthology of Prose and Verse Inspired by the People, Places, and Legends of the East*. New York: Quartet Books, 1979.

Dennis-Bryan, Kim, and Juliet Clutton-Brock. *Dogs of the Last Hundred Years at the British Museum (Natural History)*. London: British Museum, 1988.

De Ricci, Seymour, ed. *A Hand-List of a Collection of Books and Manuscripts Belonging to the Right Hon. Lord Amherst of Hackney at Didlington Hall, Norfolk*. Cambridge: Cambridge University Press, 1906.

DeSalvo, Louise, and Mitchell A. Leaska, eds. *The Letters of Vita Sackville-West to Virginia Woolf*. New York: William Morrow, 1985.

Dickie, James. *The Dog*. London: Hutchinson, 1933.

Dickson, H. R. P. *The Arab of the Desert*. London: George Allen & Unwin, 1949.

_____. *Kuwait and Her Neighbours*. London: George Allen & Unwin, 1956.

Dickson, Violet. *Forty Years in Kuwait*. London: George Allen & Unwin, 1971.

Dictionary of National Biography, 1901–1911 Supplement. 5th ed. (Oxford: Oxford University Press, 1958).

Doughty, Charles M. *Travels in Arabia Deserta*. London: J. Cape & the Medici Society, 1926.

Drummond, Cherry. *The Remarkable Life of Victoria Drummond, Marine Engineer*. London: Institute of Marine Engineers, 1994.

Dumreicher, André von. *Trackers and Smugglers in the Deserts of Egypt*. London: Methuen & Co., 1931.

Dunning, H. W. *Today on the Nile*. New York: James Pott, 1905.

El Habashi, Zaki. *Tutankhamun and the Sporting Traditions*. (New York: Peter Lang Publishing, 1992.

Farwell, Byron. *Mr. Kipling's Army*. New York: W. W. Norton, 1981.

Festival of the Saluki 2007, Art Exhibition Catalog, Kennel Club Art Gallery. London: The Kennel Club, 2007.

Freeth, Zahra. *Kuwait was My Home*. London: George Allen & Unwin, 1956.

Gibson, Katharine. *The Goldsmith of Florence*. New York: Macmillan, 1929.

Gilbert, Katherine Stoddart, Joan K. Holt, and Sara Hudson, eds. *Treasures of Tutankhamun*. New York: Metropolitan Museum of Art, 1976.

Glendinning, Victoria. *Vita: The Life of Vita Sackville West*. London: Orion Publishing Group, 2005.

Goodman, Susan. *Gertrude Bell*. Leamington Spa: Berg Publishers, 1985.

Goodrich-Freer, A. *Arabs in Tent and Town*. London: Seeley, Service, 1924.

Graves, Philip. *The Life of Sir Percy Cox*. London: Hutchinson, 1941.

Graves, Robert. *Lawrence and the Arabs*. London: Jonathan Cape, 1927.

_____, and Liddell Hart. *T. E. Lawrence to His Biographers*. Garden City & New York: Doubleday, 1963.

Griffith, Francis L. *Beni Hasan*. Pt. IV. London: Egypt Exploration Fund, 1900.

A Guide to the Domesticated Animals (other than Horses) Exhibited in the Central and North Halls of the British Museum. London: British Museum, 1912.

Haag, Michael. *Alexandria*. Cairo: American University Press, 1993.

Hall, Donald. *British Orders, Decorations, and Medals*. St. Ives, England: Balfour Books, 1973.

Hall, Rex. *The Desert Hath Pearls*. Melbourne: Hawthorne Press, 1975.

Hardiman, James. *History of Galway*. 1820. Rpt. Galway: Connacht Tribune, 1958.

Harris, R. G., and Chris Warner. *Bengal Cavalry Regiments 1857–1914*. London: Osprey Publishing, 1979.

Hart, Liddell. *Colonel Lawrence: The Man Behind the Legend*. New York: Dodd, Mead, 1934.

Hay, Ian. *One Hundred Years of Army Nursing*. London: Cassell, 1953.

Hayman, John, ed. *Sir Richard Burton's Travels in Arabia and Africa: Four Lectures from the Huntington Library Manuscripts*. San Marino: Huntington Library, 1990.

Heathcoate, T. A. *The Indian Army*. Newton Abbot: David & Charles, 1974.

Hennessy, John Pope. *Cellini*. New York: Abbeville Press, 1985.

Hodson, Joel C. *Lawrence of Arabia and American Culture*, Westport, CT: Greenwood Press, 1995.

Hoffman, Ruth, and Helen Hoffman. *We Married an Englishman*. London: Carrick & Evans, 1938.

Howard, Michael, and John Sparrow. *The Coldstream Guards 1920–1946*. London: Oxford University Press, 1951.

Hubbard, Clifford L. B. *Dogs in Britain*. London: Macmillan, 1948.

Hudson, H. *History of the 19th King George's Own Lancers 1858–1921*. Aldershot: Gale & Polden, 1937.

Inman, Eric, and Nancy Tonkin. *Beckenham*. Chichester, West Sussex: Phillimore, 2002.

James, Lawrence. *The Savage Wars: British Campaigns in Africa 1870–1920*. New York: St. Martin's Press, 1985.

James, T. G. H., ed. *Excavating in Egypt: The Egypt Exploration Society 1882–1982*. Chicago: University of Chicago Press, 1982.

_____. *Howard Carter: The Path to Tutankhamun*. London: Keegan Paul International, 1992.

Jarvis, C. S. *Arab Command*. London: Hutchinson & Co., 1942.

_____. *The Back Garden of Allah*. 9th ed. London: John Murray, 1949.

_____. *Desert and Delta*. 4th ed. London: John Murray, 1947.

_____. *Half a Life*. 2nd ed. London: John Murray, 1943.

_____. *Happy Yesterdays*. 2nd ed. London: John Murray, 1951).

_____. *Heresies and Humours*. 2nd ed. London: Country Life, 1945.

_____. *Innocent Pursuits*. London: John Murray, 1953.

_____. *Three Deserts*. 10th ed. London: John Murray, 1947.

_____. *Yesterday and Today in Sinai*. 2nd ed. Edinburgh: William Blackwood & Sons, 1931.

Jesse, Edward. *Anecdotes of Dogs*. London: Bell & Daldy, 1870.

Johnston, Maurice Andrew Brackenreed, and K.D. Yearsley. *Four-Fifty Miles to Freedom*. Edinburgh: Blackwood & Sons, 1919.

Jourdain, H. F. N. *The Connaught Rangers*. 3 vols. London: United Service Institution, 192.

Kaleski, Robert. *Dogs of the World*. Sydney: William Brooks & Co., 1946.

Kaplan, Robert D. *The Arabists: The Romance of an American Elite*. New York: Free Press, 1993.

Kelly's Directory of Kent. London: Kelly, 1930.

Kipling, Rudyard. *Kim*. Oxford: Oxford University Press, 1998.

Knox, W. T. "Proof Positive." In *Dog Stories from Punch*. 5th ed. London: Clement Ingleby, 1926.

Kuhl, Catherine, and Carlene Kuhl. "Eastern Influences on the American Saluki." In *Saluqi: Coursing Hound of the Middle East*, edited by Gail Goodman. Apache Junction, AZ: Midbar, 1995.

Lance, F. F. "The Saluki." In *Hounds and Dogs: Their Care, Training, and Working*. Lonsdale Library, Vol. XIII. Edited by A. Croxton Smith. London: Seeley, Service, 1932.

Lawrence, T. E. *The Letters of T. E. Lawrence* 2nd ed. Edited by David Garnett. New York: Doubleday, 1939.

_____. *Revolt in The Desert*. New York: George H. Doran, 1928.

_____. *Seven Pillars of Wisdom*. Complete 1922 Oxford Text. Fordingbridge, Hampshire: J. and N. Wilson, 2004.

_____. *T. E. Lawrence: The Selected Letters*. Edited by Malcolm Brown. New York: W. W. Norton, 1989.

Layard, Austen H. *Discoveries in the Ruins at Nineveh and Babylon*. New York: G. P. Putnam, 1853.

Lees, Dorothy. "The Rualla." In *The Saluqi: Coursing*

Hound of the East, edited by Gail Goodman. Apache Junction, AZ: Midbar, 1995.

Lees-Milne, James. *Harold Nicolson: A Biography 1886–1929*. London: Chatto & Windus, 1981.

Lemish, Michael G. *War Dogs: A History of Loyalty and Heroism*. Dulles, VA: Potomac Books, 1999.

Lenczowski, George. *Iran under the Pahlavis*. Stanford, CA: Hoover Institute Press, 1978.

Lovell, Mary S. *Rebel Heart: The Scandalous Life of Jane Digby*. New York: W. W. Norton, 1995.

Lucas, Jocelyn. *Pedigree Dog Breeding for Pleasure or Profit*. 2nd ed. London: Simpkin, Marshall, Hamilton, Kent, 1925.

Manning, Samuel. *Egypt Illustrated*. New York: Hurst, 1892.

Marlowe, John. *Spoiling the Egyptians*. New York: St. Martin's Press, 1975.

Massey, W. T. *The Desert Campaigns*. London: Constable, 1918.

Mathew, H. C. G., and Biran Harrison, ed. *Oxford Dictionary of National Biography*. Oxford: Oxford University Press, 2004.

McGann, Susan. *The Battle of the Nurses*. London: Scutari Press, 1992.

McLeish, J., and J. Applebee. "History of the Saluki or Gazelle Hound Club." In *The Saluki Book of British Champions 1923–1973*, edited by Ann Birrell and Hope Waters. New Malden & Haselmere, Surrey: Trendell's, 1981.

Mellini, Peter. *Sir Eldon Gorst: The Overshadowed Proconsul*. Stanford, CA: Hoover Institution Press, 1977.

Mery, Fernand. *The Life, History, and Magic of the Dog*. New York: Grosset & Dunlap, 1968.

Messenger, Charles. *Trench Fighting, 1914–1918*. London: Pan/Ballantine, 1973.

Miller, Constance O. *Gazehounds: The Search for Truth*. Wheat Ridge, CO: Hoflin, 1988.

Morris, L. Robert, and Lawrence Raskin. *Lawrence of Arabia: the 30th Anniversary Pictorial History*. New York: Doubleday, 1992.

Mosely, Charles, ed. *Burke's Peerage & Baronetage*. 106th ed. 2 vols. Crans, Switzerland: Burke's Peerage (Genealogical Books) Ltd., 1999.

Mowat, Charles Lock. *Britain Between the Wars 1918–1940*. Chicago: University of Illinois Press, 1958.

Musil, Alois. *Arabia Petraea*. Vol. 1. Vienna: Kaiserliche Akademie der Wissenshcaften, 1907.

_____. *The Manners and Customs of the Rwala Bedouins*. New York: American Geographical Society, 1928.

Naville, Edouard. *The Season's Work at Beni Hasan 1890–1891*. 4 vols. London: Egypt Exploration Fund, 1891.

_____. *The Temple of Deir El Bahari*. Part III. 12 vols. London: Egypt Exploration Fund, 1898.

_____, Percy E. Newberry, and George Willoughby Fraser. *The Season's Work at Ahnas and Beni Hasan*. London: Gilbert & Rivington for the Egyptian Exploration Fund, 1891.

Newberry, Percy E. *The Amherst Papyri: Being an Account of the Egyptian Papyri in the Collection of the Right Hon. Lord Amherst of Hackney, FSA, at Didlington Hall, Norfolk*. London: Bernard Quaritch, 1899.

_____. *The Life of Rekhmara: Vizier of Upper Egypt under Thothmes III and Amenhetep II*. London: Archibald Constable, 1900.

Nicolson, Nigel, ed. *Harold Nicolson, Diaries and Letters 1930–1939*. New York: Atheneum, 1966.

_____. *Portrait of a Marriage*. New York: Atheneum, 1974.

Northampton, William George Spencer Scott Compton, 5th marquis of, Wilhelm Spiegelberg, and Percy E. Newberry. *Report on Some Excavations in the Theban Necropolis During the Winter of 1898–9*. London: Archibald Constable, 1908.

O'Brien, Rosemary, ed. *Gertrude Bell, The Arabian Diaries 1913–1914*. New York: Syracuse University Press, 2000.

Pakenham, Thomas. *The Boer War*. New York: Random House, 1979.

Palestine and Transjordan. Geographical Handbook Series. Great Britain, Naval Intelligence Division, 1943.

Percival, Christopher Wren. *Beau Sabreur*. New York: Permabooks, 1953.

Perry, George. *The Great British Picture Show: From the 90s to the 70s*. New York: Hill and Wang, 1974.

Philby, Harry St. John Bridger. *The Empty Quarter*. New York: Henry Holt, 1933.

_____. *The Heart of Arabia: A Record of Travel and Exploration*. New York: G. P. Putnam's Sons, 1923.

Pinches, Theophilus G., and William Amhurst Tyssen-Amherst. *The Amherst Tablets: Being an Account of the Babylonian Inscriptions in the Collection of the Right Hon. Lord Amherst of Hackney, FSA, at Didlington Hall, Norfolk*. London: Bernard Quaritch, 1908.

Polk, William R., and William J. Mares. *Passing Brave*. New York: Alfred Knopf, 1973.

Ponsonby, Frederick. *The Grenadier Guards in the Great War of 1914–1918*. London: Macmillan, 1920.

Preston, R. M. P. *The Desert Mounted Corps: An Account of Cavalry Operations in Palestine and Syria, 1917–1918*. London: Constable, 1921.

Raswan, Carl R. *Black Tents of Arabia: My Life Among the Bedouins*. New York: Creative Age Press, 1947.

_____. *Drinkers of the Wind*. New York: Creative Age Press, 1942.

Reeves, Nicholas, and John H. Taylor. *Howard Carter before Tutankhamun*. New York: Harry N. Abrams, 1993.

Reynolds-Ball, Eustace A. *Cairo: The City of the Caliphs* Boston: Dana Estes, 1898.

Robson, Phyllis. *Popular Dogs*. London: Popular Dogs, 1951.

Rockley, Lady (Alicia Amherst). *Historic Gardens of England*. London: Country Life Ltd., 1938.

Rolls, S. C. *Steel Chariots in the Desert* London: J. Cape, London, 1937.

Ross, Cathy. *Twenties London: A City in the Jazz Age.* London: Philip Wilson Publishers, Museum of London, 2003.

Ross-of-Bladensburg, John Foster George. *The Coldstream Guards 1914–1918.* 2 vols. London: Oxford University Press, 1928.

Sackville-West, Vita. *Faces: Profiles of Dogs.* Garden City & New York: Doubleday, 1962.

_____. *Passenger to Teheran.* London: Leonard & Virginia Woolf at the Hogarth Press, 1926.

Saltoun, [Lord]. *Scraps.* Vol. 2. London: Longmans, 1883.

Sanderson, C. C., ed. *Pedigree Dogs as Recognized by the Kennel Club.* London: T. Werner Laurie, 1927.

Searle, Muriel V. *Beckenham and Penge in Old Picture Postcards.* Netherlands: European Library, 1989.

Serjeant, R. B., and R.L. Bidwell, eds. *Arabian Studies II.* London: C. Hurst, 1975.

Smith, A. [Arthur] Croxton. *About Our Dogs.* London: Ward, Lock, 1931.

_____. *Dogs.* London: Penguin, 1953.

_____. *Dogs Since 1900.* London: Andrew Dakers, 1950.

_____. *Everyman's Book of the Dog.* London: Hodder and Stoughton, 1909.

Smith, Charles Hamilton. "The Natural History of Dogs." Vols. XVIII–XIX. In *The Naturalist's Library, Mammalia*, edited by William Jardine. Edinburgh: W. H. Lizars, 1839–1840.

Smith, G. Rex. "The Saluqi in Islam." In *Saluqi: Coursing Hound of the East*, edited by Gail Goodman. Bramble Junction, AZ: Midbar, 1995.

Stark, Freya. *East is West.* 4th ed. London: John Murray, 1947.

_____. *The Valley of the Assassins.* 3rd ed. London: John Murray, 1947.

Stephens, John Richard. *The Dog Lover's Literary Companion.* Rocklin, CA: Prima Publishing, 1992.

Stirling, W. F. *Safety Last.* London: Hollis and Carter, 1953.

Stonehenge. *The Dogs of Great Britain, America, and Other Countries.* New York: Orange Judd, 1909.

Strouse, Jean. *Morgan: American Financier.* New York: Random House, 1999.

Swinglehurst, Edmund. *Cook's Tours: The Story of Popular Travel.* Poole: Blandford Press, 1982.

Temple, Richard. *Palestine Illustrated.* London: W. H. Allen, 1888.

Thalman, Naftali. "Introducing Modern Agriculture into Nineteenth-Century Palestine: The German Templars." In *The Land that Became Israel*, edited by Ruth Kark. New Haven, CT: Yale University Press, 1990.

Thieme, Ulrich, and Felix Becker. *Allgemeines Lexicon der Bildenden Künstler.* Vol. 1. Leipzig: E. A. Seeman, 1907.

Thomas, Bertram. *Alarms and Excursions in Arabia.* London: George Allen & Unwin, 1931.

_____. *Arabia Felix Across the "Empty Quarter" of Arabia.* New York: Charles Scribner's Sons, 1932.

Thomas, Lowell. *With Lawrence in Arabia.* New York: Garden City, 1924.

Thomas Cook & Sons. *Dahabeahs on the Nile.* London: 1891.

Trapman, A. H. *The Dog: Man's Best Friend.* London: Hutchinson, 1929.

Trench, Richard. *Arabian Travellers: The European Discovery of Arabia.* Topsfield, MA: Salem House Publishers, 1986.

Trimbee, James W., and Jean Trimbee McKenzie. *A Trail of Trials.* Edinburgh: Pentland Press, 1995.

Tuchman, Barabara W. *The Proud Tower: A Portrait of the World before the War 1890–1914.* New York: Macmillan, 1966.

Turner, J. Sidney. *The Kennel Encyclopædia.* London: Sir W. C. Leng, 1908.

Verrier, Michelle, ed. *The Orientalists* London: Academy Editions, 1979.

Wagstaff, John, and Doris Pullen, eds. *Beckenham: An Anthology of Local History.* London: Historical Association, 1984.

Wallach, Janet. *Desert Queen.* New York: Doubleday, 1996.

Walsh, E. G. *Lurchers and Longdogs.* Gloucestershire: Standfast Press, 1977.

Waters, Hope, and David Waters. *The Saluki in History, Art, and Sport.* Newton Abbot, England: David & Charles, 1969.

Watkins, Vera H. *Saluki — Companion of Kings.* Haslemere, England: Trendell's, 1974.

Watson, James. *The Dog Book.* New York: Doubleday, Page, 1906.

Welch, William M. Jr. *No Country for a Gentleman: British Rule in Egypt, 1883–1907.* New York: Greenwood Press, 1988.

Who Was Who 1897–1915. 3rd ed. London: A. & C. Black, 1935.

Who Was Who 1916–1928. London: A. & C. Black, 1929.

Who Was Who 1929–1940. London: A. & C. Black, 1941.

Who Was Who 1941–1950. 3rd ed. London: A. & C. Black, 1964.

Who Was Who 1951–1960. 3rd ed. London: A. & C. Black, 1967.

Who Was Who 1961–1979. London: A. & C. Black, 1970.

Who's Who in Kent. London: Ebeneezer Baylis & Son, 1935.

Wilfred Jennings-Bramly 1871–1960, Memorabilia. Cairo: 1970.

Wilkinson, Charles K., and Marsha Hill. *Egyptian Wall Paintings: The Metropolitan Museum of Art's Collection of Facsimiles.* New York: Metropolitan Museum of Art, 1983.

Williams, E. T., and C. S. Nicholls, eds. *Dictionary of National Biography, 1961–1970*. Oxford: Oxford University Press, 1981.

Williams, G. *Citizen Soldiers of the Royal Engineers Transportation and Movements and the Royal Army Service Corps 1859 to 1965*. Aldershot: Institution of the Royal Corps of Transport, 1969.

Wilson, Arnold T. *Loyalties: Mesopotamia 1914–1917*. 2 vols. 3rd ed. London: Oxford University Press, 1936.

Wilson, Jeremy. *Lawrence of Arabia: The Authorized Biography of T.E. Lawrence*. New York: Atheneum, 1990.

_____. *T. E. Lawrence*. London: National Portrait Gallery Publications, 1988.

Winstone, H. V. F. *Captain Shakespear: A Portrait*. London: Jonathan Cape, 1976.

Woolf, Virginia. *Orlando: A Biography*. New York: Harcourt, Brace & Jovanovich, 1956.

Yardley, Michael. *Backing into the Limelight: A Biography of T. E. Lawrence*. London: Harrap, 1985.

Youatt, William. *The Dog*. London: Longmans, Green, 1886.

Journal Articles

Arnold, Dorothea. "An Egyptian Bestiary." *Metropolitan Museum of Art Bulletin* 52, no. 4 (Spring 1995).

Cheesman, R. E. "The Fifth Battalion 'The Buffs' (East Kent Regt.) and the Wye College Contingent." *Journal of the Agricola Club* 9 no. 49 (1939).

Edmonds, C. J. "Luristan: Pish-i-Kuh and Bala Gariveh." *Geographical Journal* (London: Royal Geographical Society), 69, no.6 (June 1922).

Jennings-Bramly, W. E. "Bedouin of the Sinaitic Peninsula, Pt. XXII: 'Life.'" *Palestine Exploration Fund Quarterly Statement*, October 1908.

_____. "Sport Among the Bedawin." *Palestine Exploration Fund Quarterly Statement*, October/December 1900.

Lythgoe, Albert M. "Statues of the Goddess Sekhmet." *Bulletin of the Metropolitan Museum of Art*, October 1919.

Mark, Gordon St. George. "The Joyces of Merview, Part II." *Irish Genealogist* 9, no. 1 (1994).

McDonald, J. A. "The Late Wing Commander A.R.M. Rickards, O.B.E., A.F.C." *The Royal Air Force Quarterly,* January 1939.

Newspaper and Magazine Articles and Issues

Advertisement. *Dog World Annual*, 1960, 119.

Allan, Ken. "The Sarona Album." *Saluki International* 3, no. 6 (Spring/Summer 1995).

Amherst, Florence. "The Dog of the Burning Sands." *American Kennel Club Gazette*, August 1, 1928.

_____. "The Gazelle-Hound." *Saluki International* no. 20 (Spring/Summer 2002). Reprinted from *Every Woman's Encyclopedia*, 1910–1912.

_____. "The Gazelle Hound or Saluki Shami." *Saluki International* 5, no. 9 (Autumn/Winter 1996).

_____. "The 'Saluki Shami' or Gazelle Hound." *Dog World*, Dogs of the Year 1924–25.

"The Amherstias: Recollections and Reflections." *Saluki Heritage* no. 6 (Spring 1984).

Angel, G. M. "Saluki Subjects." *Our Dogs*, October 28, 1927; February 14, 1936; March 13, 1936; April 10, 1936; April 17, 1936; May 29, 1936; December 1, 1939; October 10, 1941.

Applebee, June. "Luman and Another." *The Saluki*, Winter/Spring 1985.

_____. "Mazuri is Swahili for Good or Beautiful." *The Saluki*, Summer/Autumn 1985.

_____. "1951." *The Saluki* 6, no.1 (Spring/Summer 1974).

Bentinck, A.W.D, "Imported Salukis." *Country Life*, 15 Nov. 1924.

Bravida. "100 Per Cent Dog." *Blackwood's Magazine*, Feb. 1924.

_____. "The Armageddon Hunt." *Blackwood's Magazine*, Jan. 1924.

"Cinema Supplement." *London Times*, February 21, 1922.

Clark, Terence. "Salukis of the Fairford Kennels." *The Saluki*, Crufts Edition, 2000.

"Col. P. C. Joyce Obituary." *The Ranger Magazine*, 1965.

Cooks Excursionist and Tourist Advisor, November 1894.

Dickson, Violet. "Arabian Remembrances." *American Saluki Association Newsletter*, July 1973.

Dog World, March 5, 1925; August 27, 1925.

"Dogs of the Bible: The Newest Fad." *Literary Digest*, February 26, 1927.

Duggan, Brian. "Dear Miss Amherst ... Yours Sincerely, T. E. Lawrence." *Saluki International*, Spring/Summer 1994.

_____. "Ordeal." *Saluki International*, Annual no. 2.

_____. "Origins of the First Breed Standard." *Saluki International* no. 18 (Spring/Summer 2001).

_____. "The Saluki Filmography." *Saluki International* 5, no. 9 (Autumn/Winter 1996).

"An Egyptian Treasure: Great Find at Thebes: Lord Carnarvon's Long Quest." *London Times*, November 30, 1922.

The Field, September 1922–July 1923.

G. G. "Astride v. Side-Saddle." *Country Life*, December 12, 1925.

"The Grevels: Recollections and Reflections." *Saluki Heritage* no. 19 (Autumn 1990).

"The Hon. Florence Amherst and her Salukis at Amherstia Kennels." *Dog World*, May 20, 1926.

"The Hound Show at Ranelagh." *Country Life Illustrated*, June 16, 1900.

Hudson, John. "From the Country of Origin." The *Saluki*, Championship Show Edition, 1999.

"The Iraqs: Recollections and Reflections." *Saluki Heritage* no. 18 (Spring 1990).

James, Jean. "'Salukis' by The Honourable Florence Amherst." *The Saluki,* 7, no.2 (Autumn/Winter 1975).

Jarvis, C. S. "A Car Patrol in the Desert" [letter to the editor]. *Country Life*, March 23, 1923.

_____. "Fishing in Egypt" [letter to the editor]. *Country Life,* June 2, 1917.

_____. "The Passing of the Sailing Ship." *Country Life*, March 1, 1913.

_____. "Quail Shooting in the Libyan Desert." *Country Life,* May 12, 1917.

_____. "Through Sinai to the Red Sea." *Country Life*, October 11, 1924.

Jarvis, Scudamore. "A Sinai Wandering." *Blackwood's Magazine*, July 1930.

Jungeling, Saskia, and Han Jungeling. "The History of the Saluki in the Netherlands, Part 1." *Saluki World*, Fall 1971.

The Kennel, April 1911.

Kennel Club Calendar and Stud Book. London, 1923–1939.

The Kennel Gazette, January 1919–October 1929.

"Kennel Notes." *Country Life Illustrated*, July 16, 1898.

"King Tutankhamen's Tomb." *Country Life*, February 3, 1923.

Knapp, Esther Bliss. "Salukis." *American Kennel Club Gazette*, July 1955.

"The Knightellingtons: Recollections and Reflections." *Saluki Heritage* no. 7 (Autumn 1984).

"Ladies Kennel Association Notes." *Tatler*, February 28, 1923.

Lance, F. Fitzhugh. "Gazelle Hunting in Palestine." *The Cavalry Journal* no. 51. Reprinted in *Saluki International*, Spring/Summer 2004.

Lance, F.F. "Salukis." *The Kennel Gazette*, October 1924.

Lance, G. M. "Salukis." *Dog World*, January 1923–October 1929.

Lawlor, J. H. C. Letter to the editor. *The Field*, March 11, 1944.

Lees, Dorothy. "Beirut via Damascus to Baghdad." *Saluki Heritage* no. 17 (Autumn 1989).

Leighton, Robert. "Cruft's Show: Persian Greyhounds." *The Kennel Gazette*, Feb. 1923.

_____. "Foreign Dogs: Salukis." The Kennel Gazette, October 1923.

Letters to the editor. "Jack Hunting in Palestine." *Country Life*, July 12, 1919; "Major H.A. Waddington's Hounds." May 28, 1921.

Lloyd, Freeman. "Dogs and their Owners." *Dress and Vanity Fair*, October 1913.

"The Mazuris: Recollections and Reflections." *Saluki Heritage* no. 9 (Autumn 1985).

McLeish, Joan. "The Ebni & Binte El Nablous Trophy." *The Saluki*, Winter/Spring 1985.

"Minutes of the Inaugural Meeting of the Saluki or Gazelle Hound Club." *The Saluki*, Champion Show Edition, 1998.

Moss, W. P. "Hunting Salugis." *Sport and Country*, January 4, 1946.

Norvel, Christina. "A Coursing History." *The Saluki*, Crufts Issue, 1997.

Obituary for Howard Carter. *The Times*, March 3, 1939.

"Obituary for Joan Mitchell, 1954." *The Saluki,* 19, no. 1 (1977).

"The Orchards: Recollections and Reflections." *Saluki Heritage* no. 16 (Spring 1989).

Pim, D. C. "Hunting with the Exodus at Habbaniya." *The Field*, June 14, 1941.

Pollard, Alfred W. "The Amherst Library." *Country Life Magazine*, October 13, 1906; October 27, 1906.

The Quarterly Indian Army List (Calcutta), January 1920.

Rook, Tom. "Back to Our Roots." *The Saluki*, Winter/Spring 1987.

"The Ruritanias: Recollections and Reflections." *Saluki Heritage* no. 17 (Autumn 1989).

"Salukis." *American Kennel Club Gazette*, January 1930–November 1947.

"The Saronas and the Press." *Saluki Heritage* no. 5 (Autumn 1983).

"The Saronas: Recollections and Reflections." *Saluki Heritage* no. 5 (Autumn 1983).

Scott, Desiree. "Early Saluki History." *Saluki Heritage* no. 20 (Spring 1991).

"The Slughi or Gazelle-Hound." *Country Life*, July 14, 1906.

Smith, A. Croxton. "The Father of the Greyhounds." *The Field*, May 1923.

_____. "A Great Show of Sporting Dogs." *Country Life*, February 18, 1922.

_____. "Kennel Notes." *Country Life*, August 27, 1910.

_____. "Ladies Kennel Association Show." *Country Life*, June 19, 1915.

_____. "Major Bell-Murray's Afghan Hounds." *Country Life*, December 2, 1922.

_____. "The Significance of Crufts." *Country Life*, February 23, 1924.

_____. "With Hawk and Hound." *Country Life*, April 22, 1922.

"The Soldier's Dog: A Perilous Privilege." *Dog World*, October 22, 1925.

Spallanzani, Marco. "Salukis Alla Corte Dei Medici Nei Secoli XV–XVI." *Mitheilungen Des Kunsthistorichen Institut in Florenz* no. 27 (1983).

Stockley, C. H. "Hunting with Salukis in Northern Anatolia." *Dog World*, December 30, 1927.

Tatler, November 1922–March 1923.

White, Horace W. H. "Reminiscence." *The Saluki*, Summer/Autumn, 1987.

Wiggins, Lesley. "Amherstia Records." *Saluki Heritage*, no. 6, Spring 1984.

_____. "The Sarona Records." *Saluki Heritage* no. 5 (Autumn 1983).

Williams, Maynard Owen. "At the Tomb of Tutankhamen." *National Geographic Magazine*, May 1923.
Winterton, [Lord]. "Arabian Nights and Days, Part I." *Blackwood's Magazine* 207 (May 1920).
———. "Arabian Nights and Days, Part II." *Blackwood's Magazine* 208 (June 1920).

Unpublished and Miscellaneous Sources

Allen, James P., Curator, Dept. of Egyptian Art, Metropolitan Museum of Art. Letter to the author, "Amhert Sekhmet Statues," Jan. 22, 1998.
———. Letter to the author, "Hound Heiroglyphics," Feb. 20, 2002.
Amherst, Alicia M. J. *The Journal*, vols. I & II. December 1894–June 1895.
Bayne-Jardine, Colin. *The Retreat from Syria*. Unpublished manuscript, undated.
Catalogue of the Amherst Collection of Egyptian & Oriental Antiquities. London: Sotheby, Wilkinson & Hodge, 1921.
Catalogue of the Galway Dog Show Society's First Annual Show, July 9, 1936.
Catalogue of the Magnificent Library of Choice and Valuable Books & Manuscripts "The property of the Rt. Hon. Lord Amherst of Hackney." London: Sotheby, Wilkinson, & Hodge, 1908–1909.
Crufts Show Catalogues, 1898, 1906, 1908, 1913, 1914, 1915, 1923.
Flower, S. S. *Report on the Zoological Service for the Year 1920*. Cairo: Government Press, 1921.
———. *Report on the Zoological Service for the Year 1921*. Cairo: Government Press, 1922.
———. *Zoological Gardens, Giza, near Cairo, Egypt: Plan and Guide Book*. 2nd ed. Cairo: Al-Mokattam Printing Office, 1903.
Member's Roll, Royal College of Nursing, 1923.
Orders, Decorations, and Campaign Medals. Sale Catalogue, Christie's London, July 25, 1989.
The Saluki or Gazelle Hound Club Annual Reports, 1923, 1927, 1928, 1929, 1930, 1931, 1932, 1933, 1934, 1935.
The Saluki or Gazelle Hound Club Members' Show Catalogue, 1929, 1930, 1932, 1934, 1935.
Saluki Racing Club Exhibition Races Catalogue, Dartford Stadium, June 21, 1933.
Sturgeon, Adrien J. G. *Frederick Fitzhugh Lance & Gladys Maud Lutwyche Waterlow*. Monograph, Stanstead Parish Archives, 2003.

Archives

American Kennel Club Library, New York.
Amherst & Tyssen Papers, Hackney Archives, Old Rose Lipman Library, London.
British Library, London.
Centre for Kentish Studies, Maidstone, Kent.
Coldstream Guards Regimental Archives, Wellington Barracks, London.
Eastern Counties Newspaper Archives, Norwich.
General Register Office, Southport, UK.
Gertrude Bell Archives, Robinson Library, University of Newcastle upon Tyne.
Getty Research Institute, Research Library, Los Angeles.
Imperial War Museum, London.
Irish Kennel Club Library, Dublin, Ireland.
Jennings-Bramly (Library Manuscript Collection), Royal Geographical Society, London.
Kennel Club Library, London.
Local Studies Library and Archives, Bromley Library, London.
Middle Eastern Centre, St. Antony's College, Oxford.
Ministry of Defence, Hayes, Middlesex.
National Archives, Kew.
National Army Museum, London.
Natural History Museum Archives, London.
Norfolk Record Office, Norfolk, England.
Papers of W. E. Jennings-Bramly, Palestine Exploration Fund, London.
Photography Collection, Harry Ransom Humanities Research Center, University of Texas at Austin.
Register of Nurses, Westminster Training School, 1899–1949, London Metropolitan Archives.
Royal Artillery Museum, Woolich, London.
Royal Military Academy Sandhurst, Camberley, Surrey.
Somerset House, London.
T.E. Lawrence Papers, Western Manuscripts, Bodleian Library, Oxford, England.
Thomas Cook UK Ltd. Archives, Peterborough.
Wye College Library, University of London.
Zoological Society of London.

Private Correspondence and Interviews

Allen, James P. (curator, Egyptian Collection, Metropolitan Museum of Art). Letters to the author, January 22, 1998; February 20, 2002.
Amherst of Hackney, [Lord]. Letter to the author, September 7, 1993.
Baldwin, Cathleen (Biltmore Estate Archives). Letters to the author, May 24, 1995; June 12, 1995.
Barrass, Eric (Rolls-Royce Enthusiasts' Club). Letter to the author, November 11, 1993.
Bayne-Jardine, Colin. Letters to the author, November 20, 2001; April 30, 2002; June 6, 2002; August 4, 2002.
Berrisford, Mrs. Geoffrey. Interview with the author, February 17, 1997.
Betti, Vivien. Interviews with the author. March 16, 1997; April 29, 1997.

Butters, David (Swaffham Museum). Letter to the author, December 17, 1996.

Cecil, George. Letters to author, December 2, 1996; December 8, 1997; February 12, 1998; April 7, 2000; February 17, 2003.

Chattey, Venetia. Letters to the author, July 28, 1995; November 25, 1996; October 18, 1999.

Cooper, G. (press officer, Kent County Fire Brigade). Letter to the author, February 5, 1997.

Elliot, Peter (Keeper of Research and Information Services, Royal Air Force Museum, Hendon). Letter to the author, July 23, 1996.

Goslett, John. Interview with the author, March 14, 1995.

_____. Letter to the author, June 6, 1995,

Hills, Daphne M. (Mammal Section, National History Museum). Letters to the author, February 22, 1995; May 17, 1995; February 12, 1997; April 15, 2002.

James, T. G. H. Letters to the author, May 12, 1995; October 11, 1995; March 24, 2000; August 1, 2001.

Kamhawi, Walid. Letter to the author, November 7, 1996.

Keegan, Frank. Letter to the author, April 8, 1996.

Lance, John W. F. Letter to the author, October 8, 1993.

Lance, Judy. Letters to the author, May 20, 1997; February 25, 1999; November 17, 2000.

Lanyon, Lady. Letter to the author, August 11, 1996.

Mark, Gordon St. George. Letter to the author, January 11, 1996; February 26, 1996; July 17, 1997; November 14, 1998.

McGann, Susan (Royal College of Nursing Archivist). Letters to the author, February 19, 1997; May 13, 1997.

Nicolson, Nigel. Letters to the author, "Vita Sackville-West and Zurcha," 3 Feb., 25 Apr., 27 & 29 Jun., & 3 Aug. 1995.

Offer, James. Letter to the author, February 16, 1999.

Portland, [Earl of]. Interview with the author, October 31, 2002.

Scovil, Jasper. Letters to the author, May 7, 1997; June 13, 1998.

Strange, Baroness. Letter to the author, January 7, 1994.

Sutcliffe, Elizabeth. Letter to the author, September 2, 1996; November 4, 1999.

Tyerman, Margaret (Mackay Historical Society and Museum, Australia). Letter to George H. V. Cecil, March 18, 2000.

Waters, David. Letter to the author, May 18, 1996.

Waters, Hope. Letter to the author, September 2, 1993.

Other Primary Sources

Vita Sackville-West and Harold Nicholson Manuscripts, Letters and Diaries, from Sissinghurst Castle, Kent, the Huntington Library, California, and Other Libraries. 15 reels. Brighton, Sussex: Harvester Microform, 1988.

Internet Sources

Gertrude Bell Archives, Newcastle University http://www.gerty.ncl.ac.uk

Great Western Archive: "Hall" Class Details http://www.greatwestern.org.uk/m_in_hal_hall69a.htm

Internet Movie Database http://www.imdb.com

Measuring Worth: Purchasing Power of British Pounds from 1264 to 2007 http://www.measuringworth.com/calculators/ppoweruk, thePeerage.com, http://www.thepeerage.com

The Statue of Liberty — Ellis Island Foundation http://www.ellisisland.org

T. E. Lawrence Studies http://telawrence.info

Index

Page numbers in ***boldface italics*** indicate illustrations.